THE TEXAS BOOK TWO

FOCUS ON AMERICAN HISTORY SERIES

The Dolph Briscoe Center for American History
University of Texas at Austin

Edited by Don Carleton

MORE PROFILES,
HISTORY, AND
REMINISCENCES
OF THE UNIVERSITY

}

The Texas Book Two

EDITED BY DAVID DETTMER
FOREWORD BY LARRY R. FAULKNER

University of Texas Press ⟡ *Austin*

The publication of this book was supported in part by the Jess and Betty Jo Hay Endowment.

Requests for permission to reproduce material from this
work should be sent to:
    Permissions
    University of Texas Press
    P.O. Box 7819
    Austin, TX 78713-7819
    www.utexas.edu/utpress/about/bpermission.html

♾ The paper used in this book meets the minimum
requirements of ANSI/NISO Z39.48-1992 (R1997)
(Permanence of Paper).

LIBRARY OF CONGRESS CATALOGING-IN-PUBLICATION DATA

The Texas book two : more profiles, history, and reminis-
cences of the university / edited by David Dettmer ; fore-
word by Larry R. Faulkner. — 1st ed.
    p.   cm.
  Includes index.
  ISBN 978-0-292-72874-5 (cloth : alk. paper) —
ISBN 978-0-292-73713-6 (e-book)
  1. University of Texas—History.   2. University of
Texas at Austin—History.   3. University of Texas—
Biography.   4. University of Texas at Austin—Biography.
I. Dettmer, David.
  LD5333.T493 2012
  378.764'31—dc23
                              2011034989

Contents

LARRY R.
FAULKNER
President Emeritus
University of Texas
at Austin

Foreword

There are, in our lives, places and people, institutions and experiences, that loom very large, that impress us indelibly and become part of our identity. The most powerful foster a distinct culture into which we are drawn, sometimes repeatedly, through decades. Even after long disengagement, the relationship can resume with unexpected familiarity and feeling. Such has been my experience with the University of Texas, and I know it also to have been the experience of countless others.

"Do not think you can escape them," one sings in "The Eyes of Texas." For me, these words have come to be the anthem's most prophetic. I rarely speak them now without wondering over them, at least fleetingly.

My personal journey with "The University" now spans five decades. I was a graduate student in the '60s, a faculty member in the '80s, president in the '90s and into the '00s, and now I enjoy "senior status." But in those years, I was away more than I was in Austin. I came and went, and came and went, and came, not ever to leave fully again.

For me, the University has always been powerful, energetic, and irresistibly lively—a place of dreams, ambition, spirit, and imagination. Though only a part of Texas, it seems to make all of Texas still bigger and more significant. The University is an institution, a distinct culture, that keeps moving on, ever subsuming and incorporating, transforming and enabling.

Human in origin and manifestation, it is, to be sure, imperfect and even occasionally irrational. It can disappoint, and it can fail to live up to its own ideals and standards. Yet it abides, broadly valued for its deep relevance to the lives and futures of individual people and to their society. Of course, every great institution manifests both remarkable powers and clear shortcomings. Despite the weaknesses, a signal feat in human history has been the evolution of working examples that can inspire and deliver on their promises for centuries. There is satisfying evidence that the University of Texas has risen to hold a place among those of our time.

What is at the core of an institution like that? How did it come together? How does it cohere? How does it keep growing and adapting through changing times and people? My sense is that the answers to such questions cannot be found by analysis. The essence of the University of

Texas seems to be one of those fascinations that just dissipate if one looks too closely. One cannot capture it by detailing its parts. But one can illuminate aspects of it by using essays and stories—about people who passed through, who became a part of the culture, and of whom the culture, in turn, became a part—about bits of history that underlie the culture.

Such is the concept that led to this book, *The Texas Book Two*, and its predecessor, *The Texas Book*. In this volume, David Dettmer has assembled a fascinating anthology of profiles, historical pieces, and reminiscences. Each can be read alone, and the collection can be read in any order. Apart, the pieces can be seen as individual threads of the University's fabric. Taken together, they provide a loose reweave, depicting more of what the institution has been over the years and what it has come to be.

The concept of the first *Texas Book* grew largely from the imagination of Susan Clagett, an associate vice president of the University. Over the past twenty years, Ms. Clagett has been the principal figure in charge of major events, including commencement, which she redesigned dramatically in the 1990s, with remarkable and lasting success. She later established wonderful additional occasions, such as Explore UT, the yearly University-wide open house; Gone to Texas, the annual welcome for new students; and UT Remembers, a ceremony honoring members of the community who died in the preceding year. A common theme through all her work is what I sometimes call "symbolic communication." She and her team are masters of the varied and powerful symbols—sites, images, music, verse and prose, allusions to people, places, and events—evoking and expressing the heritage and attributes of the University of

Texas and its community. Drawing upon these elements, Ms. Clagett and her colleagues seem consistently to imbue their big and small events with just the right significance and tone.

The first *Texas Book* was conceived in the same vein, except that the collected elements were to be essays and stories. Taken separately and together, they would generate an experience of the University and would help the reader see into the core of the place and the basis for its influence.

Susan Clagett raised the idea with me early in my presidency, probably in 1999. I encouraged her to pursue it and drew her attention to *The Harvard Book*, which had been assembled decades earlier by William Bentinck-Smith toward a similar end for a different community. Ms. Clagett pushed ahead. She was supported by Teresa Sullivan, then vice president and the dean of graduate studies, who helped to involve both Don Carleton, the director of the Dolph Briscoe Center for American History, and Joanna Hitchcock, the director of the University of Texas Press. They, in turn, recruited Richard A. Holland into the challenge of editing the book, which appeared in 2006. David Dettmer, the editor of this present volume, played a strong supporting role in that effort.

The success of the first volume and the availability of a great range of additional material encouraged further effort. David Dettmer interested Joanna Hitchcock in *The Texas Book Two* and agreed to edit it. This product, like the university that inspires it, is fascinating.

Savor these chapters, essay by essay, and all together. They will draw you toward the core of the great institution and, most likely, will connect you to your own past and future as they do.

THE TEXAS BOOK TWO

DAVID
DETTMER } **Introduction**

"A University of the first class."

Almost everyone who is associated in one way or another with the institution known as the University of Texas—or, since 1967, the University of Texas at Austin—is familiar with this constitutional call to excellence. The phrase reverberates throughout the essays in this book. In many ways, the University of Texas is undoubtedly "of the first class." In every corner of this sprawling enterprise, one can find examples of teaching, research, preservation, and artistic creation that are among the world's best.

The University's enormous, ever-densifying urban campus includes not only the nearly 850 acres the University occupies in Austin proper, but outposts hundreds of miles from Austin as well, in every direction on the compass—from the McDonald Observatory near Fort Davis in West Texas, to the Sam Rayburn Library and Museum in Bonham near the Red River, to the Winedale Historical Complex near Round Top in Fayette County, to the Marine Science Institute at Port Aransas on the Gulf Coast. For a Texan interested in progress (no, that's not an oxymoron), there could be few pleasures greater than uncovering the intellectual treasures that one can find by exploring these "Forty Acres" and all they contain.

The Texas Book Two: More Profiles, History, and Reminiscences of the University chronicles much of the excellence that the University of Texas has produced since it opened its doors in 1883. It also faces squarely some of the shortcomings of this "University of the first class." This book picks up where its predecessor, *The Texas Book: Profiles, History, and Reminiscences of the University*, edited by Richard A. Holland and published by the University of Texas Press in 2006, leaves off. Like its predecessor, this volume is a collection of essays divided into three categories—profiles, history, and reminiscences. Each essay is told by a different author in that author's unique voice and from that author's point of view. This book is not a comprehensive history of the University, nor does it claim that the following nineteen essays are necessarily about the nineteen most important people or events in the University's history. I have carefully selected the topics to give you, the reader, a cross section of UT's relatively short existence, a cut that exposes a meaningful variety of facts, personalities, and flavors that are particular to UT. The essays can be read in the order they appear (they are arranged chronologically within each section), or each can be read individually, independent of any of the other essays. My hope is that, at its best, this book lends some anthropological insight into the values and behavior of the University of Texas and the people who have made it what it is.

In his foreword to this volume, UT-Austin president emeritus Larry R. Faulkner explains how the idea for producing a book of this nature was conceived. He connects the idea for a book of essays about the history and culture of UT to a larger effort, begun during the administration of president Robert M. Berdahl (1993–1997), to connect UT-Austin more closely to the public through the use of "symbolic communication." By communicating to the public a better understanding of the essential role higher education plays in society, the enhanced use of "symbolic communication" has enabled the administrations of Berdahl and his successors—Peter Flawn, Larry Faulkner, and Bill Powers—to demonstrate to the public more effectively the power of the University to enhance and even transform the lives of those who support it. Certainly, the University enhances lives by creating and preserving knowledge. By putting much of that knowledge into practical use, it also makes the lives of Texans better by acting as an enormous economic engine that is essential to the long-term health of the state's economy. Certainly there is truth to Faulkner's assessment in his foreword that "evoking and expressing the heritage and attributes of the University of Texas and its community" gives readers of *The Texas Book* a better understanding of the core mission of the University and their relationship to it—but as Faulkner himself demonstrates, the issue of the University's potential and the public's perception of it reaches much deeper than that truth.

In his first "Address on the State of the University," on October 6, 1998, Faulkner told the assembly that

> through its history, this university has moved forward in cycles. At times, the hard work of this community, the fortunes of our state, and the leadership of those who love Texas have come together to foster periods of great advancement.

These first two volumes of *The Texas Book* contain the stories of many of those forward movements—and at its best, the University of Texas moving forward is an awesome sight to behold. When Texans marshal their creativity, skill, ambition, and courage, the result is special—it is world class, and typically it is unmistakably Texan. However, if there have been periods of great advancement in UT's history, then implicit in Faulkner's statement is the understanding that there have also been periods when the University has not fostered great advancement. Anyone who has been associated with the University for a length of time understands well the institution's ability, on occasion, to thwart its own progress—and some of those stories are told in the pages of these volumes of *The Texas Book* as well. Perhaps this ability to be so great at times and so foolish at other times is a necessary consequence of the unique history and culture of the state. Perhaps it is a by-product of a willingness to risk; of a stubborn independence; of a strange, contradictory impulse to be both cosmopolitan and insular—to take pride in being both worldly and provincial. Perhaps it is a by-product of the violence and brutal practicality that lies at the heart of the formation and development of the state.

One episode in UT-Austin's history stands out as a particularly revealing instance of the vexing ability the University has to approach greatness while simultaneously working to thwart its arrival. Several of the essays in both volumes of *The Texas Book* include a discussion of this episode—namely, the firing of UT president Homer Rainey by the UT Board of Regents in 1944, a topic that certainly merits its own essay, or full-length book, for that matter.

By all appearances, Homer Rainey was the perfect candidate to lead the University of Texas. He was a native Texan who came from humble roots. He was an ordained Baptist minister, a World War I veteran, and a standout athlete—a four-sport star at Austin College in Sherman and briefly a pitcher in the Texas League. He had impeccable academic credentials and wrote extensively about educational issues, and he had already served as the president of Franklin College in Indiana and of Bucknell University in Pennsylvania when the UT regents brought him back to Texas in 1939. The regents fired him nevertheless.

Among President Rainey's failings, in the eyes of the regents, were his refusal to fire several tenured professors whom the regents had instructed him to fire; his refusal to order the English Department to drop from its reading list John Dos Passos's respected *U.S.A.* trilogy, which contains frank descriptions of American life and criticism of big business (the third novel in the trilogy is titled *The Big Money*); his willingness to listen to rational considerations for moving the Medical Branch in Galveston to Austin; the regents' perception that he had withheld from them knowledge of the presence of homosexuals on campus, which could also, in their view, be masking an unwillingness to report on socialistic or communistic inroads being made on campus by outsiders; and their perception that perhaps he was leaning the wrong way, in their view, on the question of racial integration.

A year after the firing—as American atomic bombs were falling on Japan, three months after the surrender of Nazi Germany—Bernard De Voto attempted to sort out in the pages of *Harper's Magazine* the decision the UT regents had made:

A group of unscrupulous but very clear-minded men, then, have destroyed the University of Texas as an educational institution—destroyed it, at least, for so long as they or anyone who represents their point of view may remain in control. Mr. Frank Dobie does not scruple to call them native fascists. He is using the word carefully: they have faithfully repeated the Nazi attack on the central mechanism of democracy. The service of the regents is to entrenched wealth, privilege, powerful corporations; they are agents of ruthless industry and finance. But clearly they could neither have won nor maintained their victory if they had not succeeded in getting the support of many Texans who want no truck with fascism and are not enlisted on the side of privilege.

Many thousands of profoundly troubled Texans honestly believe that the regents have been defending their state from outside domination, that they have struck a triumphant blow for individual freedom, that they have saved Texas from terrible evils—that in a way the Republic of Texas has been renewed. To an outsider it is clear that instead they are regressive and anachronistic, that they have only reared a wall against modern government, modern thinking, modern literature—in short against the modern world. But there lingers in Texas the ghostly memory of an unindustrialized society. Of a frontier

where lack of economic and political safeguards actually worked against the hardening of class lines. Of pioneer simplicities when frugality and enterprise and minding your own business were enough in themselves to make life excellent. To that golden nostalgia the wall against the modern world seems a defense against all that has proved grievous in the experience of our generation and a promise that Sam Houston will come again.

"THE EASY CHAIR," *HARPER'S MAGAZINE*, AUGUST 1945, 136

The University of Texas is inextricably the university *of* Texas. That is what makes it so fascinating, and so vexing.

In his 1998 State of the University address, President Faulkner raised the following question and followed it with the larger goal he held for the University, of which he hoped his administration would put the University in pursuit:

So is it now true that The University is "good enough?" One hears this question out loud at times. More often it hangs as an unspoken implication in conversations about public policy in Texas. The answer is "yes" or "perhaps" only if one is also willing to admit that Texas, as a state and as a society, is already "good enough." It is a rare Texan who will admit that. I spoke earlier about the role that Texas can play, in the nation and in the world, in the decades to come. To achieve that kind of future, Texas needs to strengthen its educational assets in several ways, but it surely needs to continue to build excellence here in Austin. We have a state culture that demands the best. We have ambition and resolve. Let us exploit these strengths and strive to excel. Let us make this place more than a university of the first class. Let's take it to the head of the class!

When I say that, I'm not just talking about rankings. At UT, we are strong enough to look beyond rankings, toward the real needs of our society, and toward the real opportunities for leadership in the future. We need to answer for ourselves the question, "What makes a great university great?" In my view, it is not possible for a university to achieve greatness without a faculty of superb quality, but even with such a faculty, a university may fail its promise because it engages poorly with the society it was created to serve. My goal for The University of Texas at

Austin is that we do the best complete job of serving the real needs of the people of Texas and the nation. Greatness is to be found in what a university does, not in what it is.

From this goal arose the need to connect the University more closely with the citizens of Texas. Efforts such as enhancement of the "symbolic communication" that events such as Spring Commencement have always provided—as well as the development of new events such as Explore UT (a university-wide open house for the general public, especially K-12 students from across the state), UT Remembers (a memorial service for members of the UT community who passed away during the preceding year), and Gone to Texas (an event in August to welcome students to campus)—were intended to be steps in pursuit of this goal. Though these volumes of *The Texas Book*, unlike those events, are not an official production of the University's administration, they serve a similar purpose, in their own modest way. One of the strengths of this project—one that the books' editors have made a concerted effort to maintain—is an objectivity that a comprehensive, chronological, officially sanctioned institutional history told through a single, authoritative voice perhaps could not achieve.

It is a well-known fact that no comprehensive history of the University of Texas exists. Many notable figures have attempted to start or have been requisitioned to undertake such a work, but none has been able to complete the task. These include several University presidents—notably Walter M. W. Splawn, H. Y. Benedict, and Harry Ransom—as well as academics and professional historians. For whatever reason, the topic of the University of Texas seems to resist being explained by a lone voice or from a solitary point of view. The hope is that the inductive approach that these volumes of *The Texas Book* offer reveals a path into the University's history that has not been previously explored.

Bernard De Voto's analysis of the causes and consequences of the Rainey affair, quoted above, provides the viewpoint of someone who observed the University of Texas from the outside and who expressed that point of view in the pages of a national magazine published in New York City—a magazine known for its liberal stance on most issues, no less. However, views of the University of Texas similar to De Voto's have been voiced close to home as well. For

example, in his book *The Forty-Acre Follies* (1983), the late Joe B. Frantz includes a chapter titled "Pursuit and Persecution," which traces the history of the "Big Bear Fight" between the University and Governor James "Pa" Ferguson in 1917 (see Patrick Cox's essay "'Farmer Jim' and 'The Chief'" in this volume for a discussion of that episode), as well as the history of the Rainey affair. Frantz was a UT alumnus and longtime faculty member in UT's Department of History; he was also one of the many historians involved in one or more of the abortive attempts to produce an institutional history. He begins this chapter with the following observations:

The University of Texas has the worst reputation of any academic institution in the United States for being ridden, even overwhelmed, by politics—and it is deserved. I've spent nearly half a century trying to figure out why we have that reputation. I haven't come to a satisfactory conclusion yet.

The state of Texas has its share of ignoramuses, but so does every other state in the Union. Texas has its political divisions, but they are no more violent than those in Massachusetts or California. Texas governors and legislators too often pander to anti-intellectual forces within the state, but I have lived all over the United States and find other legislators and public officials as inflammatory and malignant as ours. Texas has its religious zealots who think that free inquiry is a renunciation of all that is Christian, but I have found equally well buckled Bible Belts in Iowa and Illinois.

Why do Texas people invariably turn on the university?

Perhaps as you, the reader, explore the various topics discussed in the essays in this volume of *The Texas Book* and listen to the voices describing them, you can begin to form your own answer to Dr. Frantz's question. Perhaps you will also develop an appreciation—or increase the appreciation you already have—for the magnificent successes that the University has achieved in its nearly 130-year history and for the seemingly unlimited potential it has, at times, to achieve even more.

{ }

Considering the development of public universities in other states in the Union, Texas got a late start.

There are clear reasons for Texas's delinquency. Before ratification of the Texas Constitution of 1876, the leaders of the Republic of Texas and the State of Texas formally acknowledged the importance of founding a flagship public university, but had little ability to make that happen, other than by setting aside income-producing land and other resources to finance such an endeavor. (Even so, those resources were plundered by the legislature on more than one occasion for other, more immediate and practical needs.) By the 1870s, the Northeast and the Old South were home to colleges and universities with traditions several generations old already, and states from New England to the Pacific Coast had established public institutions of higher learning. Some of those state institutions, such as the University of Michigan and the University of Missouri, were founded decades before the start of the Civil War and were already thriving. Furthermore, the federal government had passed the Morrill Act in 1862—a remarkable piece of legislation, enacted under the most improbable circumstances—and in the years immediately after the end of the Civil War, vibrant land-grant colleges were sprouting up across the Midwest and in the new states in the Far West. But not in Texas.

In 1866, Texas accepted the terms of the Morrill Act, which included a five-year deadline for establishing a university. In 1871, with the state reeling from the traumas of Reconstruction, the five-year deadline approaching, and the receipt of scrip for 180,000 acres of federal land in peril, the state legislature hurriedly founded an agricultural and mechanical college, to be incorporated later in the yet-to-be-founded main university. Another five years passed before this A&M college finally opened, on the outskirts of Bryan, Texas, the same year Texas ratified yet again a new state constitution, which included the following language:

The Legislature shall, as soon as practicable, establish, organize and provide for the maintenance, support and direction of a university of the first class, to be located by a vote of the people of this State, and styled, "The University of Texas," for the promotion of literature, and the arts and sciences, including an agricultural and mechanical department.

CONSTITUTION OF THE STATE OF TEXAS,
1876, ARTICLE VII, SECTION 10

It would take five more years for the state to found the University of Texas (with the lingering question whether the agricultural and mechanical college already established near Bryan was a department of the University of Texas or a separate institution). In 1881, the state assembled a board of regents, and the statewide vote resulted in Austin being selected as the site of the new university. (In a convoluted, politicized balloting process, Tyler received the second-most votes.) Two years later, UT opened its doors to students, albeit in the temporary Capitol at 11th and Congress because the west wing of the proposed Main Building—the only portion of the building the state could afford to build at that time—was not yet ready. Making matters worse, the missteps and excesses of the Reconstruction effort in Texas wrought terrible political turmoil among Texans and within their state and local governments, effectively destroying what little public primary and secondary education existed in most of the rural regions of Texas—which, of course, constituted the vast majority of the state.

Such was the environment from which most of the students who matriculated during the first decades of the University's existence emerged.

In this volume of *The Texas Book*, Nolan Porterfield's profile of John Lomax describes much of this early history of the University, because Lomax—better known today as the ballad hunter who "discovered" Huddie William "Leadbelly" Ledbetter in a Louisiana prison—played such an important role in the early development of the University's administration and its alumni association. A small army of midlevel administrators in the sprawling operations of today's University can trace the genealogy of their positions back to one person, the indefatigable—and frustrated—Lomax.

H. Y. Benedict, a contemporary of Lomax who grew up on the fading Texas frontier about one hundred miles northwest of Meridian, Lomax's hometown, and who attended the same small college in Weatherford, Texas, as Lomax before coming to Austin for a proper university education, was the first graduate of the University to become its president. In my profile of Benedict, I outline his remarkable success as the longest-serving president in UT's history and identify the roots of that success in his unique upbringing.

Another nineteenth-century man—one whose influence on the early University would affect Benedict, a trained astronomer, significantly—was banker William J. McDonald of Paris, Texas, who provided in his will the funds to create the McDonald Observatory. Frank Bash, a former director of the observatory, gives an updated history of how the McDonald gift has blossomed into a research facility that is still competitive in world-class astronomical research—and is also a leader in public outreach.

Patrick Cox examines the University's success in defending itself against James "Pa" Ferguson, the Texas governor who attempted to suffocate the University by cutting off its appropriation when UT's leaders refused to do his bidding—in particular, his demand that the University fire tenured professors and key staff members (including John Lomax) who for whatever reason had raised the governor's hackles. Cox focuses on the role that "the Chief," UT history professor Eugene C. Barker, played in that historic episode, which culminated in the impeachment of "Farmer Jim."

Don E. Carleton's profile of J. R. Parten, who served as a regent of the University from 1935 to 1941, reveals some of the deep complexities that regents and UT administrators face in finding workable common ground among the various competing interests that attempt to impose their will on the University. These interests include the state legislature, big business, the University faculty and staff, and the voters and taxpayers of the state. Carleton reveals how the University benefited from the intellectual growth Major Parten experienced during his six years on the Board of Regents, the last two as chairman.

One of the important functions of any major research university is to serve as an incubator for new ideas and new artistic and scientific endeavors. One such endeavor is the renowned Shakespeare at Winedale program, founded by James Ayres, a UT English professor. Alice Gordon's reminiscence of her experience in the early years of the program gives insight into the power of art as it has been explored since the early 1970s by "regular" students in the bucolic setting of a former farmstead in Fayette County, first settled on the outskirts of Stephen F. Austin's original colony in the days of the Republic of Texas. Her memories reveal how the program provides its participants—and the audiences of the plays that the students stage and perform—a unique freedom to learn and to grow.

Likewise, Michael Toland's history of *Austin City Limits* explains how one of America's most respected television programs was born and came of age on the Forty Acres. *ACL* has not only given television audiences the chance to hear some of the greatest artists in American music in the twentieth and twenty-first centuries and preserved it for subsequent generations, but also showcased for the nation the cultural vibe that has always made Austin unique.

Perhaps the highest goal of art—and of a good university education—is the opportunity for self-discovery. Self-discovery and tolerance (a self-discovery that the Board of Regents of 1944 would have found intolerable) is the theme of Vance Muse's reminiscence of his days as a UT student in the early 1970s. Muse thoughtfully describes his experience as a young man in the process of discovering his homosexuality. The sixties, as a cultural and political era, really didn't come to an end until the early seventies, and in describing his own personal transformation of identity, Muse captures much of the spirit of the campus in the waning days of that tumultuous period in American history. The places and attitudes he describes will no doubt be fondly remembered by many of this book's readers.

It is virtually impossible to examine the history of the University of Texas—or almost any university in the United States, for that matter—without examining the role that race and segregation played in that history. In his essay on John W. Hargis, the first African American to enroll in UT as an undergraduate student, Richard McCaslin fills in more of the story begun by Michael Gillette, who, in the first *Texas Book*, describes the successful efforts to desegregate the University that culminated in 1950 with the enrollment of Heman Sweatt in the UT Law School. McCaslin's profile reveals the humanity and courage of Hargis's effort to matriculate at UT, as well as the deep complexities that the inevitable need to desegregate the University presented its leaders.

At the same time that Hargis matriculated at UT, on his own, in the summer of 1955, the University was preparing to enroll in the fall 1956 semester its "inaugural" group of African American undergraduates. One of the members of that group was Barbara Smith from Center Point, Texas, an East Texas hamlet founded by African Americans. She received her degree from UT in 1959, and as Barbara Conrad, earned her status one of the world's foremost mezzosopranos. Her powerful reminiscence reveals her journey from the tiny East Texas communities of her childhood to the great opera houses of Europe and the Americas.

The University's greatness—its ability to be "of the first class"—depends on its willingness and ability to outgrow its provinciality—to embrace the diversity on which the world rests—whether it is a diversity of race, gender, sexual orientation, nationality, or creed. The University's greatness also depends on its willingness and ability to recognize the best talent from around the globe and attract it to Austin. Peter LaSalle, a UT English professor, gives an account of an indisputable moment of greatness in the University's history—the year that the great Argentinean writer Jorge Luis Borges spent on the Forty Acres as a visiting professor. LaSalle uses this instance of greatness to explore the question whether UT today truly is a university of the first class. Likewise, in his essay on the many uses of Gregory Gymnasium over the years, Dick Holland recalls some of the world-class artists and performers who visited the gym during this same era, including the poet T. S. Eliot, the jazz legend Louis Armstrong, and the conductor Arturo Toscanini.

The built environment, including Gregory Gym, plays an important role in shaping the lives and intellectual development of students and scholars on the UT campus. Two UT architecture professors, Richard Cleary and Larry Speck, continue the story begun by Speck in the first *Texas Book* in his essay on the "heroic decades" of campus architecture—namely, the period during which the buildings designed by Cass Gilbert, Herbert Greene, and Paul Cret were built. In this volume, Cleary and Speck examine the post-Cret decades, providing description and analysis of the buildings of the late 1950s through the 1990s—buildings that, to risk overgeneralization, always evoke strong and mixed reactions.

Among the buildings built during that era is the Academic Center and Undergraduate Library (known today as the Peter T. Flawn Academic Center), the brainchild of UT president and future UT System chancellor Harry Ransom. Richard Oram, the associate director of today's Harry Ransom Center, outlines the history of "Harry's Place," as it was popularly known in Ransom's day. Oram describes the building's original purpose, follows the ever-changing uses of the building, and describes the recent removal of the last vestiges of the AC's original

purpose, in Ransom's conception, as a unique avenue of access to books and great works of art for the University's undergraduate population.

In addition to pointing out some of the great entertainers and literary figures who have performed in Gregory Gym over the years, Dick Holland also describes how the daily business of the University—registration, varsity basketball and volleyball games, recreational sports, and "Fite Nite"—has played out over the years in Gregory, which he calls "the most important building on campus." Another important building on campus centered on physical education—one that, like the Academic Center, has undergone notorious changes—is Anna Hiss Gymnasium. Brad Buchholz's profile of Anna Hiss shows the important contributions this pioneering and quietly remarkable woman, the sister of the accused spy Alger Hiss, made to the early development of women's athletics at the University.

In stark contrast to the work of Anna Hiss—whose work in physical education for women existed in a much earlier era and reflected both her high standards for her students and her distaste for intercollegiate competition—stands the reminiscence of Cat Osterman, a UT softball great who, in my opinion, stands in the rarefied company of Earl Campbell and Clyde Littlefield as, arguably, one of the most, if not *the* most, dominant and important athletes in the history of UT athletics. Title IX changed women's collegiate athletics immeasurably, and one cannot help noting the differences in perception of the role of women's athletics between Anna Hiss, who died the year Title IX was passed, 1972, and Cat Osterman, who was born in 1983 and has never known a world in which men's and women's athletics were not expected to be on more or less equal footing.

The hallmark of a university of the first class is excellence in teaching. This volume contains accounts of many great teachers and the effects that great teaching has had on the students who benefited from it—including James Ayres and his Shakespeare at Winedale program, Edra Gustafson and the many other voice and music teachers who influenced Barbara Smith Conrad's development, and Borges's time as a visiting professor in Austin. The profile of Harvey Penick in this volume, written by his pupil Ben Crenshaw, a three-time medalist at the NCAA Division I golf championship and two-time winner of the Masters, one of professional golf's four major tournaments, is a loving tribute to a man who was a great teacher and whose subject happened to be the game of golf.

Finally, Sam Hurt's reminiscence about Hank the Hallucination—a cartoon hallucination of the comic-strip character Eyebeam—and Hank's victory in the race for student body president in 1982, as well as Wayne Butler's thoughtful memories of his years living in Married Student Housing on the Brackenridge Tract, give glimpses into the uniquely glorious and challenging experience of being a student at a major American university. Butler's reminiscence, as well as Crenshaw's profile of Harvey Penick, also touch on the current debate over the fate of the Lions Municipal Golf Course and the use of the Brackenridge Tract in the decades to come—a seminal moment for the University as it ponders its future and the values that will guide its journey into that future.

{ }

In the late 1930s, J. Frank Dobie published a small pamphlet titled *A Corner Forever Texas*. Dobie was a member of the faculty in the University's Department of English and a writer of works that captured the spirit and flavor of the old West, which, by the 1930s, was rapidly disappearing under the inexorable progress of twentieth-century modernity. In his day, Dobie was considered by many to be Texas's greatest living writer. The subject of *A Corner Forever Texas* is ostensibly the state of the Texas Collection—the collection of books, manuscripts, maps, and artwork belonging to the University's libraries that pertained specifically to Texas. The new Main Building and Tower, whose original purpose was to serve solely as the University's library, had opened just a few years earlier, and the Texas Collection was housed in the ornate rooms of the Latin American Collection in the new Main Building—in the words of Dobie, "as a kind of subsidiary of the Latin-American collection, chiefly books on Mexico," in a room that was "characterless in so far as expressing anything of Texas."

Dobie despised the new Main Building and Tower because he thought them not to be Texan, or respectful of the Texas environment. In his pamphlet, he decries them as being merely imitative of European architecture and landscaping. He was not opposed to the work of the architect, Paul Cret—in fact, he praises Cret's Home Economics Building (today

named Mary E. Gearing Hall) as being thoroughly Texan: "No building on the campus is more at home with itself and with its environment than the Home Economics Building." Dobie begins his pamphlet with the following assertions:

> Ever since the University of Texas was established, there has been much talk about making it "a university of the first class." A good deal of the talk has been made by people who seem to think that if the University could get as many books in its library as Harvard has, as high a salary for its professors as Yale pays, as large a percentage of Ph.D.'s in its faculty as Johns Hopkins catalogues, as much laboratory equipment as the Massachusetts Institute of Technology possesses, etc., all the "first class" requirements would be satisfied.
>
> A really great University is something more than a successful ape. It has a character and an individuality peculiar to itself. In great universities like Oxford and the Sorbonne, this character is an expression of the civilization that the university both represents and influences. An outstanding characteristic of a truly great university is that it belongs to its environment, as cypresses belong to the clear streams of Central Texas, as cottonwoods belong to the water courses of the West, as live oaks belong to limestone soil and post oaks to sandy soil.
>
> Physically and culturally, the University of Texas is, despite its name, still perhaps more *in* Texas than *of* Texas.

Dobie's proposed solution for the Texas Collection, in particular, was to construct a building to house it that would be unmistakably Texan in character—a building that would be "a corner forever Texas." Of course, Dobie's description of what such a home for the Texas Collection would look like—western motifs, images of life on the range, references to the heroes of the Republic of Texas and the pioneers of the Texas frontier, primarily men, no doubt, of ancestry and outlook similar to Dobie's—reflects his particular conception of what it means to be Texan.

So as the University moves forward, and as hopeful students and anxious parents find it increasingly difficult to gain admission to Texas's flagship university, the question "What does it mean to be 'of the first class'?" is inevitably joined by the question "What does it mean to be 'of Texas'?" As the state's population continues to increase, as the prestige and desirability of the University continues to grow in the minds not just of Texans but of intelligent and ambitious people around the globe as well—and as the University's administration maintains static enrollment levels of around 50,000 students or fewer on UT's urban, "landlocked," ever-densifying campus—a smaller and smaller proportion of graduates from Texas high schools will be able to attend the University of Texas at Austin.

Today the Texas Collection is housed in Sid Richardson Hall, a building whose design and intent could not be any further from the nineteenth-century western motifs of cattle and ranching that Frank Dobie envisioned for it. What does it mean for the University of Texas to be *of Texas*? What does that look like? Dobie's roundup? A homogeneous suburb of Houston or Dallas? Something else entirely? Can the University of Texas be of the world without being merely imitative of the world?

Perhaps the essays in this volume can lend some insight as we form our own answers to such questions.

Profiles

Rising from the Frontier

NOLAN
PORTERFIELD }

John A. Lomax and the University of Texas

Illiterate people, and people cut off from newspapers and books, isolated and lonely folk—thrown back on primal resources for entertainment and for the expression of emotion—express themselves through somewhat the same character of songs as did their forefathers of perhaps a thousand years ago.

JOHN A. LOMAX, *COWBOY SONGS AND OTHER FRONTIER BALLADS,* 1910

Like the pull of the moon on ocean tides, the University of Texas ruled the ebb and flow of John Lomax's life for thirty years. At the University, he was a good student, loyal employee, and tireless booster, and later became a frustrated exile. A child of the nineteenth-century Texas frontier, a man filled with talents and contradictions, John Avery Lomax was led by his ambition to Austin, toward the education that he saw as the surest path leading him away from the life of his father's farm. That ambition would also produce his lasting legacy—namely, the preservation of American cowboy and folk songs, quintessential products of the very world he hoped to escape.

Most people today have not heard of John Lomax. If they have, they likely know him not as an important figure in the early history of the University of Texas, but instead as the great ballad hunter: the honorary curator of the Archive of American Folk Song at the Library of Congress and the author of *Cowboy Songs and Other Frontier Ballads* (1910), *American Ballads and Folk Songs* (1934), *Our Singing Country* (1941),

---

Texan Nolan Porterfield is the author of the award-winning biography Jimmie Rodgers: The Life and Times of America's Blue Yodeler *(1996) and the novel* A Way of Knowing *(1971). For many years he was a professor of English and writer in residence at Southeast Missouri State University. In retirement, he continues to write, and hosts a weekly radio program,* Old Scratchy Records, *from his home in Bowling Green, Kentucky. This profile of John Lomax, written in collaboration with David Dettmer, is based on excerpts from Porterfield's* Last Cavalier: The Life and Times of John A. Lomax, 1867–1948 *(1996).*

and several other indispensable collections of American folk music. Throughout his adult life, Lomax scoured the country, alone or with his son Alan, in search of songs that were rapidly disappearing under the early twentieth century's inexorable progress. In his later years, he traveled in a car outfitted with an enormous, custom-made recording device to capture song performances from the people he met as well as to preserve the tunes and lyrics of the songs themselves.

Lomax is most widely known as the "discoverer" (some would say exploiter) of Huddie Ledbetter, a convicted murderer and longtime convict in Texas and Louisiana penitentiaries better known as Leadbelly, "king of the twelve-string guitar players." This "queerly assorted couple"—a stern, old-fashioned white southerner and a charismatic black musician who relished being a man of mystery as well as a powerful and accomplished performer—was the toast of the New York City social scene for a few heady months in 1935. Leadbelly captivated white audiences in performances at private homes and academic settings carefully devised and overseen by Lomax.

Through his song collecting, accomplished mostly outside his work as a salaried man in higher education and banking, Lomax preserved many of those lovely, sad, and funny bits of tune and line now embedded in our lives. In many instances, he was the first to publish them. In *Cowboy Songs and Other Frontier Ballads*, Lomax collected "Whoopee Ti Yi Yo, Git Along, Little Dogies," "The Old Chisholm Trail," "Jesse James," "Sweet Betsy from Pike," and, of course, "Home on the Range," among dozens of other American favorites, which he saved from doom or otherwise helped preserve and popularize. Likewise, the rich and sprawling mixture of *American Ballads and Folk Songs* produced one of the first truly great collections of American song, in its rough, robust, distinctly American character as well as in the range of titles that have become national classics: "Casey Jones," "Frankie and Albert (Johnny)," "Down in the Valley," "Rye Whiskey," "Little Brown Jug," "Shortenin' Bread," "Cotton-Eyed Joe," "Dixie," "Amazing Grace," "Swing Low, Sweet Chariot," and dozens more whose place in our culture was established through Lomax's work. In fact, *Cowboy Songs* occupies a vital place in American cultural history. Despite Lomax's often-exaggerated claims in print

about the originality and importance of his collections, one can hazard the plain assertion that what *Cowboy Songs* amounted to was—if not in fact, then certainly in substance and in effect—simply the first important collection of American folk songs.

The work of collecting folk music would take Lomax to every corner of the American landscape—from prisons and work camps to cattle ranches and backwoods shacks, from cotton farms and dusty small-town main streets to the halls of academia and the salons of Manhattan's high society. However, it was scholarly achievement and a respectable position in a first-class institution of higher education that had been Lomax's ambition from an early age. *Cowboy Songs* was a direct result of life-changing relationships he had forged at Harvard University while pursuing a master's degree, nearly ten years after his graduation from UT. Though his Harvard experience opened doors that led to his most lasting legacy, the University of Texas, for better or worse, was the object of Lomax's desire for most of his life. John Lomax, UT Class of 1897, would devote some of the best years of his working life to the University, yet suffer three separate "exiles" from the Forty Acres.

THE HARVARD CONNECTION

Like most young men who had grown up in hardscrabble circumstances on the Texas frontier in the late nineteenth century and somehow found their way to Austin to pursue a higher education, Lomax's experience as a student at the University of Texas transformed his life. He arrived on the Forty Acres in the summer of 1895—twenty-seven years old and the holder of a teaching certificate from a small, and by then already defunct, college in Granbury, Texas. After earning his bachelor's degree from the University in just two years, he accepted the job of registrar of the University. In the long run, however, the road for John Lomax at the University of Texas would always prove to be treacherous.

The first of his three exiles from the University—self-imposed, in this instance—came in 1903. David F. Houston, Lomax's former professor of political science at UT, had risen to the presidency of the Agricultural and Mechanical College of Texas, and Lomax, feeling overworked, underpaid, and underappreciated in his job as registrar, followed him to College

John Lomax as song collector (*all images courtesy of the Library of Congress, Prints and Photographs Division, Lomax Collection*): (TOP) Prison Compound No. 1, Angola, Louisiana, with Leadbelly in the foreground, 1934 (*photo by Alan Lomax, LC-DIG-ppmsc-00346 DLC*); (LEFT) Lomax (*center*) with Uncle Billy McCrea (*right*) and friends at Billy's home in Jasper, Texas, 1940 (*photo by Ruby Terrill Lomax, LC-DIG-ppmsc-00316 DLC*); (RIGHT) Huddie Ledbetter (aka "Leadbelly") and Martha Promise Ledbetter, Wilton, Connecticut, 1935 (*photographer unknown, LC-DIG-ppmsc-00660 DLC*).

John Lomax as song collector (*all images courtesy of the Library of Congress, Prints and Photographs Division, Lomax Collection*): (TOP LEFT) Lomax and Uncle Rich Brown, at the home of Mrs. Julia Killingsworth near Sumterville, Alabama, 1940 (*photo by Ruby Terrill Lomax, LC-DIG-ppmsc-00356 DLC*); (TOP RIGHT) Stavin' Chain playing guitar and singing the ballad "Batson," Lafayette, Louisiana, 1934 (*photo by Alan Lomax, LC-DIG-ppmsc-00341 DLC*); (BOTTOM LEFT) Lolo Mendoza and Chico Real, with guitars, at the home of Mrs. Sarah Kleberg Shelton, Kingsville, Texas, 1940 (*photo by Ruby Terrill Lomax, LC-DIG-ppmsc-00302 DLC*); (BOTTOM RIGHT) Wayne Perry playing fiddle, Crowley, Louisiana, ca. 1934—1950 (*photo by Alan Lomax, LC-DIG-ppmsc-00339 DLC*).

Station to become an instructor in the Texas A&M English Department. It was during this first "exile" that he first became acquainted with the forces that would lead him to collect American folksong.

For Lomax, there were two centers of the universe—one in Texas, the other in the East, emanating from Harvard. In 1906, at the relatively late age of thirty-nine, he undertook a year of graduate study at Harvard, benefiting from one of Harvard's prestigious Austin Teaching Fellowships as well as a year of unpaid leave from Texas A&M. To Lomax, who as a child and young adult had made do with the limited educational resources his upbringing on the Texas frontier had provided him, Harvard represented everything he wanted: achievement, authority, recognition among the elite. Cambridge, in contrast to the arid, flimsy-new Texas villages and towns Lomax had known, reeked of substance and an honored past, burnished in its broad brick streets and the elegant (by Texas standards) high, spacious old houses, turreted and verandaed and set on deep green lawns under leafy elms. Other men from the frontier went back East for an education; Lomax went there to be anointed.

While working toward the completion of his AM degree, Lomax was urged by two of Harvard's professors of comparative literature, Barrett Wendell and George Lyman Kittredge, to pursue a scholarly effort to collect and study cowboy songs. The scholarly interests of these two were significant, and would influence the rest of Lomax's life. Kittredge taught The English and Scottish Popular Ballads, a course that derived from the vast, pioneering work of Kittredge's mentor, Francis James Child (1825–1896). (Child had been Harvard's first professor of English, and it was he who had introduced to English-speaking countries the notion of bringing together folk songs as a means of studying the culture of those who created and sang them.) Wendell had developed what was, in effect, the nation's first course in American literature, Harvard's famous English 33—Literary History of America—in the late 1890s, drawing on his interest in the nation's colonial literature and history. In Wendell's American literature course, Lomax had gotten, for the first time in his life, official confirmation that there was meaning and value in his native culture—the raw, uncouth life of the frontier.

Given his life experiences on the Texas ranch of his youth and his spotty educational background,

Lomax could not have found himself in a more fortuitous position at a more fortuitous time. Each student enrolled in Wendell's class met with him in his office in Grays Hall to discuss a possible subject for the term paper the student would write for the course. In these meetings, Wendell stressed his weariness with reading papers about literary eminences such as Emerson and Hawthorne and encouraged students to write about regional literary efforts in their own parts of the country. Lomax—the rough-cut Texas farmer's son, with a veneer of savoir faire but beneath it bumptious, moody, insecure—first suggested that he could write about Negro music, but when he also mentioned cowboy songs and said that he had in mind songs that the cowboys "made up" while they worked, "Professor Wendell," Lomax recalls, "sprang from his chair, and, in his enthusiasm, came around the table to shake my hand."[1] So enthusiastic was Wendell that he arranged an audience with Kittredge, whose background in comparative literature was even broader than Wendell's. During the meeting, Kittredge expressed immediate interest in what Lomax told him about cowboy songs and suggested ways that Harvard—or at least Wendell and Kittredge—might support his efforts to increase his stock of material. At that time, this stock apparently consisted of little more than the few verses published in January 1898 (a few months after Lomax had graduated from UT and begun his job as the University's registrar) in "The Minstrelsy of the Mexican Border," a four-page article in the *University of Texas Magazine*, coupled with vague memories of songs Lomax had heard growing up.[2] (Though the author of this article is anonymous, I have examined it from every angle and concluded that Lomax wrote it. The coincidences between this piece and Lomax's later work are too great to ignore.)

Significantly, "The Minstrelsy of the Mexican Border" (the title an obvious allusion to Sir Walter Scott's *Minstrelsy of the Scottish Border*) recounts the grandeur of the old days, "the days of the Cattle Kings," when "some uncouth ballad of the ranch and range, or of old fights of the border outlaws, was always on the lips of the cow-boys." The piece is short, and the prose sometimes a bit ripe, in the fashion of the time, but it covers much ground and conveys the message cleanly: these songs and singers are dying away, and that is regrettable. The writer's concern is not only for his native area north of the border; attention is also given to "the songs of the Mexicans," which the author finds more numerous than those of the Anglos but having "less right to be called folk-songs" because they are more often changed by those who sing them (clear evidence that, for better or worse, the author lacked a mature sense of folk-song scholarship). Fragments of several songs, including "Bury Me Not on the Lone Prairie" and "Sam Bass," are quoted and analyzed in the article. It closes with a lament for the passing of such songs and the men who sang them. The author of the article observes:

> Better things, it may be, are coming in to take the place of the cowboys, but to these as the years go by, will be added a glamour that the things that have driven them into the west and down to death can never hold. No furrowed field can ever make a man forget the prairies and the magic of their call when Spring is breaking, no harvest gathering can ever equal the rough assemblage of the round-up, and no man in all the world can ever take the vacant place of "the last cavalier."[3]

Soon after Wendell's call for "regional literary productions," Lomax began writing to possible sources in Texas. This work would lead him to the successful completion of his Harvard AM degree, and he would return to song collecting over and over again throughout his life. The yearlong odyssey from the Texas backwoods to Harvard brought with it a change of fortune for Lomax, and life would never be quite the same again. He had already come a long way.

CULTIVATION ON THE NINETY-EIGHTH MERIDIAN

John Lomax was born in 1867 in Mississippi, a state still reeling from the horrors of the Civil War. When the Lomax family migrated to Texas, in the late fall of 1869, the Lone Star State was, strictly speaking, not even a state. Four troubled years after the Civil War, it was still under military occupation, in chaos and turmoil, its status suspended between that of conquered territory and provisional statehood. A fiercely contested and probably fraudulent election in November of that year gave dictatorial control to carpetbagger Radical Republicans, who won the statehouse by a small majority of some eight hun-

dred votes. With an administration now more or less aligned with the policies of the Reconstruction Congress in Washington, way was finally made for readmission to the Union the following spring. Still, political and economic turbulence continued to boil, even after southern Democrats managed to regain power in the mid-1870s—when the Lomaxes were still settling shakily into their new home. These years constituted, in the words of one historian, "the most disastrous period in Texas history," worse even than the terrible days of the war itself.[4]

The growing Lomax family settled on a quarter section (160 acres) of bottom land on the Bosque River ("Bosky," off the Texas tongue), a few miles north of the village of Meridian, in the fertile, rumpled hill lands southwest of Fort Worth. It was about as close as one could get in those days to deep in the heart of Texas.[5] In the early years there was a steady procession of covered wagons, trail herds, and riders on horseback along the branch of the Chisholm Trail nearby. Cowboys and other wayfaring strangers often spent the night in the Lomax home, bringing "the big, outside world [to] our door."[6] These visitors, John felt, first awakened him to the realization that there were important people and ideas beyond the Bosque Valley.

Meridian is almost at the exact center of the Bosque Valley and halfway along the river's course. The name, however, comes from the fact that it sits on the ninety-eighth meridian—which in 1870 marked the farthest reach of the Texas frontier. The ninety-eighth meridian was—and remains—an important dividing line in other respects. Just beyond it lay a harsh, unsettled land where Comanche and Kiowa raiding bands still roamed, where the annual rainfall was never more than thirty inches, where all life was subject to frequent and violent change: drought, then flood; blazing sun, then high chill winds and blowing snow; feast, then famine.

In the ensuing century, the land beyond the ninety-eighth meridian was settled, one way or another, and the Indians "disappeared." But the weather and the topography remain essentially the same, and they dictate to a large extent the nature of human existence there—not merely the day-to-day life of people, but their ideas and values and attitudes. Historians and sociologists have dealt with the ninety-eighth meridian primarily in agricultural terms, as a division between what is "farmable" and "unfarmable," but farmers speak of "cultivating" the land, and it is the question of "cultivation" in broader terms that marks the homeland of John Lomax as a dividing line between the civilized and the primitive. Growing up in "Bosky" County, Texas, in the 1870s, he absorbed some of both, and a curious mixture of refinement and coarseness shows up in almost everything he did.

Much the same can be said of Lomax's alma mater. Situated 115 miles south of Meridian and even slightly closer to the ninety-eighth meridian is Texas's capital city, Austin, and the forty acres of land on which the state founded the University of Texas. The University had a late start—opening to students in 1883, less than twelve years before Lomax's arrival there. Like Lomax, the University was conceived during the turmoil and deprivations of Reconstruction and entered the twentieth century with clear aspirations for a more modern existence, despite the serious obstacles that lay in the way.

Boys in circumstances like those of John Lomax had essentially two occupational choices: they could till the soil or ride the range. Neither had much appeal for Lomax. Awed as he was by the flamboyant cowboys of the trail herd, he knew deep down that, contrary to the romantic image, punching cattle was a difficult life. Farming was simply hard work with no romance at all.

As soon as he could, Lomax hied himself off to the city in earnest pursuit of refined society, books and ideas, the Rotary Club, indoor plumbing. He made his way to the University of Texas in the summer of 1895—relatively late in life, at age twenty-seven—to pursue a bachelor's degree. "For many years thereafter," he wrote in his autobiography, "the University of Texas was the core of my life."[7] Lomax spoke vividly of entering the University of Texas as one of his greatest adventures; he was awkward and self-conscious, but happy beyond belief because he was fulfilling a lifelong dream.[8] He also revealed the deep insecurity that never left him, remarking that he felt students who were better dressed and had better manners were superior to him. Despite the achievements and honors that came to him later in life—he cofounded the Texas Folklore Society and served an unprecedented two terms as its president, published eight books and more than a dozen scholarly articles, was named honorary curator of the Archive of American Folk Song at the Library of Congress, knew and socialized with many national figures, from Teddy Roosevelt to Carl Sandburg—he never overcame his sense of inferiority or felt that his work was adequately recognized.

While the Lomaxes were struggling to start their life on a small farm in a new state, the state was struggling to start up a university. Although in 1839 the Republic of Texas had set aside land to support a university, nothing was ever founded or built. In the immediate wake of the Civil War, the state constitution of 1866 provided for the legislature to establish a university, and that same year the legislature accepted the terms of the federal government's Morrill Act of 1862. To address immediate practical needs, the state founded the Agricultural and Mechanical College of Texas in 1871, specifying that it would be built on the outskirts of Bryan, but it was still not yet ready to establish the main university or a medical branch. (The coming decades would see bitter fights over the question whether Texas A&M, which first offered classes in 1876, was an independent institution or merely a department of the University of Texas. Of course, even after that question was settled there would be even more bitter fights over the question of how state funds would be shared between the two schools.) The 1876 Texas Constitution specified that the legislature establish a university ("of the first class") as soon as practical, its location to be decided by a statewide popular vote. Seven more years passed before students finally matriculated at the University of Texas, in the fall of 1883. Classes were quartered at the temporary Capitol in Austin until the new building was ready for occupancy six months later (and even then, only the west wing of it had been built) on College Hill, a few blocks north of the Capitol.

Far north of Austin, amid that region's vast expanse of prairies and hills, the purchase of 183 acres of Bosque River bottomland had taken a fourth of the capital of John Lomax's father, James. He planted cotton and corn, and his older sons were put to work cutting timber to sell for firewood. As the boy John grew to it, chopping and hauling firewood to town became one of his major responsibilities, and by the time he was six, he was laboring alongside his brothers in the field. He herded the family's work stock, tended the milk cows, and helped clear new ground, a terrible job that required grubbing the trees out of the ground by their roots with pick and mattock. "Broken to work" is a country phrase used of both horses and boys; by the time he was in his teens, Johnny Lomax was qualified. Although he soon found a way to escape the drudgery of the farm, a distinguishing mark of his character throughout life was his awesome capacity for labor, an almost compulsive need for it, a seemingly tireless energy that only increased with the passing years.

As a young adult, Lomax reflected that he "forgot to be a boy" and complained that his youth had been closed off by "manual toil and frontier life."[9] Years later, still obsessed with the hardships of his childhood, he wondered to one of his sons whether his "barren background" might explain why he was "so angular, twisted mentally, [and] crude."[10] Yet his early life was not without its diversions. In his autobiography, he recounted the pleasures of roaming the cedar-clad hills and lush valleys of the Bosque tributaries in the days when the river still ran swift and clear, its banks overhung with willows and cottonwoods, elms, sycamores, and hackberries. "The beauty of the region grew in my soul," he wrote, reliving the sensations of galloping his favorite pony, Selim, across the rolling, open pasturelands, thick and vivid with native flowers. "I hunted and fished, went in swimming, and lived with my kind," he said.[11] His kind were the common run of country boys, Texas Huck Finns who, left together unattended, romped and wrestled and tumbled like pups, played risky pranks, dodged work whenever they could (which was not often), and generally behaved as boys always have.

Complementing the attractions of young Lomax's natural world was his father's insistence that his children get as much education as possible. During trips to town, John would secure from the office of the *Meridian Blade* an armful of "exchange" papers from other towns, sent to the *Blade* as trade for a complimentary subscription. His lumber wagon empty, young John would give the mules, Jack and Fan, full rein to find their way home while he slipped to the floor of the wagon and lost himself in boilerplate reports of the outside world. In due course, young John's newspaper reading habits were fed by journals of a larger scope. His father subscribed to several national papers, including the weekly *New York Sun*, with its visions of a faraway, magic metropolis. Then there were the *Louisville Courier* and the *Atlanta Constitution*, edited by the formidable Henry W. Grady, a figure of national reputa-

tion. Together with the "patent sides" of the county-seat weeklies, these papers became, as Lomax said later, "the real start of my education."[12] The rare, few books that came Lomax's way were at once treasured and consumed. Later in life, he told Lincolnesque stories of toilsome days in the fields and nights spent reading by a tiny brass lamp in his garret room when the family was asleep.

By the mid-1870s, when Lomax was old enough to start school, old-line Democrats had retaken control of the state from Reconstruction Republicans. Passionately opposed to centralized government, they made drastic cuts in state expenditures and essentially wrecked the Texas educational system.[13] While these actions retarded the intellectual climate in the state, it is unlikely that they altered the course of public education in rural Bosque County, which even under state supervision had been rudimentary. The important thing for young John was that his parents respected education and were determined that their children have as much schooling as possible. Although John claimed that he never attended a full school term until after he left home at age twenty, his father saw to it that his offspring, boys and girls alike, attended every school session when not needed for work at home.

Likewise, the Lomaxes were irregular churchgoers (despite their mother's religiosity and in large part because of their father's indifference to it). Yet fundamentalist Christian doctrine—the "hellfire and damnation of frontier Methodism"—was a strong and pervasive influence on their lives. Good and evil were strongly delineated according to Old Testament strictures. Hard work was a testing ground for the elect; retribution to the fallen was swift and certain. "We were earnest folk," said John, "and we worked hard at our religion."[14] The rural church of Lomax's time served, on the one hand, to foster this attitude of willing submission, contributing to the drab tedium and painful sameness of life, but ironically, at the heart of such strict fundamentalism was a fiery emotionalism, erupting at worst into reactionary rebellion, at best into passionate brotherhood: frontier religion in Texas was as much a force for social cohesion, an occasion for tribal gathering, as it was for the dissemination of theology. Johnny Lomax shrank from the dark, terrible doctrines of primitive Methodism, which literally caused him nightmares, but the social aspects of the church—especially its annual camp meetings—appealed to him as welcome relief from the loneliness and dull routine of his life, a source of the fellowship and camaraderie he always longed for.

Still, the pleasures of camp meetings, occasional books, and cowboy lodgers were fleeting, and always at his back Johnny Lomax heard not only Time's winged chariot but also the wrenching creak of a Georgia stock and single-row planter. Recurring bouts of imagination—an ancient affliction of bright farm boys—rendered him less and less fit for the dull tasks of frontier agriculture. As he grew aware of a world beyond Bosque County, his own existence there seemed all the more narrowed and confined, his choices limited, the route of his passage already booked and confirmed.

"HIGHER" EDUCATION: GRANBURY, WEATHERFORD, EASTMAN, AND CHAUTAUQUA

In John Lomax's favor was his parents' rule that at age twenty each child should go away to school for one year "for the common good of the family."[15] In the spring of 1887, his father set aside eleven acres of wheat land for him, and he began to lay plans to attend the so-called college in the adjoining county seat of Granbury. Heavy rains that year flooded out most of his crop, but with what he could salvage, augmented by loans from his father and an older cousin, Alonzo "Lon" Cooper, and the heartrending sale of his favorite pony, Selim, he set off in the fall to "college" in Granbury.

Throughout Texas, Methodism had been digging in for the long siege against native sin—such as the saloons and "poor men's clubs" in the frontier towns of the time—and its local bastion was Granbury College. A college in little more than name, it had been nothing more than a church-sponsored high school from its founding in 1873 until 1881, when its new president, David Switzer, added a "college" curriculum, ranging from English grammar and literature to elocution, physics, "mechanics," "mental philosophy," "moral science," and law.[16] Lomax chose and completed the one-year normal course, which covered merely "those branches that are required in order to obtain a first-class [teaching] certificate in any county of the state."[17] Armed with this "slender

equipment," and with the help of his cousin and confidant Lon Cooper, he found a teaching job in Clifton, a rural village close to both Meridian and Cousin Lon's farm, for the 1888–1889 school year.

Teaching country ruffians at a tiny, primitive school soon soured, and after a year at Clifton, Lomax asked Switzer for a position as a "professor" at Weatherford College. Facing bankruptcy, Granbury College had closed its doors earlier that year, and its Methodist directors had moved what little physical property remained to Weatherford, a thriving city more than three times the size of Clifton, merging it with Cleveland College—another erstwhile grammar and high school, founded in 1869 by the Masonic lodge in Weatherford. The consolidated, reorganized institution was renamed Weatherford College, with Switzer again in the president's chair. Conditions there, however, were not much better than at Granbury: a minuscule library, a poorly trained faculty, rigid discipline (even professors were required to attend every church service), with each teacher given a load of twelve to fifteen classes and expected to teach six days a week. Even Lomax, conditioned to the hard physical labor of the farm, found the load difficult.[18]

Lomax endured this "professorship" for six years, relieved to some extent when the college paid his expenses for a course titled Commercial Penmanship and Bookkeeping by Double-entry, offered during the summer session at Eastman Business College in Poughkeepsie, New York. After that, he went off for each of five summers to Chautauqua, New York, for the lecture-and-concert series originated by the Methodist Church, with its philosophy of "every man his own college," which appealed to those in quest of "self-improvement."[19] The sessions were often more entertainment than education, or entertainment disguised as education: lectures on high-minded subjects were given elevated titles but shortened and leavened for easy consumption. In time, Lomax came to realize this, but he also improved his mathematics and Latin, learned about light opera, and was exposed to serious poetry of the day. Still, his situation at Weatherford continued to deteriorate.

Curiously, Lomax never wrote about these first trips back East, and the very absence of such an account from a man who dwelt on himself in countless letters, journals, and jottings, who saved almost every scrap of biographical paper, is in itself illuminating. One can only suppose that his reactions to the cultural distance between rural Texas and the cosmopolitan East were true to character: part awe, part happy enthusiasm, part anger and embarrassment. He was still poor and shabby, and all too conscious of his inadequacies, social and intellectual, for such an experience. But he was also a young man with a vision who had sold his best pony to buy books and braved surly oafs in country schoolrooms and come all the way to Weatherford, Texas, to be called "professor."

In the spring of 1895, Lomax made a visit to Cousin Lon's farm near Clifton that changed forever the course of his life. When he poured out his troubles to Lon, the older man said simply, "Go and make your plans. I'll back you."[20] In Fort Worth to change trains on his way home, Lomax struck up a conversation with Joe Etter, a young hardware salesman from Sherman, just two years out of the University of Texas. When Lomax mentioned that he might try to qualify for Vanderbilt University—located in Nashville, the "Athens of the South"—with its Methodist connections and wide reputation for excellence, Etter said, "The University of Texas is the only place for you."[21] Back in Weatherford, Lomax went at once to David Switzer and gave notice that he was leaving. When the spring semester ended in early June, Lomax was on the train to Austin.

ON TO AUSTIN AND TEXAS'S "UNIVERSITY OF THE FIRST CLASS"

When John Lomax arrived in Austin that summer of 1895, the University of Texas was not yet twelve years old, still rough at the edges and struggling. But it was also energetic and ambitious, asserting for itself a place of prominence among its peers in the region. There weren't many—Vanderbilt and Tulane were the only comparable institutions in the South and Southwest. The University of Missouri, in the distant Midwest, claimed a comparable reputation (and perhaps more importantly to the student body, it provided flesh-and-blood rivals for UT's fledgling football team).[22] In Texas, the Agricultural and Mechanical College at College Station drew small numbers of future farmers, soldiers, and engineers, but as an all-male school that required every student to join its military cadet corps, it earned little academic re-

spect. The recently chartered Rice Institute in Houston would eventually become known as the state's most select and academically rigorous institution of higher learning when it finally opened in 1912, a mecca for Texas's handful of genuine intellectuals. But as the twentieth century loomed on the horizon, standards at the University of Texas were sufficient to give it a serious reputation, and it was certainly more fun than the church schools, Baylor and Texas Christian.

The atmosphere in which the University of Texas hoped to flourish was not always clear and sunny, as Lomax soon found out. His burning desire for education was not shared by other Texans, especially in rural areas, where the majority of the state's population still lived. Rank-and-file citizens, notoriously unbookish, found many reasons to oppose higher education, suspicious of anything that lurked about in the guise of "refinement," laid claim to tax dollars, and offered no clear and immediate promise of cash return. Resentment toward the University was fed, ironically, by the state's older institutions of learning, especially Baylor and Texas Christian, which got no tax money and saw the state university as unfair competition. Their opposition was frequently voiced in moral terms, reflecting concern for what many viewed as lax behavior on the Austin campus and dangerously liberal thinking ("secular humanism" is the charge today). This was a message more powerful than finances, confirming the worst fears in the minds of the rustic and fundamental, whose numbers were legion.

Even stronger resistance came from Texas A&M, which did have to compete for state funds. Although the Agricultural and Mechanical College was, on paper at least, a branch of the state university, its existence preceded that of the University of Texas by seven years, and its prerogatives, real or imagined, were jealously guarded by faculty, administration, and a loyal cadre of alumni that included prominent farmers, military leaders, and professional men. The University, on the other hand, had not been in business long enough to produce a body of influential graduates and lacked an effective alumni organization—a situation that, in time, John Lomax would play a central role in correcting.

These problems and conflicts coalesced in the state legislature, which held the purse strings and was prone to act, often irrationally, at times outrageously, as an agent of transmittal for all that was best and worst in the Texas body politic. The University, situated at the back door of the Capitol, became a ready target, subject to all sorts of legislative whims and machinations in the biennial struggle over appropriations. Some lawmakers had noble but wrongheaded intentions while others were merely populist crackpots, and a few were genuine friends of the University. The relationship was that of a nervous protégé and an affluent but quirky benefactor: the University tried to be dutiful, but sometimes failed; its moods swung from sycophantic to resentful to defiant, while the legislature could always be expected to do the unexpected. One result was to instill a certain esprit de corps among students, faculty, and administration, who at times felt themselves drawn together in a unified front—outnumbered and outgunned, not unlike the defenders of the Alamo—against a common enemy.

To the degree that the University of Texas established itself as an institution of growing promise, its success was due not so much to any truly progressive attitude among the citizens of the state as to a pervasive spirit of enthusiasm for learning that was in the air all across the nation. In the aftermath of the Civil War and Reconstruction had come a renewed faith in the old Jeffersonian ideal of education as inoculation against social and political ills, or at the very least as a prescription for "success in life"—a mighty potion that could induce, as it were, the American Dream. Yet pragmatic representatives in the statehouse spoke for the majority in rejecting fuzzy-headed intellectualism, asserting the popular notion that colleges should train people for something useful in the rough-and-tumble world of commerce and industry. That attitude was nothing new to John Lomax (in later years it had even greater appeal to him), but his initial elation at finally arriving at what he saw as a first-class university was more than a little dampened when, in his second semester there, the governor vetoed funds for the UT library, declaring with a straight face that the students would get no more books until they had read the ones they had.

Still, the physical requirements of higher education—buildings, faculties, and curriculum—were in some ways more accessible in Lomax's time than now. A developing state—in this case, Texas—could get its Olympian venture underway for a quite modest sum. Texas did it for less than $100,000. The

second necessity was a small cadre of hirsute professors in stiff collars, necessarily from the East or South and preferably sprinkled with Harvard graduates. When Lomax arrived at UT, there were, in fact, more Harvardians (eight) among the faculty of some twenty-two than graduates of any other school. Nine were from southern universities; the remainder came from Johns Hopkins, Cornell, and Syracuse. The diversity of Lomax's professors reinforced the cultural complexities begun in Bosque County and extended by his jaunts between Texas and the East.

When Lomax arrived in Austin, it did not take him long to survey the campus then taking form on College Hill. It amounted to only four buildings scattered across the wide expanse of the famous "Forty Acres" set aside by the Texas legislature in 1881, when Austin was chosen as the site for the new state university. High on the skyline was the four-story Main Building, still under construction—the tightfisted Texans had begun not with the building proper but with a smaller, cheaper west wing, then later added the central portion and a small auditorium jutting from the back of it. Now work was underway on the east wing, to be completed in 1899. Farther east was Brackenridge Hall, the new boys' dormitory, squat, flat-topped, and plain (later, as the famous "B. Hall," it would acquire decorative wings and cupolas). Northwest of the Main Building was the gable-roofed Chemistry Building, and to the northeast, the Power House and tall smokestack. Although electricity had come to Austin as early as 1889, the University buildings were still lighted by gas and heated by steam. Dust from the cattle trails was still settling, figuratively at least, and everywhere there was lingering evidence of frontier days.

Like Washington, D.C., which in time would become Lomax's second base of operations through his work with the Library of Congress, Austin was a city created primarily as a seat of government. There was the rough-and-tumble element of Texas politics connected with the Capitol, but the city had distinctly urbane tendencies, a cosmopolitan atmosphere further enhanced by the establishment of the University of Texas. The cultural diversity of the population (some 17,000 when Lomax arrived) could be seen in their ethnic celebrations: Texas Independence, Cinco de Mayo, St. Patrick's Day, Friedrich von Schiller's birthday, Diez y Seis, Rosh Hashanah, and Juneteenth.[23] The landscape reminded Lomax of Bosque

John A. Lomax, registrar of the University of Texas, ca. 1902. *From the John Avery Lomax Sr. Papers, Dolph Briscoe Center for American History, University of Texas at Austin. (DI 04238)*

County: wooded, rolling hills, running streams, and distinctive landmarks that appealed to his sense of place. West of the city stood a line of high, tree-covered bluffs and singularly imposing Mount Bonnell (elevation 785 feet), where the more athletic and amorous of the college set hiked for romance and a stunning panorama of the countryside. Southwest of town was McDonald Dam, which spanned the Colorado River to form Lake McDonald, a popular site for picnics, regattas, and steamboat excursions on the triple-decked side-wheeler *Ben Hur*.

The city offered numerous civic attractions, a variety of interesting architectural styles, and the pleasant vista of broad, tree-lined streets. The broadest and busiest was Congress Avenue, stretching north from the river up through the center of town

for eleven blocks to the handsome new pink-granite Capitol, which dominated the skyline. But most of the streets, Congress Avenue included, were yet unpaved in 1895, and the town had its seamier, more raucous districts. Along the river west of Congress and south of Fifth Street was an area known as Guy Town, lined with saloons and gambling dens populated by cattlemen, prostitutes, and hustlers of varied stripe. About the time Lomax came to Austin, William S. Porter (better known as O. Henry) was writing in his whimsical newspaper *Rolling Stone*, "Austin has one soap factory, one electric light works, one cemetery, one race track, two beer gardens, one capitol, two city councils, one cocaine factory, and will probably some day have a newspaper."[24]

It was Culture, however, that had drawn John Lomax to Austin. That summer, waiting for classes to begin, he joined an informal town-and-gown group that read and discussed Shakespeare. Through this society, he met one of the University stalwarts, Professor Leslie Waggener of the English Department, who was also serving that year as interim president of the University. Waggener's brief but significant influence on Lomax was perhaps more important than Shakespeare's. In time, Waggener's son, Leslie Jr., then a senior at the University, would play an even larger role in Lomax's destiny after his third and final exile from UT.

Anxious to overcome his intellectual shortcomings and leap ahead of his lowly freshman status, Lomax signed up for almost a double load, undertaking courses in English, history, math, chemistry, Greek, Latin, and Anglo-Saxon. Later he wrote:

> Never was there such a hopeless hodge-podge. There I was, a Chautauqua-educated country boy who couldn't conjugate an English verb or decline a pronoun, attempting to master three other languages at the same time[, but] I plunged on through the year, for, since I was older than the average freshman, I must hurry, hurry, hurry. I don't think I ever stopped to think how foolish it all was.[25]

The hectic pace never slackened, but as he grew more secure in his academic work, Lomax became increasingly involved in extracurricular activities. He joined the Rusk Society, one of three campus groups that together published the monthly *Texas University*, and soon became one of its six associate editors.

He was also initiated into the oldest and most prestigious fraternity, Phi Delta Theta. Among its members, he met several men who became lifelong friends and affected the course of both his personal and professional life: the future historian and scholar Eugene C. Barker; Norman Crozier, later a longtime superintendent of Dallas schools; Rhodes Baker, who established a prominent law practice in the same city. His Phi Delta Theta circle was soon enlarged by the arrival of two law students, Edward Crane and Edgar E. Witt (later a state legislator and lieutenant governor), as well as the brilliant but ill-fated littérateur Harry Peyton Steger, and funny, wonderful Roy Bedichek, a man for all seasons. Two of Lomax's instructors, Morgan Callaway and David Houston, were Phi Delta Theta *fratres in facultate*; in disparate ways, both had a strong impact on Lomax during this period. (According to the dubious story Lomax tells in his autobiography, it was Callaway, a professor of English, who informed Lomax that the cowboy songs he supposedly brought with him in a "tightly rolled batch of manuscript" when he first arrived on the Forty Acres were "tawdry, cheap, and unworthy," apparently crushing Lomax and spurring him to carry the manuscripts behind B. Hall and set them on fire—though in later years, the man Lomax referred to in private as "His Doctorship" occasionally lent his support to Lomax's song-collecting endeavors.)

In his second year on campus, Lomax contributed a monthly column on alumni affairs in the *Texas University* (later renamed the *University of Texas Magazine*) and also submitted poems and other material. He later assumed editorship of the publication and, with a skeleton staff, took it on himself to write articles on the intellectual climate in the South, academic integrity, the merits of the honor system, and the future of higher education. He also wrote for the campus yearbook, the *Cactus*, and got himself named associate editor of the *Alcalde*, which was essentially the private enterprise of a student who managed the UT baseball team and served as general factotum for campus athletics. (This version of the *Alcalde* soon folded, but a dozen years later, as "secretary of faculties" at UT, Lomax revived the name as the title of the alumni magazine. The *Alcalde* continues today as the bimonthly magazine of the Texas Exes, the alumni association of the University of Texas at Austin.) Lomax's outlook in these early publications was invariably that of the unabashed Univer-

sity booster: a strong supporter of popular student issues and a high-minded champion of everything that bespoke "a noble manhood, a pure womanhood, an unfaltering devotion to the Truth." The only negative note sounded was on athletics—more precisely, the lamentable emphasis on football at the expense of academics.[26] This was an issue that dogged him intermittently for years and would eventually hasten his final departure from the University.

HOLDING THE KEYS TO THE UNIVERSITY

When Lomax graduated from the University in 1897 (cramming four years of work into two), he was offered and accepted the position of "registrar" at the University, a job that was little more than that of a gofer, involving a mind-numbing variety of chores for the president and the proctor. As a student, Lomax had spent considerable time in the office of Judge James B. Clark, one of the most respected figures on the campus, loved and admired by everyone. Clark was in effect the University's operating officer—his nominal title was that of proctor, but he also performed the duties of registrar, librarian, secretary to the faculty, and general custodian. The president was George Tayloe Winston, with whom Clark had helped Lomax come into close contact as a student and whose stock John had invariably boosted in the *University of Texas Magazine* and the *Alcalde*. As registrar, Lomax soon had the responsibility for all official University correspondence, served as the president's personal secretary, and in time was charged with managing the affairs of the men's dormitory, B. Hall, in addition to the nominal business of enrolling and maintaining records on each of the University's five hundred or so students.

It was Lomax's cozy relationship with President Winston, however, that marks the first of his various struggles with the University. For the first twelve years of its existence, the University was led by a chairman of the faculty rather than a president, with Leslie Waggener serving as chairman for ten of those years. In 1895, the University established the office of president, with an ailing, fifty-four-year-old Waggener serving ad interim for a year until a permanent president was hired. (A Confederate veteran, Waggener had been left for dead on the Shiloh battlefield in 1862, and a year later he was wounded again at the Battle of Chickamauga. He died on August 19, 1896, shortly after stepping down as UT's president.) The regents hired Winston, who at the time was president of the University of North Carolina in Chapel Hill. Winston was an accomplished scholar and administrator, and his liberal attitudes had at first won him strong support with students, many of whom, like John Lomax, were less conformable than older generations and eager to slip the bonds of narrow puritanism.

But the president's strong hand eventually began to thrust itself into student affairs, and Lomax, trying to work up support for the administration and besieged on all sides by critics, felt himself increasingly alone in his defense of the president. Winston's troubles came to a head when he refused a petition from a delegation of juniors from the Law Department, led by Lomax's young friend and fraternity brother Tom Connally, asking the University to give the students the day off from classes on March 2 in order to hold a campus ceremony honoring Texas Independence Day.[27] Winston, a foreigner from North Carolina with a broader view of patriotism, thought the Fourth of July more fitting, and holiday enough. The delegation dragged an old army cannon from Camp Mabry to campus anyway, making ready to fire it off the next morning. Winston, discovering the plot, personally undertook to sneak up in the night and spike the cannon. The aroused students found the obstruction in time to remove it and fire the cannon on schedule, but such treachery sorely offended them. They were even madder several weeks later when Winston casually confessed that he was the culprit. The *Alcalde*'s editor, L. E. Hill, who had been writing outraged editorials on the matter, referred to Winston as "the wily President" and hinted that had the guilty party been less highly placed, he would have answered to a vigilante band. Winston responded by calling Hill "a stupid ass."[28]

Even as a student, Lomax had cast his lot with the University's administration, and as Winston's future as president of the University became increasingly imperiled, Lomax suffered the ramifications. By the spring of 1898, it was increasingly clear that Winston's days as president were numbered. His rigorous efforts toward campus reform had alienated the faculty and student populations, and the regents were offended by his officious manner and high-

George Tayloe Winston, president of the University of Texas. *From the Prints and Photographs Collection— George Tayloe Winston, Dolph Briscoe Center for American History, University of Texas at Austin. (DI 06854)*

handed tactics. As registrar, Lomax, seen by many as Winston's toady and an administration spy in the student camp, shared in the president's unpopularity. After scarcely six months on the job, Lomax reported himself "the reviled and despised personage of the University."[29] The state legislature was in session in the spring and summer of 1899, which meant that the University's budget had to be submitted and defended. Much of that burden fell to Lomax. Lawmakers—in the face of growing animosity toward Winston and general discontent on the campus—had even less reason than usual to act generously toward the school. But largely as a result of much extra work by Lomax, who stayed busy "providing our friends in the House with statistics and arguments," the legislators approved an increased appropriation for the University.[30] But even that was not enough to save Winston.

Winston's resignation was announced in the August 1899 *University Record*. Lomax's view was that the president's decision to leave had come as a great shock and disappointment, but the failure was not Winston's alone; neither faculty nor students had given him their full support and cooperation. Winston was going away a disappointed man, and he left Lomax "no less disappointed both in myself and in him."[31] Winston, who had managed to transfer himself to the presidency of the North Carolina College of Agriculture and Mechanic Arts, hinted he might find a place there for Lomax.[32] John said that if an offer materialized, he just might consider it, so great was his disgust with the University of Texas.

There was yet another disappointment. Lomax had hoped that Winston's vacated place would be offered to David F. Houston, the brilliant thirty-three-year-old professor of political science who was Lomax's friend, fraternity brother, and former teacher. But Houston's considerable destiny as a president of major universities and a high Cabinet official in national government lay yet some years ahead.[33] To succeed Winston, the University's board of regents named its chairman, Colonel William Lambdin Prather, as acting president, and the following year Prather was permanently installed in the post. The choice was reasonable enough (and historically significant—it was Prather's moral earnestness that inspired Lomax's friend John Lang Sinclair to write the famed "Eyes of Texas"), but at the time, Lomax saw him mostly as little more than another aging fuddy-duddy who would only add to his woes.

Lomax later characterized his six-year tenure as registrar of the University of Texas—from the spring of 1897 to the spring of 1903—as "the worst absolutely soul-repressing, life-killing, truth-crushing situation" he had experienced up to that time.[34] And the major turmoil of Winston's administration simply passed into an endless series of lesser crises under Winston's successor. Further, in defending the former president, Lomax had compromised himself, and the friction between the registrar and others on the campus did not end with Winston's departure. Lomax could pretend to ignore the dissension, but he could not avoid a steadily increasing workload; Prather had a reputation for getting things done, but all too often it was Lomax who had to do them.

Continuing under President Prather, Lomax's job involved an even greater mind-numbing variety of chores. The registrar's office constituted only a small

part of his duties.[35] Much of what he did related to students' personal lives, work that today is performed by batteries of deans, counselors, advisers, and their staffs. An immense amount of time was spent dealing with prospective students and handling the huge volume of mail that came from poor but ambitious youth across the state ("Can a boy get [a] place down there to work for his bord [*sic*]. And what is the total expense of the school. I am willing to do anything honorable.").[36] Many were letters John Lomax himself might have written only ten years earlier. These school-hungry, poor but honest boys and girls were symptomatic of a rising new order that at first glance seems at odds with the conventional picture of turn-of-the-century Texas as a rough-and-tumble backwater of civilization. It may have been true, as a leading historian has it, that the state "entered the 20th century with its basic society a full two generations, or about sixty years, behind the development of the American mainstream," but little rivulets of progressivism had begun to bubble up all over: there were any number of Texans who wanted their cultural vistas broadened, their cities modernized, their children sent to college.[37]

Texas would remain predominantly rural for several decades, but it was no longer a frontier state. Young Texans who came to Austin in quest of education were propelled by motives similar to those that had driven John Lomax off to Granbury and Weatherford and Eastman and Chautauqua a dozen years earlier. Many were serious in their regard for knowledge as truth and beauty, but equally strong was the peculiarly American notion that knowledge was also money, that the surest way to commercial success in the modern world was through the classroom and across the graduation stage. Whatever their motives, increasing numbers were eager to go to college, and the existence of state universities such as the one in Austin made that once-remote dream closer to reality. By the school year of 1901–1902, enrollment at the University of Texas had reached 1,240, making it the largest institution of higher learning in the South, just ahead of Vanderbilt. And it was men like John Lomax who, in effect, held the keys to the academy and stood at the gates to anoint the chosen.

Much as he grumbled about his long hours and low pay, Lomax found the work rewarding. The job had one very positive aspect, and he was not unaware of its potential. "The brain and power" that

The campus of the University of Texas, ca. 1900. *From the John Mattias Kuehne Photograph Collection, Dolph Briscoe Center for American History, University of Texas at Austin. (DI 06818)*

would soon run Texas was being trained at the University, he wrote. "It is great work . . . to control this power."[38] He referred to nothing less than the state's young intellectual and professional elite, rich and poor alike—its future businessmen, mayors, county judges, teachers and school administrators, state commissioners, legal corps, and statehouse politicians (including at least one governor-to-be). These were the people who would run things in the twentieth century; many rose to success performing cultural and technological functions that simply had not existed before their generation. They were coming of age at a crucial juncture in the history of the state, which was poised on the verge of a rapid transition from raw frontier to a modern empire of oil and commerce.

Through Lomax's hands filtered the letters of application—indeed, the lives and ambitions and destinies—of those who in a few years would control

Texas from courthouse to statehouse, from schoolroom to boardroom. To the extent that he could accommodate them—get them admitted to the University, find them work and housing, lend them money, offer them counsel and comfort—he earned the immediate gratitude of two generations—theirs and their parents'—and invested heavily in the loyalty of still a third, their children yet to be born. It was the beginning of a legendary reputation. John Lomax soon became one of the most visible figures on campus, as well known as President Prather himself.

HEAVEN AND HELL IN TEXAS

When Lomax left the University of Texas early in the summer of 1903 for Texas A&M, he was gone almost before anyone knew it. In 1904, he married Bess Brown and began the family that eventually numbered four children—Shirley, John Jr., Alan, and "Bess Brown Jr." In the first years of their marriage, Bess helped see her husband through his Harvard experience and the publication of *Cowboy Songs*. The book was a success and brought him a certain amount of national fame—except, ironically, at the University of Texas, where "this crude product of the West had no interest, no value, no charm whatsoever."[39]

Apparently, such judgments had no bearing on Sidney Mezes. Just two years after Lomax followed David Houston to College Station, Houston was named president of the University of Texas, in the summer of 1905, in the weeks following President Prather's untimely death. In 1908, Houston left Texas to become chancellor of Washington University in St.

Louis, and the UT Board of Regents promoted Mezes, a professor of philosophy and dean of the College of Arts, to the presidency. In May 1910, President Mezes wrote to Lomax and offered him an administrative job back on the Austin campus. Lomax had always felt that he was in exile at lowly Texas A&M; he preserved Mezes's letter for posterity and wrote across it, "This is the letter that brought me back from A&M College to the University."[40] Mezes was an old UT hand—and a Harvard man to boot. He was well acquainted with Lomax's considerable skills and capacity for hard work, and it is not difficult to imagine Houston leaving a strong recommendation on Lomax's behalf.

President Mezes had offered Lomax the newly cre-

Members of the Parker County Club at the University of Texas in 1913, including John A. Lomax (*center, with hat*), Professors C. S. Potts (*front, second man from left*), T. U. Taylor (*rear, with mustache*), and E. T. Miller (*right, with hat*), and thirteen UT students. Weatherford is the seat of Parker County. *From the John Matthias Kuehne Photograph Collection, Dolph Briscoe Center for American History, University of Texas at Austin. (DI 06845)*

John A. Lomax, director of the Ex-Students' Association of the University of Texas, undated photo. *From the John Avery Lomax Sr. Papers, Dolph Briscoe Center for American History, University of Texas at Austin. (DI 04236)*

ated position of "Secretary of the University Faculties and Assistant Director of the Department of Extension." On first accepting the position, Lomax negotiated to ensure that he would have some time for song collecting and attending academic conferences (*Cowboy Songs* led to an almost annual series of summer lecture tours by Lomax that took him all around the country), but those pursuits soon gave way to the duties of his job at UT. Settling in, he built for his growing family a fine new home at 910 West 26th Street, a few blocks from campus, with a backyard menagerie of chickens, turkeys, and cows. As assistant director of extension, he dealt with curricular matters related to "self-study" classes conducted at various places around the state. A natural outgrowth of this work involved issuing publicity and recruiting for the University, and that in turn led to his being elected secretary-treasurer of the Alumni Association, an organization that then existed in little more than name, propped up by a few former students—notably Will C. Hogg (son of James Stephen

Hogg, the first Texas governor who was a native of the state) and Dexter Hamilton, both old friends and schoolmates of Lomax. Very soon the Alumni Association began to thrive.

One of Lomax's ploys for enlarging the membership involved changing the name from the Alumni Association to the Ex-Students' Association, a seemingly trivial matter of terminology, but one that had far-reaching effects. In that era in Texas, hundreds of young men and women found their college careers interrupted by various circumstances, and many accumulated several years of credit at the University only to leave finally without a degree, but with their loyalty to the institution intact. The name change increased the pool of prospective members by many dozens. (The name of the association has since been changed to the Texas Exes.) Similarly, Lomax recognized very early the need for a regular publication that would serve as a focal point and source of esprit for the organization. For the slick new monthly magazine, compiled and produced largely by Lomax himself, he chose the name *Alcalde,* recalling the short-lived student newspaper he had worked on as an undergraduate.

This work, though, would be interrupted when James "Pa" Ferguson, known to many as "Farmer Jim," took up residence in the Texas Governor's Mansion in 1915. From the start, the University incurred the anger of Governor Ferguson, a man whose Texas frontier upbringing in Bell County, on a farm near Salado, had been much like Lomax's—but who, in the words of J. Frank Dobie, had "the brutal self-assertiveness of a man used to forcing men, because of his financial power, to their knees."[41] The UT Board of Regents had refused to follow Ferguson's directive to fire William J. Battle, a distinguished professor of classics and former dean, widely known as a man of unimpeachable integrity, who had agreed to serve as interim president when Sidney Mezes resigned in 1914 to become president of the City College of New York. The governor then seethed when, in 1916, the regents named Dr. Robert E. Vinson, a minister and respected educator who headed the Austin Presbyterian Theological Seminary, to the permanent post of president. The reasons for the governor's vehement disapproval of Vinson were never quite clear, unless it was that, in Ferguson's eyes, Vinson wouldn't "stand hitched"—that is, he wouldn't take orders. The conflict that ensued became known as the "Big Bear Fight," and it shook the University and the Governor's Mansion to the core.[42]

Lomax was drawn into the fight when Governor Ferguson appeared at the October 1916 meeting of the board of regents and demanded that seven men at the University—including Battle and Lomax—be fired. Lomax's inclusion in this group seemed directly related to his high profile as de facto assistant to the president, publicity agent for the University, and secretary of the Ex-Students' Association. Otherwise, the board concluded that "the Governor's disapproval of Mr. Lomax is obscure" and the charges against him "so trivial that it is hardly believable they represent [Ferguson's] real reasons."[43] In any event, the governor's appearance before the regents, spouting vague charges and carrying on about the "unholy spree of the educated hierarchy out there," made one thing clear: his real objective was not merely to have seven men fired, but also to bring the entire University to heel and assert absolute control over it.

When President Vinson refused to fire the seven men, Ferguson stacked the board of regents and accomplished his end. The board carried out the firings in the summer of 1917, and thus Lomax was exiled from the Forty Acres for a second time. Ferguson's tendencies ran to the absolute and tyrannical; indeed, at times he seems to have exhibited symptoms of classic megalomania. "I don't have to give any reasons!" he was known to storm. "I am the Governor of Texas!"[44]

With the help of Barrett Wendell, Jr., Lomax went off to Chicago to sell bonds for the distinguished investment firm of Lee, Higginson, and Co. In due course, Governor Ferguson was impeached, and the firings were rescinded later that year—events influenced in no small part by the work Lomax had done to publicize the University's plight during the "Big Bear Fight" and arouse the leadership of the Ex-Students' Association. On September 15, President Vinson wrote to Lomax informing him that the board of regents had rescinded his firing and reinstated him and the others who had been fired, but out of pride, Lomax declined to return to UT.[45]

HE HAD GIVEN HIS BEST TO ACADEMIA

Selling bonds in Chicago was even more foreign to Lomax than teaching English at Texas A&M. He lasted eighteen months before he was recruited by his old friend and classmate Will Hogg to come back to Austin at a substantial salary and direct the Ex-Students' Association, which was struggling once again without his indefatigable leadership. After a protracted negotiation about his salary, Lomax agreed to return to Texas. He found the directorship ideal; his salary was higher than that of a full professor, and influential backers had insisted that the association be moved off campus and away from the meddling of University officials and state legislators. Within weeks he had breathed new life into the dying association, resuming full-scale production of the *Alcalde,* beginning a vigorous membership drive, and soon juggling his usual dozen or more balls in the air at once. He also fell back into his old habit of looking after struggling students—lending them money, finding them jobs, helping them cope with homesickness and poor grades.

Nevertheless, trouble continued to follow him around like a faithful old dog. He couldn't resist dabbling in national and local politics, and he managed to alienate two powerful factions within the student body—fraternities and athletes—whose ranks in time would supply the most active and influential Exes. Lomax felt that in addition to being a waste of money, fraternities interfered with study, created class feeling, and did "little, if any good"—a curious position to be taken by a man who in his undergraduate days had been a dutiful, ambitious Phi Delt.[46] Likewise, as college athletic programs expanded in the 1920s, drawing dollars and attention away from the classroom, Lomax grew disturbed by what he considered an excessive emphasis on sports, and he also had to contend with campus politics and personalities while the athletic department went about building its empire. Articles critical of the UT sports program appeared in the *Alcalde*, to the consternation of many, most notably the athletic director, L. Theo Bellmont. Furthermore, students complained that Lomax spent too much time away from Austin and catered to the older generation—Exes of his own era—rather than taking an interest in current student affairs. By the mid-1920s, the University of Texas bore little resemblance to the raw little state college that Lomax had come to thirty years before. Although he was always one of the University's biggest boosters, now even he complained that the campus of 9,250 students had become "big and complicated, and everyone is busy, or thinks he is."[47]

The senior class, the athletic director, and ultimately the campus newspaper, the *Daily Texan*, called for Lomax's head. His duties were diminished, and in 1925 he was, for the third time in twenty years, driven from the University of Texas under pressure. This time he left the University for good, rescued by Leslie Waggener, Jr., the son of the former UT president, who was a director of the prospering Republic National Bank in Dallas. The bank was opening a bond department, and Waggener felt that Lomax was just the man to run it.

Leaving the University of Texas was bound to cause grief and inner turmoil in a man as emotional and tradition bound as Lomax. Yet he said little about his feelings. He was weary of battle and weary of time, weary of his old dreams of some high place in education or literary scholarship. He had given his best to academia, and it had only spurned him, again

and again. *Cowboy Songs* had brought him a modest reputation in some circles, but he had never been able to build on it. There was no real money in that, anyway, and he had always been too distracted or disorganized to focus on song collecting. Now nearing sixty, he felt it was time to put away old dreams, time to think of his family and storing up for old age. He was going to take care of business, literally, to the exclusion of all else—devote himself, with a vengeance, to making money. Dallas in the Roaring Twenties was a good place to do it.

Lomax thrived for a while. By the late 1920s, business was booming, and Lomax built a fine home, famous in the family as "The House in the Woods," in the Forest Hills development, some six miles from downtown Dallas. He referred to it as "a lovely refuge amid towering trees" and, for him, "the end of the trail."[48] An elaborate prototype of the design later so widely copied (and deprecated) as "ranch style," the House in the Woods was designed by David Reichard Williams, a young Texas architect just then at the beginning of a long and distinguished career. As one might suspect, Williams had attended the University of Texas. Further, Dave Williams's twin brother, Dan, had been the editor of the *Daily Texan* at the time of the Big Bear Fight and had vigorously supported the Lomax forces against Farmer Jim Ferguson. When Dan Williams taught English at the University briefly in the early 1920s, he often invited the Texas Exes' secretary to visit his classes and demonstrate cowboy songs. A decade or so later, as a prominent newspaperman on the staff of the *New York World-Telegram*, he would host—and help promote—Lomax and his new folk-singing sensation, Huddie Ledbetter, when they made their foray into the big city.

Indeed, it was Lomax's long service to the University—from his student days and his job as registrar to his positions of responsibility at some of the highest levels of the administration in both the University and the Ex-Students' Association—that had laid the groundwork for his later prominence across the state. It was at the University of Texas that he gained the experience—and the contacts—that would eventually establish him as a Texas institution.

Lomax had not reckoned with the Depression or with his beloved wife Bess's declining health. She died in May 1931, and Lomax, disconsolate, asked for an indefinite leave of absence from the bank.

His son John Jr. had also lost his banking job in Corpus Christi, but he was young and healthy, with no family to support and some money saved up. Johnny urged his father—who would remarry in 1933, to Miss Ruby Terrill, the dean of women at the University of Texas—to resume his song-collecting activities and offered to help. For John Lomax, Sr., that was a turning point: in effect, he got up from his deathbed and set upon the work that would occupy him for the next sixteen years of his life—work that finally brought him the rewards he had long sought. From his song-collecting trips throughout the nation in the 1930s emerged his two masterpieces, *American Ballads and Folk Songs* and *Our Singing Country*, as well as his appointment as honorary curator of the Archive of American Folk Song at the Library of Congress.

ONE LAST BATTLE:
THE RAINEY AFFAIR

There was one last battle to be fought—and for the first time, Lomax was on the wrong side. In 1932, on one of his lecture and collecting tours, Lomax had spoken at Bucknell University in Lewisburg, Pennsylvania, and met its president, Dr. Homer P. Rainey, a native Texan and rising star in the field of education. Lomax was much impressed with Rainey; seven years later, in April 1939, he wrote to Rainey: "For several weeks I have had in mind to tell you how pleased I am that you decided to come back to Texas as President of our University."[49]

Within a year, Lomax was one of Homer Rainey's most implacable enemies.

Rainey came to the University with an outstanding record—not only was he a Texan but, as one writer observed, he also had "all the credentials of that local ideal, 'a good old boy'."[50] Born poor, he had worked his way through college, excelling as both a scholar and an athlete. By the time he was twenty-one, he had been ordained as a Baptist minister and played professional baseball briefly. After service in World War I, he earned a PhD at the University of Chicago and launched an impressive career as scholar, educator, and university administrator. In the eyes of the Old Guard at the University of Texas, his only shortcoming was that, as later events would show, he also had liberal tendencies.

Almost from the beginning, Rainey could do nothing to please the powers that be at UT. By the time he arrived in Austin, the governorship of Texas had passed from the moderately liberal administration of James Allred to that of W. Lee "Pappy" O'Daniel, a reactionary of the first rank. In the spring of 1942, a group of right-wing Texas business interests held a rally in Dallas to protest Roosevelt's Fair Labor Standards Act, claiming that it prohibited anyone in defense industries from working more than forty hours a week while Texas boys were fighting overseas and dying for lack of the guns they needed because of oppressive governmental labor regulations. Four young economics professors from the University asked for time on the program to explain that anyone could work more than forty hours a week; the Fair Labor Standards Act merely required that employers pay time and a half to anyone who worked more than forty hours a week. Their request was denied, whereupon the four professors took a written statement to the *Dallas News*, protesting that the rally had been rigged, as indeed it had, in favor of speakers who were known to be antilabor. The University's board of regents demanded that they apologize to the rally's organizers. When they declined, their contracts were not renewed for the coming year, despite their department's recommendations and strong support from President Rainey, who viewed the affair as a serious threat to academic freedom.

Lomax vigorously defended the board's action; in his view, the men were fired because of their "outrageous attack on Texas citizens." Moreover, they weren't even citizens of the state. The very idea of outsiders coming to a local meeting, demanding to speak, then insulting everyone when they were refused—any community in Texas would resent such a thing.[51]

The dust had scarcely settled when another donnybrook erupted. The reading list for an English course at UT included *The Big Money*, part of the widely praised *U.S.A.* trilogy by John Dos Passos, which the *Saturday Review of Literature* ranked among the five best novels of the day. But members of the board of regents discovered that it depicted all sorts of seamy carryings-on between men and women, many of whom were not married, or not married to each other, and it said bad things about Big Business, which, as most Texans knew, was what had made this country great. Those who taught the course were subjected to a minor inquisition by the regents, during which each teacher was vigorously grilled about place of birth (non-Texans were immediately suspect), family and educational background, marital status, and whether the teacher knew who had placed *Big Money* on the reading list. When no individual could be singled out—the book had been chosen by group action—the regents wisely hesitated to fire the whole department, but to show their authority, they ordered the book banned immediately, ignoring the fact that the department had already decided to remove it from the reading list. Again, Lomax backed the regents, calling *U.S.A.* a "foul, sluttish, putrid obscenity," sprinkled with communist propaganda, and said it repeatedly showed vile contempt for the flag, the church, and the nation's most sacred institutions.[52]

Rainey, of course, saw this as another attack on academic freedom, but he had more to worry about than textbooks. Over the next eighteen months, he and the regents were locked in combat over one issue after another—tenure and promotion, the administration of the medical school at Galveston, "outside agitators" and immorality on the campus, and suspected "Communism." (J. Frank Dobie, a Rainey ally, said, "All the Communists [in Texas] together couldn't elect a county commissioner in the whole damn state. A great deal of talk of isms is based not on distrust of Communism but in distrust of Democracy.")[53] There were also ill-founded charges that Rainey wanted to admit black students to the staunchly all-white University.

Off in Dallas, hors de combat because of his health and distance from the firing line in Austin, John Lomax kept himself busy rallying the troops, comforting the wounded, and passing ammunition. Throughout, he kept up a steady correspondence with his friend Orville Bullington, a regent in Wichita Falls, carrying on a mutually grumpy dialogue in which they complained to each other about Roosevelt's third term, labor unions, and the generally sorry state of things.

By the fall of 1944, Rainey had come to realize that he could no longer function under the present state of affairs. He called the faculty together and presented a list of sixteen instances in which the board of regents had violated academic freedom, arbitrarily meddled with the running of the University, or otherwise acted improperly. The faculty responded with a standing ovation and afterward gave

him a unanimous vote of confidence. In turn, the regents met in closed session and voted six to two for his dismissal.

EPILOGUE

John Lomax in his later years grew increasingly bitter and narrow, yet attempted to stay busy despite failing health and a sense that the world had passed him by. In 1947, he published his autobiography, *Adventures of a Ballad Hunter*, which was generally well received despite its being something less than a full and accurate account of his life and career. His base of operations remained the House in the Woods—a mark of his affluence, the suburban achievement of the man who had come of age on his father's small farm along the Bosque River on the ninety-eighth meridian in the cruel years of post–Civil War Texas.

Lomax suffered a heart attack on January 23, 1948, while singing "Big Leg Rose" to a delegation that had met him at the Hotel Greenville in Greenville, Mississippi, where he was to be honored the following day. (Greenville is about sixty miles from Goodman, Mississippi, the place of Lomax's birth.) He passed away in the King's Daughter's Hospital in Greenville two days later, at age eighty. As he lay dying, "John Lomax Day" had come and gone. Again, for one last time, he had missed the cheering crowds.

In his lifetime, Lomax acquired substantial learning and a veneer of sophistication, spent time in the magic metropolises he once knew only from the country newspapers of his childhood, stayed in fine hotels, was entertained in exclusive clubs, and rubbed shoulders with elite society. Yet like Texas, like its cowboys whose traditional songs he preserved, he had his distinctly cruder qualities. He was in many ways an American primitive—raw, bumptious, xenophobic. On the other hand, it was his very faith in traditional values, his love of things native and openhearted, that pointed him toward his most famous work. In still another paradoxical sense, he was a true pioneer—true American, true Texan—in his eagerness to break new ground, to go where others hadn't, and do what they had not. If, in later years, he became rigidly conservative, throughout his life he harbored many liberal—that is, humanistic—points of view.

Lomax was, in short, like most accomplished human beings, a mass of contradictions. Yet it was his early experiences at the University of Texas—an institution not without its own contradictions—that formed the root of the extravagant character and unique mix of opposing elements that gave John Avery Lomax's life the force of legend. A man of his time and place, Lomax never entirely betrayed his roots on the ninety-eighth meridian.

In the spirit of the words he published anonymously in the *University of Texas Magazine* in 1898, John Lomax was himself caught between competing forces—on the one hand, "the prairies and the magic of their call when Spring is breaking" and "the rough assemblage of the round-up," and, on the other hand, "the glamour [of] the things that have driven [the cowboys] into the west and down to death." Like Lomax, the University of Texas came of age in the fading daylight of the American frontier. Today, Texas and its university in Austin are predominantly urban—that is, they are "civilized," in the word's original sense. Even so, evidence of the deep roots that the state and the University have in the nineteenth-century frontier—such as the images of Longhorn skulls, famous cattle brands, and the flora and fauna of the American Southwest seen in abundance in the architectural details of many of the campus's older buildings—can still be found on campus among the glamorous achievements of the University's twenty-first-century modernity. Memory of the romance and hardship that the frontier provided still persists at the University of Texas at Austin. Likewise, through the work of one of the most prominent figures in the University's early history, the songs of the vanishing cowboy—"the last cavalier"—survive.

NOTES

Unless otherwise indicated, materials cited are from the collections of the Dolph Briscoe Center for American History at the University of Texas at Austin.

1. John A. Lomax (hereafter JAL), *Adventures of a Ballad Hunter* (New York: Macmillan, 1947), 33.

2. Just when Lomax actually began collecting folk music may always be a mystery. His autobiographical story, first related in 1934, of coming to the University of Texas with a "tightly rolled batch of manuscript of cowboy songs" in his trunk was widely discredited almost as soon as it appeared, and among the scoffers were those who knew Lomax at close range. According to Lomax's account, he took the roll of cowboy songs to Morgan Callaway, an English professor, who pronounced them "tawdry, cheap, and unworthy," whereupon young Lomax, crushed and embarrassed, carried the roll out behind Brackenridge Hall (the men's dormitory he would oversee a few years later) and burned it. After his first work began to appear in print, Lomax offered various accounts that suggest that his collecting interests developed during his early years at Texas A&M. All of these, however, are ex post facto; what is lacking is a single shred of external evidence dated before October 1906. There is one small, indirect hint that he was looking for cowboy songs in the summer of 1906: in November, after the search was clearly on, one of his former students at A&M wrote to apologize that he had "totally neglected to get those songs for you last summer. I got out on the ranch and forgot all about it" (W. Bogel to JAL, Nov. 21, 1906).

3. *University of Texas Magazine*, Jan. 1898, 126.

4. T. R. Fehrenbach, *Lone Star: A History of Texas and the Texans* (New York: Macmillan, 1968), 408.

5. "In the 1870s and 80s, [its] geographical features made Bosque County a nexus of socio-economic frontiers, and gave it a heightened, if not unique, sense of cultural contrasts" (James Charles McNutt, "Beyond Regionalism: Texas Folklorists and the Emergence of a Post-Regional Consciousness," PhD diss., University of Texas, 1982, 19–22). The geographic center of the state is in fact less than ninety miles southwest of Meridian—scarcely a hop, skip, and jump in an area the size of Texas.

6. JAL, *Adventures of a Ballad Hunter*, 4.

7. Ibid., 28.

8. JAL to Bess Lomax [Hawes], Sept. 20, 1936, (Lomax Family Papers, American Folklife Center, Library of Congress).

9. JAL to Shirley Green, Aug. 22, 1898.

10. JAL to Alan Lomax, Apr. 22, 1942 (Lomax Family Papers, American Folklife Center, Library of Congress).

11. JAL, *Adventures of a Ballad Hunter*, 4, 5.

12. JAL, "Of Books and People: John A. Lomax Tells of the Reading That Influenced Him in His Early Life; A Tribute to the Newspapers," *Dallas Times-Herald*, Aug. 19, 1945.

13. Charles William Ramsdell, *Reconstruction in Texas* (New York: Columbia Univ. Press, 1910; reprint, Austin: Univ. of Texas Press, 1970), 312; Fehrenbach, *Lone Star*, 433–34.

14. JAL, *Adventures of a Ballad Hunter*, 6.

15. Ibid., pp. 22.

16. *Catalogue of the Officers and Members of Granbury College* (Fort Worth, 1886), 15–17.

17. Ibid.

18. JAL, *Adventures of a Ballad Hunter*, 25–26.

19. Charles W. Ferguson, *Organizing to Beat the Devil* (Garden City, N.Y.: Doubleday, 1971), 305–6.

20. JAL to Shirley Green, Apr. 27, 1902.

21. JAL, *Adventures of a Ballad Hunter*, 27–28.

22. Editor's note: The first defeat the University of Texas football team ever suffered, a 28–0 home loss to the University of Missouri, came in the team's second season of intercollegiate play, 1894. After again being shut out at home by Missouri, 10–0, in 1896, UT eventually got the upper hand, defeating Missouri 17–11 in Austin in 1900 and 11–0 in Columbia in 1901.

23. David C. Humphrey, *Austin: An Illustrated History* (Northridge, Calif.: Windsor Publication, 1985), 82.

24. Quoted in ibid., 149–50.

25. JAL, *Adventures of a Ballad Hunter*, 30.

26. See *Texas University* 11, no. 8 (May 1896): 302; and *Texas University* 12, no. 4 (Jan. 1897): 145.

27. Tom Connally, as told to Alfred Steinberg, *My Name Is Tom Connally* (New York: Crowell, 1954), 30.

28. "A Damaging Confession," *Alcalde*, Apr. 28, 1897, 3; and "Below the Belt," *Alcalde*, Apr. 21, 1897, 3.

29. JAL to Shirley Green, July 16, 1899.

30. JAL to Shirley Green, May 4, 1899.

31. JAL to Shirley Green, July 13 and 16, 1899.

32. Editor's note: This institution is known today as North Carolina State University. Winston was the second person to serve as the chief executive of North Carolina's land-grant college, which opened in 1889.

33. Editor's note: A native of North Carolina, David Franklin Houston served as president of the Agricultural and Mechanical College of Texas (1902–1905), president of the University of Texas (1905–1908), and chancellor of Washington University in St. Louis (1908–1917); he also served in President Woodrow Wilson's Cabinet, as secretary of agriculture (1913–1920) and secretary of the treasury (1920–1921).

34. JAL to Bess Brown, Feb. 3, 1904.

35. JAL to Shirley Green, undated (probably fall 1899).

36. Dozens of such letters are found among Lomax's business correspondence for the period.

37. Fehrenbach, *Lone Star*, 633.

38. JAL to Shirley Green, undated (probably fall 1899).

39. JAL, *Adventures of a Ballad Hunter*, 40–41.

40. Sidney E. Mezes to JAL, May 17, 1910.

41. Quoted in Lon Tinkle, *An American Original: The Life of J. Frank Dobie* (Boston: Little, Brown, 1978), 63–64.

42. Editor's note: For a larger discussion of the struggle between Governor Ferguson and the University, see Patrick Cox's "'Farmer Jim' and 'The Chief': Governor Jim Ferguson and His Battle with Eugene C. Barker and the University of Texas" in this volume.

43. "His Own Words to Discover His Motives," *Alcalde* 5, no. 8 (Aug. 1917): 697–721; quotation from 714.

44. Testimony of Will C. Hogg in the case John Lomax vs. G. S. McReynolds, et al., 174–75. See "His Own Words," 715.

45. R. E. Vinson to JAL, Sept. 15, 1917; JAL to R. E. Vinson, Sept. 18, 1917.

46. JAL to Norman Crozier, Oct. 3, 1921.

47. JAL to Hester Joynes Means, Apr. 23, 1924.

48. JAL, *Adventures of a Ballad Hunter*, 101.

49. JAL to Homer Rainey, Apr. 14, 1939.

50. Tinkle, *American Original*, 175.

51. JAL to (Ms.) Hal March, May 30, 1945.

52. JAL to Orville Bullington, Nov. 22, 1944.

53. "An Educational Crisis: Summary of Testimony before a [Texas] Senate Committee Investigating the University of Texas Controversy," Nov. 1944, 2. See also James Charles McNutt, "John Henry Faulk: An Interview," in *Folklife Annual 1987*, ed. Alan Jabbour and James Hardin (Washington, D.C.: Library of Congress, 1988), 129.

DAVID
DETTMER }

Benedicere Benedictus

A Profile of H. Y. Benedict

His death came as a great shock to everyone on the Forty Acres.

On Monday, May 10, 1937, after wrapping up a meeting with Dean
W. R. Woolrich of the College of Engineering late in the afternoon, University of Texas president Harry Yandell Benedict (known to folks variously as "H. Y.," "Yandell," or just plain "Benny") left his office in Sutton Hall and stepped across Guadalupe Street with Donald Coney, the
director of the University of Texas library. They waited beside the YMCA
on the corner of West 22nd Street for Dr. Charles Hackett, a professor of
Latin American history, who was bringing his car around from San Antonio Street to whisk them to the Capitol for a conference with Senator (and future UT regent) John Sayers Redditt, of Lufkin. The legislature
was in session, and the University's leadership was engaged in its usual
biannual task of endearing itself to the members and persuading them to
protect the University's appropriation.

As Coney took the president's arm to help him into the car, Benedict
leaned forward wordlessly and fell to the pavement. Coney and Hackett helped him to the shade alongside the YMCA, and Coney dashed inside to call for an ambulance. Benedict was rushed to St. David's Hospital, where, within minutes, a small group had gathered along with Coney
and Hackett, including William J. Battle, a classics professor and former
UT president; H. T. Parlin, the dean of the UT College of Arts and Sciences; and William L. McGill, the director of Texas Student Publications.
(The next day, a special edition of the *Daily Texan* reported that Benedict's only words in the ambulance were "My head, my head.") Before
long, the doctor emerged, announcing that President Benedict had died of
a cerebral hemorrhage at 4:45 p.m. Benedict's fourteen-year-old son, Yan-

---

*David Dettmer currently serves as a staff member in the Office of the President at the University of Texas at Austin. Every day on his way to work, he
glances at H. Y. Benedict's name chiseled into the cornerstone of the Main
Building's south portico and embossed on a nearby bronze plaque titled "A
Building Era 1925–1937."*

dell Jr., arrived shortly after the announcement had been made and waited patiently beside Dean Parlin for Mrs. Benedict to arrive. President Benedict was sixty-seven years old.

It is chance that attaches glory to us according to its caprice. I have very often seen it go ahead of merit, and often surpass merit by a long distance. . . . I do not care so much what I am to others as I care what I am to myself.

MICHEL DE MONTAIGNE, "OF GLORY" (1578–1580)

Chance has attached glory to H. Y. Benedict modestly. The only obvious monument to him on today's enormous urban campus is Benedict Hall, built sixteen years after his death. It hides in plain sight along the South Mall, near the Littlefield Fountain, and has never had a direct connection to its namesake or his work. It has been occupied by a number of departments and programs over the years, though not by departments in Benedict's academic areas—mathematics and astronomy. The current tenant of Benedict Hall, the Department of Spanish and Portuguese, moved in just a couple years ago, following a renovation to the building's interior.

The only aspect of Benedict Hall relevant to Benedict himself is the naming of its companions on the east side of the South Mall for H. Y. Benedict's companions in life—namely, Sidney Mezes, a philosophy professor, and Robert Batts, an attorney. (Two sets of three contiguous buildings frame the South Mall: Batts Hall, Mezes Hall, and Benedict Hall on the east; Parlin Hall, Calhoun Hall, and Homer Rainey Hall on the west. In the parlance of today's students, they are known collectively as the "Six-Pack.") Sidney Mezes was the University's chief academic officer from 1902 to 1908, which were the early years of Benedict's long career as a professor of mathematics and astronomy at UT. Dean Mezes was named UT's president in 1908, and in 1911 he recommended to the regents that they elect young Professor Benedict dean of the College of Arts, which they did. Benedict is reported to have been Mezes's favorite to replace him when Mezes resigned the UT presidency in 1914 to become the president of the College of the City of New York.[1] Robert Batts began his six-year term as a member of the UT Board of Regents in 1927, the same year Benedict was named president of the University, and was the board's chairman from 1930 to

Harry Yandell Benedict, president of the University of Texas. *From the Prints and Photographs Collection—H. Y. Benedict, Dolph Briscoe Center for American History, University of Texas at Austin. (DI 06883)*

1933, the crucial middle years of Benedict's presidency. Batts was instrumental in the success of the unprecedented building program that took place during that period.

Finding further evidence of Benedict's historic contribution to the University of Texas takes a bit of effort. A profile of Benedict carved in walnut by Peter Mansbendel hangs in the Texas Union among the portrait medallions of all the other former University presidents. These medallions are affixed to the support beams in the dim light of the President's Lobby, near the entrance to the grand ballroom. Outside, in the daylight, particularly observant pedestrians walking across the original Forty Acres may notice that the cornerstones of most of the finest red-roofed buildings—the ones that give the campus its identity—have "H. Y. Benedict, President" chiseled into them. No other remembrances exist.

When President Benedict concluded his meeting with Dean Woolrich on that last afternoon of his life and gathered his notes and hat to hurry down to the Capitol, his office was not in the Main Building, where one might expect it to have been. For three years, from 1934 to 1937, the Office of the President was quartered temporarily in Sutton Hall, Cass Gilbert's artfully designed but strictly utilitarian education building that stood then, as it does now, perpendicular to busy Guadalupe Street, tucked below Gilbert's magnificent but already antiquated University Library building (today named Battle Hall). The University's administrative offices were relocated to Sutton Hall because the original Main Building—the rickety, buff-yellow, College Gothic brick structure that Benedict had known as a student when he first matriculated at UT, in 1889—had been razed in 1934 to make way for new construction. One of Sutton Hall's great advantages for Benedict was that it provided easy access for the legions of faculty and students who would seek out the president to discuss whatever needs they had (this was an era in which university presidents were much more accessible)—and, of course, it gave the president quick access to cars that could whisk him down to the Capitol at a moment's notice. It also put him on the same level, literally, as the people he served.

The razing of the original Main Building was—and still is—one of the most pivotal moments in the history of the University of Texas. When Benedict assumed the presidency in 1927, the University's library was housed in Gilbert's University Library building. Though the building was still relatively new, the needs of the University's library in the late 1920s had already outgrown it. Chairman Batts, President Benedict, and Professor Battle, chair of the Faculty Building Committee—working with architect Paul Cret and his master plan for the University—approached the problem by thinking big. A larger, more functional, and even more spectacular new library would be built on the site of the (original) Main Building, but in two phases.

In the first phase, completed in 1933, the decrepit auditorium and defunct basement gymnasium jutting from the back of the original Main Building were razed, and the core of the new library facility—specifically, the service desk and card catalogs flanked by two enormous reading rooms, book stacks, offices for the library staff, and several floors for special collections, archives, and research—was built directly behind the (original) Main Building. This structure included the lower levels of book stacks, which would eventually serve as the base on which the upper levels of books stacks—the Tower—would be built.

The second phase of the project would attach a second structure to the south side of the 1933 structure, providing additional office space for the library and archives, classrooms, and an ornate suite of rooms to house the University's collections of rare books, as well as a new grand façade (the one that announces "Ye shall know the truth and the truth shall make you free"). Furthermore, two magnificent colonnaded wings with open-air study areas would embrace a plaza from which one could look in a direct line down to the dome of the Capitol. This second phase would also include the removal of the red-tiled roof above the existing core of book stacks in order to allow for construction of the iconic UT Tower, which would be capped by a carillon and four gold-leaf clock faces. The planners' assumption was that the second phase could not be undertaken—for both financial and political reasons—until many years later.[2]

However, to the considerable dismay of most of UT's loyal older alumni—for whom the original Main Building had housed virtually their entire collegiate experience—an opportunity arose to undertake the second phase just as the first phase was being completed. With the entire nation in the grip of the Great Depression, Franklin D. Roosevelt was sworn in as president of the United States on March 4, 1933, and he immediately began putting into action the first of his New Deal programs. Faced with the opportunity to sell bonds to the federal government's Public Works Administration (PWA) through the National Industrial Recovery Act in 1934,[3] the UT regents and Benedict's administration made the controversial decision to move forward years, or even decades, ahead of schedule by razing the original Main Building, constructing the southern portion of the library, and completing the Tower. It was a badly needed development for a University that was growing in both size and ambition, and it meant much more than added square footage and increased shelf space.

This new library facility—named the Main Building and Tower—was designed by Paul Cret to serve as the University's central library and archive. It was conceived as a temple of learning—collections of books rising toward the heavens—with only a

Under UT president H. Y. Benedict's leadership, the original Main Building was demolished in the summer of 1934 to make way for the southern portion of the new library facility. In the bottom image, the northern portion of the new library, built directly behind Old Main in 1932, can be seen at the far right edge of the photograph. *From the Prints and Photographs Collection—UT Buildings—Old Main, Dolph Briscoe Center for American History, University of Texas at Austin. (Top: DI 07024; bottom: DI 06901)*

The demolition of Old Main reveals the already-finished northern portion of the new library facility, opened in 1933. Jutting from the front of this structure is what is now the central staircase of the Main Building. When the southern portion of the new Main Building was built on the footprint of Old Main, the Tower would be built where the tallest tile roof can be seen in these photographs. *From the Prints and Photographs Collection—UT Buildings—Old Main, Dolph Briscoe Center for American History, University of Texas at Austin. (Top: DI 07008; bottom: DI 07009)*

The new Main Building and Tower, completed in 1937. The two phases of its construction are apparent in this photo: the 1933 library facility, under the tile roof to the right of the Tower, and the Tower and southern addition. *From the Prints and Photographs Collection—UT Buildings—Main Building and Tower, Dolph Briscoe Center for American History, University of Texas at Austin. (DI 01459)*

modest amount of space devoted to administrative offices. This structure was the crowning achievement of the remarkable progress that had occurred during the nearly ten years that Benedict had served as president. The success that Benedict's administration achieved would have been noteworthy in any era—but considering that it coincided with the onset and depths of the Great Depression, its scope and completeness are to this day nothing short of remarkable.

The achievements of Benedict's presidency laid the groundwork for the University of Texas to be considered among the ranks of the nation's finest universities. As one might expect, though, they did not come without costs.

In the days following Benedict's untimely death, the editor of the magazine of the University's Ex-Students' Association, the *Alcalde*, selected Roy Bedichek to write a memorial for the June 1937 issue. Then in the middle of his long career as the director of the University Interscholastic League, Bedichek possessed a wonderfully generous and gregarious character that always found its way into his writing, and he had a lifelong and diverse relationship with the University. A former student of Benedict's, Bedichek had over the years become a colleague and friend, often accompanying Benedict on cherished bird-watching and egg-collecting excursions during the rare times when the president could somehow slip the duties of office for a day or two to escape into the wilds of nature. It was often difficult to convince President Benedict to take such trips. In the summer of 1935, for example, several regents corresponded with one another privately, conspiring to force the president to take a long vacation and agreeing that he looked mentally and physically exhausted. Likewise, Bedichek recounts in his memorial how he, Benedict, and Benjamin C. Tharp, a UT botany professor, were once en route to Green Island in "the Brownsville country" near South Padre Island for a two-week camping trip when some unfinished business suddenly flashed into Benedict's mind; the traveling party, lumbering along in an old truck through the Kenedy Ranch, had to stop immediately and find a small way station at which Benedict could board a train to hurry back to Austin.[4]

In his memorial, Bedichek summarizes the Benedict administration's major accomplishments as follows:

1. The University's improved relationship to the public and the establishment for a basis for greater public support; 2. An immense building program completed with a dollar's worth of building to show for every dollar expended; 3. A fairly harmonious internal administration, meanwhile, with no concessions to "witchburners," meaning those who would impose opinions and throttle free discussion.[5]

In any era, being the president of a large state university is an enormously complex and difficult job. Considering the University's tendency to politicize its internal affairs and the Texas citizenry's historically persistent skepticism toward the idea of spending tax money on higher education, the presidency of the University of Texas is no less difficult than the presidency at any other major public research university—and probably more difficult than most. At any institution of higher learning, being president requires keeping a constant eye on the big picture as well as on any of the thousands of details—each of which may or may not be within the president's direct control—that at any moment could advance or retard the work of the institution. Typically, the Office of the President taxes its occupant with impunity—politically, mentally, emotionally, and even physically.

The period of nearly ten years during which Benedict held the presidency, 1927 to 1937, was no less difficult than any other; in fact, it might have been the most difficult in the history of the University (the brief fight in 1917 that his predecessor R. E. Vinson had with Governor Jim "Pa" Ferguson and his desire to shut down the University by cutting off its entire state appropriation notwithstanding). Oil had begun flowing from the University's barren West Texas lands four years before Benedict took office, but the conditions that would lead to the ravages that the Dust Bowl and the Great Depression inflicted across Texas—one of the greatest environmental and social disasters in American history—were already in place in 1927, needing just a severe lack of rain and the shenanigans of a poorly regulated stock market back east to set them in motion. (Benedict often quipped that in Texas the Depression didn't start in 1929—it just moved from the countryside into the city.)

In addition to being the first graduate of the University to be elected its president, Benedict served as president of The University of Texas longer than any other man or woman to hold the office—a record that, at the time of this writing, still stands. At any moment during the nine years, nine months, and twenty-one days he was president, the institution could have been seriously imperiled by failed leadership in those fragile times—whether from fiscal mismanagement, graft, internal squabbling, interference from the legislature or big business, or excessive greed.[6]

In the memorial to his friend, Bedichek elaborates on his three points. He notes that the "'cost per student' unit of measurement for the work of an educational institution became a working hypothesis"[7] during the Benedict administration, helping University administrators keep costs low, and that the state legislature had just passed a bill recognizing the effectiveness of this practice. He also notes that Benedict's administration had completed the first handbook of operations in the institution's history and had instituted a modern accounting system, both of which brought a transparency to the University's operations and stability to the working lives of faculty and students that had not existed theretofore (a transparency and stability that, one could argue, some of the University's subsequent generations have struggled to replicate).

However, Bedichek reserves his greatest praise for the Benedict administration's transformation of the physical campus. When Benedict took office, the University had just begun a massive building program, started under the guidance of Benedict's immedi-

President H. Y. Benedict (*second from right*) poses with the UT regents and key University administrators in front of the last "shack" on the Forty Acres, 1935. *From the UT Richard I. Fleming University Writings Collection Photographs, Dolph Briscoe Center for American History, University of Texas at Austin. (DI 07523)*

ate predecessor, Walter M. W. Splawn, to transform the campus into a more modern institution. Before this program, the campus consisted of a hodgepodge of scattered, outdated, and largely undistinguished buildings—Cass Gilbert's wonderful University Library (Battle Hall) and Education Building (Sutton Hall) being the lone exceptions—with much of the work of the University being conducted in classrooms and laboratories housed in deplorable wooden barracks, referred to as "shacks," crowding the Forty Acres. The plan was to demolish several of the buildings inside the campus core, as well as all the shacks, and replace them with an ambitious suite of magnificent structures designed by the architects Herbert Greene and Paul Cret, organized within Cret's long-

range master plan for campus development.[8] A large bronze plaque inside the south portico of today's Main Building describes the effort:

A Building Era 1925–1937
From 1925 to 1933 the University Available Fund was by law dedicated mainly to the construction of buildings. A constitutional amendment adopted in 1930 authorized the Regents to borrow from the University Permanent Fund for building purposes. During 1933–36 funds by loan and grant were received from the United States government for the construction of six buildings. Funds for building were also received by bequest from Major George W. Littlefield, by gifts secured by the Ex-Students' Association, and

by the sale of a Centennial half-dollar promoted by the American Legion of Texas. From these resources twenty-four buildings were erected.

This effort began under President Splawn with the construction of the Biology Laboratory (1925), Garrison Hall (1926), and Texas Memorial Stadium (1926).[9] The building program continued under President Benedict, resulting in a core set of structures that continues to define the identity and aesthetic of today's enormous twenty-first-century campus; here they are, as listed on the bronze plaque:

1927 Littlefield Memorial Dormitory
1928 Power Plant [renamed the Hal C. Weaver Power Plant]
1928 & 1933 Engineering Building [T. U. Taylor Hall, demolished][10]
1930 Gregory Gymnasium
1931 Women's Gymnasium [Anna Hiss Gymnasium][11]
1931 Waggener Hall
1931 Chemistry Building [Robert A. Welch Hall]
1932 Brackenridge Hall
1933 Architecture Building [Goldsmith Hall]
1933 Geology Building [Will C. Hogg Building]
1933 Hogg Memorial Auditorium
1933 Home Economics Building [Mary E. Gearing Hall]
1933 & 1937 Library—Main Building [Main Building and Tower]
1933 Physics Building [T. S. Painter Hall]
1933 Union—Cafeteria [Texas Union]
1933 University High School [School of Social Work Building]
1936 Roberts Hall
1936 Jessie Andrews Dormitory
1937 Asenath Carothers Dormitory
1937 Prather Hall
1937 Texas Memorial Museum

It is remarkable that this suite of buildings was planned and constructed in such a short period of time. To have done it when the state was reeling from the insults inflicted by the failed national economy and the record heat and drought of the 1920s and '30s makes the result even more noteworthy.

Regarding this achievement, Bedichek makes the following observations in his memorial piece:

To his administration came the opportunity to rebuild the physical plant of the University; the opportunity, in the words of former President Vinson, to "unshackle the University." It was merely the opportunity that was offered. The whole affair might have been bungled and blasted a dozen times.

There was the money, but how to make it available? There was the half century old feud with A. & M. College to be adjusted.[12] There was the composing of a hundred differences of opinion from responsible groups and deep-cutting compromises that looked to the uninitiate like a sell-out. There was the guarding of the oil resources from selfish exploitation, and there was the enormous building program to guard against graft.

It was all done in a masterly fashion. Seeing that oil attracts corruption and that huge sums of money made available to be spent suddenly in the public's behalf offer an ideal opportunity for the grafter, the piloting of this immense program through without giving scandal a word or a breath is a testimony to President Benedict's skill as an administrator that the future historian cannot overlook. It is true that he had perhaps the ablest group of men ever assembled in a public enterprise in Texas to fight this thing through with him, but is not that, again, a testimony to his own worth? Ability to attract and to work with able men is in itself the mark of the superior executive.[13]

One could easily argue that no leader of the University of Texas with as much on his plate under such difficult circumstances has executed the duties of the office more expertly than Benedict. His only rival would perhaps be Harry Ransom in the 1960s. Ransom built an enormous intellectual edifice on the Forty Acres through the exceptional academic talent he coaxed to Austin and the world-class literary collections he amassed in his prized Humanities Research Center. However, he built this edifice in an era in which universities were expanding rapidly in the size of their student populations and the scope of their mission, transforming themselves into the "multi-versities" that we know today. Immense resources were made available to Ransom's administration in the 1960s by the regents and a legislature that together, for perhaps the first and only time in history, were willing to turn a blind eye to over-the-top spending by the University. (In his book

Our Invaded Universities, Ronnie Dugger writes that Norman Hackerman, Ransom's successor as UT president, told him in an interview that some of the regents in the 1960s who backed Ransom's profligate spending on rare books and manuscripts were "doing repentance for their redneck days."[14] Furthermore, much of the institutional infrastructure Ransom needed was already in place, and the time was right in the nascent global economy for unprecedented growth by American universities in the aftermath of World War II, a moment in time that was dominated by America economically and (for better or worse) culturally.

By comparison, Benedict was a nineteenth-century man with a twentieth-century outlook, leading the University into a modernity that it had not yet experienced. He had to sell the University's mission over and over again to the citizenry of a state that was still predominantly rural. Their fathers and grandfathers having fought and died in the Civil War, the older generations of Texans at that time still remembered keenly the deprivations of Reconstruction-era Texas—and their view of the necessity for higher education and its attendant costs was often trumped by their memories of doing what was necessary to "keep the wolf from the door." If that weren't enough, Benedict led the University with what by today's standards would be an impossibly small support staff, working from an un-air-conditioned office in the searing heat of Texas in the 1930s.

"G. T. T.," (gone to Texas,) was the slang appendage, within the reader's recollection, to every man's name who had disappeared before the discovery of some rascality. Did a man emigrate thither, every one was on the watch for the discreditable reason to turn up.

FREDERICK LAW OLMSTED,
A JOURNEY THROUGH TEXAS (1857)

Virginia is populated by the "Have Beens," and Texas by the "Going to Be's."

DR. L. P. YANDELL, JR., OF LOUISVILLE, KENTUCKY,
LETTER TO THE LOUISVILLE *COURIER-JOURNAL*,
DECEMBER 22, 1877

In *The Forty-Acre Follies*, his informal history of the University, Joe B. Frantz, a UT history professor,

gives the following description of Benedict, who was president when Frantz was a student at UT:

He was a quiet man with a rueful smile who always looked as if he had slept in his clothes. I had two landladies who had once mattered in Austin society, and they always denigrated him because he looked uncomfortable in a tuxedo. He looked uncomfortable in anything that men wore in public in those days. He looked like all the country men I have known through the years when they put on seldom-worn coats and ties to attend a funeral. Men who look so vigorous out in the cotton field or behind a horse are suddenly transformed into something that doesn't quite belong, and show it.

But Benedict belonged. He had a brain, he had breadth, he knew his constituency, and he made people around him feel comfortable. President Benny was as Texan as it is possible to be. Not River Oaks, Texas; not Petroleum Club, Texas; not King Ranch, Texas; just plain old Weatherford, Texas, where people scratch before going out to milk and then return by daylight to eat fried cornbread and fried side meat for breakfast. He was known back home [Frantz grew up in Weatherford] for having once locked a calf in the Weatherford College auditorium over Thanksgiving (with results that don't strain the imagination) and in Austin for his informal astronomy lectures and stargazing in front of the Main Building for whoever showed up. He was a rural sophisticate.[15]

Bedichek, who first encountered Benedict at UT in 1900 as a student in one of the recently hired adjunct professor's sections of freshman math, recalls that Benedict "drawled in a curiously modified West Texanese, but not even the most critical listener could set down any errors in his grammar or pronunciation."[16] He was always deeply impressed by the precision that defined everything Benedict did. Benedict was quintessentially a Texan, and yet in many ways he could not have been further from the stereotype. He was not a native, nor had he "Gone to Texas."

Benedict was born in Louisville, Kentucky, on November 14, 1869, into a white-collar, middle-class family. His mother, Adele Peters Benedict, was an accomplished musician who knew Italian and had been schooled in the social graces of her time. Her relatives had been in the music business in Louisville for years, and it was in the music store of her uncle

Yandell Benedict and his mother, Adele Peters Benedict, Louisville, Kentucky, 1872. *Photo courtesy of Cynthia Benedict Thompson.*

W. C. Peters that a scheme was hatched by her immigrant English grandfather, William Smalling Peters, and his sons to recruit five other American and eleven English investors to petition the Republic of Texas in 1841 for "An Act Granting Land to Emigrants." The Louisville musicians envisioned a vast colony—the Peters Colony—that would become an enormous swath of settlement developed across the virgin northern plains of the Republic, including the area where the Dallas-Fort Worth Metroplex stands today. The Kentuckians, filled with dreams of success that they might realize in Texas far beyond what they could have achieved at home, were giddy with excitement over the grandiose possibilities of their scheme. Similarly, the investors in England hoped that in addition to fulfilling their idealistic intentions to provide opportunities in this new

republic for immigrants from Great Britain's industrial middle class, they would get rich.[17]

However, the realities of the North American frontier—and the perturbations wrought by grasping hands and conflicting desires—trumped the dreams of those *empresarios* manqué, though one can drive around the polished suburbs of today's Metroplex and see "Peters Colony" on the signs of schools and streets and businesses, bearing witness to the enterprise's failed frontier ambitions. (The municipality of The Colony, Texas, founded in the 1970s among the sprawling suburbs north of Dallas, is on the site of the Hedgcoxe War of 1852, an armed uprising of colonists against the Texas Emigration and Land Company.) The tale of the Peters Colony is a sad one.

In 1874, Yandell Benedict's only sibling, a brother, Carl, was born. Soon thereafter, their father, Joseph E. "Cap" Benedict—a former Mississippi River steamboat operator who had fought for four years with the Confederate Army, rising from private to lieutenant—headed west to Texas to establish a ranch in the tattered remains of the Peters Colony. In 1874, the U.S. Army was still vigorously pursuing its intentions to subdue the Comanche, Kiowa, Kiowa Apache, Cheyenne, and Arapaho peoples and drive them onto reservations across the Red River, in Indian Territory; that year saw the infamous second battle at Adobe Walls, which led to the Red River War and the tragic Battle of Palo Duro Canyon.

In 1877, Yandell, Carl, and their mother headed west as well, accompanied by Adele's father, Henry J. Peters, the longtime organist at Christ Church and the Cathedral of the Assumption in Louisville. Amid reports of riverboat traffic, opera reviews, advertisements for gentlemen's white ties and cotton drawers, and the scores of the Louisville Grays' baseball games, the Louisville *Courier-Journal* carried news of Indian depredations in Texas, including lurid narratives of excursions by troops commanded by General Edward Ord across the Rio Grande in pursuit of "Indian marauders," with tales of scalpings and bloody guerilla engagements. Nevertheless, the members of the Benedict-Peters family arrived safely at their ranch, set among the stony hills, pristine tributaries, and vacant seas of prairie grass along the upper Brazos River, eighty-five miles west of the recently incorporated town of Fort Worth, which the railroad had reached just the year before.

As a young boy forming his first impressions of

the world, Yandell would have been accustomed to the bustling streets, the busy river traffic of steamboats and barges, the variety of goods sold in the local stores, the promise of proper schools and friends and classmates, the delights of the many opera houses, and the crack of the bat to be heard at the professional baseball games in Louisville, a thriving city on the Ohio River. One can only imagine what the thoughts of this seven-year-old boy must have been as their wagon bumped and jostled its way to the family's new home in Texas, where the embers of the retreating frontier were still glowing on the western horizon and the call of the native tribes was still resonating off the scattered, solitary hills of that region.

Remarkably, the Benedict-Peters family brought a library of a thousand volumes to their new home on a ranch along the Brazos, near what would become the villages of Eliasville, South Bend, and South Prairie.

If a man would be alone, let him look at the stars. . . . The stars awaken a certain reverence, because though always present, they are inaccessible; but all natural objects make a kindred impression, when the mind is open to their influence. Neither does the wisest man extort her secret, and lose his curiosity by finding out all her perfection. Nature never becomes a toy to a wise spirit. The flowers, the animals, the mountains, reflected the wisdom of his best hour, as much as they had delighted the simplicity of his childhood.

RALPH WALDO EMERSON, "NATURE" (1836)

Two things fill the mind with ever new and increasing admiration and awe, the oftener and more steadily we reflect on them: the starry heavens above me and the moral law within me.

IMMANUEL KANT, *CRITIQUE OF PRACTICAL REASON* (1788)

Yandell's education consisted primarily of the hard work that survival on a frontier ranch demanded. Adele Peters Benedict tutored him and his brother skillfully, as did the natural world in which Yandell and Carl lived and worked. In his memorial to Benedict, Bedichek recounts a car trip that he talked the busy president into taking in May 1934 to visit the place of Benedict's youth, which he had not seen in more than thirty years:

His boyhood memories came in a flood as we approached the old ranch. Here in the swamp on the Titus place he had seen his first swallow-tailed kite; at another point he had killed eight Gambel's geese; in this tree he had robbed a red-tailed hawk's nest for his egg-collection; and down in the great red gulch, the "Devil's Washbasin," he pointed out the bed of crinoids that had first stimulated his interest in geology. . . . He pointed out the place in the Clear Fork where his mother was seriously injured while being transferred from a wagon caught in a sudden flood to a boat.[18]

Even as a child, Benedict had been an avid birdwatcher and egg collector, building an impressive collection of eggs and nests, all carefully preserved. Decades later, he gave this collection to the University of Texas in the interest of science. In a poignant section of the reminiscence, Bedichek captures the unusual complexity of Benedict's mind and his insistence on precision in everything he did:

We camped the first night at Finis, and [Benedict] indulged in long and melancholy speculations on the old pioneer ford at the creek and the stage-station fallen into complete dilapidation. "Ill fares the land to hastening ills a prey," he quoted, and I stopped him short. The poet, I said, would not repeat "ills" in the same line. We disputed the point a little while and forgot it—at least I did. Six months later I got a card from him quoting the lines and underscoring both "ills," and that's the way Goldsmith wrote it.[19]

Only the natural world, coupled with the remarkable skill with which Adele Peters Benedict guided her sons' learning, can supply the completeness of education that young Yandell received. Only through observation of the natural world and interaction with it can a pupil understand in a meaningful way the relationship that the knowledge in books has to reality outside those books—namely, the deep, metaphorical connections among the things that exist in this world, an understanding of which the especially keen and well-trained mind is able to grasp and use productively. The tender sprouts of Benedict's greatest accomplishments as an adult were watered generously on the Peters ranch along the Clear Fork of the Brazos River.

When Yandell was eleven years old, the family moved into Graham, the seat of Young County, so that he could attend public school, which he did for only five months. The next year he attended the Hendricks private school for a just a few months, and in the fall of 1884, he enrolled in Cleveland College in Weatherford, Texas. This institution, whose curriculum in those days was more like what we today would consider a high school curriculum, was renamed Weatherford College in 1889 and still exists today as the state's oldest junior college. After only three months, he was expelled by the president for refusing to divulge the names of classmates whom he knew had spread match heads on the chapel floor.

In his teenage years, when not ruminating over the origins of the crinoid fossils in the Devil's Washbasin, Benedict engaged in the real work of a typical Texas ranch. Bedichek describes the boy's responsibilities:

There was much riding and general ranch work to be done, and there was the still more gruelling task of grubbing mesquite and building miles of rock fences out of boulders which strew the surface of the foothills. There were the endless chores of the pioneer home: wood, water, milking, care of stock, etc., and there were the excitements of feuds, killings, cattle stealing, and terrible catastrophes, such as the long drouth of 1886–87, in which nearly all the cattle of the country perished, and is remembered to this day by the old-timers as "The Great Die."[20]

A letter dated June 25, 1935, that President Benedict received from W. G. Swenson, inviting him to attend the Texas Cowboy Reunion in Stamford, gives a clear indication of the gulf between the world in which the men of Benedict's generation were reared and the world in which they lived their later years. Forty-five miles north of Abilene, Stamford was in 1935 a well-established town of about 4,500 citizens. In his reply to Swenson, Benedict writes: "I think I camped one night almost exactly where Stamford now is. We had cattle in the late Eighties at the 7 Diamond L Ranch in Stonewall County, our home

place being in Young and Stephens Counties. Hence I travelled in my youth the Eliasville, Throckmorton, Haskell and Double Mountain road frequently."[21]

Benedict's relationship with the University of Texas began when he was nineteen years old. In January 1889, he accompanied his mother on a trip to San Antonio, and somewhat serendipitously, they stopped in Austin on their return to the ranch in Young and Stephens Counties. (Benedict always took delight in pointing out that when he was a child, Tom Brown, the surveyor of Stephens County, determined that the county line ran directly through their house on the Clear Fork, and so he slept with his head in Stephens County and his feet in Young. In a letter to Claude Peeler dated June 14, 1934, Benedict writes that it was Tom Brown's "use of a Traverse Table while running this line that set me to studying Trigonometry, which in later life I tried to teach for about thirty years to successive generations of University freshmen.")[22] While in Austin, Benedict earned his entrance to the University of Texas by examination, and returned to Austin to matriculate, midterm, a month later. At that time, the University consisted of nothing more than a partially finished Main Building, a small power plant, and a fence to keep cattle from wandering onto the campus.

The year after Benedict arrived on campus, a UT regent, George Washington Brackenridge, donated funds to build a men's dormitory and mess hall of purely utilitarian design. Its official name was University Hall, though everyone called it Brackenridge Hall, or B. Hall. The young man from a ranch on the Stephens-Young county line won the lottery for first pick of a room in the new building, and he selected the one that caught the most southerly breezes and had the best protection against the brutal afternoon sun.[23]

Despite his almost complete lack of formal education, Benedict was a brilliant student. He earned his degree in three years—taking a BS in civil engineering, with honors, in 1892—and stayed for one more year to complete an MA in civil engineering. Anyone with a UT library card can still examine in the UT libraries the stiff, ruled pages of his 1893 master's thesis, "A Design for a Rim-bearing Swing Bridge of 220' Span," its text and diagrams written out entirely in longhand, as well as his BS thesis, "The Deflection of Beams under a Transverse Stress. Being an Appli-

The original Main Building at the University of Texas as it appeared about the time that H. Y. Benedict matriculated at UT. The west wing had been constructed in 1882–1884, and the central section and auditorium were nearing completion in early 1889. The east wing would not be completed until 1899, the year Benedict returned to UT as a member of its faculty. *From the John Matthias Kuehne Photograph Collection, Dolph Briscoe Center for American History, University of Texas at Austin. (DI 06817)*

cation of the Common Theory of Flexure to a Number of Special Problems." So rapid was Benedict's academic advancement that he served as fellow in pure mathematics at the University during his final year as an undergraduate, and as a tutor during the year of his master's.

Since arriving in a wagon with his mother, brother, and grandfather at the family ranch on the lonely western edge of the failed Peter's Colony sixteen years earlier, the only time Benedict had traveled outside the state of Texas was during a four-month camping trip by wagon to Colorado with his beloved uncle Carl Peters (who was the second-most powerful force in his intellectual development, behind his mother) and W. M. Sager (for whom the town of Sagerton, Texas, is named). After receiving his MA,

Benedict accepted a position as an assistant at the prestigious McCormick Observatory at the University of Virginia. Dedicated just nine years earlier, the McCormick had a twenty-six-inch astronomic refractor, the world's second-largest telescope. Within a year of beginning his work at the McCormick, just west of Thomas Jefferson's historic campus, he was encouraged by peers to apply to the PhD program in astronomy at Harvard University. He did—and was accepted, in 1895.

"One can imagine her solicitude for the two boys she brought with her from Louisville, one seven the other only two [sic] years old," Bedichek writes of the Benedict brothers' mother, Adele, in the book *Peregrinusings*, a collection of humorous columns Benedict wrote for the *Alcalde* during his years as dean.

Her father and mother dying almost immediately after reaching Texas, the responsibility for the care and education of her children was put upon her. The final product certainly attested her skill, although she lived to see only a partial proof of the efficiency of her work. She died in 1894.[24]

While Benedict was at Virginia, the year his mother died, his brother Carl began his lifelong career as a West Texas cattle rancher. In 1943, with the help of J. Frank Dobie, Carl Peters Benedict wrote and published a memoir of his first experience as an apprentice cowpuncher, helping the Figure 8 Ranch gather its cattle from the Pease River range in West Texas in the summer of 1894. The account captures the romance and trials of life on the range and provides a powerful contrast to the life his brother was undertaking.[25]

Benedict studied mathematical astronomy at Harvard, taking his PhD in 1898. The following academic year, he served as an instructor ad interim of mathematics and astronomy at Vanderbilt University. During this time, he was a serious candidate for a professorship at the Naval Observatory in Washington, D.C., and was also looking at an attractive position at the University of Missouri, one of the leading universities in the Midwest in that era. A flood of letters of recommendation poured in to the Naval Observatory on his behalf. W. E. Byerly, a professor of mathematics at Harvard, wrote to John D. Long, the secretary of the navy, that Benedict "is one of the best equipped astronomers we have sent out for many years."[26] Yet throughout the year, he also kept up a steady correspondence with his old acquaintances at the University of Texas.

Texas was like a magnet; the attraction was irre-

H. Y. Benedict (*second row, second from left*) posing in May 1891 with fellow members of the University of Texas Class of 1892. *From the Prints and Photographs Collection—Class Portraits, Dolph Briscoe Center for American History, University of Texas at Austin. (DI 06881)*

Harvard PhD candidate H. Y. Benedict (*left*) and a friend, Cannon, visiting Daniel Chester French's statue *The Minute Man* in Concord, Massachusetts, ca. 1890s. *Photo courtesy of Cynthia Benedict Thompson.*

sistible. Despite other, more prestigious opportunities, he returned to the still fledgling University of Texas to take a position as instructor of pure mathematics and astronomy for the 1899–1900 academic year. No doubt other influences piqued his interest in returning to Texas as well. As a student at UT, he had courted a young woman from Henderson, Miss Ada Eliza Stone, who had since graduated from the University and who, regardless of the limited professional opportunities for women of her time, was in many respects his intellectual equal. In a letter to Bess Lomax, Jeannette S. Greer wrote of Miss Stone:

> In childhood she was bright, happy, and merry, adored by parents, brothers, and sisters. She went to the public schools in Henderson, graduating from them before the age of 15, and consequently too young to enter the University of Texas for another year—she studied at home, however, without an instructor and entered the Sophomore class just as she reached her 16th birthday, taking her degree before she was 19,

and when Phi Beta Kappa was organized in the Univ., her grades entitled her to this honor.

> Not only was she a good student, but she had a merry happy time with many friends and admirers, and it was during their student days that she and Dr. Benedict became interested in one another. Ada was an especial favorite of Judge Clark, Prof. Garrison, and Mrs. Kirby from the time she entered the U. as a student, and as long as they lived.[27]

They were married at St. Mark's Church in Beaumont on June 27, 1900, the orphaned bride given away by her brother-in-law, Robert A. Greer of Beaumont, with Lester Bugbee, a promising young historian on the UT faculty who would succumb to tuberculosis only two years later, serving as best man. The happy couple honeymooned in Saltillo, Mexico, with a side trip to Topochico. Very soon, the Benedicts welcomed a son into their lives—Carl Stone Benedict, born October 18, 1901. The Benedicts lived for many years in a house at 2525 University Avenue, roughly where Burdine Hall stands today. Tragedy struck this home when Carl, their only child, died in the great influenza epidemic just a few weeks after he arrived in Annapolis to begin his studies at the United States Naval Academy, in 1918.

Three years later, Yandell and Ada purchased an antebellum stone farmhouse at 3401 Guadalupe Street, a property on the northern outskirts of the city, which in those days was being rapidly swallowed by suburban sprawl. (By that time, to the alarm of some Austinites, the sprawl had recently leapt 45th Street in its rapid push to the north.) Even in 1921, the University coveted properties beyond the borders of its campus, and even deans were not exempt from the institution's appetite for land. Benedict describes in his book *Peregrinusings* how he came to relocate to this new home: "The Peregrinuser, selling his humble home to the Purchasing Board for what it offered, because he didn't see much chance of getting more, fled away from the society of University students and college professors to the more congenial and fitting vicinity of the Lunatic Asylum," which, in that era, was the name by which the State Hospital on 38th Street was known.[28] He took great delight in the small creek that ran through the backyard and in the number of birds that were attracted to the towering cypress trees and lush vegetation that he cultivated there. He had carved at the front door the motto "*Parva sed apta mihi*," which translates roughly as "Small but suiting me." In 1922, Yandell and Ada would be blessed with a second son, H. Y. Benedict, Jr.

The Benedict house still stands on the northeast corner of the intersection of 34th and Guadalupe. It remains a private home, the deep backyard now a graceful courtyard bounded by bungalows, where its previous owner once cared for the native cypress trees and tended his water lilies and elephant's ears. (Regrettably, many years ago, previous owners sold the front yard and circle drive to a developer, who razed the front porch and built a commercial strip mall against the front of the house.) When Benedict was named UT president, he, Ada, and Yandell Jr. moved into the president's official residence on Whitis Avenue, but five years later, the family chose to move back to 3401 Guadalupe, where they were much happier.

As the University entered the twentieth century and began to spread its wings as the state's flagship institution of higher learning, the young instructor of pure mathematics and astronomy advanced steadily through the ranks. He was named adjunct professor in 1900, associate professor in 1902, and professor of applied mathematics in 1907. He served as director of extension from 1909 to 1911. In 1911, he was named dean of the College of Arts (renamed the College of Arts and Sciences in 1920)—a position he would hold for sixteen years, before rising to the presidency of the University. During his time as college dean, he also served stints as dean of men and chairman of the University Athletic Council. He was a fine tennis player, though troubles with the football team—three seasons with losing records and public outrage over the behavior and exorbitant salary ($5,000 a year) of the head coach, Jack Chevigny—would plague his presidency in years to come.

During his entire career at UT, Benedict was a trained astronomer at a university that had neither a department of astronomy nor a proper telescope. In 1926, benefiting from the happy coincidence that the sole astronomer on the University faculty was also dean of the College of Arts and Sciences, the University was able to protect its interests when the will of William J. McDonald—a bachelor who was the president of banks in the East Texas towns of Paris, Clarksville, and Cooper and who had no connections to the University or Austin—was read, revealing that he had left virtually his entire estate of more than one million dollars to the University to fund the construction of a first-rate observatory. Of course, the de-

cedent's family contested the will, and after a series of court battles, the University eventually settled for an amount of more than $800,000. Construction on the McDonald Observatory would begin in a few years in the Davis Mountains in West Texas. However, just as he would not live to occupy his office in the new Main Building, the dean-turned-president died before construction of the McDonald Observatory was completed.[29]

In April 1927, President Splawn announced to the board of regents his intention to resign, and on July 19, 1927, H. Y. Benedict was selected by the board by acclamation, unanimously, to serve as president of the University of Texas. Many close observers thought that he should have been selected in 1923, following the resignation of President Vinson, or perhaps even as early as 1914, following the resignation of President Mezes. A closer look into the actions of the board of regents reveals why Benedict's expected rise to the presidency may have been thwarted. Remarkably, the board had voted 7–1 at its meeting on July 10, 1923 (less than two weeks after Vinson, an ordained Presbyterian clergyman, had left office, and four years before Benedict would finally achieve the office) to adopt the following resolution—against the strong advice of acting president William Seneca Sutton:

> Be it resolved by the Board of Regents that no infidel, atheist or agnostic be employed in any capacity in the University of Texas, and that while no sectarian qualification shall ever be required of persons now serving or who shall in future be elected or appointed to positions in this institution, no person who does not believe in God as the Supreme Being and the Ruler of the Universe shall hereafter be employed or at any time continue in or be elected or appointed to any office or position of any character in this University.[30]

The philosophical position held by the dean—a mathematician and astronomer—regarding the question of religion had no doubt always caused him to be considered suspect by the University's highest decision makers. Even after finally securing the office, in 1927, President Benedict received letters from local clergy as well as laypersons expressing their concern over their perception of his faith—and their doubts, therefore, about his ability to perform the duties of president. In his reply to a letter of concern he received from George Green, the pastor of the First Baptist Church in Austin, Benedict confided that he was "a fairly advanced modernist." In response to the Reverend Green's promise to pray for him every day, Benedict noted: "Concerning the efficacy of prayer my mind points not always in the same direction but I do think that more things may be wrought by prayer than some materially minded men suppose. Perhaps not all the things thought of by revivalists, but some-things [*sic*] too wonderful yet to be understood."[31]

Nevertheless, every Christmas during which Dr. Benedict held the office of president—the holidays of 1927 through 1936—he and Mrs. Benedict sent out an official Christmas card from the Office of the President, featuring an original poem penned by the president. Here is the poem he wrote for his eighth year in office:

A Merry Christmas
And A Happy New Year

Men have sought and found about the stars
Fact after fact, for many hundred years,
With ever greater telescopes to help:
And each new fact reveals immensities
That shrivel up the mean and low in Man,
By showing him how small his selfishness.

Wise, just, truth-seeking, this McDonald knew
And, passing out into the Infinite,
Left wealth he had for study of the stars:
Like Kepler and like Kant, he was convinced
That search for Truth means also search for God,
That Goodness and the Stars are somehow kin.

At Christmas time, when selfishness is cast
As far as may be from the hearts of men,
In memory of the Child in stable born
We warm our hearts by grasping friendly hands,
We lift our souls by gazing at the stars,
And so obey the Child's two great commands.

MR. AND MRS. H. Y. BENEDICT
DECEMBER 25, 1934
THE UNIVERSITY OF TEXAS[32]

When he penned that 1934 holiday greeting, the mathematician-astronomer-president who had come of age on a ranch on the open range west of Fort Worth might have had in mind Johannes Kepler's defense of his belief in the Copernican understanding

of the universe, as expressed in his 1609 treatise *Astronomia Nova*—specifically, the understanding that the earth revolves around the sun:

I, too, implore my reader, when he departs from the temple and enters astronomical studies, not to forget the divine goodness conferred upon men . . . I hope that, with me, he will praise and celebrate the Creator's wisdom and greatness, which I unfold for him in the more perspicacious explanation of the world's form, the investigation of causes, and the detection of errors of vision. Let him not only extol the Creator's divine beneficence in His concern for the well-being of all living things, expressed in the firmness and stability of the earth, but also acknowledge His wisdom expressed in its motion, at once so well hidden and so admirable.

But whoever is too stupid to understand astronomical science, or too weak to believe Copernicus without affecting his faith, I would advise him that, having dismissed astronomical studies and having damned whatever philosophical opinions he pleases, he mind his own business and betake himself home to scratch in his own dirt patch, abandoning this wandering about the world. He should raise his eyes (his only means of vision) to this visible heaven and with his whole heart burst forth in giving thanks and praising God the Creator. He can be sure that he worships God no less than the astronomer, to whom God has granted the more penetrating vision of the mind's eye, and an ability and desire to celebrate God above those things he has discovered.[33]

This view, even to some people today, is upsetting when it is interpreted to mean that man is no longer deemed the central achievement of God's creation. As an intellectual working in the politically charged environment of the University's upper administration, Benedict possessed the remarkable ability to embrace what a not insignificant number of folks might see as contradictory positions—namely, the scientific mindset that is indispensable to a twentieth-century astronomer and to the mathematician's ability to pursue his or her academic work, and the Everyman's notion of common sense (and the Everyman's faith in Protestant Christian doctrines) that was generally revered in Benedict's era by those Texans who had a voice in the University's affairs.

There is an amusing exchange that supposedly took place between Dean Benedict and Lutcher Stark, the chairman of the board of regents—which in its day was a well-known bit of campus lore. After the board passed in the summer of 1923 that infamous resolution requiring all employees of the University to believe in its particular conception of God, it conducted an inquisition of sorts, intended to root out any non-Christians among the faculty (no doubt hoping to catch some "Reds," "Pinks," leftists, homosexuals, and race mixers along the way). Perhaps the first place this campus legend was put down in print is in *Texas Merry-Go-Round*, a waggish little book of short anecdotes published anonymously in 1933, its material mined from the rich veins of absurd behavior found among the leaders and institutions of the state of Texas. The book's author gives the following short profile of UT's president:

> Wisecracker, Ph. D.—H. Y. Benedict, so far as is recorded, makes no contributions to Life or Judge and the greater part of his jests bring laughter rather because of their author than their excellence. He is president of the University and the most persistent wisecracker who ever dwelt thereabouts. He is exceedingly popular for a president and was equally popular when he was dean of the college of arts, a place he held for many years.
>
> Benedict more than once has been under suspicion of heresy. Lutcher Stark, multimillionaire regent and fairy godfather to football players, once summoned Benedict before the board for interrogation.
>
> "Do you believe in God?" demanded Lutcher.
>
> "Do you mean an anthropomorphic God?" Benedict parried.
>
> The inquisition was adjourned until Mr. Stark could find a dictionary. It was never resumed.[34]

Assuming that this incident did in fact occur, Dean Benedict not only survived the board's inquiries, but eventually endeared himself to them sufficiently enough that they would elect him president unanimously four years later.

In his lifetime, Benedict was as beloved a figure as someone at his level of power and influence could be. His papers archived at the University are filled with letters attesting to this affection, from ordinary folks as well as important figures on the Forty Acres and around the state. One such letter is a handwritten note from Annie Webb Blanton, a professor in the Department of Educational Administration, dated November 17, 1930, thanking the president for tak-

ing the time to serve on the program of a meeting of the State Federation of Women's Clubs that she had recently sponsored. (Blanton Dormitory was named for Professor Blanton, posthumously, in 1954). She closed her short thank-you note with the following observations:

> I heard many expressions of satisfaction after your address. The members were pleased actually to have seen the president of the University. They liked your talk and your friendly way of taking them seriously and explaining the business side of college administration. They liked your humor, and many said that they didn't know that a college president could be so unaffected and *human*.[35]

Another such letter is one that Benedict received from August Charles Krey, a nationally respected medievalist at the University of Minnesota whose first teaching job had been at the University of Texas. He taught at UT for two academic years, 1910–1911 and 1911–1912—with Benedict as his dean during the second year. Before leaving Austin, he married Laura Letitia Smith, a brilliant student from Brookshire, Texas, who received her BA from the University in 1912 and would years later write two well-received romantic novels about her native state, *And Tell of Time* and *On the Long Tide*. Professor Krey's letter captures the significance of Benedict's achievement—and Benedict's reply, written a year later, conveys his typical congeniality, wisdom, and goodwill:

> University of Minnesota
> College of Science, Literature, and the Arts
> Minneapolis
>
> 316 Library
> May 7, 1935
>
> Department of History
>
> President H.Y. Benedict
> University of Texas
> Austin, Minnesota [*sic*]
>
> Dear Prexy:
>
> Laura Lettie was greatly disappointed not to have seen you during her visit at Austin a month ago. Though she called at your office four different times

she was deprived of the pleasure of seeing you. I suppose that the legislative session engrossed your attention as it has a way of doing with university presidents.

Her account of what had been done on the Campus at the University of Texas, however, was so glowing that I cannot resist the temptation to pass on her opinion, which becomes my opinion also, for I fear that she will not have done it. She thinks the Campus of the University of Texas is now one of the most beautiful in the United States. I am not certain that she didn't say the most beautiful, despite her very pleasant acquaintance with the campuses of the University of Virginia, of Stanford, of Princeton, as well as of Wisconsin. She was particularly impressed with the way in which the architecture fits the landscape and, in doing so, has retained much of the spirit of Texas tradition while at the same time meeting the most advanced requirements of a modern university and modern architecture. In fact, her description of the Campus was so glowing that I shall not feel happy again until I have seen it myself.

But she saw more than the externals of the Campus. A slight illness of our son Fort detained her at Austin several days longer than she had expected to be able to stay there. She was thus enabled to visit with friends and relatives and in their company to penetrate some of the arcana of the institution which are usually concealed from superficial view. Like most good Phi Beta Kappans, she has a sturdy veneration for the sacred traditions of scholarship as well as of society. She is not so hide-bound, however, in this veneration as not to recognize that the changing years must be given their place as well. It is her impression that you have moved forward, retaining most of what she regards as lovely in the old South, which to her means manners, standards, and respect for culture, and at the same time that you are meeting the needs of a heterogeneous society with its notions of progress, its insistence upon the vocational, and its urge to make money. It is her settled conviction that Texas is bound to be the best university in the South and that it may take leadership in the nation as a whole, a position which some of the universities of this middle northern section have been tacitly accorded in the past generation.

I cannot believe that this degree of progress has been achieved without a good many heart aches and even disappointments to individual views, for your faculty, as I recall it, has some very strong and even

uncompromising representatives of several points of view. Apparently you have resisted with their help the danger of moving over to the lunatic fringe of so-called progressive ideas while at the same time moving forward from any stick-in-the-mud position. To me this seems the highest praise that anyone in the command of an American university could wish, and since she has not written to you I feel that you ought to know that somewhere among the one hundred and twenty-eight millions and in the forty-eight states your achievement has been recognized.

With best wishes for a long life and a full realization of your dreams for Texas, I am

Sincerely yours,
A. C. Krey[36]

View of the Main Building and Tower from the north, 1940s. In the foreground are the Home Economics Building (*right*), the Experimental Science Building (*left*), and the Physics Building (*center, with observatory on roof*). The dome of the Capitol is visible to the right of the observatory. *From the Prints and Photographs Collection— UT Buildings—Main Building and Tower, Dolph Briscoe Center for American History, University of Texas at Austin. (DI 04911)*

View of the southern façade of the Main Building, 1930s. *From the Prints and Photographs Collection—UT Buildings— Main Building and Tower, Dolph Briscoe Center for American History, University of Texas at Austin. (DI 07011)*

The "Prexy" replied:

May 11, 1936

Professor A. C. Krey
University of Minnesota
Minneapolis, Minnesota

Dear Krey:

Pittenger's return from a visit to Minnesota bringing the sweet news that he had had the great pleasure of seeing Laura Lettie and you prompts this belated and feeble reply to your letter of exactly one year ago.[37] Unanswered but not unread (read several times), your letter has reposed in my ponderous unanswered file until the earth has travelled 2π times 93 million miles around the sun and the sun has

travelled 400 million miles toward Cygnus and the New Deal has travelled several billions of dollars towards I know not what and I have fallen many parsecs behind filling the job I have both the honor and the pain of pretending to fill.

My failure to answer is symptomatic, not of any failing affection for the Kreys, which neither oxidizes nor sulphates nor carbonates but retains its stainless steel metallic brilliancy [*sic*] undiminished through the years. The current troubles are so numerous that I fortunately can't remember them as they flit by, but the old friendships I do remember. I fear this means I ought to take to reading *De Senectute* (in English) for a regular diet.

I was mighty sorry to miss Laura Lettie when she was here last spring, but very much pleased to hear that she found the work of Paul Cret on the Campus greatly to her satisfaction. She is right, I think, in feeling that the University is destined to be the greatest in the South. I hope she is right in feeling that there is such a thing as manners left on the Campus. The history of the University during the last fifteen years, that is its fiscal-legislature-oil-P.W.A.-A. & M., is interesting, some features of it being unique and very little known. When next I see you, this can be told to you, an historian with a flair for the currents that affect the course of events.

Which reminds me of my latest dig at the historians: "An historian is a fellow that laboriously misrepresents the past. His intentions are good, he tries to tell the truth, he fails."

With unfailing affection and best of wishes for both of you.

Come to Texas!

Yours,
H. Y. Benedict, President[38]

One year after sending his reply to Professor Krey, whose letter wished him a long life and a full realization of his dreams for Texas, President Benedict was dead.

When Harry Yandell Benedict passed away, he left behind a wife and a son and a life filled with happiness and lasting accomplishments. His life saw fundamental, paradigm-shifting changes in not only his University, but also most of the world around him. The pastoral—and, in Texas, the often downright primitive—world of the nineteenth-century American West had been replaced by the mechanized world of the twentieth century. As Roy Bedichek wrote in the *Alcalde,* "Dr. Benedict's death was timed to round out an era, a perfectly unified period, in the history of the University of Texas, an institution with which he had been identified for nearly fifty years. He died in harness, actually in the service of the institution."[39]

Yet the man who was born in the age of the covered wagon and telegraph and whale-oil lamp, and who died just sixty-seven years later as the head of a modern state university buzzing with cars and telephones and electric lights, left behind no record of regrets for the loss of the many things that had been dear to him. These might have included the Benedict-Peters family ranch; the South Prairie community in Young and Stephens Counties; Old Main and B. Hall, the two structures that contained all his memories

as a student, young professor, and dean; and even his childhood collection of bird nests and eggs—which he gave as a gift to the University and which the University then neglected and allowed to deteriorate during his life. Of course, he had also lost his parents, Cap and Adele Benedict, at an early age; his beloved uncle Carl Peters; and his and Ada's dearly beloved son, Carl Stone Benedict. To the end, he was known by his cheerfulness and his optimism.

Faith in progress—personal and institutional—defined him.

NOTES

Background information for this essay was gathered from several primary sources, including various issues of the *Courier Journal* (Louisville, Kentucky) from 1869 and 1877 and the *Daily Texan* from May 11, 1937; an interview with Harry Yandell Benedict, Jr. by the author (Sept. 6, 2008); an interview with Cynthia Benedict Thompson by the author (Mar. 16, 2009); and the William James Battle Papers, 1870–1959 (Dolph Briscoe Center for American History, University of Texas at Austin). Secondary sources consulted but not cited include the *Handbook of Texas* (The Texas State Historical Association, online at http://www.tshaonline.org/handbook); H. Y. Benedict and John A. Lomax, *The Book of Texas* (Garden City, N.Y.: Doubleday, Page, 1916); Carrie J. Crouch, *A History of Young County, Texas* (Austin: Texas State Historical Association, 1956); H. Y. Benedict, "The Deflection of Beams under a Transverse Stress. Being an Application of the Common Theory of Flexure to a Number of Special Problems" (BS thesis, The University of Texas, 1892); H. Y. Benedict, "A Design for a Rim-bearing Swing Bridge of 220' Span" (MA thesis, The University of Texas, 1893).

1. In an editorial in the June 1937 issue of the *Alcalde,* William B. Ruggles remarks:

The University of Texas was the life-work of Dr. Harry Yandell Benedict. Few of his mature years were spent away from it. He was its son once—he became its friend and adviser, eventually its head. Those associated with him through the long years of his wise and scholarly work saw in him the elements of leadership. As an evidence of this fact Dr. Sidney E. Mezes wanted Benny to follow him in the President's chair. ("In All Our Hearts," 194)

2. Today, the structure that is the finished product of these two phases—the Main Building and Tower—houses only one department of the general libraries—the Life Sciences Library—as well as a warren of offices used by the sprawling proliferation of administrators and their staffs that the modern University demands. The University moved its central library from the Main Building and Tower to the newly constructed Perry-Castañeda Library facility in 1977. Most of

Benedict's generation no doubt would have found this modern proliferation of administrators—and the fact that the University's library outgrew the massive Main Building and Tower only forty years after it was built—difficult to comprehend.

3. See Board of Regents, Minutes, University of Texas System, Mar. 31, 1934, 25–39. http://www.utsystem.edu/borminutes/1881–1939/1934Minutes.pdf.

4. Roy Bedichek, "President H. Y. Benedict: In Memoriam," *Alcalde* 25, no. 9 (June 1937), 195–201.

5. Bedichek, "President Benedict," 196.

6. For a discussion of some particularly challenging controversies President Benedict had to manage during his presidency, see Don E. Carleton, "Communism, Fruit Flies, and Academic Freedom: J. R. Parten's 'Second Education,'" in this volume.

7. Bedichek, "President Benedict," 195.

8. For a deeper discussion of this building program, see Larry Speck, "Campus Architecture: The Heroic Decades," in the first volume of *The Texas Book*.

9. Since 1926, the original stadium has undergone several major renovations and expansions. In 1996, it was renamed Darrell K Royal–Texas Memorial Stadium.

10. The T. U. Taylor Hall Annex (1933) was razed in 1998 to make way for the Applied Computational Engineering and Sciences Building, and T. U. Taylor Hall (1928) was razed in 2011 to make way for the Bill and Melinda Gates Computer Science Complex.

11. Anna Hiss Gymnasium's natatorium—the east wing of the building—was razed in 1994 for construction of the Louise and James Robert Moffett Molecular Biology Building.

12. Bedichek refers here to the dispute over how to distribute the earnings from the Permanent University Fund equitably between the two state universities. Only a generation earlier, the two institutions and the state government had still been battling over the question whether Texas A&M was an independent college or merely a department of the University of Texas.

13. Bedichek, "President Benedict," 195.

14. Ronnie Dugger, *Our Invaded Universities: Form, Reform and New Starts* (New York: Norton, 1974), 78.

15. Joe B. Frantz, *The Forty-Acre Follies* (Austin: Texas Monthly Press, 1983), 139.

16. Bedichek, "President Benedict," 199.

17. The Harry Yandell Benedict Papers, 1855–1865, 1874–1940, Dolph Briscoe Center for American History, University of Texas at Austin; see also Seymour V. Connor, *The Peters Colony of Texas: A History and Biographical Sketches of the Early Settlers* (Austin: Texas State Historical Association, 1959) and the *Handbook of Texas*.

18. Bedichek, "President Benedict," 200.

19. Ibid.

20. Ibid., 197.

21. Benedict to W. G. Swenson, June 25, 1935, Benedict Papers, Box 2B64.

22. Benedict to Claude Peeler, June 14, 1934, Benedict Papers, Box 2B63.

23. For more about the raucous history of B. Hall, see David Dettmer, "When the Poor Boys Ruled the Campus: A Requiem for B. Hall," in the first volume of *The Texas Book*.

24. Harry Yandell Benedict, *Peregrinusings: A Queer Title for Some Moronic Essays* (Austin: Ex-Students' Association of the University of Texas, 1924), xxiv. Quotation is from Roy Bedichek's essay "The Peregrinuser."

25. Carl Peters Benedict, *A Tenderfoot Kid on Gyp Water*, introduction by J. Frank Dobie (Austin: Texas Folklore Society, 1943).

26. W. E. Byerly to John D. Long, March 11, 1899, Benedict Family Papers, Cynthia Benedict Thompson private collection.

27. Jeannette S. Greer to Bess Lomax, October 13, 1927, Benedict Family Papers, Cynthia Benedict Thompson private collection. Judge James B. Clark was a beloved regent, proctor, and "custodian general" of the early University; Professor George P. Garrison was chairman of the Department of History; and Helen Marr Kirby was the first dean of women at the University.

28. Benedict, *Peregrinusings*, 183.

29. For more about the history of the McDonald Observatory and the gift of William J. McDonald, see Frank Bash, "McDonald Observatory: Bigger and Brighter," in this volume.

30. Board of Regents, University of Texas System, Meeting Minutes and Dockets, 1923, 141. http://www.utsystem.edu/borminutes/1851–1939/1923Minutes.pdf.

31. Benedict to the Rev. George Green, August 8, 1927, Benedict Papers, Box 2B62.

32. Benedict Papers, Box 2B53.

33. Johannes Kepler, *New Astronomy*, trans. William H. Donahue (Cambridge: Cambridge University Press, 1992), 65–66.

34. *Texas Merry-Go-Round* (Houston: Sun, 1933), 77–78.

35. Annie Webb Blanton to Benedict, Nov. 17, 1930, Benedict Papers, unprocessed materials.

36. Benedict Papers, Box 2B62.

37. Benjamin Pittenger, the dean of the UT College of Education.

38. Benedict Papers, Box 2B62.

39. Bedichek, "President Benedict," 201.

A view of one of the courts in the Women's Gymnasium, ca. 1930s. *From the UT Texas Student Publications, Inc. Photographs Collection—Intramural Sports for Women, Dolph Briscoe Center for American History, University of Texas at Austin. (DI 06838)*

BRAD
BUCHHOLZ }

A Feminist,
before Her Time
The Journey of Anna Hiss

Anna Hiss was an independent woman who came of age in austere, less liberated times. She taught her first class at the University of Texas before women's suffrage and died before the passage of Title IX. So it is sometimes difficult to see her clearly in the blazing light of the twenty-first century. Her legacy lies in the shadows; her moment has passed.

Still: I've always felt one could step into her story—and touch Hiss's spirit, just a bit—by visiting the elegant, sienna-brick gymnasium complex that bears her name. The Anna Hiss Gymnasium is one of the oldest structures on campus, dedicated in 1931. In its prime, it was a graceful, strikingly feminine structure, a gym that at first impression evokes the spirit of a Mediterranean spa.

In search of Anna Hiss, I have lingered in its Spanish-style portico, paused at the door of her old office, admired the sheets of light streaming through the floor-to-ceiling windows of the dance studio. The soul of the gym, however, was its inner courtyard—compromised, forever, by the destruction of the complex's east wing in 1994. It was nature's space, a stately rectangular lawn at the bottom of a winding double staircase, shaded by towering deodar cedars.

Anna Hiss loved this place, its practical grace. And that only makes sense, since she conceived it. Hiss traveled the country at her own expense in the service of design. She studied other structures, shared notes with the UT architects, selected plants and trees to landscape it. Most of

---

Brad Buchholz, who received his bachelor of journalism degree from the University in 1978, discovered Anna Hiss's story during the first days of his freshman year, when a fraternity rush event drew him inside Anna Hiss Gymnasium, the first building he visited as a new student. While a student at UT, he wrote for the Daily Texan *at a time when Title IX was transforming women's athletics. Today he is a feature writer for the* Austin American-Statesman *and serves on the UT Women's Athletics Hall of Honor Selection Committee. This profile has its roots in Buchholz's "Basketball, White Gloves and Espionage," an article that appeared in the August 31, 1990, issue of the* Dallas Morning News.

Anna Hiss, ca. 1935. *From the UT Texas Student Publications, Inc. Photographs Collection—Anna Hiss (Faculty), Dolph Briscoe Center for American History, University of Texas at Austin. (DI 06868)*

all, she persuaded the men who sat on the board of regents that the women of the University *deserved* this gym, which so eloquently mirrored her essence, her values, her egalitarian social aims.

As UT's director of physical training for women, Anna Hiss was very much of her time—but also ahead of her time. She was white gloves and discipline, piano and art, the grit of nature and an ardent champion of social graces. She advocated recreation in all its forms—hiking, team sports, music, folk dance, crafts, literature—to the entire female student body. Hiss was instrumental in founding the Orange Jackets service group, the campus League of Women Voters. She was a cofounder of Delta Kappa Gamma, the national teachers honor society, and remained involved in it throughout her career.

Raised in Baltimore, the eldest of five children, Hiss was a strikingly erect woman—her dark wavy hair, cropped short, always—who stood tall for UT women from 1918 to 1957. At the same time, she won the respect of the University's most powerful men: Thomas Gregory, William Battle, Harry Ransom. Texas football coach D. X. Bible referred to her as "my quarterback" for her ability to get things done.

Although Hiss won national renown for her work in Austin, she wrestled always with private sorrows. Her father, a wholesale grocer named Charles Hiss, committed suicide at home—calling to his wife to contact the family physician, then cutting his throat with his razor—when Anna was thirteen years old. Her brother was Alger Hiss, a prominent aide in the Franklin Roosevelt administration who was accused of espionage and of harboring communist allegiances while in federal service. He was ultimately sentenced to five years in prison for perjury after a pair of sensational trials in 1949 and 1950.

Anna Hiss stood by her brother throughout the ordeal. Alger Hiss visited her in Austin several times, in fact, in secret. Yet that connection is merely a footnote, secondary to Anna Hiss's "enterprising personality"—and to the physical and holistic empowerment of women through four decades at the University of Texas.

"'Feminist' is a term that suggests the women's movement, here and now," Betty Thompson, the late director of UT Recreational Sports, observed in 1987 in the midst of the women's intercollegiate sports boom. "But sometimes we forget that there were feminists long ago, women who were dynamic and influential, task-oriented, objective-oriented. Anna Hiss was such a woman."

Anna Hiss moved to Austin, for reasons we will probably never know, in the summer of 1918. She was twenty-five and single, a recent graduate of the Sargent School of Physical Training in Cambridge, Massachusetts, where she had served as student-government president and edited the school's first yearbook. Hiss was clearly ready to make her own way in life—good-bye to Baltimore, good-bye to the memory of her father's suicide, good-bye to her mother's expectation that she marry well and marry young.

"Anna's mother wanted all her children to do well, to go to the finest schools," says Anna's niece, Joanna Hoople, whose father, Donald Hiss, and uncle Alger Hiss both attended Harvard Law School, both clerked for Supreme Court Justice Oliver Wendell Holmes as young men. "I remember my father telling me that Anna, as the oldest child, got that [message] from her in spades." In the end, "the family reaction was kind of 'wow.' I know my father and mother were very impressed that a young woman had the courage to take a step [into Texas] like that."

Hiss was hired as an instructor to teach physical training for women for the fall term of 1918. It was a turbulent time. America was at war; UT students were fighting in Europe. The campus was lined with barracks, dotted with tents, bustling with student soldiers in training. The flu epidemic shut down the campus for two weeks. Ten members of the faculty and student body died. This was her introduction to academic life.

Yet by 1921, Hiss had made such an impression that she was promoted to director—instilling the idea of fitness, recreation, and club sports as an essential part of University life, even as male satirists in the *Cactus* yearbook sometimes cracked wise about the wisdom of funneling student blanket taxes to something as insignificant as women's athletics. Many women, however, saw the young Anna Hiss (circa 1922) as "a fairy princess" whose castle "stands on the firm foundations of health, truth, and loyalty."

Between 1919 and 1929, Hiss founded nearly a dozen sports clubs: the Turtle Club for swimming, the Orchesus Club for interpretive dance, the Robin Hood Club for archery, the Te-WAA-Hiss club for hiking and camping, the Racquet Club for tennis, the Bit and Spur for horseback riding, the Tee Club for golf, the Touché Club for fencing. She saw these clubs—run by the students under an umbrella organization called the Women's Athletic Council—as a means of bringing women together in community in an era before big dormitories, when most female students were scattered around town, living in various boardinghouses.

The outdoor component was clearly important to her. Members of the Te-WAA-Hiss club staged ten-mile walks, learned camping skills, scheduled weekend retreats in a rustic cabins or houseboats outside the city. Hiss lobbied UT to utilize some of its wild lands for the use of her students.

Fiercely dedicated, Hiss adhered to the philosophy that "each of life's moments is precious and it is a sin to be wasteful." She "had a clear disdain for the status quo" as she sought to revolutionize women's athletics on the university level. "Above all," faculty member Harold C. Bold wrote years later in reminiscence, "she had the ability to sell herself and her program." She was a highly disciplined, highly motivated woman, stately in every way, even in the face of tragedy. Hiss returned to Baltimore for a time in 1926, the year her twenty-six-year-old brother Bosley died of kidney disease. Her thirty-four-year-old sister Mary committed suicide in 1929, leaving behind a husband and two children.

Yet for all her self-control, Hiss was popular on campus. Faculty friends remembered her as vivacious, "a fascinating conversationalist . . . rich in her awareness of life and other people." Hiss engaged with other departments and other teachers, and supported men's athletics. She used her first savings from UT to buy a piano and cultivated a record collection. Hiss believed an appreciation for literature and the arts was as much a part of recreation as team sports or physical fitness.

She liked to sing—for her students, and at parties, and around campfires. "She loved social gatherings and frequently became the life of the party," wrote Bold, "whether telling stories, leading singing, presenting dramatizations, or drawing each guest into the enjoyment of the occasion."

In the late 1920s, Hiss persuaded the University to set aside funds for a "first of its kind" women's gymnasium, no small task in an era when some considered it immoral for men to watch women participate in sports. With the financial support of the UT Ex-Students' Association and the board of regents, UT had already committed to a new gymnasium for the men—the future Gregory Gym. But would it fund a women's facility?

Toward that end, Hiss summoned her diplomatic skills, set up a meeting with Thomas Watt Gregory, and then had her students make the point of how little the University was providing them in terms of support. They successfully made the point that the current structure, N Hall—a holdover from UT's World War I barracks-building days in 1918—

Women's Sports Faculty Committee, 1934: *(left to right)* Mary McKee, Leah Gregg, Dorothy Gebauer, Anna Hiss (chair, and intramural staff director), and Agnes Stacy (secretary, coach, and referee). *From the UT Texas Student Publications, Inc. Photographs Collection—Intramural Sports for Women, Dolph Briscoe Center for American History, University of Texas at Austin. (DI 06831)*

had all the charm of a dilapidated wooden barn. And in the end, Anna Hiss won support for her dream gymnasium.

The Women's Gymnasium, dedicated the week of Round-Up in 1931, was a revolutionary place in its day—not just for its pleasing architectural lines, but for its abiding spirit, for the way its decor and its essence blended Hiss's sense of discipline with a kind of feminine grace.

"The building had a charm and dignity about it that was truly impressive," Betty Thompson—who worked with both Anna Hiss and Donna Lopiano, an iconoclast from the Northeast who created the modern UT women's athletics department—recalled in 1987.

I wish people could have seen it the way it was—the way the light streamed in from those huge windows. The building has been allowed to run down . . . but

when Anna was there, you could have eaten off the floors. I kid you not. Her touch was everywhere.

Mary McKee Stewart, who worked as an assistant on Hiss's staff from 1929 to 1941 and helped her design the gym's nationally renowned dance studio, recalled (during a 1990 interview) a similar picture: long, gray curtains swaying over the tall windows of the studio. Awnings stretched over the windows facing the courtyard. A piano playing a Strauss waltz. Or a polka. Or a march.

Hiss placed mirrors everywhere, even in the wing that housed the swimming pool—so that students would be forever mindful of their posture. As a woman devoted to manners and style, "Miss Hiss" made it a policy to evaluate the posture of all incoming freshmen—creating a posture photograph of each woman as part of the required "Posture Test." There were even end-of-semester Posture Pageants.

"The posture picture was actually three photographs—front, back and side views, basically taken in the nude. You wore white cotton panties, but that was it," says Josephine Crouch Sherfy, UT Class of '45, remembering the posture-photo experience, circa 1942.

> Then you had a one-on-one meeting with Anna Hiss in her office, where she presented you with the photos.
>
> Miss Anna always addressed everyone by their last name. She said to me, "Crouch"—that was my last name then, Crouch—"you need to take some weight off." I really wasn't tubby at all. But according to her charts—let me tell you, she had *all* these charts on height and weight and nutrition—I was maybe five pounds overweight. She told me I needed more exercise. She was big on walking, floor exercises . . . and drills. I played basketball, too. And a lot of volleyball.
>
> At the end of the year, they took a new posture photograph and returned the "before" and "after" shots to us in little white envelopes. You could tell the difference, too. No doubt about it. Almost everybody had straightened up, lost weight. Looking back, I realize what a big impact it made on me, personally. I have adopted and maintained a lifestyle of nutrition and weight and exercise that all started with her. Before then, no one had ever talked to me seriously about walking and exercise. I still take a walk, every day, because of Anna Hiss.

The foundation of Anna Hiss's three-year physical-training curriculum was a mandatory course known as Freshman Fundamentals. Although the course varied according to generation and instructor, Freshman Fundamentals was part aerobics, part dance, and part exercise class, with plenty of attention to posture.

"The things I remember best about Miss Dodge [an instructor] and that gym are the miles we walked in a circle around the edges, and the way it felt with rib cage lifted, chin up, stomach in, hips pulled under, knees in line, and weight on the outsides of the feet, arches lifted," Jane Homeyer Weems recalled in a story about Hiss and her gym that appeared in the *Alcalde* in 1993. "Each time a mirror was passed, a check of posture was made."

Anna Hiss encouraged individual and team sports, constructing tennis courts for women just south of her gym and transforming the open land east of the gym into playing fields for field hockey, archery, golf, and outdoor volleyball. Her curriculum at times included indoor baseball and touch football. "I like to think of what a team sport can mean to an individual," she once wrote, "over and above the good physical development."

Hiss, a prolific scorer who came to love the game for its egalitarian values, played basketball through high school and college. She championed the sport for its "loyalty, vigorous effort, freedom of action within the bounds of the rules (a good democratic principle for us all!), knowing the strong and weak points of 'our team mates,' using and depending on the former to the fullest"—the score and the game "a very small part of a thrilling whole."

Despite this enthusiasm for team sports, Hiss was apprehensive about intercollegiate competition. She believed it tainted the pure essence of sport and excluded too many students from participation. According to legend, she altered the dimensions of the basketball court and the swimming pool when they built her gym—intentionally constructing facilities that could not be used to stage official intercollegiate competitions of the day.

"That's true," Mary McKee Stewart, her longtime assistant, said emphatically during our 1990 interview, in which she talked about the craftsmanship and construction of the dance floor with the precision of an engineer.

> She [Anna Hiss] did not believe in intercollegiate athletics. . . . She was more concerned with other things. Her idea was to expose her students to at least two sports, to give them something they could pursue after school.
>
> Most of the girls came into that gym wearing high heels and silk dresses. Practically none of them knew how to swim. They had no knowledge of any sport at all.

Forever looking forward, Hiss had already designed a model for a Women's Gymnasium annex—it sat on her desk for years—before the showcase gymnasium was even completed. Every woman on campus knew her—for, as Josephine Crouch Sherfy pointed out, Hiss and her staff in physical training were the only female instructors she ever had in college. By

Women's intramural sports, 1937 and 1938. Swimming: Austex, 1938 team champion (*DI 06834*); tennis: 1938 champion Edith Fordtran and runner-up Dorothy Baldridge (*left to right*) (DI 06842); softball: pitcher (*DI 06841*). *All images from the UT Texas Student Publications, Inc. Photographs Collection—Intramural Sports for Women, Dolph Briscoe Center for American History, University of Texas at Austin.*

Women's intramural sports, 1937 and 1938. Archery: Anne Fleming, 1937, who would be named president of the 1937–1938 University of Texas Sports Association (*DI 06835*); table tennis, doubles: 1938 champions Dorothy Perkins and Glenn Appling (*front, left to right*), runners-up Margaret Sheffield and Therese Dean (*back, left to right*) (*DI 06832*); equestrian: jumping (DI 06843). *All images from the UT Texas Student Publications, Inc. Photographs Collection— Intramural Sports for Women, Dolph Briscoe Center for American History, University of Texas at Austin.*

the 1940s, Hiss was a commanding figure to UT students: formidable, even intimidating, yet surrounded by an aura of secrecy and mystery. She didn't smile very much. But Anna Hiss had presence. She wielded power still.

As Austin grew, Hiss fretted about increasing automobile traffic on Speedway and the potential for an accident as her students crossed the street from the gym to the playing fields. So she went to the city council. She told the council that Speedway was "unsuitable" as a public route through campus. Sure enough, the city designated San Jacinto as the preferred route. Speedway has been closed to through traffic ever since.

By the summer of 1948, Anna Hiss had already devoted thirty years of her life to the University of Texas. Hiss was a full professor now—a rare accomplishment for a woman outside the Home Economics Department in those days—and had just received an honorary degree from Boston University. She was publishing, developing training curricula for a new generation of teachers, enjoying a national reputation.

Hiss was fifty-five and still single. As her nephew Tony Hiss would write years later, "Anna never went near a man." She lived west of campus in Pemberton Heights on a quiet bluff above Shoal Creek with her longtime staff associate Leah Gregg. The two had been roommates in four different campus-area homes over the course of seventeen years. Dorothy Gebauer, the women's dean of students, was another of her close friends, an occasional companion for a horseback ride.

And it was that summer—in August 1948—that Whittaker Chambers brought Alger Hiss's name before the House Committee on Un-American Activities—first labeling him a communist sympathizer, later accusing him of espionage. Though Hiss was never formally charged as a spy (the statute of limitations had expired), his perjury trials were a national sensation, the launching point of Richard Nixon's political career. To some, Hiss is forever a victim, a man whose civil liberties were sacrificed to a prevailing national sense of fear at the dawn of the Cold War. To others, he was notorious: a calculating communist intellectual who betrayed his country.

"I understand at the point in time when he was brought to trial [in May 1949] she began to pull back,

to become less and less visible at any level, even here on campus," Betty Thompson recalled in 1987. "It was my understanding that she never allowed her picture to be taken, or appear in the newspaper, or grant an interview. Anything like that. She did not want to embarrass the University or draw attention to herself on that account."

In fact, Anna Hiss's name and photo appeared prominently in Austin newspapers in the spring of 1949. It was announced that she would be spending the summer abroad, representing UT at several prestigious education conferences in Europe. No mention of her brother. No mention of a trial.

After Alger Hiss's conviction in 1950, Anna spent part of the summer with him at a family retreat in Peacham, Vermont. She was one of only seven people Alger was allowed to correspond with after he entered federal prison in 1951. Yet Betty Risley, an instructor hired in 1953, says Anna Hiss did not talk about her brother at UT, "and I don't remember anyone else talking about it very much." Anna Hiss's legacy and her feelings were more important.

Recounting the final four years of Hiss's UT tenure—1953 to 1957—Betty Thompson recalls that the director ran her department like "a benevolent dictator." At the same time, Hiss took great care to give her staff moments to talk—and shine—in meetings with University brass. Betty Risley describes Hiss in affectionate terms, with colors that suggest discipline, punctuality, diplomacy, sense of purpose . . . and eccentricity.

"One of the first things [Miss Hiss] asked me was what I was called," recalls Risley.

I said, "Everybody calls me Betty." And she said, "We're going to call you Mary. That was my sister's name, and I was very fond of her." So she called me Mary that whole time I was there. . . .

She was more the mentor to me, though, not a sister. You couldn't pass the open door of her office—and that door was *always* open—without her calling you in. She'd always have a few notes written of things she wanted to tell you. . . . And yes, she was meticulous. She advised me at one time that I should always have a paper and pencil next to my bed, in case I woke up at night with an idea, I should be able to write it down.

Risley thought the gym "most unusual"—"so light and airy, the way it was built, because of the courtyard, it was a very welcoming building." She remembers the light and the big windows, the piano music in the dance studio, a prevailing sense of rhythm in all things.

Risley also remembers the day Anna Hiss called her into the office and asked whether she wouldn't mind playing tennis with her brother. Alger Hiss, released from prison in 1954, was in town, visiting his sister.

"I said I'd be glad to play tennis with him," says Risley, who had long felt a sense of compassion for Alger Hiss and his journey.

And then [Miss Hiss] said, "Don't say anything about laundry." Apparently, that's what he did in prison . . . laundry. . . . And of course, it never would have occurred to me. But after she said that, the whole time we played tennis the only thing I could think about was laundry.

I had the feeling that [Miss Hiss] talked him into it, thinking it would be good for him. . . . She was very sensitive about Alger Hiss, though I had the sense that they had been very close. . . . It was still a very painful time for him. I don't think he was ready yet for social interaction. . . . We met at the courts at the appointed time. . . . It was quiet, it must have been the afternoon, because there were no classes. . . . I don't even know if anyone knew we were there . . . and when it was over we shook hands and said, "It's a pleasure." That was it.

"I don't feel retired, as I will always be greatly interested in 'department' . . . and what makes it 'tick,'" Anna Hiss wrote upon retirement in 1957. "I realize how fortunate I have been in knowing so many remarkable people, and what great influences they have had on my life. I know that the field of teaching, especially Physical Education, has the greatest of privileges and responsibilities."

Harry Ransom led the move to designate Hiss as a director emeritus—and then she left her Austin cottage on Hollywood Street and returned at last to Baltimore. When she died in January 1972, the Women's Gymnasium was quickly renamed in her honor. Not long afterward, the incoming UT women's athletics director, Donna Lopiano, occupied Hiss's old offices in the gym—initiating a movement that would make Texas a front-runner in the realm of intercollegiate athletics.

Yet Anna Hiss's gym has never fit comfortably into twenty-first-century thinking or conformed to twenty-first-century functionality. When the University considered demolishing the entire building in the late 1980s—how to modify those tiny classrooms, those funky gyms?—the late Barbara Jordan joined the movement to preserve it. Not only in the name of Anna Hiss, but for the sake of her times.

"I strongly believe modernity and progress should not be destructive of a past that is worth preserving," Jordan said in 1990. "The presence on campus of this building provides a keyhole to the University's past, and a refreshing change from the modern architecture that crops up around it."

Although most of the footprint remains, Jordan and her friends lost the battle to save the building's integrity when the natatorium was destroyed to make way for new construction in 1994. The courtyard is rutted and ruined, no longer tranquil, no longer even a courtyard. The air around the gym is filled with the hum of cooling units. The building itself is dwarfed by blockish, industrial-style buildings devoted to molecular biology, neural molecular science, and pharmacy—which offer a different kind of bounty to the women of the twenty-first century.

Twenty years ago, the building imperiled, I walked the entire gym with a maintenance worker named Margaret—assuming it would be for the last time. We lingered a long time in the deserted natatorium. Even in the dark, the original hand-painted tiles still glistened in the bottom of the pool. Iron figures of fish, designed by Austin's famous Weigl blacksmiths, danced on the back wall. The room was like a grand, faded photograph, real and yet somehow distant after the passage of so many years.

Margaret told me that a few years back—some time in the 1980s—an older gentleman, soft-spoken and strikingly tall, came to visit the gym. All the way from the Northeast. He remarked that he knew a woman who had worked in the place and wanted to visit one last time, a tribute to her memory.

She said his name was Alger Hiss.

NOTE ON SOURCES

Unless otherwise noted, all quotations are from interviews or correspondence with the author.

Members of the University of Texas Board of Regents, January 1940: (*left to right*) J. R. Parten (chairman), George Morgan, H. J. Lutcher Stark, E. J. Blackert, Hilmer H. Weinert, Homer Rainey (president, University of Texas), Leslie C. Waggener, Jr., Kenneth H. Aynesworth, Edward Randall, Sr., Marguerite S. Fairchild, and Leo C. Haynes (secretary). *From the UT Texas Student Publications, Inc. Photographs Collection—Board of Regents, Dolph Briscoe Center for American History, University of Texas at Austin. (DI 06872)*

Communism, Fruit Flies, and Academic Freedom

DON E.
CARLETON

J. R. Parten's "Second Education"

Before J. R. Parten was appointed in 1935 to the University of Texas Board of Regents, his business interests had guided his involvement in public affairs. He had little experience in dealing with issues such as academic freedom. On the few occasions before 1935 when he was known to have expressed a formal opinion on academic freedom, his views were decidedly intolerant and self-serving.

During his service on the board, from 1935 to 1941, Parten used his knowledge of the oil business to increase greatly the University's income from its oil holdings. Convinced that Texas's prosperity and civic health required a great state university, Parten worked hard to make his alma mater a "university of the first class."

However, as the main public university in a state where religious fundamentalism and a strong strain of anti-intellectualism have made their marks, the University of Texas has often been the target of those who feared change, free inquiry and expression, and "non-Texan" influences. The University's board of regents frequently serves as a lightning rod for highly charged attacks on the institution by these elements of reaction and fear. On the other hand, the regents also deal with a frequently hostile faculty never satisfied with any budget. In addition, the University of Texas has always been seen by a large percentage of state legislators as an unreasonable financial burden on the state treasury. Every two years, the University and the legislature engage in an often-acrimonious struggle over appropriations. Those regents who have become leaders on the board usually serve as the institution's most important lobbyists in this ex-

Don E. Carleton has been the executive director of the University's Dolph Briscoe Center for American History since its creation, in 1991. From 1979 to 1991, he was the head of the University's Eugene C. Barker Texas History Center. He has published and lectured extensively in the fields of local history, archives, historical research methods and sources, urban history, the history of broadcast journalism, and twentieth-century U.S. political history. This profile of J. R. Parten is drawn from his biography A Breed So Rare: The Life of J. R. Parten, Liberal Texas Oil Man, 1896–1992 *(1998).*

hausting battle. Service on the board, therefore, can be hard and thankless work for those regents who take a leadership role.

During his tenure on the board, Parten developed an understanding and a deep appreciation of freedom of expression and inquiry, and he continued to the end of his life to staunchly defend both. The years Parten spent on the board of regents would have a profound effect on his political views and would be indicative of the deep love he had throughout his life for the University of Texas. He would spend six hectic and eventful years as one of the most active regents in the history of the University.

THE APPOINTMENT:
FROM MADISON COUNTY
TO THE BOARD OF REGENTS

Jubal Richard "J. R." Parten was born in 1896 in Madisonville, the seat of Madison County, which is located on the western edge of the Piney Woods of East Texas; he died in his bed at home in Madisonville in 1992. He was the sixth of eleven children—and the first son—of Wayne and Ella Parten, his mother an active member of several of Madisonville's community organizations and his father a prosperous merchant with substantial land holdings. The county and the town are named for James Madison, the fourth president of the United States. Parten often referred to Madison, the primary author of the U.S. Constitution, as "the greatest of all Americans." Though J. R. Parten's name never became a household word in Texas, he was a man of considerable achievements. He was a quiet gentleman, loyal to his friends, and a man of honor and principle—but also a highly successful entrepreneur capable of playing hardball with the sharpest of the Texas oilmen.

Parten studied government and law at the University of Texas from 1913 to 1917, but without finishing his degree, he left school to join the army, becoming the youngest major in the field artillery during World War I. In 1919, he entered the oil business as a young man and brought in the discovery well at the fabled El Dorado field in southern Arkansas in 1922. Starting with the Woodley Petroleum Company in the 1920s, Parten founded several highly successful businesses. As they grew, they came to earn mil-

lions of dollars and employ thousands of people. One of these ventures was Pan American Sulphur, which he founded in 1947, several years after his service as a regent. Competing directly with Texas Gulf Sulphur, it operated one of North America's most prolific and profitable sulfur mines.

Governor James Allred appointed Parten to the University of Texas Board of Regents to replace Beauford Jester, a future Texas governor, whom Allred decided not to reappoint because he felt Jester had not supported him during his campaign the year before. The board that Parten joined was generally one of the most harmonious and stable in the University's politically turbulent history. Regents serve staggered terms, with three positions up for appointment every two years, but six of Parten's colleagues served as regents for the entire six-year period he was on the board, and a seventh member served for nearly five of those six years. This unusual degree of continuity was the result partially of Parten's influence with Allred, who reappointed several regents at Parten's urging. Parten got along well with all his colleagues, but his closest allies on the board were Dr. George Morgan, Marguerite S. Fairchild, Leslie C. Waggener, Jr., and Kenneth H. Aynesworth. Those regents with whom Parten occasionally clashed were Hilmer H. Weinert, Henry J. Lutcher Stark, and Edward Randall, Sr.

THE FIRST TEST:
LEFT-WING "RADICALS" ON CAMPUS

A number of issues that confronted the board of regents during Parten's tenure transformed his understanding of the role of a university in an advanced society—and of the necessity of particular freedoms if a university's faculty and students are to be able to fulfill that role. But in the beginning, his views were more pragmatic. Two years before his appointment to the board, for example, Parten had complained to Jimmy Allred about a speech made by George Ward Stocking, a UT economics professor who had called for compulsory unitization of oil fields. Outraged, Parten asked then–attorney general Allred why the state allowed university professors to "take sides on such a highly controversial question." There is no record of an Allred reply, and the matter seems to have ended there, but Parten's complaint indicates that

UT professor of economics George Ward Stocking, 1938. *From the UT Texas Student Publications, Inc. Photographs Collection—George Ward Stocking (Faculty: Economics), Dolph Briscoe Center for American History, University of Texas at Austin. (DI 06869)*

UT professor of economics Bob Montgomery. *From the UT Texas Student Publications, Inc. Photographs Collection—Robert Hargrove Montgomery, Dolph Briscoe Center for American History, University of Texas at Austin. (DI 06884)*

his view of academic freedom was extremely narrow at this point in his life. As a regent of the state's most important institution of higher learning, however, Parten now had an opportunity to expand his intellectual and political horizons. His frequent meetings with University faculty members and administrators presented him with ideas and perspectives vastly different from those to which he had been exposed in the oil industry.[1]

Parten's initial confrontation with the issue of academic freedom as a regent came only four months after his first board meeting. The problem stemmed from public statements issued by a member of the University's Department of Economics, which in the 1930s and 1940s had a reputation as a haven of leftist ideologues and intellectual bomb throwers. In his memoirs, the liberal Harvard economist John Kenneth Galbraith recalled that during these years, the University of Texas had "the most radical of the major economic departments in the United States . . . even active Marxists were tolerated." This is an exaggeration. In reality, anticommunist New Deal liberals dominated the department. The most promi-

nent of this group were Clarence Ayres and Robert Montgomery. Because these well-known economists were highly visible critics of laissez-faire capitalism and the conservative policies of the Republican Party, they were frequent targets of conservatives, who accused them of teaching radical and even subversive economic ideas.[2]

Ayres, who was one of the nation's leading scholars in economics, attracted much attention in Texas as a proponent of the income tax as a tool to redistribute wealth, while Montgomery was equally well known as a critic of monopolies. Montgomery's favorite target in his antimonopoly lectures and writings was the Texas sulfur industry and its lobbyist, Roy Miller. Montgomery was a master teacher and an energetic political activist, but he was not as highly regarded a scholar as Ayres. The latter, on the other hand, was not as politically active as Montgomery. Although very liberal for Texas, neither man was a communist. The reason for their radical reputations stems more from the attacks made upon them by their conservative critics than from their actual economic philosophies. Conservative Texans tended to categorize anyone espousing the ideals of the progressive wing of the national Democratic Party as a left-wing radical. If they happened to be professors at the University, that made them *dangerous* left-wing radicals.[3]

Robert Montgomery in particular seemed to cause many sleepless nights for the state's economic reactionaries. The popular teacher, known by his students as "Dr. Bob," was a scourge of the Texas business establishment. Montgomery had been a student of Thorstein Veblen and Charles A. Beard, and his politics were firmly rooted in the progressive tradition. He was a primary influence in the lives of a generation of students who later became leaders of the postwar liberal wing of the Democratic Party in Texas, including the political strategist Creekmore Fath and the seven-term congressman Robert C. Eckhardt.

Montgomery was a gifted public speaker who often spoke at banquets and civic-club meetings around the state. At a public meeting in Fort Worth on July 1, 1935, Montgomery gave one of his standard talks about taxation policy, arguing that inheritance taxes should be increased enough to redistribute the wealth hoarded by the nation's richest families. Two days later, an acquaintance of Parten's living in Fort Worth wrote to the new regent, complaining that Montgomery's lecture had been "socialistic in the extreme" and that his demands for a "soak-the-rich" taxation policy might lead to "nationalization of the country as advocated by all true socialists." He asked Parten whether he thought such men should be employed by the University.[4]

The complaint about Montgomery's speech was similar in substance to Parten's earlier criticism of Stocking. Parten's immediate reaction to the complaint revealed that his thinking had not changed during the intervening two years. Replying to his friend in Fort Worth that he had received "several complaints about Dr. Montgomery's speeches," Parten declared that he was "very sympathetic with the ideas expressed" about whether faculty members should be allowed to give speeches on public issues. He explained that the University followed the same rules of academic freedom adopted by other schools, but he believed "that there should be limitations upon this privilege which should require professors not to go so far as to advocate destruction of our form of government." Parten promised to "do all within my power to stop the activities of professors that might bring discredit to the university."[5]

Parten met with University of Texas president Harry Yandell Benedict to discuss the complaint. Benedict told Parten that as a political conservative, he disagreed with Montgomery's economic philosophy, and as an administrator, he preferred that Montgomery keep his political opinions to himself. Nevertheless, the president was a defender of academic freedom as that concept was broadly defined on most campuses in the 1930s, and he supported Montgomery's right to speak out on political and economic issues. Benedict explained that the preservation of such faculty rights was essential to the University's mission to pursue truth and to extend the boundaries of knowledge. "I can't say that it made a deep impression right away," Parten admitted, "but Benny gave me something to think about."[6]

Determined to know more about Montgomery, Parten hired a stenographer to transcribe one of Montgomery's speeches. When Parten read the transcript, he was surprised to discover that Montgomery's economic views closely resembled some of his own. The economics professor had called for a federal tax on the profits of monopolies at a rate "as close as possible to 100 percent," arguing that such a confiscatory tax would stop monopolistic practices. "Remove monopolies and we shall have a democracy again," Montgomery declared, "we have none today!" Montgomery also charged that "grasping capitalists" were conspiring to produce less simply in order to drive up prices, an argument Parten had made previously about the practices of the major oil companies. Parten also learned that Montgomery was a close ally of Jimmy Allred's and that he had drafted the governor's public-utilities-regulation bill, then making its way through the legislature. At the end of July, Parten met with "Dr. Bob" and determined that although the economics professor was too supportive of federal regulation of all business activities to suit Parten's taste, he shared Parten's views on trust busting and the need to protect the "little guy" in business. Parten and Montgomery soon became friends, and their relationship grew as Montgomery became more involved as an adviser to Governor Allred.[7]

Parten's change of opinion about Montgomery did not indicate that he had developed a new understanding of the tenets of academic freedom. At this stage of his life, Parten's support for academic freedom applied to those whose opinions he favored, rather than to those who espoused an opinion with which he strongly disagreed. His behavior in a similar affair only four months after the Montgomery incident is evidence of this unchanged mind-set. In November 1935, a headline in the *Daily Texan* titled "Dr. Stocking Urges Federal Oil Control" seized Parten's attention. The story alleged that Stocking told the student Social Justice Club that he not only supported compulsory unified operation of oil fields, but that he also believed those fields should be controlled by the federal government. Stocking was quoted as saying that the oil industry "is conducted on the principle of robbery," the same statement Stocking had made two years earlier in a speech to the American Economics Association and so outraged Parten. As soon as he saw the *Daily Texan* story, Parten called his longtime friend and attorney Jack Blalock and requested him to contact the *Daily Texan* to demand an opportunity to counter Stocking's statements. Parten believed that it would be inappropriate as a regent for him to make a public statement on the subject. The *Daily Texan* subsequently published Blalock's statement against federal control. "The only ones who favor federal control today," Blalock declared, "are . . . Harold Ickes . . . and a few professors who know nothing about the oil industry." Parten complained to Benedict that Stocking was "championing one side of the highly controversial issue of 'Federal Control of Oil Production.' Such utterances . . . are calculated to do great harm to the University." Claiming that Stocking was a "propagandist" rather than "a seeker of truth," Parten wanted Stocking's head.[8]

As in the episode with Montgomery, Benedict counseled Parten to calm down and to get Stocking's version of what he had said. Parten agreed to talk to Stocking, but the meeting was postponed several times because of the regent's hectic schedule and Stocking's own professional obligations. Stocking eventually wrote a long letter to Parten, explaining that he had given a lecture to the student group about issues related to regulation of the oil industry and that he had carefully explained every side of the controversy. The problem occurred when a student asked him after the lecture what his personal opinion was and he gave it. "I do sincerely regret," Stocking wrote, "that the *Texan* account left the impression that I was appearing in the role of an agitator for any particular program for the control of oil." By the time Parten received Stocking's written explanation in May 1936, he was eager to put the incident behind him. This was partly because Benedict had educated Parten about Stocking's considerable talents

as a scholar and teacher, but it also stemmed from the fact that Parten was angry with the *Daily Texan* for reasons having nothing to do with the Stocking story, and he was more than willing to shift blame for the incident to the student paper. "This is just another instance of where the *Daily Texan* recently has been unfair with a member of the Faculty," Parten wrote to Stocking.[9]

As a result of the influence of Benedict, Montgomery, and others, Parten gradually developed an understanding about the importance of preserving academic freedom. But he also understood the problems that academic freedom created for a highly visible public university funded by legislative appropriations. Most of the University's budget remained dependent on the goodwill of a legislature highly sensitive to complaints from constituents about radicalism at the University. Parten and his board colleagues were preparing another major effort to increase the amount of its state appropriation, and Parten did not want the budget to get tangled in a political spiderweb. Accordingly, Parten's desire to keep the University out of politics and away from controversial public issues guided most of his actions.

As Parten's understanding of academic freedom evolved, he devised a strategy that sought to protect the faculty while making it seem as though he and his fellow regents were sympathetic to those who complained about the politics of individual teachers. Typical of this strategy was the way Parten handled two incidents in December 1935 involving Montgomery. Earl P. Adams, the chairman of the State Industrial Accident Board, complained to the board of regents about a speech Montgomery had given to UT's Progressive Democrat Club. Adams claimed that the professor, who was on leave from the University to serve on the Federal Planning Board in Washington, was a radical who was "teaching class prejudices and hatreds . . . that men who have accumulated wealth are enemies of society." He demanded his dismissal. Replying for the board, Parten thanked Adams for not taking his complaint to the press and assured him that Montgomery's activities would be thoroughly investigated. Parten, however, actually did nothing, and the matter was dropped quietly.[10]

That same month, Parten received a letter from J. O. Guleke, of Amarillo, a member of the State Board of Education and the author of a recently published pamphlet titled *Federal Encroachment upon the Field of Education in Texas*. The pamphlet's basic theme was that federal aid to education would end individual freedoms and turn the innocent children of Texas into Bolsheviks. Guleke, who had sent Parten one of his pamphlets, warned the regent that there were certain left-wing University faculty members who favored the idea of federal aid to education. He advised Parten to consult with J. Evetts Haley, a gifted writer of western history and passionate political reactionary who was working as a Texana collector for the University library, to learn the names of faculty members guilty of harboring such subversive ideas. Two months later, after Parten had failed to respond to this suggestion, Guleke and Haley went to Parten's office in Houston to press their case about subversives on the University faculty. Parten listened politely to their accusations, which were aimed mainly at Bob Montgomery. Comparing federal control of education to federal control of oil production, Parten assured Guleke and Haley that he opposed it as much as they. His "pride" in Texas, Parten said, had prevented him from "going to Washington begging for Federal funds for anything." Parten's assurances about his own beliefs and his rhetoric about Texas pride satisfied Guleke and Haley that something would be done about Montgomery and some of his colleagues. Parten, however, had no such intention, and he did nothing. "I figured that these people who were so riled up about these teachers would go on with their business once they had time to calm down," Parten stated.[11]

Parten generally ignored accusations about communist subversion on campus because he knew that the faculty members always under attack were not communists. He also rejected the idea that communism posed any domestic threat to the United States. Instead, Parten believed that a form of corporate fascism similar to that in Mussolini's Italy posed a far greater threat to freedom in the United States. A few weeks before Parten's meeting with Guleke and Haley, Governor Allred had given him a copy of Elizabeth Dilling's *The Red Network* with a request for Parten to let him know what he thought about it. Dilling charged that with the active aid of the Roosevelt administration, the "Communist-Socialist world conspiracy . . . is boring within our churches, schools, and government and is undermining America like a cancerous growth." Parten told Allred that he was unimpressed. "Personally," Parten declared, "I have little fear of Communism in this country."

Instead, he warned Allred about the threat from the extreme right. Parten argued that "any time . . . capital comes into violent conflict with Communism it has and will take shelter under the cloak of Fascism . . . as a means to protect itself."[12]

THE PROFESSOR IN MOSCOW: UT GENETICIST HERMAN J. MULLER

Activities by another professor would soon cause much more serious political concerns for the University than any associated with Montgomery or Stocking.

On January 10, 1936, the state representative from Corpus Christi, Walter Elmer Pope, complained to reporters that "rank communism" was being taught at the University. He warned that the legislature would investigate the situation as soon as possible. "Uncle Elmer," as he was known affectionately by his friends and colleagues, was well acquainted with the Partens of Madison County. Born and reared in neighboring Leon County, he had begun his law career in Madisonville, in 1902, after graduating from the University of Texas Law School that same year.

When Parten met with his family's longtime friend a few days later, Uncle Elmer told him that it would be difficult to prevent the legislature from cutting the University's budget because of the "Bolsheviks" on the faculty. Parten assured Pope that there were no communist faculty members currently at the University. He told Pope that the University had nothing to hide and that it would not oppose a legislative investigation of the faculty if doing so would be necessary to prevent a budget cut. His friendship with the Parten family made no difference to Pope in this matter. "Uncle Elmer just shrugged his shoulders," Parten recalled. "Hell, I knew what was going on. The old man just didn't want the University to get any more money."[13]

In mid-January, with Pope's threat hanging in the air and the University planning to launch another campaign for increased appropriations in the next legislative session, Parten and his regental colleagues were presented with a very unwelcome development in the form of a newly published book titled *Out of the Night: A Biologist's View of the Future.* Written by internationally famed geneticist Herman J. Muller, who was on a leave of absence from

Professor of zoology Herman J. Muller (*second from left*) in his UT lab with visiting colleagues (*left to right*) Israel Agol, director of the Timiryasev Biological Institute of Moscow; Carlos Offermann, University of Buenos Aires; and Solomon Levit, director of the Biomedical Institute in Moscow, 1931. *From the Prints and Photographs Collection—Herman J. Muller, Dolph Briscoe Center for American History, University of Texas at Austin. (DI 06851)*

the University of Texas, *Out of the Night* was a vision of a future world shaped and governed by scientific practices known today as genetic engineering. Although disconcerting to many, Muller viewed such developments positively, predicting the eventual betterment of the human race through eugenics. Muller predicted, for example, that in the future women could be artificially inseminated. Muller's opinions about eugenics meant little to the University of Texas Board of Regents. What was bothersome about *Out of the Night* was not only the fact that Muller was working in Moscow when it was published, but also that the book included a section in which he praised "the great and solid actualities of collective achievement" in the Soviet Union. On the title page of his new book, Muller was identified prominently as a professor of zoology at the University of Texas and a "member of the Academy of Sciences of the U.S.S.R."[14]

At a meeting in mid-January, President Benedict warned the regents that Muller's book could prove

to be very damaging to the University. Benedict explained that Muller was a Communist Party member who had been actively promoting the party as a University professor. A legislative investigation of Muller would provide much ammunition for the University's enemies to use in their fight against an increased appropriation. Parten knew nothing about Muller, so Benedict gave him the background.

Muller, who was described by Julian Huxley as the world's "greatest living geneticist," was one of the most prestigious scientists ever to serve on the University's faculty. He came to Texas as an associate professor of zoology in 1920 after earning his doctorate at Columbia University. Muller bombarded fruit flies with X-rays in his University laboratory in 1926 and discovered that radiation could change the structure of genes. For this discovery, he was elected to the American Academy of Sciences in 1931, and he was eventually awarded the Nobel Prize in Physiology or Medicine, in 1946, "for the discovery of the production of mutations by means of X-ray irradiation." From all accounts, Muller was a shy and quiet workaholic who pushed his physical and mental abilities to the limit. Early in 1932, he apparently suffered a nervous breakdown. After disappearing for two days, he was found wandering in the hills west of Austin, bruised and dazed. Muller's physician determined that he was suffering from "melancholia" and concluded that the geneticist had tried to kill himself. Muller quickly recovered. A few weeks after this incident, he learned that he had won a prestigious Guggenheim Fellowship for 1932–1933 to conduct research in Europe. The University granted Muller a year's leave of absence.[15]

In June 1932, before Muller's scheduled departure for Germany, an unauthorized student newspaper titled the *Spark* was distributed on campus. The four-page publication denounced the low wages paid to construction workers employed on University building projects, the impoverished living conditions of Austin's African Americans, and the reactionary activities of Maco Stewart, a Galveston businessman who was trying to get the legislature to pass a law against "subversive speech." Appearance of the *Spark* caused an immediate uproar. The regents, led by Chairman R. L. Batts, quickly passed a rule against student membership in "secret political organizations" and student participation in the production and distribution on campus of anonymously published material. A few days after the appearance of the *Spark*, an agent of the U.S. Immigration and Naturalization Service made available to the regents photostats of papers seized in a raid in San Antonio, including a handwritten letter signed by Herman Muller that not only implicated him in the publication of the *Spark*, but also provided conclusive evidence that he was a member of the Communist Party of the USA. Muller's party membership was not illegal, but University policy prohibited the employment of party members, and it was cause for dismissal. President Benedict wanted to fire Muller, but Chairman Batts feared that Muller's mental condition might cause him to commit suicide if he was dismissed, resulting in "much unpleasant notoriety" for the University. The regents finally decided to keep silent about the matter and allow Muller to go to Europe for a year. "Almost anything can happen during a year," Batts advised a fellow regent.[16]

Muller proceeded to Germany, unmolested by the regents. After Muller's year in Berlin, the regents ex-

Front page of the *Spark*, volume 1, number 1, June 1932. *From the Eugene C. Barker Texas History Collection, Dolph Briscoe Center for American History, University of Texas at Austin. (DI 06890)*

tended his leave of absence for another year so that he could continue his research. Unknown to Benedict, Muller was headed for Moscow to conduct research at the Soviet Institute of Genetics. After he had spent several months in the Soviet Union, the regents granted Muller an additional year's leave. Muller was still in Moscow at the Soviet Institute of Genetics when *Out of the Night* was published in late 1935.[17]

Publication of *Out of the Night* threatened to expose the theretofore-successful effort to hide Muller and his activities in the hope that he would never return from Moscow. Benedict proposed to Parten and his board colleagues that he should inform Muller about the University's evidence of his Communist Party membership and his role in the *Spark* affair. He would tell Muller that his leave of absence would not be extended another year and that he would have to return to Austin by September 1, 1935, to be tried by a faculty committee on the charge that he had conspired to produce a second issue of the *Spark*, in violation of the regents' rules, before he went on leave. This charge was obviously flimsy and would be difficult to prove, but Benedict hoped that the specter of being subjected to a public hearing would persuade Muller to resign and remain in Moscow. A few days after the regents approved Benedict's letter to Muller, the situation took on some urgency when the *Daily Texan* spread the news of Muller's affiliation with a Soviet scientific institute in a front-page story about *Out of the Night*. To many Texans, it was damning enough simply to be working in the Soviet Union, much less to praise its government in a book.[18]

Muller replied quickly to Benedict's letter. He denied any association with the *Spark*, but he verified his belief in communism. Much to Benedict's relief, Muller also stated his intention to resign from the faculty. In a follow-up letter, Benedict assured Muller that if he resigned, the University would drop the matter and nothing would be made public. Accordingly, on April 3, Muller submitted his resignation to Benedict, stating that the official reason was that his position in Moscow gave him better opportunities for research. He added, however, that staying in Moscow also gave him "greater freedom . . . in expressing what I consider to be the cardinal truths which must require recognition by the world today." The regents authorized a press release claiming that the scientist had resigned to become "the national genetics expert of Soviet Russia." There was no hint of controversy. Parten later explained that Benedict "just figured that Texans were so provincial that they just could not tolerate this Communist on the faculty, and he thought he was doing the best thing for the University and the best thing for Muller." The best thing for the University meant that Muller's resignation would spare it from the inevitable firestorm of protest during the next session of the legislature.[19]

When Parten was asked years later whether he had any regrets about the way the Muller case had been handled, he answered: "Things have changed a whole lot from that day to this. I might not feel the same way now. But I went along with Benedict, and the whole Board did." Parten's support of Benedict's action stemmed from his fear that the University's legislative enemies would use Muller as a weapon in their effort to keep the University's budget from growing. It was easy to sacrifice a man who held an-

other prestigious post and therefore would not be unemployed, who was several thousand miles away, who did not protest publicly, and who was a communist. Parten eventually moderated his position, but in 1936 he did not believe a Communist Party member should hold a teaching position at a public university.[20]

THE COMPROMISE: CENSORING THE *DAILY TEXAN*

During this time, Parten and his fellow regents faced other issues that were as complex and challenging as the Muller affair had been.

In early July 1936, an editorial in the *Daily Texan* created a public controversy that ultimately led the board of regents to impose censorship on the student newspaper. On July 9, the *Daily Texan* published an editorial titled "Leeches Don't Like Light," which implied that the directors of the Lower Colorado River Authority (LCRA) were involved in graft and the misuse of three million dollars. The editorial also referred to the powerful Texas congressman James "Buck" Buchanan as the "pork barrel chairman" of the House Appropriations Committee. The regents were especially sensitive to any student or faculty criticism of Buchanan—not only because he represented the congressional district in which the University was located, but also because his committee had control over Public Works Administration (PWA) appropriations. Buchanan had played a key role in the University's successful request for three hundred thousand dollars for the Texas Memorial Museum. The University had several other applications pending for PWA grants to build dormitories and other facilities. To make matters worse, the LCRA's legal counsel was Alvin J. Wirtz, perceived by many to be the most influential lobbyist in the state capitol. Wirtz made it clear that the *Daily Texan*'s comments were offensive, and he demanded an official apology from the regents.[21]

Almost as soon as Parten became a regent, he realized how damaging the *Daily Texan*'s political editorials could be to the University's relationship with the Texas legislature. The editors of the *Daily Texan* loved to single out individual legislators as prime examples of corruption, indolence, and ignorance. Inflaming the situation was the fact that copies of the

Daily Texan were placed on the desks of legislators every morning the legislature was in session. What the representatives read in the *Daily Texan* did not predispose them to be generous to the University at budget time, which was a problem of overriding concern to Parten. During most of the spring semester of 1935, when the University was trying to coax additional money out of the legislature, Parten and his regental colleagues were forced to apologize to legislators for statements made in the student newspaper.

With the next budget fight in mind, Parten had made an unofficial attempt late in the fall semester of 1935 to prevent a repeat of the problems caused by the *Daily Texan*'s editorials. In early November, he asked William McGill, the director of student publications, to explain to the *Daily Texan* editor and to other Student Publications Board members that their editorials and other published writings were damaging efforts to improve the University's financial condition. Accordingly, McGill met with the *Daily Texan* editor, Joe Storm, and the student association president, Jenkins Garrett, and reported back to Parten that "the Editor has agreed to put forth every effort to avoid printing material which might be harmful to the University." He also reported that the Student Publications Board had passed a resolution stating that the board "feels that the news and editorials can be presented without antagonizing state officials and without stirring up controversies."[22]

Seven months later, however, Parten discovered that his problems with the *Daily Texan* were far from over. After he read the editorial on the LCRA, Parten called McGill and told him to issue an official apology for it as soon as possible. McGill subsequently printed the apology in the July 23 edition of the *Daily Texan*, stating that the comment about Buchanan was "poorly phrased and that the *Daily Texan* knows of no blemish on the Congressman's . . . record." Parten and Benedict were not finished, however. "It appalls me to know that the editors of the *Daily Texan* are guilty of gross misconduct," Parten complained to Leslie Waggener. "It evolves upon the administration to alleviate this condition."[23]

As soon as the first presidential primary campaign ended, Parten decided to put an end to the *Daily Texan*'s troublemaking. At Parten's suggestion, Benedict drafted a censorship policy and submitted it to the board of regents for discussion and action on July 27, 1936. At the meeting, Benedict offered

the view that the *Daily Texan* was not a real newspaper but merely a practical journalism lab, a teaching tool. Therefore, Benedict explained, it needed direct faculty supervision. The newspaper should also restrict itself to harmless "campus" news. Such a restriction would not prevent the student journalists from learning the mechanics of writing and editing a news story. During the discussion, Parten reminded his colleagues that the University faced a difficult struggle in the next legislative session in its attempt to get increased state appropriations. Parten's old family friend Elmer Pope had already warned him that some members of the legislature were upset by what they were hearing about radical faculty members. They were also receiving complaints from other legislators and powerful lobbyists about *Daily Texan* editorials and stories. The Texas Gulf Sulphur Company was especially insistent that the regents muzzle the newspaper.[24]

Without dissent, the regents accepted Benedict's censorship regulation. The regents also created an editorial advisory committee of two faculty members and one student whose charge was to select an "agent" to screen the *Daily Texan* for any material containing "improper personal attacks, reckless accusations, opinion not based on fact." Also forbidden were articles on national, state, and local political questions as well as those covering a whole range of transgressions, including violations of "good taste" and "material prejudicial to the best interests of the University." This action, which was discussed and voted on in an executive session, was withheld from the public. The next day, Benedict called *Daily Texan* editor Ed Hodge into his office and handed him a letter announcing the regents' new rule. The president told Hodge that "the *Daily Texan* is not a newspaper, but it is an annex of the University." Referring to problems with the legislature, Benedict said that he did not want the University "to suffer when the paper forgets this." In a letter to Parten, Leslie Waggener referred to this regents' rule as a "censorship regulation," and censorship it was. A journalism professor, Granville Price, agreed to serve as the censor and immediately axed an editorial against a proposed state sales tax and another editorial critical of the Texas sulfur lobby. News about the censorship policy was likewise ruled off-limits.[25]

On July 30, the *Austin American-Statesman* broke the news that the regents had placed the *Daily Texan* under official censorship. The wire services picked up the story and made it national news, bringing forth an avalanche of criticism from the press, educational leaders, politicians, and civil libertarians from around the country. Censoring the *Daily Texan* quickly became a public relations blunder that hurt the University's image far more than anything any student had written in the newspaper. The most vocal denunciation of the censorship policy came from Congressman Maury Maverick, of San Antonio, who accused the regents of "nazifying" the University of Texas. "That my university should adopt the policies of communists and fascists in suppressing the freedom of speech and press is astonishing," Maverick declared. Other critical voices joined Maverick's. The pastor of the University Methodist Church denounced the regents' action in a sermon. Claiming that the censorship was "out of harmony with the trends in American university life," the Academic Freedom Committee of the American Civil Liberties Union urged the regents to reconsider their "extraordinary" action.[26]

Censoring the *Daily Texan* even brought forth the wrath of the state's conservative press. Influential establishment journals such as the *Dallas News* and the *Houston Post* condemned the regents' policy. The *Houston Press* published the editorials that had been censored out of the *Daily Texan* with the observation that "if they are anything more than thought-provoking without being in the least damaging to anyone except a few selfish vested interests, we do not know the meaning of the English language." Noting that "the University is not a kindergarten," the *Houston Press* demanded an end to "petty academic tyranny."[27]

Despite the storm of criticism, Parten urged his fellow regents to hold fast and reminded them that they had merely exercised their obligations as regents to ensure proper control of student behavior. When he heard that some of the students were calling on Governor Allred to intervene, he contacted his friend in the Governor's Mansion and explained why the regents had passed the new regulations. When the press asked Allred for a statement, he declared that "the censorship of the *Daily Texan* is the business of the University Board of Regents and none of mine."[28]

Members of the Travis County delegation to the State Democratic Convention refused to stay out of the controversy. They announced that they would ask the state convention to pass a resolution condemning the regents for censoring the student newspaper. Parten worked hard behind the scenes to stop the resolution. Fortunately for Parten, Myron Blalock was slated to serve as chairman of the state convention. Blalock, who exerted much influence within the state's Democratic Party leadership, argued that it was "not censorship for the regents to tell immature youths the point beyond which they may not go." He mustered enough votes to defeat the motion of condemnation.[29]

When school began in the fall, President Benedict met with student leaders and the editors of student publications, including the *Daily Texan*, to explain the censorship rule, which had been passed while most of the students were away from campus on summer vacation. He explained that the *Daily Texan* was "not an ordinary newspaper whose owners are entitled to the liberty of the press." Benedict told Parten after the meeting that he would grade the success of the meeting "at C+ or B-." He was afraid the issue would continue to simmer among the student activists. Benedict was also concerned about a rumor that students were trying to persuade members of the legislature to file a resolution criticizing the regents during the next session, which was scheduled to open in January 1937. He urged Parten to head off such a move.[30]

Parten contacted several of his allies in the legislature and urged them to suppress any attempts to condemn the regents. Parten explained that it was important that the *Daily Texan* be subject to faculty supervision. "For several years," Parten stressed, "the administration was rather lax in the enforcement of this rule." The *Daily Texan* staff had abused the rules often in the last two or three years. "I refer particularly to *Daily Texan* personal attacks on Congressmen and Legislators," Parten stated, "and the taking of strong sided positions on political questions that are highly controversial." The regents believed that "academic freedom does not imply license to damage one's fellows," and they were not going to allow "a partisan newspaper to be run on the campus."[31]

THE AGITATOR: J. EVETTS HALEY

While Parten worked to minimize the public relations damage resulting from the censorship policy, a controversy hit the University from another political direction. In early September 1936, J. Evetts Haley announced to the press that because of his opposition to Franklin Roosevelt's reelection, the board of regents was forcing him to resign his job as a collector of historical materials for the University library. While liberals such as Maury Maverick were criticizing the regents for "nazifying" the campus, Haley attracted newspaper headlines by accusing them of being leftist toadies for the New Deal.

Haley, a nonfaculty employee of the University, was an impulsive and highly opinionated man who held extremely conservative political views and had become a vocal and active critic of the Roosevelt administration, and his working relationships with two of his equally strong-willed colleagues in the library—Winnie Allen, an archivist, and Fannie Ratchford, a rare-books librarian—kept the library staff in constant turmoil.[32] Additionally, Haley had been appointed chairman of the Jeffersonian Democrats, a conservative organization bitterly opposed to President Roosevelt's reelection. Two of the founders of the Jeffersonian Democrats—Orville Bullington, a Wichita Falls businessman, the Republican candidate for governor in 1932, and a future UT regent, and J. M. West, Sr., a rancher and oilman from Houston—were paying Haley to run their anti-Roosevelt campaign full time.[33]

Haley had been looking for an excuse to leave the University. It came when President Benedict delayed giving Haley, a staff member in UT's Bureau of Social Science Research, a requested leave of absence for the upcoming academic year until the regents approved the bureau's budget—approval that would not come until after the new academic year had started. Seeing an opportunity to make some political points and garner publicity for the Jeffersonian Democrats, Haley called a press conference and announced that his request for a leave had been denied, which was untrue. "It may be that in declining to grant me leave of absence to fight the Roosevelt regime the university has taken the easy course of firing me by inaction," he declared. "If so, that alone is an indication of the danger of the New Deal tactics. When a bushy-headed . . . economist [Bob Montgomery] is hired by the new deal to propagandize the farmers, that is merely in accord with planning. But when I take leave to fight for constitutional government on my own time and at my own expense, that must be partisan politics."[34]

For the next two months, Haley traveled across the state, attracting headlines by attacking the University almost as much as the Roosevelt administration, implying that the campus was awash with communists and race mixers. Haley's accusations implied that the regents had either ignored or endorsed the subversion on campus. During the fall of 1936, therefore, one could consider the regents either a band of fascists because of the censorship of the *Daily Texan* or communist dupes because of the Haley incident. It was the latter charge that bothered Parten most, because he knew that the legislature, which was scheduled to meet in special session in late September, was more inclined to see the campus the way Haley saw it.[35]

THE INVESTIGATION: REPRESENTATIVE JOE CALDWELL AND THE SULFUR INDUSTRY

Just as Parten had long feared, the day after the special legislative session opened, state representative Joe Caldwell, of Asherton, introduced a resolution calling for an investigation of rumors that communism and atheism were being taught on the campuses of the state's universities. Haley's campaign-trail rhetoric and the *Daily Texan* editorials critical of the legislature helped to make conditions ripe for the investigation, but Caldwell made it clear that his resolution was the direct result of the activity of Bob Montgomery and the University's chapter of the Progressive Democrats of Texas. Caldwell declared that he had "conclusive documentary proof" that at least one professor was teaching communism and that he had "gathered about him a group of young zealots who have pledged to devote their lives to the cause."[36]

Caldwell's demand for an investigation of the University was motivated by a series of attacks by the *Daily Texan* (before it had been censored) on the powerful sulfur lobbyist Roy Miller. The *Daily Texan* had published documents revealing details of some of Miller's lobbying tactics. Miller, whose official position with the Texas Gulf Sulphur Company was "public relations director," was alleged to have spent the then staggering sum of $173,000 for "publicity" in Austin during a previous legislative session. Because there had been little evidence of Miller's "publicity" efforts, some of his critics charged that he had used the money to entertain and even bribe key members of the legislature. One of Montgomery's protégés, Creekmore Fath, has claimed that Miller reserved entire floors of the Stephen F. Austin and Driskill hotels. Any legislator could have a room and charge anything he wanted on Miller's tab. "That's how Miller took care of the Legislature," Fath charged, "it was the most outrageous thing in the world."

Just before the opening of the special legislative session, Fath and some other Montgomery protégés organized a free dance at Gregory Gym and officially dedicated it to "A Higher Tax on Sulphur." A huge crowd of students showed up. When Miller heard about the event the next morning, he erupted with anger, immediately blaming his nemesis Bob Montgomery, who had earlier pinned the title of "Sulphurcrat" on Miller. The lobbyist had frequently been the target of some of the economics professor's most scathing speeches. The next morning, President Benedict called Fath and asked him to come to his office at once. When he arrived, the exasperated Benedict asked, "Young man, what are you trying to do to the University? Do you know how much trouble you've caused me with your dance? [Lieutenant Governor] Woodul called me this morning and said Roy Miller was raising hell all over the Capitol." Fath replied that he had hoped it would cause trouble over at the legislature, not with the University. Caldwell's demand for an investigation soon followed this incident.[37]

Benedict asked Parten to check with his friends in the legislature to see whether there was any way to stop the investigation. Parten persuaded a small group of legislators to make an attempt to kill Caldwell's resolution. One of them, Congressman Bryan Bradberry, of Abilene, used Parten's information to charge that Caldwell's resolution was actually "the voice of J. Evetts Haley." He declared that Caldwell and Haley were trying to discredit the Roosevelt administration, which had hired university professors to serve as advisers. Despite Bradberry's and others' efforts to stop Caldwell's resolution through various legislative maneuvers—Roy Hofheinz, of Houston,

tried to send it to oblivion in the Committee on Livestock and Stock Raisers—it passed on October 2 by a vote of 67–61. Speaker Coke Stevenson, whose rulings thwarted most of the efforts to kill the resolution, appointed Caldwell chairman of the special investigatory committee.[38]

The special committee opened its investigation on October 13, 1936, with testimony by Bob Montgomery and his former students Herman Wright and Otto Mullinax. When Montgomery received his summons to appear before the legislative committee, he walked to Benedict's office to tell him about it. Benedict replied: "My God, Bob. They're accusing you of teaching communism. I'd be pleased if some of these old farts [on the faculty] taught anything!" When Montgomery appeared before the committee, Caldwell demanded to know whether the professor favored "private profit." Montgomery smiled and replied, "So much that I'd like to see it extended to where 120 million people could have it." As the audience roared with laughter, Caldwell quickly shifted gears. Ignoring the communism issue, Caldwell focused instead on attacks made by the University's Progressive Democrats on Roy Miller. A reporter for the *Houston Press* noted that the committee seemed to be concerned only about criticisms of Roy Miller by University students.[39]

The House of Representatives eventually tired of Caldwell's investigation, which failed to find anything subversive at the University. A majority voted on October 27 to disband the committee and to commend the University's faculty members for their "patience" and their "fine work." After the investigation ended, the reason for Caldwell's interest in Roy Miller rather than communism soon became apparent. A lobbyist named Hulen R. Carroll claimed that the Jeffersonian Democrats and unnamed investors in the Texas Gulf Sulphur Company had hired him to stir up problems for the University and Montgomery in the legislature. He told the *Daily Texan* that "the Sulphur company is out for Dr. Montgomery's scalp" because of his call for a tax on monopolies. Carroll also stated that Texas Gulf Sulphur wanted to discredit the University because of the company's fears that the plan to increase its appropriations might result in higher corporate taxes. The Jeffersonian Democrats wanted to discredit Montgomery for political reasons. He had worked as a consultant for the

New Deal for several months in 1936, and they had hoped to tie the charge of communism to the Roosevelt administration by making it look as though one of its economists was a subversive. Of course, Evetts Haley, head of the Jeffersonian Democrats, also had personal motives for encouraging a legislative investigation of the University that he claimed had "fired" him for political reasons.[40]

THE DENOUEMENT: HOMER RAINEY AND BEYOND

With political controversy swirling about the University, Parten now searched for a way for the board to get out of the censorship debacle while maintaining some level of administrative control over the *Daily Texan*'s editorial page. He still believed that if the regents allowed the *Daily Texan* to print stories and editorials highly critical of legislators, it would doom their efforts to get increased funding for the University in the upcoming regular session. Accordingly, in early February 1937, Parten, Stark, Randall, and Benedict worked out a compromise with student leaders that allowed censorship to be lifted. Future editors of the *Daily Texan* would continue to be elected, but to be eligible, students had to meet certain grade-average and course-work qualifications. The editor could be removed at any time by vote of the Student Publications Board, which consisted of three faculty members and three students. The dean of student life had the authority to break a tie vote. It was agreed that the *Daily Texan* would "exclude . . . unduly violent and partisan material" from its pages.

A significant part of the new plan required that censorship had to remain in place until June 1, which meant the newspaper would be censored until the legislature adjourned on May 31. When student leaders accepted this reorganization proposal, Parten went to work on his fellow regents. He was so anxious to resolve the matter before it caused any problems with the legislature that he did not wait until the next board meeting to get regental consent. He contacted the regents by telephone and by mail, asking for their agreement to lift censorship, arguing that he believed it was necessary "to act on this plan immediately." The compromise plan was quickly approved.[41]

In later years, Parten admitted that the censoring of the *Daily Texan* had been wrong, not because of the public relations damage, but because of its violation of the principle of freedom of the press. "The *Daily Texan*'s editorials seemed to threaten the University's financial health," he explained. "But I was wrong. Preserving freedom of the press, even for a school newspaper, is more important than any increase in a legislative appropriation."[42]

As a regent, Parten was forced to confront and make decisions about these and other controversial issues relating to intellectual, economic, and political freedom, including press censorship, race relations, and free speech. The most profound influence on his political views, however, would come three years after Parten had left the board of regents. Homer Rainey's dismissal in 1944 as University of Texas president after five years in office and his subsequent defeat in the 1946 Democratic Party primary election for governor of Texas dramatically affected the University's national reputation and polarized the Texas Democratic Party, and it profoundly influenced Parten's political views and the role he would play in state politics as a fund-raiser and campaign organizer in the years to come.

Following President Benedict's untimely death in 1937, Parten championed Rainey's candidacy for the UT presidency, and subsequently, as chairman of the board of regents, he had worked closely with Rainey, who took office in 1939, to promote a strong belief in the principles of academic freedom and the responsibility of the University to the people of Texas as an instrument of democracy. Together they recognized the University's critical importance as an active leader and shaper of a progressive "New Texas." The New Texas needed trained professionals, scientists, and technicians not only to provide the intellectual and skilled support necessary for the state to exploit and benefit from its own natural resources, but also to engage in research that would develop new industries, create jobs, and raise the overall standard of living of all Texans.[43]

However, by 1944, three years after Parten had finished his term as regent, there was a new majority on the board, and it believed the University was overrun with politically subversive undesirables who advocated such dangerous ideas as labor unionism, civil rights for blacks, federal fair-labor standards and antitrust laws, and corporate and personal in-

J. R. Parten (*fourth from left*) at the inauguration of University of Texas president Homer Rainey (*second from left*). *From the J. R. Parten Photograph Collection—Homer Price Rainey, Dolph Briscoe Center for American History, University of Texas at Austin. (DI 06878)*

come taxes. This majority—which included Orville Bullington and Dan Harrison, an independent oil-man from of Houston (who had replaced Parten on the Board), longtime regents Hilmer Weinert and Lutcher Stark (who disputed with Rainey over matters regarding UT athletics), and newly appointed regents Judge D. Frank Strickland, an attorney and corporate lobbyist from Mission, Texas, and Scott Schreiner, a conservative rancher from Kerrville— had no intention of allowing the state's dominant institution of higher education to be run by people who threatened the state's political, social, and economic status quo.[44]

At the heart of the firing of Rainey by the board of regents was a demand by this new majority to fire four tenured professors in the Department of Economics, including Bob Montgomery and Clarence Ayres, of

whose teaching they did not approve. Though tenure protected those professors, the regents later attacked four nontenured instructors in the Department of Economics who, three months earlier, had publicly criticized an antilabor rally in Dallas presided over by Karl Hoblitzelle, the owner of an extensive chain of movie theaters and one of Strickland's clients. Federal district judge T. Whitfield Davidson demanded a purge of the Department of Economics, and Bullington was happy to comply. After a token hearing and over President Rainey's heated objections, the instructors were dismissed. Rainey's spirited defense of the dismissed instructors and a series of further confrontations with the regents, including a highly publicized squabble that resulted in the removal of John Dos Passos's acclaimed novel *The Big Money* (part of the *U.S.A.* trilogy) from a list of recommended readings in the Department of English, culminated in Rainey's firing.[45]

During the tumultuous weeks that followed—which were marked by student protests, state Senate hearings, and widespread public debate—Parten received a letter from a real estate agent in San Antonio, asking him to answer three questions. How could he defend the conduct of the economics instructors who had been fired? Did he believe that a professor should be able to ask his students to write a theme on the advantages of socialism in government? And did he believe Dos Passos's *U.S.A.* should be part of the curriculum? Parten's answer reveals how much his view of academic freedom had changed since he first joined the board of regents in 1935. In regard to the economics instructors, Parten declared that college teachers had the same right to protest as every other citizen "under our democracy and under the freedoms guaranteed by our constitution." On teaching about socialism, Parten stated that "in a university Socialism, Communism, Fascism and all other forms of government should be taught objectively." As for *U.S.A.*, Parten declared that "the issue of this book has no significance whatsoever in the university controversy other than . . . that the Regents made it an issue." These and all the other issues and incidents, Parten concluded, obscured the real reason for the controversy at the University. At the heart of the Rainey affair, Parten argued, was the effort by big business interests "to eliminate from the university the teaching of so-called New Deal economics." This was not the same J. R. Parten who in 1933 had complained to Jimmy Allred about George Stocking's endorsement of the unit operation of oil fields by asking "why should our college professors take sides on such a highly controversial question?"[46]

Frank Dobie, a member of the faculty in the Department of English who had watched Parten closely for many years (and who would be dismissed from the University two years later after the regents refused his request for a continuation of his leave of absence in Europe), wrote to him during the Rainey affair to say: "Jube, I have watched your intellectual development with great pride."[47]

Parten provided valuable service to his country immediately after stepping down from the Board of Regents. During World War II, he was a dominant figure in the development of the "Big Inch" and "Little Inch" pipelines, which stretched from East Texas to New York and Pennsylvania and provided a se-

cure system of transportation for American oil and fuel, which were critical to the Allied war effort. In 1945, Parten served as chief of staff for the U.S. delegation to the Allied War Reparations Commission in Moscow and later participated in the Potsdam Conference in Berlin. During the Korean War, Parten organized the Petroleum Administration for Defense, which ensured that the military efforts in Korea were supported by adequate supplies of oil. Parten also served as an oil policy adviser during the Kennedy administration.

A lifelong Democrat of moderately liberal cast, Parten was extremely active behind the scenes in promoting candidates and ideas. In 1954, he joined other wealthy supporters of the national Democratic Party to establish the *Texas Observer*. His support for the *Observer*, his support for sometimes-unpopular politicians and ideas, and his work with the Fund for the Republic and the Center for the Study of Democratic Institutions, a think tank for the study of public policy, brought important liberal ideas to the forefront on a state and national level. As a philanthropist, Parten supported a wide range of nonprofit programs and institutions, including the University of Texas, which named Parten a Distinguished Alumnus on October 2, 1987.

Throughout the remainder of his long and extraordinarily productive life, Parten's experiences as a University of Texas regent fostered his liberal views on civil liberties, his opposition to the Vietnam War, his criticism of American policy toward the Soviet Union, his respect for learning and higher education, and his identification with the liberal wing of the Democratic Party—an image in stark contrast to the popular stereotype of the wealthy Texas oilman.

When he recalled his time as a regent many years later, Parten admitted that the experience caused him to look at the world in new ways. "I didn't get a degree," Parten said, "but it was really my second university education."[48]

NOTES

1. Stocking's speech was reprinted as "Stabilization of the Oil Industry: Its Economic and Legal Aspects," *American Economic Review*, 23 (Mar. 1933): 70; a condensed and revised version was printed as "Chaos in the Oil Industry," *Nation* (June 1936), 634–636; J. R. Parten (hereafter JRP) to Allred, Jan. 17, 1933, James V. Allred Papers (M. D. Anderson Library, Uni-

versity of Houston); JRP, interview by Anthony Champagne, Jan. 19, 1980, Madisonville.

2. John Kenneth Galbraith, *A Life in Our Times* (New York: Houghton Mifflin, 1981), 24.

3. Creekmore Fath, interview by the author, Nov. 2, 1990, Austin; Ronnie Dugger, interview by the author, Nov. 29, 1989, Austin; Robert C. Eckhardt, interview by the author, Dec. 1, 1989, Austin; Ronnie Dugger, *Our Invaded Universities: Form, Reform, and New Starts* (New York: Norton, 1974), 39–41.

4. Don E. Carleton, *Red Scare! Right Wing Hysteria, Fifties Fanaticism, and Their Legacy in Texas* (Austin: Texas Monthly Press, 1985), 22; Dugger, *Our Invaded Universities*, 39–41; Clarence R. Wharton to J. Evetts Haley, Dec. 2, 1935, box 2D264, J. Evetts Haley Papers (Dolph Briscoe Center for American History, University of Texas at Austin; hereafter DBCAH).

5. *Fort Worth Star-Telegram*, July 2, 1935; Frazier Moss to JRP, July 2, 1935, J. R. Parten Papers, DBCAH (hereafter JRP Papers); JRP to Frazier Moss, July 3, 1935 (JRP Papers); JRP to Scott, July 3, 1935 (JRP Papers); Scott to JRP, July 5, 1935 (JRP Papers).

6. Benedict's interpretation of academic freedom did not apply to communists or to those strongly suspected of having communist sympathies. Official University policy prohibited the employment of members of the Communist Party (JRP interview).

7. Parten later secured an appointment for Montgomery as an economic consultant to a branch of the Federal Reserve; *Daily Texan*, July 5, 1935; JRP interview.

8. *Daily Texan*, Nov. 17, 1935; JRP to Benedict, Nov. 21, 1935 (JRP Papers).

9. Frances Perkins, Roosevelt's secretary of labor, appointed Stocking to serve as a mediator in a longshoremen's strike in Galveston in December. Stocking to JRP, Jan. 20 and May 23, 1936 (JRP Papers); JRP to Stocking, Jan. 25 and May 29, 1936 (JRP Papers).

10. Adams to Morgan, Dec. 17, 1935 (copy in JRP Papers); JRP to Adams, Dec. 20, 1935 (JRP Papers); *Daily Texan*, Nov. 27, 1935.

11. JRP to J. O. Guleke, Dec. 19, 1935 (JRP Papers); Guleke to JRP, Dec. 30, 1935 (JRP Papers); Haley to W. C. Murphy, Jr., Nov. 25, 1935 (box 2D264, Haley Papers); and JRP to Dean William Masterson, Feb. 17, 1936 (JRP Papers); Don E. Carleton, *Who Shot the Bear? J. Evetts Haley and the Eugene C. Barker Texas History Center* (Austin: Wind River Press, 1984); JRP interview.

12. Elizabeth Dilling, *The Red Network: A "Who's Who" and Handbook of Radicalism for Patriots* (Kenilworth, Ill.: self-published, 1935), 5; JRP to Allred, Dec. 20, 1935 (JRP Papers).

13. JRP interview.

14. *Daily Texan*, Jan. 30 and Apr. 28, 1936; Muller, *Out of the Night: A Biologist's View of the Future* (New York: Vanguard, 1935), vii, 74; JRP interview.

15. *Daily Texan*, Jan. 30 and Apr. 28, 1936; Herman J. Muller to Benedict, Mar. 30, 1932 ("Investigations" file, University of Texas, Records of the Office of the President, DBCAH; hereafter, "Investigations" file); Benedict to Muller, Apr. 11, 1932

("Investigations" file); R. L. Batts to Edward Crane, July 13, 1932 ("Investigations" file); Dugger, *Our Invaded Universities*, 32.

16. The June 1932 number is the only known issue of the *Spark*—a rare copy is in the Texas Newspaper Collection (DBCAH); *Austin American*, June 28, 1932; *Dallas News*, June 29, 1932; Batts to Benedict, June 23, 1932 ("Investigations" file); Crane to Batts, July 12, 1932 ("Investigations" file); Batts to Crane, July 13, 1932 ("Investigations" file).

17. Maco Stewart to Edward Randall, Sept. 30, 1932; Randall to Benedict, Oct. 6, 1932; Muller to Benedict, Feb. 22, 1933 (all in "Investigations" file).

18. *Daily Texan*, Jan. 10, Jan. 30, Apr. 28, 1936; Benedict to Muller, Jan. 18 and Apr. 27, 1936 (Muller folder, "Investigations" file); Muller to Benedict, Feb. 23 and Apr. 3, 1936 ("Investigations" file).

19. Ibid.; JRP interview.

20. Muller (1890–1967) fled to Scotland in 1939 as a result of Stalin's purges and eventually denounced the Soviet Communist Party. He was awarded the Nobel Prize in 1946 and retired as a professor at the University of Indiana in the 1960s. The real reason for his resignation from the University of Texas faculty remained confidential until the publication of Dugger's *Our Invaded Universities* in 1974. See Dugger, 26–32; see also the *Daily Texan*, Mar. 24, 1967; JRP interview.

21. *Daily Texan*, July 9 and Sept. 18, 1936; Richard B. Henderson, *Maury Maverick: A Political Biography* (Austin: Univ. of Texas Press, 1970), 125; for more on Wirtz, see Robert A. Caro, *The Years of Lyndon Johnson: The Path to Power* (New York: Knopf, 1982), 373–379; JRP interview.

22. JRP interview; William McGill to JRP, Nov. 8, 1935 (JRP Papers); Jenkins Garrett, interview by the author, Oct. 26, 1989, Fort Worth.

23. JRP interview; *Daily Texan*, July 23, 1936; JRP to Waggener, Sept. 8, 1936 (JRP Papers).

24. JRP interview; *Daily Texan*, Aug. 6, 1936.

25. Waggener to JRP, Sept. 4, 1936 (JRP Papers); *Daily Texan*, Aug. 6 and Aug. 9, 1936; Henderson, *Maury Maverick*, 124; JRP interview.

26. *Austin American-Statesman*, July 30, 1936; *Daily Texan*, Aug. 6, 1936; *San Antonio Light*, Aug. 2, 1936; Henderson, *Maury Maverick*, 126; *Longview Daily News*, Aug. 5, 1936; *Daily Texan*, Aug. 30, 1936.

27. *Daily Texan*, Aug. 11, 1936; Houston *Press*, n.d. (clipping in JRP Papers).

28. JRP to Waggener, Sept. 8, 1936 (JRP Papers); JRP interview; *Daily Texan*, Aug. 9, 1936.

29. Tom Dailey, Jr., to Blalock, Sept. 3, 1936 (JRP Papers); Myron Blalock biographical file (DBCAH); *Houston Chronicle*, Sept. 16, 1936.

30. Press release, UT Free News Service, Sept. 16, 1936 (JRP Papers); Benedict to JRP, Sept. 18, 1936 (JRP Papers); *Daily Texan*, Sept. 17, 1936.

31. JRP to George F. Howard, Dec. 2, 1936 (JRP Papers).

32. Carleton, *Who Shot the Bear?*, 7; Don E. Carleton and Katherine J. Adams, "'A Work Peculiarly Our Own': Origins of the Barker Texas History Center, 1883–1950," *Southwestern Historical Quarterly* 86 (Oct. 1982): 197–230.

33. Haley to Benedict, Aug. 24, 1936 (box 2D263, Haley

Papers); *Daily Texan*, Sept. 18, 1936; Carleton, *Who Shot the Bear?*, 9, 11; JRP interview.

34. Haley to Ruby Mixon, Sept. 10, 1935 (box 2D264, Haley Papers); Haley to Dobie, Dec. 4, 1936, J. Frank Dobie Papers (Harry Ransom Center, University of Texas at Austin); Carleton, *Who Shot the Bear?*, 11–13; J. Evetts Haley, interview with the author, Apr. 14, 1989, Midland, Texas; *Dallas News*, Sept. 13, 1936.

35. JRP interview.

36. JRP interview.

37. Roy Miller (1884–1946), the mayor of Corpus Christi (1913-1917) and publisher of the *Corpus Christi Caller*, was also a lobbyist for the Port of Corpus Christi. He played a key role in getting the Texas portion of the Intracoastal Canal completed. "Roy Miller," biographical file (DBCAH); John E. Lyle, interview (oral history transcript, Lyndon Baines Johnson Library and Museum, Austin); for Miller's expenses, see *Daily Texan*, Feb. 4, 1937; Fath interview.

38. JRP interview; *House Journal*, 44th Legislature, special session 3 (1936), 28, 43, 50–54, 78; *Daily Texan*, Sept. 30, Oct. 2, Oct. 7, 1936.

39. Benedict quotation from Fath interview; *Daily Texan*, Oct. 14, 1936; *Houston Post*, Oct. 13, 14, 1936; *Cuero Record*, Oct. 14, 1936; *Houston Press*, Oct. 14, 1936.

40. *House Journal*, 44th Legislature, special session 3 (1936), 491–493; George Norris Green, *The Establishment in Texas Politics: The Primitive Years, 1938–1957* (Westport, Conn.: Greenwood, 1979), 72; *Daily Texan*, Oct. 28 and Oct. 29, 1936; Fath interview.

41. *Daily Texan*, Dec. 8, 1936, Feb. 6, Mar. 7, and June 1, 1937; JRP to Marguerite Fairchild, Mar. 5, 1937 (copy in the Texas Student Publications files, VF-5, Records of Office of the President); Henderson, *Maury Maverick*, 126.

42. JRP interview.

43. Homer Rainey, interview (oral history transcript, library, University of North Texas, Denton); JRP interview.

44. *Austin American-Statesman*, Dec. 12, 1971; *Dallas News*, June 15, 1942; *Daily Texan*, June 20, 1942; JRP interview.

45. Homer P. Rainey, *The Tower and the Dome: A Free University versus Political Control* (Boulder, Colo.: Pruett, 1971), 7, 8; Green, *Establishment in Texas Politics*, 84, 86; Alice Carol Cox, "The Rainey Affair: A History of the Academic Freedom Controversy at the University of Texas, 1938–1946" (PhD diss., University of Denver, 1970), 41–42; Davidson to Bullington, Mar. 25, 1942; Bullington to Davidson, Mar. 26, 1942 (both in the J. Evetts Haley Papers, Haley Library, Midland, Texas).

46. Joe Sheldon to JRP, Jan. 18, 1945; JRP to Joe Sheldon, Feb. 17, 1945 (both in JRP Papers).

47. Dobie to JRP, Feb. 22, 1945 (JRP Papers).

48. JRP interview.

BEN
CRENSHAW } # Harvey Was My Friend

Ben came to me when he was about 8 years old. We cut off a 7-iron for him. I showed him a good grip, and we went outside.

There was a green about 75 yards away. I asked Ben to tee up a ball and hit it onto the green. He did. Then I said, "Now, let's go to the green and putt the ball into the hole."

"If you wanted it in the hole, why didn't you tell me the first time!" little Ben asked.

HARVEY PENICK, FROM *HARVEY PENICK'S LITTLE RED BOOK*

I still have that little club Harvey made for me. Half a century now has passed since the day he put it in my hand and showed me a good grip. I keep it in a special place, hidden away among the books and photos and trophies that I've collected over the years.

I became a professional golfer in 1973, after my junior year at the University of Texas. Ever since then, I've been a touring pro. I competed on the regular PGA Tour until I reached my early fifties, and I now compete on the PGA's Senior Tour. I've had the good fortune to enjoy a successful career in the game—a fine career, with some memorable wins. Through it all, Harvey Penick has been a special, special person in my life. He is special not just for me, but for thousands of people—golfers of all abilities, and people from all walks of life—whose lives he touched.

Harvey guided my learning. He always said he didn't teach; he guided

---

Before embarking on a highly successful career as a professional golfer, Ben Crenshaw attended the University from 1970 to 1973, where, as a member of the Longhorn golf team, he was a three-time NCAA champion. His nineteen wins on the PGA Tour—and twenty-nine overall as a professional—include his emotional and highly popular victories at the Masters in 1984 and 1995. His firm, Coore & Crenshaw, has built championship courses throughout the United States and done restoration work on some of the nation's finest courses. In 1997, Crenshaw was named a Distinguished Alumnus by the Texas Exes. This profile is drawn from a September 2008 interview with David Dettmer, who collaborated on the writing and supplied additional historical information.

Harvey Penick, ca. 1953. *From the UT Texas Student Publications, Inc. Photographs Collection—Golf, Dolph Briscoe Center for American History, University of Texas at Austin. (DI 06844)*

people's learning. Although he wasn't a highly educated man—his formal schooling didn't extend beyond his high school years—Harvey was a scholar in the correct use of words that applied to his craft. He knew that words have a certain connotation to them, and he always had a wonderful way of putting things. No one ever went to Harvey for a "lesson"; students went to Harvey "to get some help." He never wanted golf to seem like work.

Harvey was born in Austin in 1904, in an era when the capital of Texas was still a very small city and golf was just beginning to be established as a sport and pastime in America. Austin is the only place he ever called home. He had a long and productive life. His was a quiet life, but one that meant so much to so many people. Harvey has meant a lot to this community as well. In the spring of 1995, he died peace-

fully at his home near Austin Country Club, surrounded by loved ones. I'll have more to say about Harvey's passing later in this essay.

When he was just a young boy, Harvey wanted to join his older brothers Tom and Tinsley in the caddy yard at Austin Country Club, but he said his mother wouldn't let him until he was eight years old, well after he had started school at Pease Elementary. After caddying as a child and teenager, he was made the head professional in 1923, when he was just eighteen years old. His association with the club spanned eighty-two years. For thirty-two seasons, from 1931 to 1963, he was also the head coach of the golf team at the University of Texas. After he turned over the job of head pro of Austin Country Club to his son, Tinsley, in 1971, he remained as professional emeritus, guiding the learning of members, visiting professionals, college athletes, and anyone else who sought him out for help.

Everyone listened to Harvey when he spoke. He had a very gentle touch. Even apart from his teaching, he was such an incredible person. He didn't say many words, but there was so much meaning in what he said. He was *so* humble, *so* meek and soft-spoken, and *softhearted*. Basically, he was a very simple person. He always said he was just an overgrown caddy. That never left him—his humility. He always said he was so happy because he had a fine place to work and three square meals a day and he was teaching others and got to be around a lot of fine people. He was offered the job of head professional at River Oaks Country Club in Houston when he was in his late thirties, but he said, "No, I'm from Austin. I want to just stay here."

Golf was Harvey's occupation, and in a very real way, Harvey was the living embodiment of the best aspects of the game. Even though golf is around six hundred years old, it has always been a game in which the golfer uses a club to hit a stationary object by a swing of some sort, trying to get that object in the hole in the fewest number of strokes possible. The clubs and balls have changed quite a bit, but the essence of the game has not. Early on, it turned out to be a sociable game. There was a code of honor attached to golf that is still upheld by golfers worldwide. Because there are sets of rules and people abide by them, many games have been likened to the game of life—but golf has an especially clear parallel with life, because golfers play against nature. The golfer knows that there are hazards on the golf course—in the form of water, trees, bunkers—and if he or she falls into them, there is a penalty involved. Just as in life, there are bunkers, there are hazards out there, and these extract a penalty. There are pitfalls, and the honest golfer readily accepts them—accepts penalties—because it's the honor of the game.

Golf's inventors knew there was an element of chance inherent in the game. That's the game's fascination—the golfer is responsible for making the ball go, but he or she is never sure what is going to happen to it once it's in motion. If luck were ever taken out of the game, it would cease to be golf. I have built up a nice library of books about golf over the years—I'm very proud of it—and one of my favorites is a book by Charles McDonald, who was one of the five charter members of the United States Golf Association and who built many of the early golf courses in the United States. He describes recreations as being either sports or games—and sport is what you do against nature. Therefore, golf and yachting are sports; tennis, for example, is a game. Therefore, he says that the golfer should tee off with the ball and then not touch it again until lifting it out of the hole. In other words, the golfer should "play the ball as it lies."

From Harvey Penick's *And If You Play Golf, You're My Friend*:

I was watching four of my University of Texas players getting ready to hit on the first tee one afternoon in the early spring.

They were discussing whether to play "winter" rules or "summer" rules.

"What do you think, Coach?"

I said, "Well, you boys can go play golf. Or else you can make up some other game and go play that, instead."

They understood my meaning.

In the game of golf, the ball is played as you find it.

The first written, recorded rules of the game were set down in 1744 by the Honourable Company of Edinburgh Golfers. Ten years later, the Society of St. Andrews Golfers (known today as the Royal and Ancient Golf Club of St. Andrews, home of the famous Old Course) adopted those rules, and St. Andrews became the seat of the game. The game is structured so that the golfer plays on his or her honor. You play the very best that's within you, but there are penalties involved. If the golfer commits an infraction, that act must be accorded with the golfer's honor if the game is to go on. I can say for sure that among those of us who play golf as an occupation and all golfers who genuinely love the game, when we know that someone has knowingly cheated, the reaction is swift and severe. If the golfer violates a rule and doesn't know it, that's one thing. But if a golfer *knowingly* violates a rule, that infraction becomes known and society shuns that person—and I can't imagine anything more severe than that. Golf involves the *conscience*.

From Harvey Penick's *And If You Play Golf, You're My Friend*:

During the third round of the Kemper Open in 1993, Tommy Kite was leading and was paired with Grant Waite of New Zealand.

Near the fourth green, Waite took a drop from a Ground Under Repair area. As Waite prepared to hit the green, Tommy looked over and noticed Waite's heel was still inside the Ground Under Repair marker.

This was a tournament Tommy wanted very much to win. It was his first strong showing since a back injury in the spring. It would have been so easy to glance away and pretend he hadn't seen where Waite was standing.

That is, it would have been easy for some people. For Tommy Kite, it was not even a consideration.

"We don't need any penalties here," Tommy said, pointing out the location of the New Zealander's heel.

If Waite had hit that shot, it would have been a two-stroke penalty. The penalty would have put Tommy in the lead by three. But, as I said, Tommy never gave it a thought.

Tommy said, "It would have been pretty chicken for me to stand by and watch a guy accidentally break a rule and then say, 'By the way, add two strokes.' That's not golf. That's other sports where guys are trying to get every advantage they can."

Waite won the tournament by one shot. Tommy finished second.

I think I'm more proud of Tommy for that tournament than I am for his U.S. Open victory. An Open champion is a winner on the golf course. A person of honor is a winner everywhere.

There are enough people who think enough of the game to have made its traditions last this long, and at the heart of that tradition is the game's honor. Harvey very quietly extolled that virtue, not so much by word, but by example. By example, he touched all of us so much. What poured out of him was simple goodness—simple goodness that he carried with him and expressed through his word and his deed to everyone with whom he came in contact. He never raised his voice to anybody—ever. If a caddy or an employee needed correcting, he would explain very carefully what he wanted them to do, but he never raised his voice. I think about the employees at the Austin Country Club when I was growing up, and I remember how happy they were. Like a good golf swing, Harvey's life revealed a very gentle touch in everything he did. He commanded so much respect from the life he led. Everyone who has spoken or written about Harvey manages to find powerful words to express their feelings about him. The common theme is love—we loved this man.

Many of those words can be found in the introductions I and others wrote for *Harvey Penick's Little Red Book*, a wonderful collaboration Harvey did near the end of his life with the great writer and journalist Edwin "Bud" Shrake. Shortly after he became the head professional at Austin Country Club, Harvey began writing notes and observations to himself in a little red Scribbletex notebook that he kept locked in his briefcase. People knew about "the little red book," but Harvey would show it to no one. Then one spring day in 1991, Harvey decided to share the contents of his book with the world. *Harvey Penick's Little Red Book*, published in 1992 by Simon and Schuster, has since become the best-selling sports book of all time. Harvey didn't decide to publish his notes for money or fame—after all, this is the man who continued to give lessons for no more than fifteen dollars, if he charged anything at all, until the end of his life. He just didn't care about money at all. He says in his introduction to *The Little Red Book* that he decided he was being *selfish*. He writes, "Maybe it was wrong to hoard the knowledge I had accumulated. Maybe I had been granted these eighty-seven years of life and this wonderful career in order that I should pass on to everyone what I had learned. This gift had not been given me to keep secret." That's pure Harvey. He and Bud Shrake would publish two more books in his lifetime—*And If You Play Golf, You're My Friend*

in 1993, and *For All Who Love the Game: Lessons and Teachings for Women* in 1995. A fourth book, *The Game for a Lifetime: More Lessons and Teachings*, would appear posthumously.

Those brilliant little books perfectly typify who Harvey was and what he thought about and how hard he really tried to *teach* people. Bud just did an outstanding job putting them together. All of us who knew Harvey are so thankful that these treasures have preserved his thoughts and his words.

From *Harvey Penick's Little Red Book*:

I learn teaching from teachers.
   I learn golf from golfers.
   I learning winning from coaches.
   There are many good teachers of golf who teach quite differently from each other. I prefer listening to one who teaches differently than I do. I might learn from him. I already know my own way. . . .
   I'll always remember what my cousin, Dr. D. A. Penick, said when he turned over the reins as University of Texas tennis coach to Wilmer Allison:
   "Wilmer, I know you'll make better players of your students in four years. But will they be better people? That's the important thing."

Harvey knew me very well, and early on he knew that I enjoy history, especially the history of the game of golf. He encouraged this interest. When I was about sixteen, I started reading about golf and golf architecture. My head has been in a book ever since—I can't get enough of it! He also encouraged me to read about Bobby Jones. Those who know the game know that Jones is one of the greatest golfers of all time. Jones is my favorite golfer, not just because of his skill as a player, but because there has never been anyone else in the game like him. I think he's been one of the few golfers who have ever had three degrees. He studied law at Emory, earned a BA in English literature at Harvard, and earned his BS in mechanical engineering at Georgia Tech. He never relinquished his amateur status, and in 1930 he won the "grand slam"—all four major tournaments in the same year. He retired after that, at age twenty-eight. He really had a tragic life, being diagnosed in his mid-forties with syringomyelia, a progressive disease of the spinal cord that caused him unimaginable pain, suffering, and increasing paralysis for the last twenty-five years of his life. But he had such an educated taste about everything he did. That sophistication in his outlook on life influenced his approach to the game, I'm sure. It was Jones who said, "Always the toughest golf course I ever played was the space between my ears."

Harvey was much the same way. He could be as technical in his teaching of the game as the pupil wanted to make it, but he knew that teaching in technicalities was usually detrimental to the golfer. He knew that a modicum of rudimentary fundamentals, conveyed with the greatest economy, was going to produce the best results in most people. He knew that when a golfer is standing over the ball, his or her mind is going to wander. He knew the psyche and the intellect of a golfer. He knew that the golfer's mind just races—often to the wrong things. He knew how to train the mind.

When Harvey was helping someone learn to putt, he would tell the pupil never to try to imitate someone else's putting form. I never heard any other teacher say that. Harvey would say, "I can't tell a person how to get in there and be comfortable. Only the player knows that." I think that's brilliant. The game is overtaught so much these days. Those of us who had the good fortune to be around Harvey know that a little bit goes a long way—and what he told us lasts forever.

People would go to Harvey for a lesson, and Harvey would just tell them a few words. They would come away with a nice thought, but would leave thinking, "Gosh, why didn't he tell me more?" Two or three weeks later, they would be practicing or playing with Harvey nowhere in sight, and the meaning of what Harvey had told them would reveal itself to them. They would say, "Oh, now I understand."

One of my favorite people in the world is Jack Burke, Jr., who was the 1956 Masters champion and is now in his late eighties. Harvey learned a lot from Jackie's father, Jack Burke, Sr., who came from Philadelphia and was the first pro at River Oaks in Houston, where early Texas golf was started. Jack Burke, Sr., was a great player—he finished second in the 1920 U.S. Open. A lot of professionals like Harvey would go down to Houston and go to the Burke household to learn to teach. Harvey was just seeking help all the while, in the interest of furthering his occupation.

Harvey had a fascination with the immigrant pros, Scottish and English, because they gave us the game, and he knew many of the original importers of the sport to America personally. He hung on their every word because he knew that they knew the game. He liked them because usually Scots are fairly direct and use an economy of words, but the words they choose, they mean. He liked that—those are the kind of people he enjoyed. Early golf professionals were servants to the game, servants to their club.

Because golf began in Scotland over six hundred years ago, we tend to think of it as being an old sport, which it is. But it's amazing to consider how little removed we Americans are from its arrival here in the United States. Golf started in this country only around 1880 or so, and that was on the Eastern seaboard, really: Boston, New York, and Pittsburgh. Baseball is older in America than golf is. Golf was a new pastime, one that didn't reach Texas until the very end of the nineteenth century. Considering that Harvey was born in 1904, Texas golf was still very much in its formative period when he took up the game.

The Austin community picked up golf early. Austin Country Club was chartered in 1898 as one of the first two golf clubs in Texas. In 1899, the club opened to its members a nine-hole, sand-green golf course designed by Lewis Hancock, a local businessman who had served a term as Austin's mayor. The site chosen for the course was a property along Waller Creek, well beyond the northern outskirts of the city. In those days, it truly was a country club. Today, these holes are a small municipal course—Hancock Golf Course—the oldest surviving golf course in Texas. They are played today in a different order than they were in 1899, but with only a couple exceptions, they are still laid out in their original configuration.

In 1914, the members acquired the pastureland adjacent to the northeast corner of their course and built a new front nine. Those nine have succumbed to time, but the original nine holes survive, bounded now by 41st Street, Red River Street, 38th Street, and Peck Avenue. Of course, people today consider this location to be in the heart of the city. I can only imagine what the atmosphere at that course must have been like in the 1920s, with young Harvey helping members improve their game and no doubt introducing this new sport to many folks in the Austin community who were just learning about it.

It's amazing to consider how tightly interconnected Austin's early history is and how close to that history we still are. For example, I was amazed

Harvey Penick at the Austin Country Club, 1928. *From the Daniel Allen Penick biographical file, Austin History Center, Austin Public Library. (C07692)*

to learn that Lewis Hancock's father, George Hancock, was a veteran of the Battle of San Jacinto. He then became a surveyor of frontier Texas and an early Austin merchant. In 1845, he opened a grocery and dry-goods store at Congress Avenue and Pecan Street (which long ago was renamed 6th Street). His son Lewis eventually sold this property to E. M. Scarbrough, who developed on it Austin's first "skyscraper," the famous Scarbrough Building. The Scarbrough Building is still there on what one could consider to be Austin's most important intersection, standing catty-corner to the beautiful Littlefield Building, built by banker and cattleman George Littlefield, whose relationship with the University of

Texas in its early days as a regent and benefactor is well known.

Lewis Hancock helped the city grow northward by developing neighborhoods between the University and Austin Country Club, including Aldridge Place. In downtown Austin, he built the Hancock Opera House, which is famous in UT history as the place where a quartet of students first sang "The Eyes of Texas" by John Lang Sinclair at a minstrel show fund-raiser for the UT track team. The wonderful little clubhouse that still stands at the municipal Hancock Golf Course, with its beautiful little hardwood-floored ballroom, was built by Austin Country Club in the 1930s after the first clubhouse on that site burned down. The new clubhouse was constructed with bricks salvaged from the original Main Building at UT, which was razed in the summer of 1934 to make way for the southern portion of the new Main Building and Tower. I can picture Harvey in his shop in that clubhouse, making clubs for members by hand by shaving down the wooden shafts with a piece of glass to achieve a custom fit for each golfer.

In the history of Austin—and Texas—the roots of the Hancocks and Austin Country Club run deep.

Change is inevitable, though. The world was transforming rapidly—as was Austin—in the years immediately after World War II, and the members of Austin Country Club decided that the club needed more space. They built a new course, designed by Perry Maxwell, four miles east of downtown Austin on Riverside Drive. The club officially opened there in 1950 and sold its old course—today's Hancock Golf Course, which at that time still included the 1914 addition—to the City of Austin.

The original home of Austin Country Club has seen many changes since then. In the early 1960s, as U.S. 81 was being expanded into the Interregional Highway (known today as I-35), the City of Austin sold the 1914 addition to the development arm of Sears, Roebuck. On that property, the developer built Hancock Shopping Center, Austin's first mall. After a period of decline in the 1980s and 1990s, it has been refurbished in recent years, still standing in the middle of busy parking lots in the shadow, literally, of the congested upper deck of I-35. Happily, the City retained the original nine holes at Hancock, which remain a beloved, historic green space and place of recreation for the people of Austin.

In 1984, Austin Country Club relocated again,

moving from the Riverside Drive site to the club's current Davenport Ranch location along Loop 360. The new place features a beautiful Pete Dye–designed course along the Colorado River, just below the Pennybacker Bridge. The property around the old Riverside clubhouse is now a campus of Austin Community College. The golf course is still there, but with many modifications to the original Perry Maxwell design. The place by the first tee where Harvey would stand with his clipboard and start the golfers is now covered by asphalt. At the time of the relocation, a lot of us got together and tried to persuade the University of Texas to buy the old club, but the University wasn't in an acquisition mode at that time.

Each place Austin Country Club has been—Hancock, Riverside, and Davenport Ranch—is filled with special memories for tens of thousands of golfers, in no small part because Harvey was a fixture at all three. The club's location on Riverside Drive in East Austin is where I learned the game. It's where Harvey made that cut-down seven iron for me in his little shop tucked down amid a grove of trees below the clubhouse.

Like many golfers of earlier generations, Harvey learned the game by caddying. Caddy yards in his day were tough—very rough-and-tumble. Money was scarce, and caddies had to try hard to get a job carrying a bag. The leading caddies ran the caddy yards by authority—and the meekest would be picked on. It was a highly competitive environment. I've read that the great golfer Ben Hogan—who was born in Stephenville and grew up in Dublin, Texas, and Fort Worth—said he was always the smallest boy in the caddy yard, and was picked on all the time. The older boys would put him in a barrel and roll him down the hill and beat him up. It was rough, really rough. But Harvey's brother Tom was the caddy master at Austin Country Club—and a strict taskmaster, too. Harvey said Tom was a stern guy, which I always found fascinating. He was very much the antithesis of Harvey.

Something Harvey showed me when I was a boy has always stuck with me, and I'm reminded of it when I find myself in competitive situations. There was a little caddy yard out by the back of the club at Riverside, and Harvey took me out there once and told me to watch the fifteen or so caddies who were there. While they were waiting on a bag, they set up a little golf course—a little pitch-and-putt course, re-ally—in these trees in the bottom there by the clubhouse. As they were playing their little games, he said, "Ben, I want you to watch these guys. Do you see the common theme here? These guys don't chip the ball way up in the air. They keep the ball along the ground." He said, "Do you know why?" and I said "No." He said, "That's because they're playing for *their money*—and that's the safest shot they can play." The simplest, surest way is to hit that chip-and-run. He said it's not the prettiest shot by far, but it's the most effective.

Many times as he was guiding a pupil's learning, Harvey would place a bench a short distance from the pupil and ask, "What do you think I want you to do with this shot?" And they would all say, "Oh, you want me to chip it over the bench." And Harvey would say, "No, I want you to chip it *under* the bench." That's just very simple, but effective. It's proper, because it involves the proper set of fundamentals. The brilliance of his guidance for the little junior golfer in learning that simple chip shot is that he or she is not trying to loft the ball—the golfer isn't trying to do anything to that shot other than simply scooting the ball along the ground. Sometime later, the pupil will realize on his or her own the correlation between the position of the hands at impact of that shot and their position at impact in a full stroke—they're no different. Harvey's methods of teaching were just wonderful.

From *Harvey Penick's Little Red Book*:

Betsy Rawls came to the University of Texas out of high school with a very strong grip. She was a talented player who loved golf, and I began gradually to change her grip. Betsy improved fast and won the city tournament in Austin, followed by the state championship.

I taught her that she must learn to play on all kinds of courses—good and bad—with all different sorts of people. I learned a lot from Betsy in return. She was a Phi Beta Kappa in physics.

One thing I learned from Betsy was that you don't win a tournament with good golf shots only. There are many more things of importance, and they grow even more important when you start playing against the whole world. . . .

I learned from Betsy not to give a pupil too many things to think about in one lesson. One day I was teaching her two or three things at once. She said,

"Harvey, let's learn one or two things this week and save the third thing for next week."

That was a real lesson for me. If a Phi Beta Kappa and talented golfer like Betsy can't concentrate on more than two things at once, what chance would an ordinary student have?

This became a cornerstone of my teaching—one thing at a time.

In knowing Harvey and growing up around Harvey, I was the beneficiary of the appreciation he gave to my golf and my learning. Because of that, I always

Harvey Penick and Betsy Rawls. *From the Daniel Allen Penick biographical file, Austin History Center, Austin Public Library. (PICB 06812)*

worked harder at it to try to become a better golfer. But there are other things intrinsic to the game that are just as important as playing. As a golfer realizes how great the game is, it's hard not to think about other people and how people and places matter to the game—and what effect the game and the people who love it have on the community. I really do believe that Austin is unique in that it has been led by people like Harvey. They have shaped its personality. Austin is a very embracing society. It has always been a learned society—we all know that—and it's our place of government, here in Texas. I've always considered Austin to be a place where people have a keen sense of others. "Tolerant" is maybe not quite the right word in this sense, but there is an awareness of others here, a caring about our fellow man—whether that comes through education or state government or one's own existence as one's life intertwines with other people. Kindness and humility. When we realize what a beautiful place we live in—when we focus on an awareness of our surroundings—I think most Austinites believe in the end that we've had it really good, our way of life here in Austin.

The shadow of those two institutions—the University and the Capitol—was just as strong in Harvey's younger days as it is today, probably even more so. Harvey was a product of watching people's enjoyment of the game, but he was also formed by the ideologies of the people who were his practitioners—club members, politicians, professors, or whatever. All sorts of people would come out to play golf, and Harvey would be sure to learn as much from each of them as he could. It was very much a two-way street—Harvey benefited immensely from the community, the people he met by way of the University and the Capitol. There's no question it was a simpler life when Harvey began his career. But through it all, Austin's beauty and its geography and the people who have been committed to keeping those intact have been a huge part of our community. We've been really lucky to have people in this community like Harvey. We have had people to learn from who have formed the basis of how we think today and how we reflect on the importance of Austin's past.

Harvey was there to see the game of golf become a part of the fabric of the Austin community. When he was made the head professional in 1923, Austin Country Club was the only golf course in the Austin area, and it was for members only. The next year, though, the local Lions Club formed the Austin Municipal Golf and Amusement Association, which built what would become an eighteen-hole public course in the bend of the Colorado River just west of the city, on the parcel of land owned by the University of Texas known as the Brackenridge Tract. The course had grass greens, which spurred Harvey to encourage Austin Country Club to replace its sand greens with grass. There is speculation that either Tom Penick or John Bredemus designed the Lions Club course, or that it was a collaboration of the two. In 1936, the association transferred its lease with the University to the City of Austin, and it has been a true municipal course—Lions Municipal Golf Course, more commonly referred to simply as "Muny"—ever since. Muny has a long and rich history with the Penick brothers, Austin, and the University of Texas.

Tom Penick served as the head professional at Lions Municipal Golf Course from 1928 to 1961. In the spring of 1927, the University of Texas made golf a conference sport for the first time in the school's history, and Tom Penick served as the new team's coach. The team practiced at Lions Municipal and, in those early days, competed in a limited number of matches, some held at Lions Municipal. In addition to this early history with the UT golf team, Muny has welcomed hundreds of thousands of golfers from the entire Austin community over the years. In 2009, the Texas Historical Commission placed a marker near the entrance indicating that in 1951 Muny quietly became the first integrated golf course in the South—a clear example of the power a municipal course has to bring the community together.

I think it is important for me to point out the degree to which Lions Municipal has made a great difference in people's lives. It has provided a lot of enjoyment to a lot of people from all walks of life in our community. It has been so accommodating, in terms of location, price, and its availability as a municipal golf experience. As a physical resource, it gives so much to West Austin through its absorption of storm events and noise. Of even greater significance, it connects Lady Bird Lake, West Austin, and the ever-densifying downtown by way of a public green space. It is an important physical resource, but perhaps its greater importance is as a *mental* resource. It is one of those indispensably vital places that make a community what it is—those places that

have helped ensure the unique character that makes Austin what it is. Austin is unique, largely because of places like Muny. It is sad to read about municipal courses in different parts of the country going by the wayside, either because their rounds are down or because other uses are being found for the properties. Muny remains one of the busiest courses in the area, a favorite for thousands of golfers. The City continues to lease from the University of Texas the land on which Muny stands, and once again the University is giving serious consideration to not renewing the lease when it expires in order to develop the property into something other than a golf course. My views on this issue are well known around town. I think a vital part of Austin—and the University, too—would be lost if Muny ceased to exist.

The successes of the University of Texas and the city of Austin are inextricably tied to each other. Neither can flourish without the other. For over three-quarters of a century, Muny has been a shining example of that relationship.

Under Tom Penick, Texas was the team champion at the inaugural Southwest Conference championship, in 1927. In 1928, UT won the team title again, and UT's Gib Payne was medalist. In 1931, Harvey took over the reins of the UT golf team from his brother. Like Tom, Harvey served as coach without pay during his early tenure.

From its beginning in 1897 and up through the 1920s, the NCAA championship was dominated by the Ivy League schools, especially Harvard and Yale, but among Harvey's early successes as coach of the UT golf team was Ed White, a remarkable talent who was the medalist at the 1935 NCAA championship.

From Harvey Penick's *The Game for a Lifetime*:

I had been teaching the game for several years, but I was new to being a university golf coach in 1931 when a black-haired boy named Ed White, from Bonham, Texas, started playing at the first Austin Country Club on a junior membership that his father had bought for fifteen dollars. . . .

I learned later that Ed had taught himself to play golf while caddying at the Bonham Country Club. Because he was a caddie, Ed wasn't allowed to play at the club, but he and four friends fashioned a six-hole layout of their own in a pasture. Ed read *The American Golfer* magazine and studied the photographs and drawings of Jones and Hagen and other great players. One day his father saw Ed playing golf in the pasture and recognized a natural talent. Soon Ed was on his way to Austin. He still had never met a golf pro, much less taken a lesson. . . .

Ed enrolled at the University of Texas as a petroleum engineering student. In February 1932, Ed turned out for our 72-hole qualifying tournament for the Texas golf team. The low six scores would make the squad, and from then on they would have challenge matches among themselves to determine their rankings from week to week.

In the tournament, Ed shot 61-64-65-62 and finished first by about a mile and a half.

His 72-hole total of 252 has never been threatened in the Massengill Trophy, which is given to the low qualifier on the Texas team.

However, the money to be won on the professional tour in those days was nothing like it is today, and Ed never turned pro. Harvey was convinced that if he had turned pro, he would have been the best of his time.

It's remarkable to realize today that despite all the success his teams had, Harvey almost never traveled with his teams to their out-of-town matches. He had his duties at Austin Country Club to attend to, and of course this was simply a different era in intercollegiate athletics in terms of travel and budgets than what exists today.

From *Harvey Penick's Little Red Book*:

One of my University of Texas golfers was playing in a tournament in North Carolina. He won his first match handily.

He phoned me and said, "The guy I play tomorrow I can beat easily. He has a bad grip and also a bad swing."

My boy lost the next match.

"The lesson to be learned," I told my golfer later, "is don't be afraid of the player with a good grip and a bad swing. Don't be afraid of a player with a bad grip and a good swing. The player to beware of is the one with the bad grip and the bad swing. If he's reached your level, he has grooved his faults and knows how to score."

In 1963, Harvey passed the reins over to George Hannon, who was my coach at UT. Harvey had had a remarkable run as coach of the UT golf team. In the thirty-two seasons he was coach, the Longhorns won the Southwest Conference championship twenty times. His teams also recorded eight top-ten finishes at the NCAA championship—the highest in 1949, a second-place finish behind North Texas—in addition to Ed White being the individual medalist in 1935.

I was very fortunate to have had success on the UT golf team as well. I was medalist at the NCAA Championship in 1971, the first Longhorn to win the individual championship since Ed White, and our team that year was the first in school history to win the team championship. The next year at the NCAA tournament, Harvey was pleased to see two of his protégés from Austin Country Club—my UT teammate Tom Kite and me—tie for the individual championship. We won the team championship again as well. Then in 1973, I was once again NCAA medalist. As of this writing, only one other Longhorn golfer has been NCAA medalist—Justin Leonard, in 1994—and our team titles in 1971 and 1972 remain the only two in school history.

Though there was no varsity women's golf team at UT during the time he coached there, Harvey had the privilege of guiding the learning of several Longhorns who had great success after seeking him out at Austin Country Club. In the years before the NCAA held championships for women's golf, Debbie Petrizzi was the 1978 Association for Intercollegiate Athletics for Women champion, and Kelli Kuehne won the 1994 U.S. Junior Girls Championship and the 1995 U.S. Women's Amateur Championship. Though her career occurred before UT had a women's team, Betsy Rawls won eight majors as a professional in the 1950s and 1960s. LPGA Tour cofounder Betty Jameson, who won the U.S. Women's Amateur in 1939 and 1940, sought out Harvey's help as well.

I have also had the good fortune in my life to be able to play on both the Austin Country Club Riverside course and on Lions Municipal. I grew up in my parents' house on Bridle Path, just a few blocks from Muny, and I attended O. Henry Junior High. O. Henry is across the street from Muny, so I could hop the fence and walk onto the course. It has always been a part of my life. I've lived in Austin my entire life—and my home today is still less than a mile from Muny. I drive by Muny every day when I'm home.

As much as I love them, I'm convinced that golf cannot advance on private clubs alone. Golf cannot flourish if there are not places where everyone can play, people of all ages and skill levels. I really think we see that today. There are going to be products of purely private country clubs who have lots of instruction, and a few of those are going to do well professionally—but on the same token, there are also going to be players who learned the game and competed as a municipal player on, let's say, less than ideal conditions, who will do just as well. If that municipal player is a little more self-taught and competes, well, I think I'd bet with that person. I cannot stress enough the value of having this type of golf course. Municipal courses are still some of the most wonderful forms of golf that we have in this country.

I'm reminded of the way that Harvey taught us the game. He encouraged us to go out on our own—to learn things for ourselves. A tournament is seventy-two holes in a week. Success comes from mastering the ability to make a series of minute little adjustments, and you can't have somebody pointing all those things out all the time. With many of today's younger professionals, I see them play their round and then go right to the practice tee, where the coach has a camera out. That's a tough way to learn. Believe me, if the next day you're facing a five-iron shot and that wind's blowing right to left and the green is firm and you have to play a certain shot into it, no teacher in the world is going to tell you how to do that. The golfer has to trust his or her ability—his or her judgment and instincts—in order to play that shot. The golfer has to *imagine* that shot. And that imagination has to be cultivated, which can happen only through developing competitive skills and playing the game.

I'll never forget this as long as I live. When I was about twelve, I had gone out to the country club, and I somehow found about six golf balls that day, which was amazing, and I had a couple more in my bag. So I took those golf balls and I went to the putting green. I had this little spot over there on one part of the green, and I was putting the same putt over and over and over. I'd been there about an hour—same putt, same putt. Harvey came out of the shop and he said, "Ben, I see what you're doing down here. Your stroke looks pretty good. But you know something? You won't have that putt the rest of your life. I want you to putt to different holes and make a game out of it." That's just perfect! Harvey was interested in seeing me cultivate my imagination—the ability to *imagine*

the shot. He said the best putting practice a player can do is to putt against a buddy, because each player is playing a different hole with each putt. A chip, a putt—with one ball. You're putting yourself on the line, and you're competing—you're imagining. Cultivation of the touch. In that way, Harvey was always making things real for us.

I met Harvey through my father, who was a member of Austin Country Club. He was a lawyer in town and a good athlete; he played golf at Baylor. My brother Charlie, who's fifteen months older than I am, and I would go with our father to the club on Riverside, and Harvey would let us hit a few balls— just barely get us into the game. There were no formal lessons; they kind of watched us and gave us occasional guidance. I have a distinct remembrance of my father and Harvey both sort of looking at my hands on the club; I arrived at one position and they both said, "That's good—now just leave them there." And that was it. After that, both of them said, "Just wind up and hit it." There was nothing technical at all. We knew that some shots certainly pleased our father, and then there were some little shots that pleased Harvey. If we hit a good little chip, he'd just say, "That's fun!"—so we knew we must be doing something right, and we'd go on. They encouraged us to get out there and just play.

Harvey always thought that the best way to see if a kid likes the game is if he has a little buddy. If you've got a little buddy, he said, you can go do something together. In my case, it was my brother. Harvey said it's hard to learn golf alone—and it's hard to do with just father there, because fathers can be tough on sons. The best way is to let the child go loose, where he can cultivate his imagination. Of course, a parent has to find a place for them to do that, which is tough these days. A lot of places don't let it happen.

From *Harvey Penick's Little Red Book*:

The best age to start a child in golf is the time he or she becomes interested in the game.

I don't believe in parents forcing the game on kids who would rather be doing something else. But if a little child four or five years old is eager to go out and play with Dad or Mom, then it's time to start.

Don't be too exacting on the grip or anything else. Just let the kids use their natural ability. Hands together.

Be sure the club you give them has plenty of loft.

Problems start when the child uses too little loft and tries to scoop the ball up into the air. The more the child tries to help the ball up, the less it'll get up.

Also be sure the club is light enough. A small child will learn a bad grip by trying to swing a club that is too heavy. My cousin, Dr. D. A. Penick, a professor of Greek who rode around town on a bicycle and was the tennis coach at the University of Texas for fifty years, discouraged toddlers from swinging a tennis racket for that same reason.

When you take your youngster to see a teaching pro, say that you're going to get some "help." The word "lessons" sounds too much like going to school, which is not always fun. Golf should be fun. With a child I never say "teach" or "lessons." . . .

Practicing is an individual matter. When they were kids, Ben Crenshaw was always playing more than he practiced, and Tom Kite was always practicing at least as much as he played. Hogan was a practicer. Byron Nelson was a player and also a practicer.

Whatever the child wants to do—play or practice—that's what he or she should do.

Worst of all is when I see Dad, on the range or the course, constantly nagging the child to keep his head down, keep his left arm straight, stare at the ball—bad information, all of it. This may be fun for Dad, but it is hurting the child's development.

Harvey never let Tom Kite and me practice together, because our individual styles were so different.

I had a wonderful existence growing up—a very normal upbringing. Just like any other kids, we enjoyed a variety of sports. We were always competing. We had fun. My friends and Charlie and I had some really caring parents, too—you know, parents who allowed us to play. A lot of them were coaches. My father was our Little League coach. There were some great little baseball players and football players in my neighborhood.

My brother played baseball at Austin High School. He played in the outfield with Don Baylor, an unbelievable player who went on to have a long career in the Major Leagues, winning the American League Most Valuable Player award in 1979. When we were in high school, Austin High was at 12th and Rio Grande, in the building that is now a campus of Austin Community College. It had a wonderful little baseball stadium just down the hill, next to House Park. It was the neatest little stadium—it had as much personality as the old Clark Field at UT. Coach Cliff Gustafson offered Charlie a scholarship to play baseball at Texas, and because he was an outfielder, Charlie had to learn how to climb Billy Goat Hill, the outcropping of rock in the outfield of Clark Field. Those quirky, asymmetrical parks are the ones that stick in your memory—and Austin had two of the best.

Another unique place in Austin is the Butler Pitch and Putt course, just south of the river on Lamar Boulevard. Harvey always told us, if we couldn't find some place to play, just go to Butler Pitch and Putt. He said that's ideal for juniors to learn the game. Harvey wanted the game to be learned from the hole backwards; that's not something that's done today. Butler Pitch and Putt is still a wonderful place to go to play—there might be students over there, little kids, older people, all playing the game. The longest hole is only about 135 yards, so it's a place to go to master the short game. People can talk about spectacular long shots all they want, but getting the ball in the hole is the name of the game, and whoever has the hot hand in the short game is going to win the match. Like Muny and old Clark Field, Butler Pitch and Putt is one of those places that have made Austin unique.

When we were at the club, Harvey was always there. He always said he was "looking after" us, which meant that he was always observing. It was as if he always had his eyes on the whole place. When I got older, I was blessed because Bill Munn, who played for Harvey at UT, would come and pick me up at my house, and I'd go shag balls for him and his group and watch them play. They knew my father and were very kind to let me tag along. As a twelve-year-old, I was watching some really good shots. Bill is in the oil business in Midland now, and he is still one of my best friends. We talk on the phone at least once a week, and I can't remember a single conversation we've ever had in which we didn't eventually end up talking about Harvey. He has told me many times, "Ben, I just can't tell you how much of a difference he's made in my life. I see it in the way I carry on my business. I'll be in a business transaction, and I'll try to think about what Harvey would say."

Harvey always believed in the value of competition and watching other players hit good shots. He always wanted juniors and newcomers to learn the game by developing first their touch and their little

Harvey Penick (*center*) with his longtime pupils and friends Tom Kite (*left*) and Ben Crenshaw (*right*) at Austin Country Club, ca. 1992. Photo by Bob Daemmrich.

shots, because those are the shots that will stay with the golfer for the rest of his or her life. Harvey always stressed that he got just as much pleasure helping a novice get the ball in the air as he did helping those of us who would go on to win championships.

When I turned pro, Harvey was always so supportive of everything I did. I won some tournaments right out of the gate, but like most professionals, my career has always had its ups and downs. In 1984, I had the honor of winning the Masters—one of the four major tournaments in professional men's golf—on the fiftieth anniversary of the event's founding. The Masters was founded by Bobby Jones, and it is played on Augusta National, a demanding, picture-perfect course in Augusta, Georgia, that Jones designed with one of the game's greatest architects, Dr. Alister MacKenzie. When I returned to Austin after winning the famous Green Jacket, Harvey met me at the airport. He always had a very unusual handshake—he would present his hand with his palm facing upward, and

then grasp your hand. We shook hands and he said, "Ben, I'm mighty proud of you." I'm sure he did the same thing for Tom Kite after Tom won the U.S. Open in 1992. Tom's family had moved to Austin when he was young, and we grew up together playing at Austin Country Club under Harvey's watchful eye.

My victory in the 1984 Masters was an important moment in my life. I had had heartbreaks before that, in about seven other majors. Winning a major was a great relief because even for a really good golfer, you just never know for sure if it's going to happen. Majors are the most difficult events to win because the course itself is set up to be such a greater test of one's golf skills, but also because the pressure is so much greater. Bobby Jones said it best: regular tournaments and the majors are two entirely different things. He said playing in a major is like being a trapeze artist—the trapeze artist has a net for the tournaments, but the majors take that net away. A golfer has to trust himself in a major because every aspect of it is so much more difficult. I truly do believe in fate. My books are filled with accounts of tournaments that have been decided by a twist of fate. Grantland Rice, one of the great sportswriters of all time, wrote about fate; Jones believed in it, and talked about it during his Grand Slam year. There are some things in golf you just can't explain. When things hang in the balance, a golfer can attempt at the production of a good golf shot—but sometimes there's something else that takes over. I really believe that.

With that 1984 Masters victory, I was the first former Longhorn to win a major. In 1992, my childhood friend and competitor Tom Kite became the second, staying unbelievably focused in brutal weather conditions at one of the most famous and beautiful courses in the world, Pebble Beach, to win the U.S. Open. For many years, Tom was the all-time leading money winner on the PGA Tour as well. Two other former Longhorns have won majors: Mark Brooks won the 1996 PGA Championship at Valhalla Golf Club in Louisville, Kentucky, in a playoff over Kentuckian Kenny Perry, and in 1997 Justin Leonard carded a final-round 65 to win the British Open at the Royal Troon Golf Club in Troon, Scotland.

I was thirty-two in 1984, and I had some good wins in the years after that, but not a victory in a major. Harvey turned eighty later that year, and I continued to seek his guidance for my golf swing and enjoy the friendship of a man who had already had such a profound effect on my life.

Harvey's health began to decline in the late 1980s, though he was still at Austin Country Club almost every day, guiding the learning of so many golfers of all abilities who sought him out. Even before the publication of his books, he had developed a reputation throughout golf circles as one of the greatest teachers who had ever lived. He was in great physical pain for much of his later years. In 1972, he had had broken his back in a golf-cart accident, going to check on some youngsters who were picking up balls. Harvey was always opposed to the use of golf carts, so he said it was ironic that he would suffer an injury in that way.

By the spring of 1995, Harvey's health was failing. As the 1995 Masters approached, we all knew that Harvey was reaching the end of his life. I had visited him in his home two weeks earlier, and as he lay in his bed, he watched me putt some balls across the carpet, guiding my learning for one last time. I flew to Augusta with a heavy heart.

In his last days, Harvey enjoyed watching the telecast of Davis Love III winning at the Freeport-McMoRan Classic in New Orleans. Davis's father had been one of Harvey's players at Texas in the 1950s, and Harvey had known the younger Davis since he was a boy. Davis had not yet qualified for the Masters that year, but his victory at New Orleans earned him a last-chance entry in the field at Augusta.

Harvey died in his home on Sunday, April 2, 1995. After receiving the phone call I was dreading, my wife and I hurried back to Austin. Tom Kite and I served as pallbearers at the funeral, which was on Wednesday, and then I caught a flight back to Augusta. The first round of the Masters was the next morning.

Even now, fifteen years later, expressing my thoughts on the events of that week is very difficult for me. Every time I speak or write about it, my emotions overwhelm me.

I can't explain what happened next. I simply can't. Somehow, I won the tournament.

I've said many times that I had a lot of help from a lot of different places that week. Something made me remember the joy of playing golf that week. It was just amazing—I had not a technical thought, really, in my brain. I was just reacting and playing the golf course. I can't believe I was allowed to play that well that week, after we had buried Harvey.

Over the four rounds, I made only five bogeys. I've never had a golf tournament—certainly not a major tournament—where I made only five bogeys the whole week. But whenever I made a little mistake, I would retrieve it on the next hole, and it somehow calmed me down again. Making a silly mistake and then letting it stay with me for several holes has cost me a lot of tournaments. But I've never had a more even-keel frame of mind than I did that week—and as I said before, I've had some ups and downs in my career. Much has been written about the amazing number of lucky bounces I got that week as well. It just happened. I can't explain it.

On the back nine of the final round, I was tied for the lead with, as fate would have it, Davis Love III. I birdied the sixteenth and seventeenth holes to take a two-stroke lead over Davis, which proved to be enough. Anyone who knows me knows I'm the most sentimental guy in the world. Somehow, some way, I held myself together through those last several holes—through the whole week, really. I sank a short putt for bogey on the eighteenth to win by one shot. Somehow, everything culminated right there in that moment—at my favorite tournament and on my favorite course, both of them created by my favorite player. Out there on Bobby Jones's course, at his tournament, I was a trapeze artist performing without a net. And to have won it for a second time, at the age of forty-three. I still just cannot believe it. I can't believe it.

Harvey was obviously on a lot of people's minds that week. Maybe my achievement reminded people of the mentors they had in their life—teachers, professors, or whoever it might be. They witnessed a pupil having an opportunity to do something for the memory of his teacher. I can't tell you what a nice feeling it is to do something for the memory of somebody like Harvey. I don't know how it happened.

Harvey had this incredible ability to take the self out of the equation. He would much prefer to talk about others, other than himself. He got excited talking about others. For example, someone would ask him how he learned, and he would give examples of going down to Clark Field at UT to watch Billy Disch and Bibb Falk. There was once a skinny outfielder on the UT baseball team who would lunge at the pitch, losing all his power, so Coach Falk tied a clothesline around him, and when the pitch came in, Coach Falk would dig in his heels and yank him backward, like a cowboy tying a calf. Harvey never used that technique on his lunging golfers, but he just loved that kind of stuff! He was always trying to get himself to learn so that he would be a better teacher.

In his book *And If You Play Golf, You're My Friend*, Harvey tells the story of how one day, in 1929, he lost his patience with a stubborn pupil and blurted out a hurtful comment; he said, "I wish your brain and muscles were as coordinated as the clothes you're wearing!" He was so troubled by what he had done that he apologized to the pupil, told him he was making progress, and ended the lesson early. He then walked straight to the clubhouse and wrote down in a ledger a list of principles that he would remind himself of every few days for the rest of his life. The principles are now in the book, for all of us to read.

A lot of us were surprised to read that confession by Harvey. But, you know, his life was not without trial and tribulation in his experiences with people. He kept working at it, working at it, working at it, to be effective. I'm sure he got angry with people—he was real, he was human—but he had such effective traits in his life that when you encountered them, they couldn't help but stay with you. People who encounter a teacher who has a lasting effect on them are very fortunate. I've had many wonderful teachers in my life, but there was nobody like Harvey.

I may be completely wrong about this, but I'm not sure there could ever again be someone quite like Harvey in the world of Austin golf. He came along at such a unique moment in history and was such a uniquely special person. I don't know what a modern Harvey would be like. I wish one would come along for people. I will say this: I would love to give people my experience around a person like Harvey, to be able to give that to a future generation. That gift would be really good.

John W. Hargis. *Courtesy of University Communications,*
University of Texas at Austin.

Steadfast in His Intent

RICHARD B.
MCCASLIN

John W. Hargis and the Integration of the University of Texas at Austin

On June 5, 1950, the United States Supreme Court ordered the Law School of the University of Texas at Austin to admit black applicant Heman M. Sweatt. Although this decision was a crucial step in the desegregation of all admissions by the University, it did not repudiate the doctrine of separate but equal established in *Plessy v. Ferguson*, adjudicated by the Court in 1896. The University continued to segregate undergraduate admissions for five more years, referring blacks to state institutions of higher education elsewhere in the state. In June 1955, John W. Hargis became the first black undergraduate admitted to the University, completing the process of judicial integration begun by Sweatt. During his struggle to gain admission, and while becoming the first black to earn a degree in chemical engineering from the University, Hargis remained "steadfast in his intent," as a colleague later recalled, to establish blacks as a vital part of the University community. This determination led him to return to Austin after retiring early from a successful business career and resume playing an active role in minority affairs at the University until his untimely death in 1986.[1]

The initial assault on the color line at the University of Texas occurred when Sweatt, a veteran who held a bachelor of arts from Wiley College and had completed twelve hours of graduate work at the University of

Richard B. McCaslin, a University of North Texas professor, received his PhD in history from the University of Texas at Austin in 1988. He wrote Lee in the Shadow of Washington *(2001), which was nominated for a Pulitzer Prize and won the Slatten Award and Laney Prize. Other works include* Tainted Breeze: The Great Hanging at Gainesville, Texas *(1994), which received a Tullis Prize and an American Association for State and Local History commendation, and* At the Heart of Texas: One Hundred Years of the Texas State Historical Association *(2007), which won an Award of Merit from the Texas Philosophical Society. He interviewed John W. Hargis for* Commitment to Excellence: One Hundred Years of Engineering Education at the University of Texas *(1986), written with Earnest F. Gloyna. This article first appeared in the* Southwestern Historical Quarterly *95 (July 1991).*

Michigan, applied for admission to the law school in February 1946. After his application was rejected, he filed suit in the 126th District Court, in Travis County, on May 16, 1946. The National Association for the Advancement of Colored People (NAACP) gave him strong support during his campaign to attend the University, as part of their broad-based efforts to eradicate racial barriers through court action. His case reached the U.S. Supreme Court in March 1949, where it was filed on behalf of the NAACP by a team of attorneys led by Thurgood Marshall. The Court, in its opinion delivered on June 5, 1950, agreed that a hastily organized law school under the aegis of the nascent Texas State University for Negroes, later renamed Texas Southern University, did not offer a legal education equal to that available from the University of Texas, and ordered that Sweatt be admitted to the UT Law School.[2]

Although the University of Texas became the first institution of higher education in the South to admit blacks to its graduate and professional degree programs, the doctrine of separate but equal, set forth in *Plessy v. Ferguson*, had not been repudiated. In his briefs, Marshall stressed the inequality of the separate law schools, focusing not only on physical differences between the two institutions but also on intangibles, such as reputation. He coupled this argument with a direct assault on *Plessy*, submitting an amicus curiae brief signed by law faculty from all over the United States and a statement from the Department of Justice condemning the doctrine of separate but equal. The opinion of the Court, written by Chief Justice Fred M. Vinson, ignored the attack on *Plessy*, however, and concentrated on the question of inequality. Marshall won an important victory in persuading the justices to declare that equity in education required more than just equitable facilities, thereby laying the groundwork for the eventual repudiation of the doctrine of separate by equal; but for the immediate future, "*Plessy* was still the law."[3]

Sweatt enrolled in the University of Texas Law School in the fall of 1950. Although he left after two years because of poor grades, many others followed. The number of black graduate students enrolled at the University increased within a few years to nearly a hundred during the summer and about sixty-five during regular sessions. The Supreme Court's decision, however, did not prevent the exclusion of many blacks who attempted to enroll in academic programs

at the University. A black student was admitted only if his or her chosen curriculum was not available at a public institution of higher education for blacks elsewhere in Texas. These schools could not afford graduate and professional programs that required expensive equipment and a well-developed library for research, but did offer undergraduate curricula of varying quality. Chief Justice Vinson's decision allowed the University to remain within the law in its exclusion of blacks, especially undergraduates.[4]

On May 17, 1954, the Supreme Court, in a unanimous opinion written by Chief Justice Earl Warren, struck down the doctrine of separate but equal by ruling in *Brown v. Board of Education of Topeka* that segregated educational facilities were "inherently unequal." Public reaction in southern states indicated that desegregation would be difficult to enact. In Texas, state representative Jack Fisk, anticipating the Court's decree, had urged in March 1954 that his state secede, if necessary, to thwart federal integration efforts. Governor Allan Shivers was less histrionic, but he did insist that it would be "years" before desegregation could take place. The primary consolation for proponents of segregation was the justices' decision to hold a hearing in the fall of 1954 before decreeing how desegregation would be implemented.[5]

A challenge to the policy of separate but equal in undergraduate admissions at the University of Texas came quickly in the wake of *Brown*. Marion G. Ford, Jr., a black football standout and honor graduate from Phillis Wheatley High School in Houston, applied and was refused admission to the University on June 29, 1954. His protest drew national attention before Henry Y. McCown, the registrar and dean of admissions for the University, wrote to Ford on July 23 to admit him, ending with an admonition "that you will get over your inferiority complex and the idea that you are being discriminated against." Within a few weeks, five more black freshmen from Austin and a transfer student from Morehouse College in Atlanta, John W. Hargis, were admitted as well.[6]

The admissions occurred not because the University of Texas was abandoning its segregationist stance, but because a runoff was to be held in the Democratic gubernatorial primary in August 1954. Governor Shivers, whose political allies included influential University regents such as Chairman Tom Sealy, had failed to win his party's nomination in July. Sealy telephoned University president Logan

Wilson as the crucial date approached, then reported to fellow regent Leroy Jeffers that Wilson, in admitting the blacks, had managed the situation "beautifully so as to avoid any adverse publicity pending the August 28th run-off." After a solid primary victory, Shivers consolidated support for the upcoming general election by reaffirming himself as a segregationist. Texas Democrats within a few weeks adopted a campaign plank condoning segregation and condemning the Supreme Court's May 1954 ruling as an "unwarranted invasion of states' rights." By that time, the University's board of regents had already demonstrated its endorsement of Shivers, and the doctrine of separate but equal, by rescinding the admission of the seven black applicants.[7]

An overwhelming majority of Texas voters endorsed segregation by returning Shivers to the governor's office for an unprecedented fourth term. Conversely, many University students, many of whom had supported Sweatt, publicly condemned President Wilson for the rejection of the seven blacks. Five southwestern delegates to the National Student Council of the YMCA-YWCA, including the president of the University of Texas YWCA, telegraphed a formal protest on September 6, 1954. Wilson replied, "We are as yet not authorized to admit Negroes as undergraduates for lower-division courses or programs which are readily available at Prairie View [College] or Texas Southern [University]." The seven applicants had been referred to colleges elsewhere in Texas and "would be privileged to make another application" if they became eligible for admission to the University of Texas. Although many other University supporters and alumni congratulated Wilson for his stand, not a few joined with those students who denounced him, despite his insistence that his hands were tied in the matter.[8]

Wilson was being truthful when he explained that he lacked the authority to admit black undergraduates. As Willie Morris, then student editor of the *Daily Texan*, later recalled, Wilson was under great pressure to "heal the wounds of the calamitous Rainey era with analgesic balm and periodic injections of Novocain." President Homer P. Rainey, who had clashed openly with Governor W. Lee O'Daniel and the regents, had been dismissed in 1944. Many believed that one of the primary reasons for Rainey's removal was his ambivalent position on interracial relations. Wilson would not make the same mistakes; he intended to follow the regents' directives explicitly.[9]

What Wilson did not explain was that his recommendations were the basis for the policy adopted by the regents pending the Supreme Court's second hearing. The Texas commissioner of education, J. W. Edgar, in a widely circulated memorandum of May 1954, declared that the doctrine of separate but equal would remain in effect in Texas public schools until the Court said otherwise. Dean McCown recommended to Wilson that this course of action be adopted by the University, and proposed a strategy to cope with blacks who would apply for admission following the Supreme Court's May 1954 decision. To exclude "as many Negro undergraduates as possible," McCown would order black applicants for programs not offered by Texas Southern or Prairie View to take at least one year of the basic courses required for every University of Texas degree at those schools. Wilson tabled the proposal until late summer, when Chairman Sealy asked for an evaluation of McCown's plan. Wilson, together with Dean C. Paul Boner and W. Byron Shipp, the assistant registrar, assured Sealy that McCown's scheme was viable.[10]

Sealy presented Wilson's report to the executive committee of the board of regents, who endorsed reversing the admission of the seven blacks in September 1954. A memorandum from Sealy made clear the public policy to be promulgated by the regents and President Wilson: blacks would be admitted to the University only after completing their freshman year elsewhere and only if their chosen degree programs were not offered at public institutions of higher education for blacks in Texas. Wilson, then, was not entirely candid in his reply to a protest from H. M. Ratliff, a Methodist minister whose seven children had graduated from the University of Texas. Wilson declared that the rejection of the seven blacks was "not an administrative decision, but simply an action consistent with the policy set forth by the Board of Regents several years ago after the Sweatt case." In fact, until the Supreme Court made a final decision, he and the regents would work together to maintain the policy of separate but equal in undergraduate admissions, despite the opposition of Ratliff and others to the exclusion of blacks.[11]

Having reversed the admission of the seven black applicants, the University of Texas assigned them to the two state institutions of higher education for blacks in Texas. Two of the black freshmen from Austin, Norcell D. Haywood and John A. Searcy, were referred to Texas Southern for their course work in architecture. Four other freshmen were advised to attend Prairie View: Marion G. Ford, Jr., for chemical engineering; Robert R. Norwood for aeronautical engineering; Herman C. Smith for electrical engineering; and John W. Walker for petroleum engineering. The seventh applicant, John W. Hargis, was told to enroll at Prairie View ostensibly because he could not get the required chemistry course for his chosen degree program, chemical engineering, at the University of Texas in the fall of 1954. As Wilson wrote to McCown, it was the University's position that Hargis, though a transfer student from Morehouse, "would be no more handicapped at Prairie View than here."[12]

Two of the seven rejected applicants contested the decision of the University. Walker filed suit in federal district court in San Antonio in September 1954, demanding an injunction that would allow him to enroll in the College of Engineering at the University while his case was heard. His attorney argued that Prairie View, where Walker had been told to enroll, was academically inferior. Judge Ben H. Rice refused his petition on September 25, 1954, and the case was dropped. Ford appealed to the regents, then quickly abandoned his protest and enrolled at Wiley College, from which Sweatt had graduated. More than a few eyebrows had been raised when Ford said during a Houston press conference that he wanted to be the first black man to play football in Texas Memorial Stadium. Ironically, the regents failed to postpone that milestone in desegregation. A black halfback from Washington State University got the honor in the fall of 1954 because a contract for the game had been signed before University of Texas officials were aware of him. Rather than risk additional public protest, the University allowed him to play.[13]

An unlikely radical emerged from the debacle in September 1954: Hargis, then just nineteen years of age. He had been reared in predominantly black and Hispanic East Austin but, by his own admission, was remarkably naïve about segregation. He lived only a few doors down from Sweatt, but paid scant attention to the landmark decision of 1950, about which he learned in classes at old Anderson High School, then a school for blacks, from which he graduated as valedictorian in 1953. He enrolled at Morehouse, a liberal arts institution for blacks founded in Atlanta dur-

ing Reconstruction, solely because of its reputation for medical education. Among the alumni of Morehouse was Martin Luther King, Jr., but Hargis, who was preoccupied with his studies, absorbed little of the spirit of civil disobedience brewing there. After a year, he decided to focus on chemical engineering rather than continue in medicine. He knew that the University of Texas had one of the finest engineering schools in the United States, and his mother, a custodian there, told him that the institution was integrated, so he decided to return home.[14]

The furor over the initial rejection of Ford had died down after his admittance to the University in July, so Hargis was stunned when his own admission, as well as Ford's, was reversed in September, just one day before he was to have registered for classes. Reflecting perhaps his political naïveté, Hargis, unlike Sweatt, did not turn to the NAACP for aid. Instead, he enrolled at Prairie View along with Robert R. Norwood and Norcell D. Haywood. Their absence from the University was not noticed by the student body, which was preoccupied with protesting Ford's plight, but the Austin blacks were resented by many of their classmates at Prairie View. Because it was anticipated that the trio would be admitted to the University of Texas, they were enrolled in upper-division courses as freshmen and received preferential treatment, such as eating in the faculty cafeteria. During the spring of 1955, they shared a dormitory room because no one else welcomed their company. In addition to his personal discomfort, Hargis found that Prairie View offered few courses in his field that he had not already taken at Morehouse. In October 1954, he asked to be admitted to the University of Texas for the spring semester of 1955, but his request was denied.[15]

While at Prairie View, Hargis began to read more extensively on the struggle to desegregate higher education. The progress of judicial integration offered little hope that his dilemma would be resolved. The second hearing on desegregation was postponed from December 1954 until April 1955 because the Senate had delayed its confirmation of John M. Harlan, nominated to succeed Justice Robert H. Jackson, who had died in October 1954. Popular and official sentiment favored gradual integration supervised by the federal district courts. After President Dwight D. Eisenhower endorsed that approach in November 1954, the Justice Department, together with six southern states, including Texas, submitted amicus curiae

On October 2, 1954, Carl Talmadge "Duke" Washington (*above*) became the first African American to participate in a collegiate football game in Texas Memorial Stadium. In the second quarter of a lackluster 40–14 Longhorn rout, the Washington State fullback out-sprinted the Longhorn secondary (*left*) on a spectacular 73-yard touchdown run after having taken a delayed handoff and shaken off several would-be tacklers. Both the *Daily Texan* and the *Austin American-Statesman* reported the next morning that this play drew the greatest ovation of the day from the partisan Longhorn crowd. *Both images from Manuscripts, Archives, and Special Collections, Washington State University Libraries (Publicity photo, above: WSU University Publications Photographs Collection—PC 1, #19768. Frame from Washington State College coaches' game-film, left: WSU Football Films Collections—UA 29, Box 50.)*

briefs in favor of such a policy. Texas attorney general John B. Sheppard described rapid desegregation as "rash, imprudent, and unrealistic" and added that a poll conducted by his office revealed that seven out of ten Texans anticipated violence if segregation were to be abolished immediately. A survey of University of Texas students also indicated that most of them wanted gradual integration. The justices bowed to public opinion, and on May 31, 1955, decided in favor of gradual desegregation policed by federal district courts. They required that a "prompt and reasonable start" be made toward integration, but following that, officials were admonished only to proceed "with all deliberate speed."[16]

Desegregation of public education in Texas did gain some momentum following the Supreme Court's ruling in May 1955. The number of integrated community colleges in Texas increased to twelve, out of thirty, while nineteen public and ten private four-year colleges and universities formally desegregated within a year. A number of public school districts won praise for their immediate integration. To be sure, most of these were located in southern and western Texas, where few blacks had settled, but the racial prejudice against Mexican Americans had proved to be almost as virulent. On October 12, 1955, the Texas Supreme Court ruled that state funds could be appropriated for desegregated public school districts, upholding a state district court ruling against a request by the White Citizens' Council to block funding for the Big Spring school district. That same month, the U.S. Supreme Court voided Article VII, Section 7, of the Texas Constitution and Article 2900 of the Texas statutes, both of which provided for educational segregation in Texas.[17]

The University of Texas joined only halfheartedly in expanding the opportunities for blacks in higher education. In an open meeting on July 7, 1955, the regents decreed that integration of their institution would take place in September 1956 and would be accompanied by admissions tests, the first ever administered by a public university in Texas. They pointedly insisted that no black undergraduates would be allowed to enroll before that time, and Chairman Sealy pledged to oppose in court any attempt to do so. At the same time, the regents immediately desegregated Texas Western College, a branch of the University of Texas system located in El Paso, where, in June 1955, the first Texas public school district had integrated. A racial discrimination suit had been filed against Texas Western in April 1955, and President Dysart E. Holcomb considered it unwinnable. By integrating that campus, the regents hoped to provide clear evidence of a "prompt and reasonable start." True to their word, however, they denied requests for admission to the University in Austin for the fall of 1955 from three black undergraduate and two black graduate students, since they could obtain some of their required courses at state institutions for blacks elsewhere in Texas.[18]

Despite the regents' insistence that black undergraduates would not be admitted before the fall of 1956, one applicant, Hargis, forced them to make an exception. After completing his second semester at Prairie View, he applied to the University of Texas for admission. Officials there pigeonholed his request until the conclusion of the Supreme Court's second hearing. In the meantime, Prairie View officials promised him substantial compensation—including an automobile and monthly payments—if he would remain there. When he insisted on entering the University, they became abusive, but he stood his ground. Seven days after the Court's second ruling, on June 7, 1955, he was admitted to the University for the summer session. The regents had no alternative. He had taken the basic requirements for a chemical engineering degree from UT, a curriculum that was not offered at either Prairie View or Texas Southern, and had refused the former's offer to establish a program for him.[19]

Hargis had learned some hard lessons since his return to Texas. He no longer trusted university administrators, and he believed that the wisest course was to register as soon as possible. At the same time, he had observed the toll that being a "test case" could take on litigants. Many, like Sweatt, benefited little from their victories, which were won only after long years of conflict and at the expense of their academic plans. While he realized the value of their achievements for others, he decided that his greatest contribution would be to obtain a degree. His roommates at Prairie View, Norcell D. Haywood and Robert R. Norwood, waited until September 1955 to enter the University, but Hargis enrolled in June. President Wilson tried halfheartedly to dissuade him from enrolling. When Hargis came to the University to register, he was told that he would have to go to Wilson's office because his records were there. Wilson, intrigued that Hargis was not accompanied by an NAACP attorney, informed him that his credit in physics from Prairie View would be disallowed because it was an inferior school. Hargis agreed, but pointed out that it had not been his choice to go there; he had been virtually exiled. When he remained adamant, Wilson conceded the point and allowed him to transfer the credit.[20]

Hargis, by enrolling in the summer of 1955 despite the regents' pledge to maintain segregation until the fall of 1956, breached the barrier against black undergraduates before the University could prepare itself.

Logan Wilson, president of the University of Texas, ca. 1959. *From the Prints and Photographs Collection—Logan Wilson, Dolph Briscoe Center for American History, University of Texas at Austin. (DI 06852)*

Because no policy to govern integration had been adopted, the first year proved especially unpleasant for Hargis and other blacks attending the University. They suffered not only from the actions of several recalcitrant faculty members toward blacks, for which there was no official recourse, but also from the passive ostracism of many students. Hargis later recalled that he believed that he could not afford to relax his guard. Two black veterans who had attended Prairie View enrolled with Hargis in June 1955: David Wallace and Herman C. Smith, one of the six freshmen who had been rejected in September 1954. The tension proved too much, and both of them withdrew before the end of that summer. Haywood and Norwood joined Hargis in September 1955, but only the former earned his degree. Norwood suffered a nervous breakdown after one year and withdrew.[21]

The tension within the University of Texas mirrored that in the state as a whole. Desegregation of public education in Texas stalled after 1956 as a conservative backlash swept the South. The "Southern

Manifesto," which declared the May 1954 decision by the Supreme Court to be a "clear abuse of judicial power," was signed by ninety-six southern congressmen and senators in March 1956. Included in this group were four representatives from Texas as well as Senator Price Daniel, who had represented the University of Texas against Sweatt and would succeed Shivers as governor in 1957. A majority of the Texas legislature—which convened January 8, 1957, for the first time since the May 1955 Supreme Court hearing—endorsed several bills to stall desegregation. They circumvented the earlier Texas Supreme Court decision by denying funds to any school district in which integration was undertaken without the prior approval of a majority of the voters in that district. This statute remained in effect until Texas attorney general Will Wilson declared it unconstitutional on January 1, 1963. Also in 1957, the Texas legislature, like that of Florida and Virginia, adopted a law mandating the closure of any public school occupied by federal troops, a belligerent response to President Eisenhower's show of force in Little Rock, Arkansas.[22]

This conservatism among Texas's politicians was accompanied by sporadic outbreaks of violent opposition to desegregation in the fall of 1956. Support for segregation was most prevalent in East Texas, where a majority of the state's blacks lived. Ordered in November 1955 to admit three blacks, Texarkana Community College president Henry W. Stillwell encouraged the local White Citizens' Council to protest. A shotgun blast riddled a gasoline station owned by a black man, crosses were burned, and a black figure was hanged in effigy on campus, but the would-be students were unable to secure assistance from four Texas Rangers present when a mob of whites blocked their entrance into the school in the fall of 1956. In Mansfield, another chapter of the White Citizens' Council employed similar tactics to dissuade three blacks from attending the local high school under a federal court order. Two Texas Rangers were sent by Governor Shivers, but he gave them the same instructions as those in Texarkana: they were to keep order, not to assist in integration. None of the blacks attempted to register, and the school board, upon the advice of Shivers, transferred them to another district. A confrontation at Lamar Technical College in Beaumont became violent when two black students were beaten by white picketers when they tried to attend classes. A few days later, black students were driven through the picket line in taxicabs; several black drivers and students were subsequently jailed. Lamar College, like the other two institutions, remained segregated through the end of the decade.[23]

Blacks encountered more insidious resistance at the University of Texas. The admission tests authorized by the regents in July 1955 were defended as a measure to limit burgeoning enrollment, but were used primarily to restrict the number of blacks at the University. As F. Lanier Cox, a close adviser of President Wilson, admitted, the primary reason for the delay in integrating the University was to provide time to implement this admissions screening. The examinations ostensibly were to be administered "equally to all regardless of racial origin" and were to selectively admit applicants "based on merit." Despite the University's official stance against segregated testing facilities, however, the regents insisted that Texas public school superintendents be quietly informed "without any publicity" that separate rooms would be required. Herschel T. Manuel, the director of the University Testing and Guidance Bureau, telephoned four superintendents of East Texas districts with large black populations and prevailed upon them to segregate the students. The tests had the desired effect: of the students tested from February to September 1956, 45.6 percent of whites were admitted, but only 19.6 percent of blacks were accepted.[24]

In spite of admission tests, and futile attempts by two Houston antidesegregation groups to gain injunctions against the formal integration of the University of Texas, 110 black freshmen and transfer students were admitted in September 1956. Like Hargis, most of them found campus life to be lonely and unpleasant. They could participate in intramural sporting events, join campus religious organizations, and attend University functions and Texas Student Union programs. They could not, however, play on varsity teams or in the Longhorn Band, or live on campus. The University had no dormitories for black women, but a few men lived off campus in San Jacinto Dormitories D and F and Cliff Courts, a cluster of prefabricated living units. The Human Relations Commission of the University Students' Association condemned housing conditions for black students, but University administrators in the spring of 1956 refused to integrate campus dormitories. A student committee on integration, organized for the seventy-fifth anniversary of the University, in 1957, found that "Negro students must now stay in the cheapest University owned and operated dorms available." Some blacks found alternatives; Hargis lived with his grandmother while attending the University. For all blacks, entertainment options remained few: most campus-area restaurants and theaters would not admit them, nor were they allowed in Barton Springs Pool, a popular student oasis. Confronted by stubborn and arbitrary attempts to preserve segregation, many black students withdrew.[25]

Blacks who, like Hargis, remained at the University could rely on some support from the student body on public issues. On March 9, 1956, the Students' Association adopted a resolution of solidarity with their black fellow students. White students also protested when President Wilson in April 1957 removed Barbara Smith, a black music major, from a University production of *Dido and Aeneas.* Wilson explained his decision as a measure to protect Smith, who had received threatening telephone calls, and as an action taken in response to adverse public opinion. State representative Jerry Sadler was among the most prominent in protesting against Smith. He threatened to eliminate the University's state appropriation if it continued to admit blacks, and several other legislators joined him in condemning Smith. In reply, students displayed a swastika-emblazoned flag with "No Comment" scrawled across it in front of the Administration Building and hung effigies of Sadler and Joe Chapman, another outspoken opponent of desegregation in the legislature. *Dido and Aeneas* without Smith played to only a half-full house, but she performed her senior recital the next year before a standing-room-only audience.[26]

Despite the public support of some students, the general attitude toward the black newcomers remained perceptibly cool. In response to a survey in the fall of 1952, only 26 percent of male undergraduates at UT endorsed desegregation without any qualifications. Subsequent polls in the spring of 1955 and the winter of 1958, which were conducted more systematically, indicated that the social upheavals of the period had effected "no measurable changes in degree of acceptance of the Negro for the undergraduate student body as a whole." Excluded from the ordinary social routines of campus life, Hargis and other black students frequently met in the Student Union, where a table became their customary gathering spot. Some black students refused to at-

Cabinet members of the Wesley Foundation at the University of Texas, 1958: (*left to right*) John W. Hargis, Darlene Brucks (assistant director), Kirby Perry (chairman), Helen Jones, Raymond Slaughter, the Reverend Morris Bratton (director of the Methodist Student Foundation), Betty Weide (secretary), Dexter Hill. *From the* Cactus *yearbook (1958, p. 500), Dolph Briscoe Center for American History, University of Texas at Austin. (DI 07019)*

tend, insisting that to segregate themselves at the table would be to undermine their role in the desegregation of the University. Hargis, emerging as a leader among black undergraduates by virtue of his longer tenure on campus, dismissed their protest. He understood the important support provided by the meetings; if nothing else, he and the others at the table would at least see some friendly faces and gain some relief from enforced isolation.[27]

The surveys noted that fraternity members were more intransigent than any other male students in opposing integration. It was not until the spring of 1958 that many social organizations at the University of Texas accepted black students, and the fraternities and sororities remained closed even then. Hargis was convinced that Greek organizations provided a distinct advantage to their members, both socially and academically, as support networks. Along with Norwood, he worked to establish a chapter of Alpha Phi Alpha, the national black fraternity, at the University. They obtained a charter from W. Charles Akins, a founding member of the chapter at Huston-Tillotson College, a predominantly black school in East Austin. Hargis persevered even after Norwood withdrew. Although University administrators admonished him to "'make haste slowly and carefully'"

and refused initially to recognize the group as a fraternity, it continued to function as the Alpha Upsilon Tau Club, a "pre-fraternal colony." The members could not afford to buy or rent a house, so they met at the table in the Student Union. For Hargis's achievement in organizing a chapter at the University, Alpha Phi Alpha at Huston-Tillotson elected him "Alpha Man of the Year."[28]

Although he was forced to organize his own fraternity, Hargis managed to integrate other University organizations. He joined the student chapter of the American Institute of Chemical Engineers in 1956. Remarkably, though the surveys indicated that Protestant groups at the University generally had not accepted integration, Hargis served from 1957 to 1959 in the cabinet of the Wesley Foundation, a Methodist organization. He also became one of the first vice-presidents of the University Religious Foundation, established during the 1957–1958 academic year.[29]

Hargis had been valedictorian of his class at Anderson High and had done well at Morehouse College, but encountered unexpected difficulties that delayed his graduation from the University. A contemporary later recalled that Hargis's experience was typical for blacks at the University. Although most had been exceptional students in black high schools and colleges, they often found themselves woefully unprepared for university classrooms, where the inequities of segregated education became painfully evident. Also, the racial tension that they confronted inhibited their academic performance. Many black upperclassmen tried to explain this to freshmen, but each group had to learn through experience. Hargis's founding of a fraternity, which was intended to provide academic support for blacks, provided only a partial solution. Large numbers of blacks simply withdrew from the University.[30]

Hargis's graduation from the University in January 1959 proved to be anticlimactic. There was no graduation ceremony; diplomas were mailed to the recipients' homes on January 31. The Ex-Students' Association held its first January reception ever on January 15, 1959, but Hargis did not attend. His name appeared on a list of engineering graduates published by the *Daily Texan* on January 17, 1959, but it elicited no public comment. A student editorial in the *Daily Texan* on January 13, 1959, ignored Hargis while lauding as pioneers the black undergraduates who entered the University in the fall of 1956. The article did not receive any subsequent notice in "Firing Line," the section reserved for letters from students; instead, the correspondence focused on a proposal to remove pornographic magazines from Austin newsstands. More attention was lavished on Barbara Smith, who was the subject of a laudatory front-page article in the *Daily Texan* on February 3 and also attracted notice from the *Austin American-Statesman*.[31]

After graduation, Hargis applied to his career the determination he had developed during his academic struggle. His race left him with few options other than becoming an instructor at a black college, so he accepted a temporary job with Reichhold Chemical Company in Austin as a process engineer. There he developed a facility to manufacture lauroyl and benzoyl peroxides, which was in continual use until 1985. In 1961, he joined Ampex Corporation, a manufacturer of magnetic tape in Redwood City, California. In the course of his research for Ampex, he devised a binder system for which he received a patent. Audio Devices, Inc., a producer of magnetic tape in Stamford, Connecticut, lured him away in 1964. Hargis won that company's President's Award in 1970, the next year earned a master's in business administration from the University of Bridgeport in Connecticut, and by 1972 was the senior plant manager.

In 1973, Capitol Records, Inc., acquired Audio Devices. Capitol Records appointed him vice-president in charge of manufacturing for its large, multiplant operation in Stamford, which employed 599 people and earned $30 million annually.[32]

Hargis remained politically active throughout his life. In New Canaan, Connecticut, where he resided while working for Audio Devices and Capitol Records, he served on the board of directors for the United Fund and as president of the Interchurch Services Committee from 1972 to 1975. He was treasurer of the Democratic Town Committee in 1972 and was elected its chairman in 1976. Ironically, he became president of the New Canaan Chapter of the NAACP. As its candidate, he campaigned unsuccessfully for mayor and then, in December 1972, began a four-year term as the first black appointee to the New Canaan Board of Finance. In nearby Stamford, Hargis served as president of the West Side Development Corporation from 1973 to 1975 and as a director and trustee of Family and Children's Services from 1972 to 1975. He became a director for United Way in Stamford in 1976. He also served on the board of directors for the Carver Foundation in Norwalk and was a member of the American Institute of Chemical Engineers, the Society of Plastics Engineers, and the Engineering Foundation of the University of Texas at Austin. For his achievements, Hargis proudly reported to the Ex-Students' Association that he had been listed in *Community Leaders and Noteworthy Americans* and *Black Leaders in America* in 1974 and in *Who's Who in the East* in 1976, the same year that Alpha Phi Alpha at the University of Texas conferred upon him its Ed Brookes Award.[33]

Throughout most of his career, Hargis maintained little more than a perfunctory relationship with the University of Texas, but failing health brought him to Austin once more. He described his condition as "excellent" in an alumnus update submitted to the Ex-Students' Association in 1976. He appeared to be approaching the goals he had revealed in an application for a lifetime membership in 1972: to become the president of a major corporation, then to return to the University as an instructor in the College of Engineering or the College of Business. In 1976, however, at forty years of age, he suffered a major heart attack and learned that he had a heart ailment. His doctor advised a reduced workload, so he relocated to Capitol Records' headquarters in Los Angeles and assumed new duties as corporate director of administration. He soon immersed himself again in community affairs, serving on the board of directors of the Hollywood Chamber of Commerce from 1980 to 1982. After another heart attack and open-heart surgery, he retired from Capitol Records in 1982 and returned to Austin to rest.[34]

Although Hargis realized that he was in extremely poor health, he forsook retirement when he found that black involvement in the affairs of Austin and the University had not advanced as he expected. He became a charter member of the Austin Jazz Club, then joined the board of directors of KAZI, a community radio station in East Austin. His great-uncle Eugene W. Ramey, a renowned jazz bassist who had also retired to Austin, introduced Hargis to Linda Lewis, a KAZI board member who had attended the University but had earned her bachelor's degree in sociology from Southwest Texas State University. Hargis and Lewis discovered that they shared a common concern about the lack of interest in Austin and University matters among blacks. They believed that if the black community worked together, it could be instrumental in the final integration of both the community and the University. A vital first step would be to organize the cadre of black University alumni in Austin as well as in other areas of Texas.[35]

Against his doctor's wishes, Hargis became involved in University minority affairs, working with Suzan Armstrong-West, an assistant dean of students, and Tom Backus, the director of the Minorities in Engineering program. In the fall of 1985, Hargis became the first volunteer chairman of the Black Alumni Task Force of the Ex-Students' Association. There had been several previous attempts to organize black University alumni, but they had met with apathy. The task force was Hargis's proposal, which he successfully defended in a meeting with black alumni in Austin, and he was determined that it would succeed. He professed two objectives: to begin to heal the wounds of the University experience for blacks and to try to increase black participation in the University alumni network. He decided good initial objectives would be to enlist five hundred black alumni as regular members of the Ex-Students' Association and fifty more as lifetime members like himself. Tragically, these were not achieved until after his death in November 1986. He did see another of his recommendations reach fruition: Barbara Con-

rad, nee Smith, was chosen as a Distinguished Alumnus of the University of Texas, and a scholarship was founded in her honor.[36]

Recognizing Hargis's growing influence with black UT alumni, President William H. Cunningham in October 1986 appointed him special assistant for minority affairs. Hargis's elevated status formalized the advisory role on minority retention he played as chairman of the Black Alumni Task Force. When questioned by news reporters, he commented, "I'm still on cloud nine." His physical condition continued to decline, but he refused to surrender his post. He had been hospitalized in the fall of 1985, and again spent several days in the hospital during November 1986, but still came to work as often as he could. He was in his office on Wednesday, but failed to appear on Thursday, November 13, 1986. A concerned friend found him dead in his home that afternoon.[37]

The University of Texas honored Hargis with a memorial service on November 21, 1986. Friends and onlookers filled Bates Recital Hall in the Performing Arts Center as those who had known Hargis spoke. President Cunningham remembered, "He was committed to improving and strengthening a university that has made his path very difficult." Reuben R. McDaniel, the chairman of the Faculty Senate and a distinguished member of the faculty of the College of Business, declared, "We saw in John a rare hope that things would improve and things would get better for every black." The Innervisions of Blackness Choir led the audience in singing "We Shall Overcome," followed by "The Eyes of Texas." The fact that the performance of those songs together was "a real watershed" did not go unnoticed.[38]

A memorial service was not the greatest honor accorded Hargis by the University. The Student Senate adopted a resolution in honor of Hargis, which said in part, "It can be argued that John Hargis accomplished more for minority recruitment and retention than had been accomplished to date." On November 21, 1986, representatives of the University Students' Association and the National Society of Black Engineers requested that the new Chemical and Petroleum Engineering Building be named for Hargis. President Cunningham proposed instead that the renovated Admissions and Employment Center, the focus of the revitalized Little Campus, bear Hargis's name. The regents agreed with Cunningham, and on February 12,

1987, after waiving the rule that prohibited naming a building for someone until that person had been deceased at least five years, approved the naming of the Admissions and Employment Center as John W. Hargis Hall. As a compromise with the Black Student Alliance, which wanted the center named for Heman M. Sweatt, in whose honor an annual civil rights symposium had already been designated, the regents on August 13, 1987, redesignated the Little Campus as the Heman M. Sweatt Campus.[39]

Hargis always maintained that he felt most at home as a student and as an alumnus in the College of Engineering. In the spring of 1987, the college began administering the most fitting tribute to Hargis: the John W. Hargis Endowed Presidential Scholarship, established with the transfer of $25,000 in gift funds by the University president's office. Proceeds from this endowment were made available for black undergraduates enrolled in engineering. In addition, the Black Alumni Task Force launched a drive to establish its own scholarship in honor of Hargis: the John W. Hargis Ex-Students Scholarship, generated from an endowment, was made available to a black undergraduate in any academic discipline. These scholarships ensured that the University of Texas would continue to facilitate the entry of black undergraduates into the academic community, just as Hargis had done in his lifetime.[40]

NOTES

1. John W. Hargis, interview by Richard B. McCaslin, June 20, 1985 (copy of tape and transcript in the Dolph Briscoe Center for American History, University of Texas at Austin; cited hereafter as DBCAH); quotation from "Remarks by Edwin R. Sharpe at Memorial Service for John Willis Hargis, Bates Recital Hall, November 21, 1986" (typescript, President's Office Files, University of Texas at Austin). Hargis was not the first black student to receive an undergraduate degree from the University of Texas; Edna Humphries Rhambo transferred to the University from Huston-Tillotson College in September 1956, with Hargis's encouragement, and received a bachelor of science in education in August 1958. Racial designations were not included in student records in the 1950s, so it may be that other black undergraduates received degrees before Hargis. See the *Austin American-Statesman*, Aug. 20, 1987.

2. Michael L. Gillette, "Blacks Challenge the White University," *Southwestern Historical Quarterly* 86 (Oct. 1982): 327–330; Marilyn B. Davis, "Local Approach to the Sweatt Case," *Negro History Bulletin* 23 (Mar. 1960): 133–136; Teo Furtado, "Cracking the Door of Segregation," *Alcalde* 75 (May–June 1987), 16–19; Frank L. Wright, ed., "A Study of Desegre-

gation and Integration at the University of Texas" (Religious Worker's Association, 1963; typescript, DBCAH, I-1); Richard Kluger, *Simple Justice: The History of "Brown v. Board of Education" and Black America's Struggle for Equality* (New York: Knopf, 1976), 261; Michael L. Gillette, "Heman Marion Sweatt: Civil Rights Plaintiff," in *Black Leaders: Texans for Their Times*, ed. Alwyn Barr and Robert A. Calvert (Austin: Texas State Historical Association, 1981), 161, 165–167; Raymond Wolters, *The Burden of Brown: Thirty Years of School Desegregation* (Knoxville: Univ. of Tennessee Press, 1984), 71–72; *Sweatt v. Painter*, 339 U.S. 629 (1950). For more on the role of the NAACP in civil rights reform in Texas, see Michael L. Gillette, "The NAACP in Texas, 1937–1957" (PhD diss., University of Texas at Austin, 1984).

3. Mark V. Tushnet, *The NAACP's Legal Strategy against Segregated Education, 1925–1950* (Chapel Hill: Univ. of North Carolina Press, 1987), 125–135; Joe B. Frantz, *The Forty-Acre Follies* (Austin: Texas Monthly Press, 1983), 202–203; Wolters, *Burden of Brown*, 71–72; Kluger, *Simple Justice*, 274–275 (quotation); *Sweatt v. Painter*.

4. Frantz, *Forty-Acre Follies*, 204–205; Gillette, "Blacks Challenge the White University," 342; Davis, "Local Approach to the Sweatt Case," 137; Wright, "Desegregation and Integration," I-2, IV-2; Kenneth B. Clark, *Desegregation: An Appraisal of the Evidence* (New York: Association Press, 1953), 32.

5. Benjamin Muse, *Ten Years of Prelude: The Story of Integration since the Supreme Court's 1954 Decision* (New York: Viking, 1964), 4, 24–25; *New York Times*, Mar. 22 and May 18, 1954 (2nd quotation); *Brown v. Board of Education of Topeka*, 347 U.S. 483, 495 (1954) (1st quotation).

6. Henry Y. McCown to Marion G. Ford, Jr., July 23, 1954 (quotation); W. Byron Shipp to Logan Wilson, Aug. 25, 1954 (both in General Files, "Negroes in Colleges, 1939–1952," University of Texas President's Office Records, DBCAH; cited hereafter as UTPOR).

7. Tom Sealy to Leroy Jeffers, Aug. 28, 1954 (1st quotation; General Files, "Negroes in Colleges, 1939–1952," UTPOR); *New York Times*, June 15, Aug. 29, and Sept. 19, 1954, Jan. 19, 1955; Muse, *Ten Years of Prelude*, 24 (2nd quotation).

8. Jeffers to Sealy, Aug. 25, 1954 (General Files, "Negroes in Colleges, 1939–1952," UTPOR); F. C. McConnell to Ford, Sept. 3, 1954; Peggy Rowland to Wilson, Sept. 6, 1954 (telegram); Wilson to Rowland, Sept. 10, 1954 (quotations) (all three in General Files, "Negroes in Colleges, 1952-," UTPOR); Davis, "Local Approach to the Sweatt Case," 134; *Austin American*, Sept. 10, 1954; *Daily Texan*, Aug. 24, Sept. 15, and Sept. 23, 1954; Hargis interview.

9. Willie Morris, *North toward Home* (Boston: Houghton Mifflin, 1967), 167–168, 169 (quotation), 170, 186–192; "How to Be First Class," *Time*, Jan. 27, 1958, 72; Gillette, "Blacks Challenge the White University," 322–323.

10. J. W. Edgar to "All Superintendents of Schools," May 24, 1954; McCown to Wilson, May 26, 1954 (quotation) (both in General Files, "Negroes," University of Texas Chancellor's Office Records, DBCAH; cited hereafter as UTCOR); Wilson to McCown, Aug. 31, 1954 (General Files, "Negroes in Colleges, 1952-," UTPOR).

11. H. M. Ratliff to Wilson, Sept. 22, 1954; Wilson to Ratliff, Sept. 25, 1954 (quotation) (both in General Files, "Ne-

groes in Colleges, 1952–," UTPOR); Sealy to Board of Regents, Sept. 2, 1954 (General Files, "Negroes in Colleges, 1939–1952," UTPOR).

12. Shipp to Wilson, Aug. 25, 1954 (General Files, "Negroes in Colleges, 1939–1952," UTPOR); Wilson to McCown, Aug. 31, 1954 (quotation); McCown to John W. Hargis, Sept. 7, 1954 (both in General Files, "Desegregation," UTCOR); *Daily Texan*, Sept. 26, 1954; Hargis interview.

13. Scott Gaines to Wilson, Sept. 24, 1954 (General Files, "Negroes in Colleges, 1939–1952," UTPOR); Don Shoemaker and Patrick E. McCauley, *A Statistical Summary, State-by-State, of Segregation-Desegregation Activity Affecting Southern Schools from 1954 to Present, Together with Pertinent Data on Enrollment, Teacher Pay, Etc.* (Nashville: Southern Educational Reporting Service, 1957), 25; *New York Times*, Sept. 4, 1954; *Austin American*, Sept. 10, 1954; *Daily Texan*, Sept. 15, Sept. 21, and Sept. 26, 1954; Wright, "Desegregation and Integration," III-5; *Cactus 1983, Commemorating the University of Texas Centennial* (Austin: Texas Student Publications, University of Texas at Austin, 1983), 61; "Record of Understanding with President Clement French, of Washington State College Concerning the Football Game Scheduled at The University of Texas between That Institution and This One on October 2, 1954, in Austin" (General Files, "Desegregation," UTCOR).

14. Edward A. Jones, "Morehouse College in Business Ninety Years—Building Men," *Phylon Quarterly* 18 (Oct. 1957): 231, 235; Stephen B. Oates, *Let the Trumpet Sound: The Life of Martin Luther King, Jr.* (New York: Harper and Row, 1982), 16–20; "Biographical Information on 'V.I.P.' Texas Exes: John W. Hargis" (typescript, Ex-Students' Association Office Files, Nov. 4, 1973, University of Texas at Austin). In his interview with the author on June 20, 1985, Hargis recalled with some amusement that as a youth he thought segregation "was based on religion rather than race" because most of the white and Mexican children attended Catholic schools, and he and other blacks, most of whom were Protestant, went to public schools. A lifelong Methodist, he claimed that he briefly considered converting to Catholicism so he could go to school with his friends of other races.

15. *Daily Texan*, Sept. 16 and Sept. 23, 1954; McCown to Hargis, Oct. 11, 1954 (General Files, "Desegregation," UTCOR); Hargis interview; Norcell D. Haywood, conversation with the author, Apr. 9, 1987.

16. Muse, *Ten Years of Prelude*, 25–26; *New York Times*, Nov. 23 and Nov. 28, 1954, Apr. 14 (1st quotation), June 1, and June 14, 1955; *Daily Texan*, Sept. 22, 1954; *Brown v. Board of Education of Topeka et al.*, 349 U.S. 294, 300 (1955) (2nd quotation).

17. Muse, *Ten Years of Prelude*, 77–78, 87–88, 209; *New York Times*, Oct. 10, 1954, June 26 and Oct. 13, 1955; *Cactus 1983*, 69; Henry Allen Bullock, *A History of Negro Education in the South from 1619 to the Present* (Cambridge, Mass.: Harvard Univ. Press, 1967), 263; Guadalupe San Miguel, Jr., "The Struggle against Separate and Unequal Schools: Middle Class Mexican Americans and the Desegregation Campaign in Texas, 1929–1957," *History of Education Quarterly* 23 (Fall, 1983): 343–359; Arthur D. Morse, "When Negroes Entered a Texas School," *Harper's*, Sept., 1954, 47–49; Clark, De-

segregation, 17, 32; Harry K. Wright, *Civil Rights U.S.A.: Public Schools, Southern States, 1963, Texas* (Washington, D.C.: Government Printing Office, 1963), 4.

18. *Daily Texan*, July 8 and July 12, 1955; *Dallas News*, July 9, 1955; *New York Times*, July 24, 1955; McCown to Wilson, July 6, 1955 (General Files, "Desegregation," UTCOR).

19. Shipp to McCown, May 6, 1955; McCown to C. Paul Boner, May 9, 1955 (both in General Files, "Desegregation," UTCOR); "Degree Check: John Willis Hargis," Jan. 31, 1959 (Dean's Office for Student Affairs Files, School of Engineering, University of Texas at Austin, DBCAH); Hargis interview; Haywood, conversation with the author; Teo Furtado, "Movement and Resistance: Forces of Change Sweep the University," *Alcalde* 75 (May–June, 1987), 20; Wright, *Civil Rights U.S.A.*, 3–4; *Southern School News*, July 6, 1955, 12, and Aug. 1955, 2.

20. For a synopsis of the impact of litigation on the black plaintiffs, see Reed Sarratt, *The Ordeal of Desegregation: The First Decade* (New York: Harper and Row, 1966), 126–127. In his interview with the author on June 20, 1985, John W. Hargis recounted not only his decision to enter the University of Texas and his confrontation with Wilson, but also a serio-comic sequel. In 1985, the two found themselves sitting next to each other at a commencement exercise. They spoke afterward about their first encounter, including their argument over the credit for physics. Hargis laughed while recalling how Wilson told him that he knew nothing about physics and had tried to tell him that thirty years earlier, but he was so intent upon being admitted that he would not listen.

21. McCown to Wilson, July 6, 1955 (General Files, "Desegregation," UTCOR); Hargis interview; Haywood, conversation with the author.

22. Shoemaker and McCauley, *Segregation-Desegregation Activity*, 24–25; Muse, *Ten Years of Prelude*, 63–64, 85, 146, 153–156, 275; Wright, *Civil Rights U.S.A.*, 13, 14, 16; "World Documents: Southern Declaration on Integration," *Current History* 31 (Aug. 1956): 116–118.

23. Wright, *Civil Rights U.S.A.*, 7–10; Sarratt, *Ordeal of Desegregation*, 158–159; Wallace Westfeldt, "Communities in Strife," in Southern Education Reporting Service; *With All Deliberate Speed: Segregation-Desegregation in Southern Schools*, ed. Don Shoemaker (New York: Harper, 1957), 44–47; Muse, *Ten Years of Prelude*, 87–89; *New York Times*, June 4, 1954, Nov. 27, 1955, Sept. 7, Sept. 8, Sept. 28, Oct. 3, and Oct. 5, 1956; *Southern School News*, Sept. 1956, 12, Oct. 1956, 94, and Nov. 1956, 8.

24. "A Plan for Selected Enrollment in a State University," address by McCown to the Southern Association of Colleges and Secondary Schools, Miami, Florida, Nov. 30, 1955 (2nd and 3rd quotations) (typescript, General Files, "Admissions," UTCOR); Herschel T. Manuel to Wilson, Dec. 16, 1955; Wilson to Boner, Dec. 9, 1955 (4th quotation); Sealy to Fred W. Moore, Aug. 16, 1956; F. Lanier Cox to Mrs. H. E. Brown, Feb. 27, 1956 (1st quotation) (all four in General Files, "Desegregation," UTCOR); McCown to Boner, Jan. 4, 1957 (General Files, "Admission and Degree Policies," UTCOR); *Dallas News*, July 9, 1955; *Southern School News*, Nov. 1956, 6.

25. Frantz, *Forty-Acre Follies*, 206, 208–209; Almetris Marsh Duren, with Louise Iscoe, *Overcoming: A History of Black Integration at the University of Texas at Austin* (Austin:

Univ. of Texas at Austin, 1979), 5–7; Wright, "Desegregation and Integration," I-2, I-6, IV-3, IV-4; *New York Times*, Mar. 10, Sept. 15, and Sept. 19, 1956; Hargis interview; Wayne H. Holtzman, "Attitudes of College Men toward Non-Segregation in Texas Schools," *Public Opinion Quarterly* 20 (Fall 1956): 565–568; Robert K. Young, William M. Benson, and Wayne H. Holtzman, "Change in Attitude toward the Negro in a Southern University," *Journal of Abnormal and Social Psychology* 60 (Jan. 1960): 132; Shipp to McCown, Mar. 20, 1957 (General Files, "Desegregation," UTCOR); *Southern School News*, Nov. 1955, 6, July 1956, 7, and Oct. 1956, 14.

26. Frantz, *Forty-Acre Follies*, 206–208; Duren, *Overcoming*, 5–6; *New York Times*, Mar. 10, 1956; *Daily Texan*, May 8, 1957; "The Eyes of Texas," *Time*, May 20, 1957, 50.

27. Holtzman, "Attitudes of College Men," 559–569; James G. Kelley, Jean E. Ferson, and Wayne H. Holtzman, "The Measurement of Attitudes toward the Negro in the South," *Journal of Social Psychology* 48 (Nov. 1958): 305–317; Young, Benson, and Holtzman, "Change in Attitude," 131 (quotation), 132–133; Hargis interview.

28. *Cactus 1983*, 547; W. Charles Akins, conversation with the author, Feb. 25, 1987; Hargis interview; Haywood, conversation with the author; "'V.I.P.' Texas Exes: John W. Hargis"; Wright, "Desegregation and Integration," III-7, III-14; Linda Lewis, conversation with the author, Feb. 25, 1987; Jack Holland to McCown, June 26, 1958 (1st and 2nd quotations) (General Files, "Desegregation," UTCOR).

29. *Cactus 1956* (Austin: Texas Student Publications, University of Texas at Austin, 1956), 458; *Cactus 1958* (Austin: Texas Student Publications, University of Texas at Austin, 1958), 456, 497; *Cactus 1959* (Austin: Texas Student Publications, University of Texas at Austin, 1959), 323, 359; Holtzman, "Attitudes of College Men," 565–568; "Degree Check: John Willis Hargis"; Hargis interview.

30. Hargis to R. B. M., June 20, 1985, interview; Lewis to R. B. M., Feb. 25, 1987, conversation; "Degree Check: John Willis Hargis"; *Daily Texan*, Nov. 24, 1986; Shipp to McCown, Mar. 20, 1957, General Files, "Desegregation" (UTCOR).

31. *Daily Texan*, Jan. 13, Jan. 17, and Feb. 3, 1959; *Austin American*, Jan. 27, 1959.

32. "'V.I.P.' Texas Exes: John W. Hargis"; Hargis interview; "Curriculum Vita: John W. Hargis," 1976 (typescript, Ex-Students' Association Office Files, University of Texas at Austin); *Who's Who in the East*, 15th ed. (Chicago: Marquis Who's Who, 1975), 304; *Austin American-Statesman*, Nov. 14, 1986.

33. *Austin American-Statesman*, Dec. 31, 1972; *Who's Who in the East*, 304; "Curriculum Vita: John W. Hargis"; Hargis interview; Suzan Armstrong-West, conversation with the author, Jan. 23, 1987.

34. "'V.I.P.' Texas Exes: John W. Hargis"; William H. Cunningham to Jess Hay, Jan. 22, 1987 (President's Office Files, University of Texas at Austin); Armstrong-West, conversation with the author; Hargis interview.

35. *Who's Who in the East*, 304; *Austin American-Statesman*, Sept. 27, 1979, Dec. 9, 1984, Dec. 10, 1984, and Nov. 14, 1986; Doug Ramsey, "Bass Hit," *Texas Monthly*, May 1981, 176–187; "First Black Undergraduate at the University Dies," *Alcalde* 75 (Jan.–Feb. 1987), 46; Armstrong-West, conversation with the author; Lewis, conversation with the author; Hargis interview.

36. Lewis, conversation with the author; Haywood, conversation with the author; Hargis interview. After Hargis's death, Linda Lewis succeeded him as chair of the Black Alumni Task Force.

37. *Austin American-Statesman*, Oct. 29 (quotation) and Nov. 14, 1986; "Deaths: John W. Hargis," *On Campus* 14 (Nov. 24–30, 1986), 2; Armstrong-West, conversation with the author.

38. "A Memorial Service for John Willis Hargis 1935–1986" (Vertical File: John W. Hargis, DBCAH); *Daily Texan*, Nov. 21 and Nov. 24, 1986 (1st and 2nd quotations). Hargis's funeral was held November 17 at Wesley United Methodist Church in Austin. Among the pallbearers was Norcell D. Haywood, who was turned away with Hargis from the University of Texas in 1954, shared a dormitory room with him at Prairie View, and returned after him to graduate from the University. "A Service of Praise and Thanksgiving for John W. Hargis" (Vertical File: John W. Hargis, DBCAH).

39. "Senate Resolution No. ——, Introduced by Senators Foley and Hilliard, Fifth Student Senate, Third Session, Fall 1986" (quotation) (photocopy in author's collection); Armstrong-West, conversation with the author; Craig B. Cassel and Adam Reed to Earnest F. Gloyna, Nov. 21, 1986 (photocopy in author's collection); Cunningham to Hay, Jan. 22, 1987 (President's Office Files, University of Texas at Austin); "Regents Rename Historic Building," *On Campus* 14 (Feb. 23–Mar. 1, 1987), 1; *Daily Texan*, Aug. 25, 1987.

40. "University of Texas System News Release," Feb. 12–13, 1987 (photocopy in author's collection); Cunningham to James P. Duncan, Dec. 18, 1986 (President's Office Files, University of Texas at Austin); Lewis, conversation with the author; *Daily Texan*, Nov. 24, 1986.

PETER
LASALLE } **A Desk for Borges**

Reality is not always probable—or likely.
JORGE LUIS BORGES

Some years ago, when I was living and teaching in Paris on an academic exchange, I went to a dinner party. No sooner was I handed an aperitif by the host and encouraged to help myself to the decidedly complicated hors d'oeuvres, than I was introduced to one French writer there as being somebody who was a faculty member at the University of Texas—he was *extremely* impressed. Yes, he said that he did know about the institution, and he seemed to admire the very idea of the University of Texas simply because, to paraphrase his French: "Of course, that's where Borges once taught."

His response has always stuck with me. And it might be as good a place as any to start on the story of the wonderful association with UT of the Argentinian literary giant Jorge Luis Borges, who did teach regular classes at the University as a visiting professor for a semester in 1961–1962 and whose innovative short stories—metaphysical in intent, bravely challenging common assumptions about time and space, reality and unreality, even what literature itself is—probably changed the look of serious fiction forever.

That response from the French writer has also led me to thinking about something else. It has to do with the label (buzzword?) that lately

Peter LaSalle worked as a journalist after graduating from Harvard and came to the University of Texas at Austin in 1980, where he is currently the Susan Taylor McDaniel Regents Professor in Creative Writing. His books include the novels Strange Sunlight *(1984) and* Mariposa's Song *(2012), and three short story collections:* The Graves of Famous Writers *(1980),* Hockey Sur Glace *(1996), and* Tell Borges If You See Him: Tales of Contemporary Somnambulism *(2007). In 2005, he received the Award for Distinguished Prose from the* Antioch Review *in recognition of his work in the short story genre. Some material in this essay originally appeared in "Borges and Batts Hall," a book review in the January 7, 2005, issue of the* Texas Observer.

Visiting professor Jorge Luis Borges in his office at the University of Texas, 1961. *From the Prints and Photographs Collection—Jorge Luis Borges, Dolph Briscoe Center for American History, University of Texas at Austin. (DI 06850)*

gets tossed around quite often on the Forty Acres, with the whole business of the school announcing itself on many fronts—sometimes maybe too loudly in its understandable high spirits—as "world class"; it's a consideration I'll get to in a bit here, and somewhat grumblingly, too, to forewarn you.

But first for some of the facts in an amazing twentieth-century life, that of Jorge Luis Borges.

Born in 1899 into a historically prominent family, with an ancestry that included nineteenth-century Argentinian military commanders on both sides, Borges grew up thoroughly bilingual in Buenos Aires; his grandmother was British, and his father, a sometime attorney, was a great admirer of England's literature. English was so much a part of his early life that Borges later liked to note that as a boy he had

first read some of the classics of Spanish literature in the English translations he found in his father's extensive library. The family moved to Europe for several years, where Borges attended Swiss schools and later became involved in avant-garde poetry circles in Spain while still in his teens. He returned with the family to Argentina and took up with like-minded young poets who were bent on shaking things up in what they saw as the stuffy Buenos Aires literary scene, publishing broadsides and refusing to docilely accept the beliefs of established luminaries.

Tall, as good looking as a tango crooner, he was shy by nature and also had the habit of falling head-over-heels for rich Buenos Aires socialites. They saw him as a good companion for talk about books, though when it came to marriage they inevitably opted for more well-to-do prospects. Actually, it was while he was hurrying to meet a young woman for a date that he bounded up the stairs to her apartment and struck his head on an open steel window frame, suffering a gash that became badly infected; there was an operation and long hospitalization, complete with feverish delirium. Upon recovery, he was fearful that he had lost some of his faculties, and to challenge himself and test his mind, he tried writing what would be something new for him, a short story rather than a poem. The result was "Pierre Menard, Author of the *Quixote*." In the story, a dabbling contemporary writer in Nîmes, France, sets out to do more than just rewrite the Cervantes masterpiece: he wants to create it word for word exactly and as the product of his own imagination—which he does, showing how any great book maybe taps into a universal creative consciousness and has an existence of its own, independent of even the author. Borges said the story was a breakthrough for him, and in a subsequent burst of creativity that lasted a decade or so, he wrote a couple dozen more short stories equally as challenging. "Death and the Compass" takes its erudite detective protagonist on a quest to solve the murder of a renowned Kabala scholar, with the sleuth's discovery that the solution apparently lies in understanding a timeless parallel dimension. "The Library of Babel" is about a strange and limitless library of hexagonal towers where one text only leads to another, and that to another, and so on, vertiginously, for what observers today see as a prophesying of the whole seemingly unbounded universe of information that we currently call the Computer Age. The tonguetwistingly titled "Tlön, Uqbar, Orbis Tertius" tells of a secret cult that succeeds in establishing that an invented world is a real one because articles describing that land in detail—right down to an analysis of its odd language that contains no nouns—exist in a very real encyclopedia.

This was fiction that in form and content ventured well beyond not only traditional realism, which suddenly looked as passé as a backfiring Model T, but also the writing of daringly experimental practitioners such as James Joyce and Virginia Woolf, both of whom Borges admired and translated; with Borges now using the short story to examine in depth a whole host of intriguing matters (the meaning of philosophical paradox, the implications of mathematical infinity, etc.), narrative progressed in a single high-flying leap from the still emotional tenor of modernism to the probingly intellectual one of postmodernism. The first stories were gathered together in what would prove to be the seminal volume *Fictions* in 1944, with the collection *The Aleph* following in 1949.

During those years, Borges lived modestly, bordering on monkishly, with his widowed mother in a Buenos Aires apartment. His eyesight had begun to fail him in midlife, a situation that gradually worsened and led to all-but-total blindness. He earned a living as an assistant at a branch library in a bleak end of the city. Putting his innate shyness aside, he took political stands and became a vocal opponent of Colonel Juan Domingo Perón (Borges's elderly mother and adult sister were once arrested for demonstrating against the thuggish dictator and his locally idolized wife, the former radio actress Evita Perón); he resigned from the library assistant's job when some Peronista flunkies—for a cruel joke, the way Borges saw it—tried to reassign him to another governmental position, as chief inspector of poultry and rabbits in the city's Calle Córdoba public marketplace. However, in a fitting and dramatic reversal of fortune once Perón was at last ousted in 1955, Borges was made director of Argentina's prestigious National Library, the equivalent of the U.S. Library of Congress. He held the post for almost twenty years.

Eventually, his writing would be translated and then loudly celebrated abroad. The very first to do so, as is often the case, were the spookily insightful French, who, it should be remembered, also rescued both Poe and Faulkner from impending oblivion. Borges was the spiritual godfather for the whole 1960s and '70s generation of dazzling young American experimenters in fiction—Donald Barthelme, John Barth, Robert Coover, and William Gass all acknowledged his strong influence. In fact, Borges soon became an icon for the new and culturally hip in general, and amidst the blaring rock music and confusing group sex in the 1970 Mick Jagger movie *Performance*, the star is shown in one scene stretched out in a bubbly bathtub in a London flat and studiously reading a volume of, naturally, Borges. Though his most significant writing was finished before he was fifty, the last couple of decades of Borges's long life proved to be a continual international tribute to the man and his achievement—Borges jetting all over the world, the honorary degrees and orders of merit from various governments piling up.

In 1986 he died in Switzerland. He was traveling with his longtime companion-secretary, María Kodama, whom he married several weeks before his death; she was thirty-nine and he going on eighty-seven. He's buried in Geneva, which Kodama held was his own strong wish, contending he didn't want his remains returned to his native land. Apparently, Borges was convinced Argentina had been ruined under the vicious military rule of the 1970s and 1980s, despite the fact that he himself—known for a stubborn conservative streak toward the end, once even dedicating a translation of Walt Whitman to Richard Nixon!—had publicly supported, in the name of political stability, those same generals and admirals when they first took over. His stand on that came to trouble him terribly as he gradually learned of their clandestine bloody tactics, and it's usually thought that his backing them most likely kept him from being awarded the Nobel Prize in Literature.

While Borges's time in Austin does receive some mention in the three full-length biographies of him available in English, the best and surely most heartfelt document regarding Borges and UT is a several-page memoir written by a professor in the Spanish Department in the 1960s, Miguel Enguidanos; it serves as the introduction to Borges's book *Dreamtigers*, and I'll borrow from it extensively here. Also, realizing that there are those on campus today who, without question, know a whole lot more about Borges's stay than I do and who even had firsthand experiences with the man, I'll nevertheless try my best to convey what I've learned through reading around some on my own and informally talking to people knowledgeable of Borges's visit.

Under the auspices of a Tinker Visiting Professorship in Spanish, which still operates with a mandate to bring Latin American writers to UT, Borges arrived in Austin in September 1961 and, according to the schedule of the old semester calendar, was in residence right through January 1962. His mother accompanied him, and he taught two courses in Batts Hall; one was an overview of his homeland's poetry and the other a seminar on Leopoldo Lugones, a leading Argentinian modernist. During the semester, he also delivered several open lectures on other major Argentinian writers and Walt Whitman.

Actually, placing this moment in the context of his career becomes significant, because at that time the full, loud worldwide acclaim for Borges described above was yet to come, granting he was past sixty years old. I think that it stands as a testament to the caliber of the UT Spanish Department of 1961 that by inviting him, the powers that be within the department exhibited respect for his work comparatively early and therefore had the admirable prescience to realize just how important that work would soon prove. As said, the French had given him his earliest recognition beyond Argentina, with some translations into their language in the 1950s, and shortly before coming to UT he had been named the cowinner, along with Irish writer Samuel Beckett, of a new, but not very well known, achievement award backed by publishers from several countries. However, UT was the first U.S. institution to seek him out and bring him to a campus. In fact, though he did later have academic residencies elsewhere in the United States—lecturing at Harvard, Indiana University, and Michigan State (the Harvard and Indiana appointments entailed public talks, and the Michigan State teaching position was rather brief and interrupted by considerable travel)—UT was the only American university where he actually taught scheduled classes as a faculty member for an entire regular semester, which turned out to be that significant note in Borges's curriculum vitae that the writer at the dinner party in Paris remarked to me about.

Professor Enguidanos describes well the excitement that surrounded Borges's visit. It began almost as soon as his plane touched down in Austin after a rare and metaphorically quite apt hurricane had blown in from the Gulf Coast, delaying his arrival. Enguidanos writes: "To evoke the impression he made in the many hours he lived among us is not easy. Within a week there was talk about Borges, with Borges, because of Borges, and for Borges, in every corridor of Batts Hall. Scholars felt obliged to write studies and theses on Borges's work. Poets—wasn't it inevitable?—fired dithyrambic salvos at him." People still remember his classes to this day. Quite pleased himself to be here, his very first time in the States, and fully appreciative of the attention he was being given, he showed that the enthusiasm was a two-way street, as an ever-smiling Borges immersed himself in academic duties as well as what he considered the stimulating intellectual environment overall of the comparatively small but vibrant campus town of the period. Back in Argentina Borges had recently embarked on a project to learn the Old Norse of the great Icelandic sagas, organizing a group of Buenos Aires university students to study it with him; in the person of Rudolph Willard, a professor of Old and Middle English in the UT English Department, Borges found somebody who shared his interest, resulting in extended afternoon discussions on the subject in Willard's office. Before long Professor Willard became a good friend. Thomas Whitbread, still a very active member of the English Department today, tells of attending an evening get-together with other faculty members and Borges. Upon discovering that Whitbread's field was contemporary American poetry, Borges, the inquisitive lifelong student, wanted only to hear of everything that Whitbread could tell him of Robert Frost now that he, Borges, had cornered somebody who might be an expert on the American poet who intrigued him so.

In more casual moments, Borges met with friends and students to discuss literature in the old all-night Nighthawk diner on the Drag. His mother was an elegant, albeit occasionally snooty, matron who when in Argentina never failed to remind people of her son's hallowed lineage, but she appeared to tone down her haughtiness somewhat once she was in the United States, often accompanying Borges (whom she always called "Georgie," using the English diminutive) to social gatherings; avid moviegoers, the pair of them sat through multiple screenings of Hitchcock's *Psycho* at the Varsity Theater—Borges sight was nearly gone at this point, though he was still capable of distinguishing shapes and limited color if he took a seat up front. When he did express some homesickness for Buenos Aires, colleagues would drive him to Town Lake, where he enjoyed sitting and relaxing for a while and where the water's muddy aroma reminded him of the wide, majestic, and decidedly muddy Río de la Plata in his native city. All reports speak of him of being an unassuming, good-natured man, ever the bachelor librarian at heart whose whole life was basically and nobly that of books.

One of the most amusing anecdotes about his visit involved Borges's desire to go to San Antonio, where he would visit the Alamo and give a newspaper interview. He loved the writing of the fin de siècle British aesthete Oscar Wilde, and he had read that Wilde himself had once spent time in San Antonio during a lecture tour in America. Borges asked those in the Spanish Department whether they might be able to find out where Wilde had stayed, because he would like to stay there, too. They assured Borges that it must have been at what had always been the indisputable landmark hotel in the city, the Menger. A secretary from the department called the hotel ahead of time, to ask, "Do you know if the Menger is where Oscar Wilde stayed in San Antonio?" only to be told by the desk clerk, possessor of a strong Texas twang, that he couldn't be certain, but he would get back to her. Which he did the next day, informing her, Texas twang as strong as ever, "I went through the register book for the whole past year, ma'am, and no fella by that name has been here—I'm sure of it."

Borges got a kick out of that, and he did stay at the Menger, even if he never had actual confirmation of the Wilde residency.

In his busy schedule, another trip was organized out to the South Plains and Texas Tech in Lubbock to give a lecture, and the editors of the *Texas Quarterly*—an elegantly packaged literary journal with a solid national reputation that was once published at UT and later unceremoniously disposed of by the University administration in the early 1980s—put together an issue featuring his work in translation, plus verse about him by British poet Christopher Middleton of the UT German Department. The head of the University of Texas Press at the time, Frank Wardlaw, upon the urgings of those in the Spanish Department, apparently set out on a mission to approach Borges and ask about the possibility of acquiring translation rights to any of the Borges books in

Cover of *Dreamtigers*, by Jorge Luis Borges. The book was published by the University of Texas Press in 1964. *Courtesy of the University of Texas Press.*

Spanish for the then relatively new Texas Pan American Series, devoted to important modern literature from Latin America in translation. Borges agreed to have the Press bring out in the United States in 1964 a collection of poetry and short prose pieces, *Dreamtigers* (titled *El Hacedor* in the original 1960 Spanish edition). Jointly translated by Mildred Boyer, a UT Spanish professor, and the poet Harold Morland, the slim volume remains one of the most important Borges books in English today; in its pages can be found the cryptic, and iconically Borgesian, little narrative called "Borges and I" on the idea of any author as not himself or herself but a ghostly Other—the piece has emerged for some contemporary scholars, it seems, as far more than a mere text to be analyzed and become nothing short of an indispensable pronouncement in the canon of literary theory. *Dreamtigers* has gone through close to a dozen printings and is still offered by the Press in a paperback edition with a distinctive cover that uses an original woodcut by the noted Uruguayan artist Antonio Frasconi, reproduced in bold black and russet on white and showing a wild-eyed tiger prowling through shafts of skewed, daggerlike jungle grass—expressionistically intense, the image is very appropriately the stuff of strange night-imaginings indeed. Mortimer J. Adler, the founder and guru of the Great Books Foundation, once pronounced *Dreamtigers* a "masterpiece" of the twentieth century, and Borges himself would comment on how it held a special place in his own heart, calling it his "most personal" volume of work. I myself suspect that it would be tough to name a more significant title ever published by the Press.

To return to Professor Eguidanos's account, the introduction to *Dreamtigers*, here's a passage that gives a moving concluding assessment of what Borges's visit meant to the University, as it sums up the rare effect he had on those with whom he came in contact:

> But how can I express the accents of a voice grave and sweet, the flights of an extraordinary intelligence and imagination, the candor of a good and innocent soul, the quiet ache of a darkness and a loneliness we sensed, the magic of the poet who makes dreams come to life?
>
> Many times I guided his uncertain steps through halls and down stairways, over the rough places of the island that is this out-of-the-way university. His poor sight allowed his friends the paradoxical task—misfortunate fortune—of guiding the best *seer* among modern writers in the Spanish language. To walk beside Borges, the great peripatetic conversationalist, was to enter and live in his world. The guide soon discovered, by the light that matters, that he himself was the blind one, and not the poet leaning on his arm.

That's really lovely, isn't it?

Borges never forgot his experience at UT either. The two-way street that characterized the relationship certainly didn't end when he flew back to Argentina.

He later visited many campuses in the United States to deliver lectures and attend symposiums on his writing, yet he frequently assured people that Austin remained his favorite spot in all of America, and he returned to UT for briefer visits in 1967, 1976, and 1982. On each trip, he spoke to packed audiences, and during one stay he was taken on a freewheeling picnic with some Spanish Department grad students, a lot of fun for all concerned. (I was recently told about that by one of those students in attendance, now middle-aged and a professor of Spanish literature herself in San Antonio, as excited today about the afternoon spent with Borges as when it happened.)

Sometimes there seemed to be no bounds to Borges's affection. He's said to have on one occasion told an interviewer that he found Austin to be the most beautiful city in America. The interviewer did respectfully challenge him on that, reminding him that he was nearly completely blind at that stage, so how, in fact, could he pass judgment on the city being beautiful? To which Borges, his grin wide, reportedly provided an answer fitting of an author who was the acknowledged master of metaphysical literature, somebody ever suspicious of the very concept of dominant reality: "I find it so beautiful because I *dream* well there." When the novelist Paul Theroux traveled entirely by rail from his home in Boston to Argentina specifically to interview Borges in 1978— a long, adventurous journey described in Theroux's best-selling nonfiction account *The Old Patagonia Express*—Borges asked Theroux, almost before the American writer could get through the door to Borges's book-clogged apartment in central Buenos Aires, whether he had stopped in Austin on his trip. Theroux said no, and Borges chided him for having missed it and emphasized the intellectual importance of the place, an offbeat exchange wittily related by Theroux in his book.

Homage to his Texas experience turns up several times in Borges's work as well. In the hefty, posthumously published *Selected Poems* (1998), the editor assembled the book so that the very last poem, a place of honor, is given to "The Web," where an aging Borges speculates on which of the several cities in the world that he has appreciated in life ("my cities," as he refers to them) he might one day die in: "Austin, Texas, where my mother and I / In the autumn of '61 discovered America?"; in another poem, "Elegy," he looks back on his past and mentions having been "part of" Texas. And there's, of course, his beautiful sonnet on the state, "Texas," where he finds haunting geographic, historical, and even mythic paral-

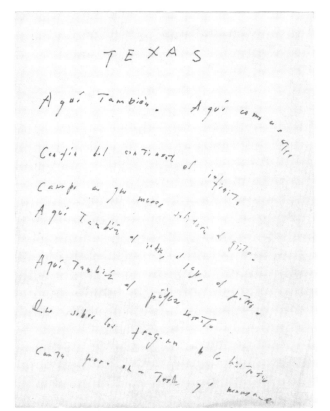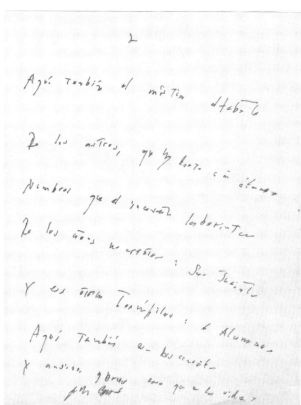

Copy of "Texas" by Jorge Luis Borges, handwritten by the author in New York in 1967 at the request of Edward L. Tinker, who later gave it to the Humanities Research Center at the University of Texas. *Copyright © 1967 María Kodama, reprinted by permission of The Wylie Agency LLC.*

lels between it and his Argentina. Often anthologized, "Texas" has been translated into English by a number of poets—and also wannabe poets, unfortunately, of the ilk who proceed with but an elementary knowledge of the other language and dictionary firmly in hand—yet nobody has ever come close to the sonorous and darkly lyrical version done by the Pulitzer Prize–winning contemporary poet Mark Strand (as a note, Strand's translation was once reproduced on a handsome little commemorative card printed by the HRC, more or less a collector's item). Borges even set an entire short story about some academic intrigue, "The Bribe," on the UT campus, with it taking place in a faculty office in Parlin Hall, home of the English Department; the main character—a venerable scholar of old New England stock—appears to have been based on Borges's good friend who discussed Norse with him, Professor Willard.

And maybe I can insert here yet another anecdote concerning Borges and UT, this one my own. It does

figure in, and it might also serve as a good way to loop my way back, at long last, to what I started this off with—how the whole idea of Borges and UT has gotten me to thinking about what does make for a truly world-class university.

It happened just a few years ago in the creative writing course that I teach every spring, E 355K: Advanced Creative Writing. It's the final course in the sequence of undergraduate creative writing offerings, and I can honestly say it's my absolutely favorite class to teach, graduate courses included, one I always intently look forward to. E 355K tends to attract some of the very best young literary talent on campus, and the students who enroll in it are inevitably, well, outright terrific.

Because E 355K is different from other creative writing courses, in that it accommodates both aspiring fiction writers and poets, I assigned as a spring-break reading project that year Borges's *Dreamtigers*. With its first half devoted to short prose pieces and its second to poems, *Dreamtigers* is one of those rare literary documents that demonstrates how a truly gifted writer can excel in both genres, which often seem quite dissimilar, even at odds, and how each genre can, in fact, feed the other in the overall creative process. (Besides the short stories he's best known for, Borges produced an impressively large body of poetry, much of it evoking the unique atmosphere of what can become his airy, dreamlike Buenos Aires; especially fine are the very early volumes from the 1920s, *Fervor of Buenos Aires* and *Moon Across the Way*.) I guess another reason I assign it is because of my own longtime obsession with Borges's work and constantly wanting to spread the word on it, plus my hoping that it will excite students the way it first excited and inspired me as a younger writer. (Having been away on leave in 1982, the one time Borges visited UT during my tenure here, I missed seeing Borges in Austin, but I did hear him deliver his Charles Eliot Norton Poetry Lectures on a succession of autumn evenings in Cambridge, Massachusetts, when I was an undergrad at Harvard in 1967, the start of my own Borges obsession. Said obsession once even led me to journey the long five thousand miles to Buenos Aires—solo and traveling with little more than a couple of changes of clothes and some Borges texts stuffed in a small suitcase—for no other reason than I wanted to reread the work *in* Buenos Aires, "on the premises," so to speak.) When assigning *Dreamtigers* before spring break, I told the students that they could respond to the experience of reading it in whatever format they wanted, but limited to a single page—a poem, a letter, or a reading journal; I planned to have each read aloud that response to the others in the class on the first day we met following the break.

This particular semester, campus construction meant that classrooms in the English Department's Parlin Hall were often used by other departments, while English classes, in turn, got shuffled somewhere else—it had something to do with the size of rooms and the time slots needed for the meetings—and wouldn't you know it, just the year that we were reading Borges, E 355K was relocated from its regular venue of Parlin Hall to a room in Batts Hall. Better yet, Batts Hall was at the time definitely the "old" Batts Hall that Borges himself must have known when the Spanish Department (then part of the Department of Romance Languages and later the Department of Spanish and Portuguese) had been located there. That meant it still had considerable

Borges outside Batts Hall with UT professor of Spanish and comparative literature Miguel Gonzalez-Gerth during a later visit to Austin, 1982. *Courtesy of University Communications, University of Texas at Austin.*

character, with fine dark woodwork and lumpy yellow plaster walls and battered kidney-bean-red linoleum floors, before Batts, like so many other campus buildings, fell prey to more of the incessant "renovation" at UT, which does have a tendency to render even the classrooms in impressive older buildings, such as those on the South Mall, clinically bland within and somehow pretty character*less*—in my opinion, anyway.

I was late getting to the class that day, hurrying from Parlin across the South Mall after the bells on the Tower had chimed three. I strode into the room on the first floor, where the big windows were shoved wide open to the balmy late-March day—blossoming and sunny and oh-so-fragrant—and I maybe muttered some apologies about having gotten tied up with a phone call back in my office, which was true. Unpacking my book bag at the teacher's desk, however, I seemed to notice something was different, though at first I wasn't sure exactly what it was. Yes, a few of the dozen or so students had acquired very good tans since I had last seen them, from time logged at the beach during spring break, but that wasn't it. And yes, they had arranged the old desks with seats attached, each all one piece, in a semicircle as they always did when they first got to the room, before the start of every class; it was the configuration we regularly used for workshop discussion of the students' short stories and poems, and the one we would use this particular class for their reading aloud their responses to *Dreamtigers*, a copy of which most of them had ready on the flat, marred desktop slabs. The book's distinctive cover with the aforementioned tiger being repeated atop the semicircle of desks did make for a rather nice fan pattern from my vantage point up front, but that wasn't it either—no, that wasn't what seemed to be different this day. Sitting down at the teacher's desk, I finally realized what it was.

A single student desk—very much so one of those ubiquitous one-piece units with seat attached that were once found in just about every American schoolroom—had been placed exactly in the center of the semicircle, which *did* look weird to me, it simply being there and empty like that. But when I asked what was the deal with it, the students explained that they had carefully positioned the desk that way; they said it was all intentional and also only right, the bunch of them agreeing—enthusiastically, near chorally—with something along the lines of:

"It's for *Borges*."

You have to understand that I hadn't even lectured on Borges at this point, so whatever they knew about his work they had discovered in their own reading of *Dreamtigers* during vacation. Nevertheless, I had no doubt that if the students had come up with something like this, on their own, I could rest assured that I didn't need to launch into any prefacing explanatory lecture on him and his work. They might have read *Dreamtigers* on a 737 flying back from their parents' home in Midland, or by the waves in Cancun, or just stuck in a grim West Campus apartment in Austin because they didn't have the money to get away for spring break, but wherever it had been, they had understood the underlying message of Borges's

writing. It's a message that announces that those common assumptions about time and space are certainly meant to be challenged (critics often note that what Einstein did for physics, Borges did for literature), as the validity of the dreaming world can become more significant than that of the waking one; it's a message that also says that art itself can indeed offer a transcendence in its shedding of the limitations of the corporeal, the thumpingly chronological too, so that for all intents and purposes once you are taken up by a book—in this case, once it is moving you into a realm of possibility and wonder with the heady power of words, as genuine literature can, and once you have subsequently assembled with fellow students in a classroom to read aloud and share one-page responses to an author's work—it makes perfect sense that the author is actually alive and right there with you.

So, just maybe a silver-haired, ever-smiling Borges, well groomed in a tailored business suit as usual and baggy eyelids half lowered in his blindness, *was* seated at that little desk in the semicircle's center that afternoon in the same building, Batts Hall, where he himself had once taught, now there again to eagerly listen to these students talk about his book.

No?

Anyway, here is what I want to get at. It's the larger something I mentioned right at the start and what lately I've been ruminating on with regard to the Borges visit.

Nowadays we frequently hear UT speaking of itself as "world class," the term turning up in all sorts of official statements and publicity items. However, it may be that it is repeated so often that possibly the whole sense of what world-class designation really entails tends to get lost in the repetition and also an off-putting note of marketing that can often accompany the assertion. So the concept bears some looking into.

What I do know is that as big a Longhorn football fan as I am (and among these ranks could also be included Borges's mother, who when in Austin with her son wanted to learn all about the American game), and while I savor as much as anybody seeing the Tower lit that incandescent orange after a sweet victory, winning at football or any other sport doesn't make a school world class. Neither do record, corporate-CEO-style salaries for coaches or the celebrated appurtenances of new luxury skyboxes in a massive state-of-the-art stadium, for that matter, especially when one considers the often startlingly low figures concerning graduation rates for student players—a questionable situation that involves young people's lives and for me erases in a deft swipe the standard counterargument that big-time athletics brings in revenue for the entire University. And what I also know—having been associated with the University, gratefully so, in the capacity of professor for over thirty years—is that spending the better part of an adult lifetime at UT can't help but mean the occasional discouraging moments, when to somebody in my position, a faculty member observing things up close, the place may not seem exactly world class.

No need to go into too much sticky detail, but the point probably requires a few supporting examples for at least minimal credibility. I suppose that when one sees the normally rigorous review process for the granting of faculty tenure quietly sidestepped, as a lifelong academic appointment has sometimes been given more or less by decree and apparently as the result of Main Building personal connections, or when one watches some of one's most promising younger colleagues leave UT to take positions at other institutions for any number of contributing reasons, like the fact that the University has never had—or appeared to have much interest in instituting—a true sabbatical system to encourage and support research, those are such moments of doubt. Ditto for witnessing, let's say, the UT Press's catalogue every season increasingly replacing serious scholarly monographs on its list with more and more rather glitzy coffee-table books of the variety that probably should best be left to publication by overtly commercial houses. Or consider when one has to watch the board of regents, surely essentially good people, make a major mistake by assuming that besides being good people, they are experts in the field of contemporary architecture. It leads them to nix a commissioned plan for what could have been a landmark building to house the University's art collection—a prize-winning European firm's daring, visionary modern design with the potential of the building becoming recognized internationally as a work of art in itself, as modern museum buildings often are—and then replace it with a generic big box of a place that, southwestern detailing to match the campus "master plan" notwithstanding, does to my eye look dangerously

akin to a glorified Home Depot store. Well, at a moment of pretty embarrassing provincialism like that, the whole premise of UT being worthy of world-class status not only seems to lose its punch but borders on the somewhat absurd.

Still, as I said, those are occasional moments, observed by one faculty member. And as almost anybody will tell you, university faculty members everywhere are often known to be grumblers. (As my own colleagues would attest, I personally can be a prime—though I hope always benevolent, affable, and contributing—grumbler, almost priding myself on it, actually; the largest danger of all on a campus, the way I see it, could be overabundant giddy boosterism and self-congratulation, with the by-product inclination—in the name of so-called team-playerism or even a shadowy code of "go along, get along"—to shy away from necessary frank appraisal now and then.) I suppose that rather than dwell on the missteps and problems, it might be better to turn to the many triumphs at UT, including, and specifically, the Borges residency and what we might all take from it.

The entire fascinating story of Borges and UT provides a valuable paradigm for how a large, strong university like ours can work to its full potential— what never should be lost sight of. It began with a specific episode when so many of the University's resources—as elaborated above: a prescient departmental administration; energetic and outstanding faculty members from several other departments; a top-notch university press; eager, inspired students; and even the larger community of the University's city itself—they all came together to produce something startling and with repercussions both lasting and undeniably international. I mean, don't forget the glowing image of the University that Borges left with and went on to tell so many others in so many places about. And don't forget either how that writer in France all but bowed to me with Gallic elegance at the dinner party, how he marveled to me about the University's excellence, simply because Borges had taught here.

Talk about a proud moment, one when, for me in faraway Paris, there was no questioning of my university being world class—and then some.

There is nothing on campus named after Borges that I know of, though I once did see a great bumper sticker, bright red, on the door of a young assistant

Borges with some of his fans at Laguna Gloria during a trip to Austin, 1976. *From the Miscellaneous Photographs Collection—Argentina, Nettie Lee Benson Latin American Collection, University of Texas Libraries, University of Texas at Austin.*

professor's office in the Spanish Department that said, "Honk If You Love Borges!" Zulfikar Ghose—a recently retired UT professor in the English Department and an exceptional novelist, poet, and essayist with twenty or so books authored, who, in all honesty, has been one of the perhaps two or three members of the department (the *only* member?) during my time here who might be considered to wield a major, genuinely global and world-class reputation, or one extending beyond the coterie of academia, anyway—has suggested that Borges be reinterred in Austin. You see, there has been a drive launched by devotees of Borges in Argentina to return Borges's remains from Switzerland to Buenos Aires and its stately Recoleta Cemetery, where famous Argentinians are laid to rest and where there exists a fine mausoleum for the illustrious Borges family. But argument has never let up—much of it from his widow, María Kodama—to keep the remains in Geneva, and some speculate that Borges traveled to Switzerland when

in failing health and shortly before his death in order to die and be buried outside Argentina, which would make a clear statement on his disillusionment concerning the brutal excesses of the military regime at home. Ghose says that his idea would solve the argument and locate the site of burial somewhere that Borges always loved, as well as put it geographically about midway between Switzerland and Argentina—Austin. Also, remember the poem mentioned earlier, where Borges does muse about which of "my cities" he might someday finally find himself in when it comes time to die, which adds some fuel to the argument.

But, of course, Borges will never be buried in Austin, and in truth, Ghose, laughing when he suggests it, is obviously only having his fun with his solution to the problem of determining Borges's final resting place, a whimsical chopping of the Gordian knot that in itself sounds, nicely so, almost like something right out of a wildly inventive Borges short story.

The acclaimed avant-garde Scottish novelist James Kelman, winner of the UK's top literary honor in fiction, the Man Booker Prize, once spent an evening with me at the Dog & Duck Pub on Guadalupe when he was in residence at UT as a visiting creative writing professor for a semester. In the course of the two of us enjoying spirited conversation on matters literary, and after maybe too many "pints" for our own good (don't worry, neither of us was driving or had classes to teach the next day), we indulged in happily fantasizing about how fine it would be to have a graduate creative writing program at UT, or anywhere else, bearing the name of Borges and therefore establishing a certain tenor for the operation.

Of course, UT does now have a vibrant new graduate creative writing program, awarding a master of fine arts degree. Since 1998 it has operated under the name of the American author who wrote many bestselling historical novels, several made into successful movies and network-TV miniseries, and who settled in Austin in his later years. No doubt whatsoever, he was a wise, respected, and extremely generous man. He donated multiple millions of dollars to the University to ensure the founding of this program, for which it's only fitting that UT proudly honor him by name, even if he himself probably would have wholeheartedly agreed, I'd say, that as a writer he wasn't to be at all confused with somebody of Borges's stature in the bigger picture of literary history. (Borges was far from being an author on the best-seller charts at any stage of his career, including when he was most celebrated; the truth of the matter is that all his ma-jor short stories, those acknowledged milestones of modern world literature, originally appeared in flimsily bound, nonpaying literary journals with a circulation of just a few hundred copies in Buenos Aires, which offers a meaningful lesson in how Art—keep that capitalization—does work, seldom much concerned with marketplace validation and, not to put too fine a point on it, money.) You know, now that I think of it, there's not an endowed chair bearing the name of Borges, though it definitely seems that it someday might be appropriate to launch a campaign to establish one in the Department of Spanish and Portuguese. On the other hand—and without intending to make light of this, and with emphasis on how the observation might take on a revelatory significance—if there isn't a chair, there was a *desk* for Borges in Batts Hall that sunny spring afternoon for a creative writing class, E 355K. Which is to say, there was the sheer magic of his writing, an enduring literature, and there was the way the bright, talented UT students, nearly a half century after he first visited Austin, were so excited about it, how they were touched and enriched and possibly changed in their own insight into life itself by that work and its dizzying suggestions of other dimensions of perception, in dreams well beyond reality or elsewhere.

I like to think that for Borges, such is the kind of invisible tribute—there in the ignited imaginations of those undergrads—that he would have ultimately found most suitable when it comes to these Forty Acres that were so very dear to him.

History

UT professor of history Eugene C. Barker. *From the Eugene C. Barker Papers, Dolph Briscoe Center for American History, University of Texas at Austin. (DI 06847)*

Texas governor James E. Ferguson, 1914. *From the James Edward Ferguson Papers, Dolph Briscoe Center for American History, University of Texas at Austin. (DI 06874)*

"Farmer Jim" and "The Chief"

Governor Jim Ferguson and His Battle with Eugene C. Barker and the University of Texas

PATRICK
COX

Texas governor James E. "Farmer Jim" Ferguson rose from political obscurity in the early twentieth century to become one of the most influential and controversial chief executives in the state's history. He forever embedded his legacy in a confrontation with the University of Texas during his two terms as governor, from January 1915 until his impeachment and his resignation from office in August 1917, the day before the state Senate was to remove him. Historians credit his tumultuous and very public battle with the University as the primary reason for the undoing of a very popular governor who had designs on a position in the U.S. Senate. It also brought the role of the University and its funding to state and national attention. Ferguson's actions and the ensuing reaction also sowed the seeds for a series of conflicts that would mar the University during the twentieth century.[1]

The University of Texas, an emerging center of higher education in the American Southwest, occupied the eye of this political hurricane. One of Ferguson's primary adversaries was a little-known professor of history at the University—Eugene C. Barker. Known as "The Chief" by his colleagues, Barker rose from humble origins as a blacksmith in rural East Texas to become one of the most recognized Texas historians. An 1899 graduate of the University of Texas, Barker ultimately became a nationally recognized historian and, at the time of his death, in 1956, was rec-

Patrick Cox recently retired from the University, where he had served as associate director of the University's Dolph Briscoe Center for American History. In that position, he had administrative responsibilities for the Congressional History Collection, the Sam Rayburn Library and Museum in Bonham, the John Nance Garner Museum in Uvalde, and historic preservation projects and programs at the Winedale Historical Complex near Round Top. He has written extensively on Texas history topics, including the biography Ralph W. Yarborough, the People's Senator *(2001) and* The First Texas News Barons *(2005), which examines independent Texas newspaper publishers and the creation of the modern Texas identity. He received a PhD in history from the University in 1996 and a BA in history in 1974.*

ognized as "the foremost authority on Texas history and one of America's most distinguished historians." Barker spent his entire academic career of sixty-one years at the University of Texas. The confrontation between The Chief and Farmer Jim became a personal battle that illustrated the larger conflicts over public support and funding for higher education, along with the values of academic freedom and the role of University faculty in public affairs.[2]

An attorney and banker from Temple, Ferguson had no record of public office before running for governor in 1914. Born near Salado in 1871, Ferguson worked on the family farm, attended Salado College, worked at a number of jobs as a young man, and began to study law. He joined the state bar in 1897, set up a law practice in Belton, and married Miriam A. Wallace in 1899. In the early 1900s, he practiced law, purchased real estate, and founded the Temple State Bank. Calling himself a "Hogg Progressive Democrat"—after a popular predecessor, Governor James S. Hogg—Ferguson ran a populist-style, energetic campaign that upset Tom Love, a veteran political leader, former congressman, and businessman from Houston. Ferguson promised to improve education and provide reforms that would help agriculture and the state's rising population of tenant farmers and sharecroppers. He also opposed prohibition. He became known as "Farmer Jim" to supporters and to the press. Ferguson won more votes than any prior candidate in a Democratic primary election and took office in January 1915.[3]

When Ferguson took office, he promised a "business-like administration." In his first term as governor, he persuaded the legislature to increase funding for public schools by one million dollars, provided for compulsory attendance, and secured a number of other reforms to expand the woefully inadequate services provided by the State of Texas. The state legislature authorized the first public institution for mental health, which became the Austin State School. Notably, he also encouraged more funding for the University of Texas. However, Ferguson sounded a cautionary note early in his first term regarding what he viewed as an imbalance in public funding for education. "When we consider the seventy thousand children in Texas who never get a chance to go to school and against this put the fact that the Texas Legislature is today being asked to appropriate over $325 per student for the benefit of those fortunate enough and

able to go to the Agricultural and Mechanical College and the University [of Texas], you can begin to see that there is a real danger of somebody going hog wild about higher education."[4]

During the early years of the twentieth century, Texas, like many other southern states, lagged behind the rest of the nation in almost every aspect of public education. Texas was in the bottom half of states in teacher salaries, length of school year, children attending school, and expenditures per pupil. Illiteracy remained high. Agriculture still dominated the state's economy, and the majority of the population resided on farms or lived and worked as tenants in rural Texas. The state school superintendent stated in 1913 that "the country schools of Texas are not rendering to the people of the State that vitalizing, effective and positive service which must be rendered if the country children are to acquire a common school education, and are to be prepared in the country schools for the responsibilities of life and for entrance into the institutions of higher learning."[5]

Ferguson's problems with the University of Texas may have been both philosophical and political in nature. They began in the spring of 1915 when he questioned acting president William J. Battle over the annual budget. The governor also demanded that President Battle dismiss six faculty members. A year later, when the University regents named Austin Presbyterian Theological Seminary president Robert A. Vinson as the new president of the University of Texas, Ferguson objected and renewed the attack. At a meeting with President Vinson and UT regent George W. Littlefield, he demanded that the six faculty members should be fired. "I am the Governor of Texas; I don't have to give reasons," Barker quoted the governor in his account of the confrontation.[6] Ferguson also predicted that they would face "the biggest bear fight that has ever taken place in the history of the State of Texas."[7]

While the fight between the governor and the University smoldered for the next two years, Barker tangled with Ferguson over the appointment of a position that most assumed would be uncontroversial—the state librarian. Ferguson wanted to replace state librarian E. W. Winkler with A. F. Cunningham, a political supporter and Presbyterian minister. Winkler and Barker had been classmates and friends at the University of Texas in the 1890s. At the time of the controversy, Barker, in his role as chairman of the UT Department of History, served on the board of the Texas State Library and Historical Commission, which administered the state agency and selected the state librarian. Barker objected to "putting an inexperienced man in charge" and sent a letter to Cunningham that challenged his credentials. Barker sent a carbon copy of the letter to Ferguson as well. The governor quickly responded. He told Barker that the letter was "an insult to him [Cunningham] and me both." Ferguson then stated, "As you have entered into a long discussion of politics in the letter, I hope that you will not hereafter complain if your wishes are not carried out." Barker undoubtedly realized that he too was now in the governor's sights.[8]

When the board of the Texas State Library and Historical Commission met in Austin on February 20, 1915, it debated the appointment of Winkler or Cunningham and deadlocked over the decision. When the members reconvened on March 3, Ferguson restated his position, and they elected Cunningham. Barker resigned his board position in protest. Barker wrote to his friend Thomas M. Marshall, describing the proceedings and the outcome, and declaring Ferguson to be "as devoid of general education as he is of any historical appreciation." He closed the account by stating, "The man is more than usually ignorant and self satisfied, but since the Governor had the appointment of three members of a board of five, the man was elected."[9]

The "Big Bear Fight" the governor predicted erupted in 1917. When Ferguson called a meeting of the UT Board of Regents on May 28, 1917, rumors quickly spread that faculty members would be dismissed and fraternities would be barred from campus. The governor was also making it known to the press, members of the legislature, and the regents that he would veto the University's state appropriation. Many of the state's newspapers carried editorials condemning the governor's threats. More than a hundred faculty members attended an emergency meeting to protest the action. That same day, University students gathered for a mass meeting and paraded through the streets of Austin and to the Capitol, where the governor was meeting with the regents. Students shouted and carried banners reading: "Kaiserism, a menace abroad; likewise, a Menace at home." Ferguson adjourned the meeting and blamed the students and faculty for the disruption.[10]

Ferguson followed through with his threats and vetoed the University's appropriation on June 2, 1917, after the end of the legislative session. In his veto message to the University regents, he stated, "If the University cannot be maintained as a democratic University, then we ought to have no University." As he later told the *Dallas Morning News*, "I do not care a damn what becomes of the University. The bats and owls can roost in it for all I care."[11]

As the battle between the University and the governor escalated that summer, Barker became more involved with the University administration and the Ex-Students' Association in challenging Ferguson's accusations. The state's newspapers carried news about the fighting in the trenches in Europe alongside accounts of the battles between the University and Ferguson. Barker consulted with President Vinson during the appropriations battle and after the governor's veto. Following the veto, Ferguson embarked on a statewide tour to defend his actions and continue his attacks on the University. Barker included the governor's statements in his chronology of Ferguson's attacks. Between June 10 and June 18, Ferguson "made an average of three speeches a day in nearly all of which he vilified the 'University crowd.'" In Kerrville on June 10, Ferguson told his audience, many of whom were of German descent, "I have found far more disloyalty in the State University at Austin than among the Germans or the people of any nationality."[12] At a speech in Lubbock on June 16, he went even further in his denunciations of faculty and students, characterizing the group as "butterfly chasers, day dreamers, educated fools and two-bit thieves." According to the *Dallas Morning News*, thousands showed up to hear Ferguson as he made speeches in West Texas and received significant applause and support. One supporter told him, "I'm glad to shake hands with a live Governor." Ferguson responded, "Well, I would be a dead one if some of those University fellows had their way."[13]

Back in Austin, Barker and the University's allies planned their attack. Part of the strategy involved emphasizing the University's wartime response and playing to Texans' patriotic sentiments. In this, they began to use the governor's strategies to their own advantage. In addition, with the assistance of the Ex-Students' Association, Barker utilized his research and historical skills to combat the governor. His pamphlet *Ferguson's War on the University of Texas* not only documented the author's criticisms, but also

Opponents of the actions of Governor Ferguson against the University of Texas rallying on campus (TOP) and marching through Austin (BOTTOM). *From the Prints and Photographs Collection—Gov. J. E. Ferguson, Dolph Briscoe Center for American History, University of Texas at Austin. (Top: DI 06861; bottom: DI 06862)*

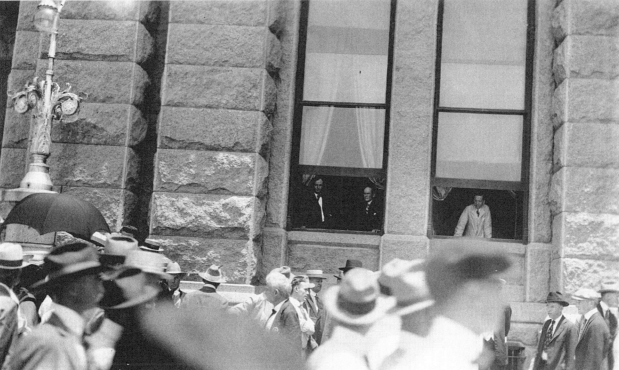

The rally on May 28, 1917, reached the grounds of the Texas State Capitol (TOP) and confronted Governor Ferguson (BOT-TOM, *standing at the windowsill, far left*). *From the Prints and Photographs Collection—J. E. Ferguson, Dolph Briscoe Center for American History, University of Texas at Austin. (Top: DI 06863; bottom: DI 06864)*

provided an extensive rebuttal to all of Ferguson's allegations against the University and its political allies. In the publication, Barker provided a chronology of events relating to the confrontation from January 1915 through July 1917.

Barker maintained that hundreds of University students and former students had enlisted in the army, purchased bonds, volunteered for the Red Cross, and allowed the University's facilities to be used for the war effort. "The University has never to this day attacked the Governor, but has merely tried to defend itself from his vicious attacks upon it," Barker stated. In answering the charges of misappropriated University funds, professors who seldom taught class, and favoritism for wealthy students over poorer ones, Barker maintained that Ferguson willfully distorted the truth to impress his audiences. Ferguson had "quite surpassed his own record of vituperation, misrepresentation and libel of University, faculty, students and ex-students," Barker concluded in his review.[14]

Following his brief history of the confrontation, Barker used Ferguson's veto of the University's appropriation to rebut allegations he had made. In his veto statement, Ferguson accused the University of being a "rich man's school" and sneered that "the student body is divided into fraternities and barbarians." He maintained that the "institution is undemocratic and snobbish and should be reformed or abolished." The governor also charged that the University "should have new blood in its faculty and a competent man at its head."[15]

Ferguson also attacked the students at the University who protested his actions. "The students who engaged in the parade were a lawless mob of rich men's sons who desire to establish an educational aristocracy. They have no respect for the legislature, for the governor, or for the Board of Regents." The governor maintained that the University should be blamed for starting the fight, because it opposed his support for rural schools and public education: "The educated autocratic highbrows who desire to maintain an educational aristocracy are opposed to the education of the masses."[16]

Barker provided a point-by-point rebuttal, using budgetary information and statistics to counter Ferguson's charges. Barker noted that the actual cost for educating a student at the University from 1913 to 1916 was $227 a year, not $545, as the gover-

nor charged. "The only fair way to study the cost of education at the University of Texas is to compare it with the cost of other universities," Barker wrote. At the University of Virginia, costs per student were twice as much at the time; at the University of Michigan, they were $394 a year; and at the University of Iowa, $354 a year. Barker also defended faculty rights for leaves of absence, their salaries, and good working conditions at the University.[17]

In addition to defending faculty rights, Barker also defended the rights of students to demonstrate and express their opinions freely and openly, noting, "The student parade was not inspired by the faculty, but was an expression of spontaneous student indignation at the attempt of the governor to coerce the Regents into doing his bidding." Noting the independent nature of the students, Barker wrote that "no one familiar with the operation of student self-government at the University will need to be told that the students are in the habit of doing their own thinking in matters that concern the University and themselves." Refuting the statement that the students were all the sons and daughters of wealthy Texans, Barker said they came from "3,000 respectable families, representing nearly every occupation followed in Texas." At the time, fully 40 percent of the students paid for their own education, Barker stated. "Parents of 1916–17 represent nearly every occupation followed in Texas, but the vast plurality of them are farmers," Barker maintained, taking a jab at "Farmer Jim." Barker said the attack on fraternities was nothing more than "a political trick." Barker charged that the governor used this charge merely as an attempt to divide the student body and the ex-students. Quite the opposite occurred, as students and alumni united in attacking the governor, regardless of their participation in or support for fraternal organizations.[18]

A strong alliance between the University and the Ex-Student's Association emerged during the struggle. Former governor Joseph D. Sayers presided over a mass meeting of the Ex-Students' Association in Austin. The organization united to protest Ferguson's attacks on the University and took out full-page ads in the state's newspapers. "The Educational Institutions of Texas must be freed from Partisan Politics and One-Man Rule," the ads proclaimed. The unity is illustrated by the alliance between Barker and Will C. Hogg, the secretary of the Ex-Students'

Association. "I have no political or personal axe to grind, no apologies or excuses to offer, but in common with a large majority of our people, I am heartily ashamed of the prevailing political conditions in this state," Hogg wrote. Arguing for the governor's impeachment and conviction, Hogg asked the following question: "What measure of personal and official misdeeds must a Governor commit before he has indisputably demonstrated his personal and official unfitness for the office?"[19]

Will Hogg spent a long, hot summer working in Austin with Barker and friends of the University to counter the governor's attacks and coordinate the impeachment movement. In an interview he provided to his biographer John A. Lomax, Hogg stated, "My prediction is that he [Ferguson] is riding to the biggest fall, personally and politically, in the short and simple annals of the misguided politicians of Texas." Hogg also issued a pamphlet titled *His Own Words to Discover His Motives—The Ferguson Idea of University Control*. The publication contained resolutions by the Ex-Students' Association and statements from Hogg and other regents that discredited Ferguson's positions.[20]

The showdown between Ferguson and the University ultimately led to a special session of the legislature to consider his impeachment. On July 23, 1917, the Speaker of the Texas House, Francis O. Fuller, called for an August session to hear charges against Ferguson. In a counter move, Ferguson called the session himself to consider the University's appropriation. The special session passed the appropriation bill and then moved to impeach Ferguson. After several weeks of heated debate, the House of Representatives voted on twenty-one charges of impeachment, most of which centered on the governor's finances and his questionable loans. Of those charges, three articles involved allegations against the board of regents and the University of Texas.[21] The state Senate convicted the governor on ten charges, primarily on violations of the law involving his personal finances. After Ferguson resigned rather than be removed, Lieutenant Governor William P. Hobby completed Ferguson's term and successfully retained the governor's office the following year.[22]

Although the legislature removed Ferguson for charges relating to his personal finances and his refusal to disclose information, his conviction can be traced to his battle with the University of Texas. De-spite the fact that he left office in disgrace, Ferguson would rise like a phoenix from the ashes and have an extended influence in Texas politics. Texans would twice elect Farmer Jim's wife, Miriam Ferguson, governor, and "Fergusonism" would remain a force in Texas politics for decades.

The Ferguson episode undoubtedly left a profound mark on the young Barker. He became a preeminent, nationally recognized historian who remained at the University and with the History Department until his death, in 1956. In 1917, only a few years into his term as chair of the History Department, the Ferguson drama provided a clear illustration of the impact of politics on Barker and the University. Barker understood that a charismatic political leader could have a profound impact on those involved in higher education. For academics, like Barker, who chose to enter the political fray, not every outcome could be easily analyzed or debated. The episode also left Barker distrustful of elected officials whom he deemed unfit for public office or who disagreed with his vision of American society. Barker also discovered that the public spotlight could be unfavorable to professional academics and their institutions.

The Chief prevailed over Farmer Jim in this battle. However, future confrontations between the University and state elected officials would not be as successful and would be more divisive for the University alumni and supporters.

NOTES

1. To date there is no scholarly biography of James E. Ferguson, but he has been the subject of significant historical studies. These include Lewis L. Gould, *Progressives and Prohibitionists: Texas Democrats in the Wilson Era* (Austin: Texas State Historical Association, 1992); Ralph W. Steen, *Twentieth-Century Texas: An Economic and Social History* (Austin: Steck, 1942); Ouida F. Nalle, *The Fergusons of Texas* (San Antonio: Naylor, 1946); Randolph B. Campbell, "Fergusonism," in *Gone to Texas* (New York: Oxford Univ. Press, 2001), 248–252; William C. Pool, *Eugene C. Barker, Historian* (Austin: Univ. of Texas Press, 1971).

2. *Austin American-Statesman*, Oct. 23, 1956, *Dallas Morning News*, Oct. 23, 1956 (clippings in the Eugene C. Barker Vertical Files, Dolph Briscoe Center for American History, University of Texas at Austin; hereafter cited as DBCAH).

3. Campbell, *Gone to Texas*, 348.

4. Ibid., 348–351; Gould, *Progressives and Prohibitionists*, 187.

5. Gould, *Progressives and Prohibitionists*, 186.

6. Eugene C. Barker, *Ferguson's War on the University of Texas: A Chronological Outline* (Austin: Ex-Students' Association of the University of Texas, 1917), 7. Barker's pamphlet consisted of a lengthy statement of events that transpired before Ferguson's impeachment and removal from office. The Ex-Students' Association printed the tract in time for it to be placed on the desks of legislators, who had been called into session for the governor's impeachment and trial.

7. Campbell, *Gone to Texas*, 351.

8. Eugene C. Barker to A. F. Cunningham, Feb. 19, 1915, and James E. Ferguson to Eugene C. Barker, Feb. 20, 1915 (Barker Papers, DBCAH). The letters and the account are quoted in Pool, *Eugene C. Barker, Historian*, 72.

9. Eugene C. Barker to Thomas M. Marshall, March 4, 1915, Barker Papers. The account and letter are quoted in Pool, *Barker, Historian*, 73.

10. Pool, *Barker, Historian*, 78; Barker, *Ferguson's War*, 22–23.

11. Campbell, *Gone to Texas*, 351.

12. Barker, *Ferguson's War*, 34–35.

13. *Dallas Morning News*, June 17, 1917.

14. Barker, *Ferguson's War*, 39.

15. Ibid., 24–25.

16. Ibid.

17. Ibid, 26–28.

18. Ibid.

19. Ibid, 46–47, *San Antonio Express*, June 27 and Aug. 6, 1917.

20. John A. Lomax, "Will Hogg—Texan," *Alcalde* (June 1968), 10–11 (William Clifford Hogg Vertical File, DBCAH); Will C. Hogg, *His Own Words to Discover His Motives—The Ferguson Idea of University Control* (James E. Ferguson Vertical File, DBCAH).

21. "Jas. E. Ferguson Impeachment," State of Texas vs. Jas. E. Ferguson (copy in James E. Ferguson Vertical File, DBCAH).

22. Campbell, *Gone to Texas*, 351–352.

"Harry's Place"

A Brief History of the Academic Center and Undergraduate Library/ Peter T. Flawn Academic Center

RICHARD W.
ORAM

The evolution of the use of the building known today as the Peter T. Flawn Academic Center (the FAC), located at the western edge of the Forty Acres, between the Main Building and the Texas Union, reflects nearly a half century of changes in the University environment and in patterns of academic library use. This building, originally known as the Academic Center and Undergraduate Library, opened in 1963, and to a person strolling down the West Mall today, it has an external appearance virtually unchanged from the day it opened. Its internal appearance and the use of its space, however, have changed dramatically over the last fifty years.

The unwieldy official name ensured from the outset that the facility would be known as the UGL or the AC, or, in its early years, familiarly as "Harry's Place," after Harry Huntt Ransom, who served as president of the University of Texas and chancellor of the University of Texas System in the 1960s. The idea for Harry's Place emerged from confident, ambitious views Ransom held concerning the need for undergraduate students to have a meaningful educational experience at the University—especially one that placed the student in close contact with rare books and other cultural treasures.

The Flawn Academic Center of today has been reincarnated as a multipurpose office facility and information technology center. In 2005, the University of Texas Libraries removed the last of the books that remained in the old UGL stacks and integrated them into other collections on campus, primarily those housed in UT's main library, the Perry-Castañeda Library (PCL). In 2010, the Harry Ransom Center, the enormous special

Richard W. Oram is associate director and Hobby Foundation Librarian at the Harry Ransom Center. He holds a PhD in English Literature from Cornell University and an MLIS from the University of Texas at Austin. He has written on special collections management, library history, and nineteenth- and twentieth-century British literature. His essay on the HRC's acquisition of the T. E. Hanley Collection appears in the first volume of The Texas Book.

View of the Academic Center/Undergraduate Library from the fourth-floor terrace of the Main Building. *From the Prints and Photographs Collection—UT Buildings—Peter T. Flawn Academic Center, Dolph Briscoe Center for American History, University of Texas at Austin. (DI 07012)*

An early conception of the design for the Academic Center, before the Women's Building (bounded by the Academic Center, the Texas Union, and Hogg Auditorium in this rendering) was razed. This drawing appeared in an article titled "An Undergraduate Academic Center" by Helen Tackett in the June 1958 issue of the *Alcalde. From the UT News and Information Services Records, Dolph Briscoe Center for American History, University of Texas at Austin. (DI 06875)*

collections library that had long maintained an outpost in the building, transferred the last of its collections, severing the FAC's last remaining connection with the University's libraries and special collections.

In this brief history of the Peter T. Flawn Academic Center/Academic Center and Undergraduate Library, I intend to examine the history of the building in the larger context of the rise and fall of the undergraduate library concept, associated with the period 1950–1980 in the history of American academic libraries. The demise of the Academic Center and Undergraduate Library was not something unique to the University of Texas, but rather was the result of changes effected by far-reaching trends in life on American campuses, in reading habits, in the evolving uses of technology, and in the way libraries are perceived and used.

The notion of an "academic center," as opposed to a conventional "undergraduate library," was something peculiar to Texas. It was the brainchild of Chancellor Harry Ransom, the initiator of the campus building boom of the 1960s. Ransom is best known for founding the Humanities Research Center (HRC), now known as the Harry Ransom Center, an internationally recognized special collections library famous for holding the literary manuscripts and correspondence of major British, American, and French writers of the modern era. Ransom had a far-reaching grasp of the importance of general academic libraries in the midcentury American university, and many of his collected talks and writings were devoted to libraries and their users. A study of Ransom's thoughts on this subject reveals both his idealistic belief in the importance of primary sources in research in the humanities and social sciences (he was himself a scholar of the history of copyright) and his more hardheaded view of research libraries as academic status symbols.

The Academic Center and Undergraduate Library grew out of a similar admixture of practicality and idealism. The immediate, practical impetus was the growth of the student body; between 1950 and 1960, the undergraduate population at Texas ballooned from 10,658 to 16,477. Texas had a strong graduate library, but stacks access for undergraduates had been restricted ever since the library's move from Cass Gilbert's elegant (but, by that time, undersized) University Library building (today named Battle Hall) to the new Main Building and Tower, in 1936. Books had to be requested from the fourteen stories of book

stacks in the Tower, then sent down to the central reading room in an elevator, and browsing of the shelves was not possible for most undergrads. The University library was not generally regarded as a social center or meeting place. The postwar explosion in undergraduate enrollments radically altered the situation at Texas and at other large state universities. In 1958, a group of desperate University of Texas students signed a petition pleading for an open-shelf undergraduate library building and calling attention to the "antiquated, inefficient, unavailable, and completely uninviting nature of our present library facilities for undergraduate reading."[1]

The first undergraduate library of the postwar era was Lamont Library, opened in 1949 at Harvard University. Over the next three decades, similar facilities were built at other large universities, such as Cornell University, the University of Michigan, and the University of Illinois at Urbana-Champaign. By 1976, there were twenty-five separate undergraduate libraries, and although a handful were added to the list after that date, there is general agreement that the undergraduate library movement had peaked by the late 1970s.[2] In its most basic conception, the undergraduate library was designed to serve as both a social and intellectual gathering place, relieving pressure on access to the research materials that were not, or so some maintained, necessary for the core undergraduate curriculum. In the undergraduate library's heyday of the 1970s, the focus shifted to the provision of services to support undergraduate learning and teaching; as Michael Engle observes, "Librarians working with undergraduates developed a variety of innovative programs to teach basic bibliographic and critical thinking skills to new students and to orient upper-level students to the literature of their major."[3]

Another component of the undergraduate library concept was more idealistic, focusing on the importance of users being able to browse collections, the easy availability of popular fiction and other new titles, and the exposure of undergraduates to the "best books" in human thought. The selection of what was termed an "opening day collection" for undergraduate readers became the subject of fascination for library schools; between 1967 and 1988, the American Library Association published three editions of its *Books for College Libraries*, which include a selection of "core" primary texts and the best secondary works in all fields, selected by a panel of librarians.

Harry Ransom examining rare books with UT students Dianne Garrett, left, and Martha Brindley, ca. 1965. *From the Harry Ransom Collection, Harry Ransom Center, University of Texas at Austin.*

In 1958, responding in part to the undergraduate pleas previously mentioned, Ransom proposed that an undergraduate library be constructed at Texas—in his words, so that it would be impossible for students to "avoid coming into contact with books."[4] Ransom often confessed that he was "deeply—almost passionately—interested in the printed word."[5] His notion was that undergraduates would benefit from books not only in the intellectual sense but also by actual exposure to the physical artifact. One must recognize that the Academic Center evolved nearly simultaneously with the Humanities Research Center, first broached by Ransom in late 1956 and emphasizing the collection of primary source materials such as first editions and manuscripts. His full vision is set forth in his 1960 *Library Chronicle* essay "The Academic Center: A Plan for an Undergraduate Library."[6] Ransom's Academic Center, "a term selected partly in the hope that the usual library functions

would be broadened," was unique in that it combined a conventional undergraduate library, which was to occupy three floors of the building, with a special fourth floor, designed to house the growing modern literature collections that had begun to overflow the storage spaces in the Tower. This was to be known (somewhat confusingly) as the Academic Center Library (ACL). Ransom's notion was that undergraduates, especially Honors and Plan II students, would be naturally drawn upward from the lower floors to experience advanced research in the ACL, which would also contain a gallery displaying the treasures steadily being accumulated on the UT campus. An unusual feature of the fourth floor of the Academic Center was the presence of several so-called special rooms. These too served both practical and idealistic ends. During the Humanities Research Center's remarkable growth during the late 1950s and 1960s, Ransom sought to attract archives, entire libraries, and other collections from public figures such as the publishers Alfred and Blanche Knopf, the mystery writer Erle Stanley Gardner, and the Texas folklorist J. Frank Dobie. Appealing both to their public-spiritedness and their egos, Ransom proposed the creation of rooms associated with particular special collections that would also serve as study spaces for undergraduates. The upshot was to be a facility that would be the opposite of "a mausoleum of dead ideas attended by the undertakers of polite scholarship."[7]

Synergism was anticipated from the Academic Center's special rooms, which were intended to feature Texana, Latin American, and literary holdings, all strengths of the Texas special collections. In the case of Frank Dobie, who had retired from the faculty following a distinguished though controversial career, Ransom suggested a Dobie Library, which would be "a corner forever Texas," featuring books, cowhides, saddles, and other reminders of western and ranching lore so dear to the historian. He added, "I would want in it a lot of humanity, some gusto, a proper sense of place . . . and above all the vitality of faith in what is alive."[8] For Edward Larocque Tinker, a New York collector of books and artifacts relating to South America and the vaqueros, Ransom created a Tinker room with vaquero blankets, saddles, and other artifacts to supplement the large Tinker Library. Until the late 1980s, the ground floor of the Academic Center featured a Hall of the Horsemen of the Americas, which has since succumbed to the University's need for space.

Alfred and Blanche Knopf, well-known publishers of many prestigious books, were responsible for the creation of another special room. In 1959, these quintessential New Yorkers, who had fallen in love with the wide-open spaces of Texas, agreed to give their collection, accumulated over forty years, of Alfred A. Knopf, Inc. titles and fine press books to the Humanities Research Center, with the understanding that it (along with their Danish modern furniture) be maintained in a special room.[9]

The most unusual of the special rooms, after it was completed in 1965, was an exact replica of the cabin study of Erle Stanley Gardner, the creator of the fictional defense attorney Perry Mason, who was made famous by Gardner's novels and the eponymous television series of the 1950s and '60s. This was meticulously re-created down to the last detail, including the author's handgun in his original desk drawer; a

visitor could press a button and hear a recorded description from "Uncle Erle."[10] Among the less well-known special rooms were the Jack Josey Honors Room, which was intended for the use of honors students, and the Esther Hoblitzelle Parlor—named for the spouse of Karl Hoblitzelle, the owner of a Texas theater chain—which was lavishly furnished with antiques and originally intended to be used for afternoon tea. Another unusual feature of the Academic Center was the 5,000-volume Ruth Stephan Poetry Collection, housed on the third floor of the building and intended to encourage the University community and the general public to appreciate poetry.

The Academic Center was designed by the Austin firm of Jessen and Associates. One striking feature of the building is the large black granite porch that extends all the way around the building. The bottom floor is enclosed in aluminum and glass, accented with granite-faced pillars, in keeping with the International Style, which dominated the architectural world of the 1960s. Another prominent feature is a large lobby, a multipurpose space used for registration, student gatherings, and informal socialization. The expansive open areas were expressions of UT's pride in its burgeoning student population and the wide-open spaces traditionally associated with Texas. On the ground level there was, and still is, a large teaching auditorium (originally labeled AC 21), which has never had much of a connection, architecturally or otherwise, to the rest of the facility.[11]

The middle floors of the Academic Center have horizontal windows obscured by large, horizontal, Moorish grille work, and they are encased in Texas shell limestone, a favorite material of the architect.[12] The fourth floor, the new home of the Academic Center Library (that is, the modern literary collections and others that would form the nucleus of the Humanities Research Center) was a penthouse with a large central atrium.[13] The open atrium, with its sculptural addition, "The Three Graces" by Charles Umlauf, an Art Department faculty member, and a terrace with a Chinese garden, accessed by doors near the Gardner and Hoblitzelle Rooms, were intended to be an attractive gathering place, but in practice, the strong Texas sun and winds, along with a complement of roosting pigeons, usually made the experience less than pleasant. Another Umlauf bronze, "The Torch Bearers," was prominently placed at a mosaic-tiled fountain at the entrance. This work of

Mrs. Erle Stanley Gardner with UT president Stephen Spurr in the Gardner Room of the Academic Center. *Photo by Frank Armstrong; Harry Ransom Center, University of Texas at Austin.*

The fourth-floor atrium of the Academic Center. *From the UT News and Information Services Records, Dolph Briscoe Center for American History, University of Texas at Austin. (DI 06876)*

art provided a focus for controversy when two faculty members wrote a letter attacking its conventional conception and execution, finding it "fit for the lawn of some country court house."[14]

The board of regents and its architects were delighted that the facility had been constructed for a cost of $17 a square foot ($4.7 million total), much less than the Business Administration and Economics Building of the same era. Other savings were achieved because the building was a sort of sandwich, with only the first and fourth floors being outfitted relatively lavishly. For example, the blue-carpeted Leeds Gallery, named for William B. Leeds and intended for the display of Humanities Research Center materials, and the various special rooms all featured large walnut doors and woodwork; the second and third floors, meanwhile, were strictly utilitarian, with linoleum floors, stacks, and spartan study carrels.

The Leeds Gallery. *Photo by Frank Armstrong; Harry Ransom Center, University of Texas at Austin.*

The opening of the Undergraduate Library on September 23, 1963, was an unqualified success. The doors were simply opened without benefit of a ribbon cutting (a formal ceremony was scheduled for the following spring), and students were allowed to occupy the space, which they did in great profusion, and to begin browsing the sixty thousand books.[15] Six students were stranded for more than an hour in one of the "plush" elevators on opening day, but this misadventure didn't detract from undergraduates' pleasure at having their "own" space. Sally Leach, a retired administrator at the Ransom Center, recalled that "it was a great thing to have a library that was specifically for undergraduates and specifically the first two years, and to have books available just for reading."[16] Not long after the opening, the *Daily Texan* reported that the social and study functions of the building were already being combined in the "stacks date."[17]

The Academic Center's early and middle years saw several evolutions in function. In 1971, the contents of the Academic Center Library, except for a collection of art by and about writers as well as the materials in the special rooms, were removed to the new Humanities Research Center building, leaving behind the Leeds Gallery, which at that time was the center's only large exhibition space.[18] The result was that for the next thirty years, visitors interested in viewing the HRC's major exhibitions (comprehensive exhibitions devoted to George Bernard Shaw and the Carlton Lake Collection of modern French literature come especially to mind) had to find their way to the Academic Center's fourth floor. Both attendance and visibility suffered, and the problem of constricted exhibition space perplexed a series of HRC directors and curators until the renovated Ransom Center building, with a ground-floor gallery dedicated to its materials, was opened in 2003.

In 1985, the Academic Center and Undergraduate Library was renamed the Peter T. Flawn Academic Center in honor of the retiring University president. The same year, the central atrium of the Academic Center and Undergraduate Library was covered with a roof and turned into a large conference and meet-

Students studying in the stacks area of the Undergraduate Library. *From the UT Texas Student Publications, Inc. Photographs Collection—Academic Center, Dolph Briscoe Center for American History, University of Texas at Austin. (DI 07015)*

ing space, a reflection of the growing need for spaces suitable for social and developmental functions. In the early 1990s, various alterations were made to the lower levels of the building, which one enters from a plaza on the west side—the one facing the Texas Union. Initially, these were class and conference rooms; they have gradually been taken over by various academic administrative offices.

From the outset, the fourth floor of the Academic Center was architecturally and atmospherically removed from the rest of the building. Those students who found their way to the Dobie, Tinker, and Knopf Rooms, each of which had an associated curator when the building was opened, were happy enough to use them as study halls, but established few if any relationships with the materials inside. These were noncirculating rare or unique materials that could not be easily browsed and whose use had to be care-

fully supervised. In later years, budgetary and security concerns meant that the positions for the curators of the special rooms were eliminated, and in time, the special rooms had to be closed to everyone except during scheduled events. In a sense, Ransom's dream of involving undergraduates with special collections was decades ahead of its time.[19] His dream languished not only because of budgetary reasons, but also because there was never a substantive plan to involve faculty and students in research, programming, or discussion of the special collections at the Flawn Academic Center. Proximity, as it turned out, was not enough.

During the 1970s, the Undergraduate Library's heyday, the focus shifted to the provision of services in support of undergraduate learning and teaching, including assistance with writing, research, and library use. Another development was the addition of an extensive audiovisual collection and laboratory. By the 1980s, the undergraduate library concept was beginning to fade on the national scene. The advent of the personal computer, coupled with changes in undergraduate reading habits, ensured its gradual demise. In the early 1990s, computers were still financially out of reach for many undergraduates, but word processing became essential for most class work. The immediate need to find a place for staff displaced from the structurally unsound Gebauer Student Services building in 1992 led to the removal of a large portion of the UGL collection from the second floor; volumes were either integrated into the PCL's collections or sent to storage at the Collections Deposit Library near the Frank C. Erwin, Jr. Special Events Center or at the Library Storage Facility on the J. J. Pickle Research Campus in north Austin. Once the student services staff moved out in late 1993, the space was converted to a huge 200-seat Student Microcomputer Facility (SMF), known affectionately as "the Smurf." This was soon popular enough to be voted one of the best places to pick up a date on any college campus.[20] *Plus ça change, plus c'est la même chose.*

In 2005, the administration of the UT Libraries decided that the remaining portion of the collection would be merged into the PCL. This was in part due to an ongoing revolution in academic libraries that has replaced printed books with electronic information resources. About the same time, a coffee shop was added to the first floor of the PCL. The announcement of the UGL's demise caused something of a stir in the national press when the *New York Times* seized upon the closure with a front-page story headlined "College Libraries Set Books Aside in a Digital Age." The article announced: "By mid-July . . . almost all of the library's 90,000 volumes [this had been 160,000+ volumes in the early 1990s] will be dispersed to other university collections to clear space for a 24-hour electronic information commons, a fast-spreading phenomenon that is transforming research and study on campuses around the country."[21] The *Times* article stirred up media attention around the time when Google was announcing its massive project to convert print materials to digital form; some media outlets had inaccurately represented that development as the death knell of the traditional library.

While some viewed the closing as apocalyptic, a completely opposite (and equally extreme) tack was taken by a reporter for the UT alumni magazine, the *Alcalde*, who emphasized the march of progress inherent in the UGL's demise: "The UGL was to be a 'Gentleman's Library,' stocked with the classic books the University considers crucial to every great education, from Aristotle and Homer to Darwin and Dickens. It was here that the University could guide undergraduates, as a parent guides a child."[22] The writer seems to imply that the millennial student, laptop or iPad in hand, had now been freed from the scourge of dusty sets of the Harvard Classics and the old-fashioned paternalism inherent in the original UGL. This ignores the throngs of students who cheered the easygoing informality of Harry's Place in 1963 and those who, for several decades after, benefited from the UGL's collections as well as its wide range of services targeted at undergraduates.

While the press, as often happens, emphasized the revolutionary nature of the event (good or bad, depending on the point of view), the demise of the Undergraduate Library was ultimately a foregone conclusion. Other universities had already undertaken to merge their graduate and undergraduate collections, notably Cornell University in the early 1990s. Such mergers were partly a consequence of changes in the information environment, and partly a result of serious financial pressures dictating that duplication of book collections and services was no longer feasible. Dennis Dillon, the associate director for collection development at the UT Libraries, reported to a professional group:

> The library side of this process was fairly uneventful. Most of the books were simply moved a couple of hundred yards to the main library, but the misunderstandings, gnashing of teeth, and blog-based accounts of the end of library civilization were interesting. Five months later, the building is still packed and most of the students using the former Undergraduate library are still studying, still using computers, and still having discussions with their colleagues, seemingly unaware of the changes that have occurred around them.[23]

After a new series of renovations to the building, in progress at this writing, are completed, the Flawn Academic Center will bear little resemblance to Harry's Place. The first and second floors have been given over to information technology spaces for the use of students, while the lower level as well as the third and fourth floors are being converted to administrative office space. Harry Ransom could not have envisioned the University's need to provide workstations and printers for thousands of students. He would most likely be dismayed that it had become theoretically possible to complete an undergraduate degree without coming into contact with books, other than textbooks, at all. On the other hand, he might well have been pleased that the notion of an "information commons" aimed at both the social and the intellectual needs of undergraduates has been taken into account in the Flawn Academic Center's expanding Student Microcomputer Facility and the recent student-friendly remodeling of the first floor of the Perry-Castañeda Library.

In that sense, Harry's Place lives!

NOTES

The author wishes to acknowledge the assistance of David Dettmer, Cathy Henderson, Sally Leach, Michele Ostrow, and James Stroud.

1. Quoted in Richard Cole, "Harry's Place Will Become Rendezvous," *Daily Texan*, Aug. 16, 1963.

2. Michael O. Engle, "Forty-Five Years after Lamont: The University Undergraduate Library in the 1990s—The Library and Undergraduate Curriculum," *Library Trends* 20, no. 2 (1995): 371.

3. Ibid.

4. Ransom to W. J. Burke, 24 July 1958; quoted in Alan Gribben, typescript draft of *Harry Huntt Ransom: Intellect in Motion*, 127 (Harry Ransom Humanities Research Center, hereafter cited as Ransom Center). Chapter Nine ("The Academic Center and the Humanities Research Center") of the unpublished version of Gribben's official biography, published by the University of Texas Press in 2008, contains much useful information omitted from the final volume about the development of the Academic Center.

5. Gribben, *Harry Huntt Ransom*, 112.

6. This work appears as "The College Library" in Harry Ransom, *Chronicles of Opinion: On Higher Education, 1955–1975*, ed. Hazel Ransom (Austin: Univ. of Texas at Austin, 1990), 229.

7. Ransom, "The College Library," 230.

8. Ransom to Dobie, 31 Dec. 1957; quoted in Gribben, *Harry Huntt Ransom*, 130. Dobie requested Texas mesquite wood trim for the room, but was overruled by the architects.

9. See "Why Texas?" in Cathy Henderson, ed., *The Company They Kept: Alfred A. and Blanche W. Knopf, Publishers* (Austin: Harry Ransom Humanities Research Center, 1995), 225–227.

10. This room has now been re-created as a virtual exhibition on the Ransom Center's website: http://www.utexas.edu/hrc/esg.

11. Editor's note: For more on the architecture of the Peter T. Flawn Academic Center, see Richard Cleary and Lawrence Speck, "Campus Architecture: Identity Crises," in this volume.

12. The limestone was also prominently used in the Humanities Research Center building (1970), designed by the same firm.

13. The volumes of the J. H. Wrenn Library, along with other pre-1900 books, were maintained in the Miriam Stark Library in the Main Building until they were brought together with the modern materials when the Humanities Research Center building was completed.

14. Quoted in Cole, "Harry's Place Will Become Rendezvous."

15. Fifty thousand volumes were purchased specially for the new building, and 10,000 were transferred from the main library.

16. Sally Leach, interview by Richard Oram, May 24, 2009.

17. Dave Wilson, "Harry's Place Opening Misses Ups and Downs," *Daily Texan*, Sept. 24, 1963.

18. Originally, part of the first floor of the Ransom Center was to be devoted to an exhibition gallery, but this was removed at the last minute so that the Michener Collection of contemporary paintings could be permanently exhibited in the same space.

19. See, for example, Anita Bartholomew, "Page Turners: Institutions Are Giving Students Greater Access to Rare Books and Manuscripts, Opening a New Chapter in Higher Education," *Continental Magazine*, May 2009, http://magazine.continental.com/200905-iom.

20. Juliana Fernandez Helton, "SMF Celebrates 10 Years of Service on Campus," Feb. 27, 2004, http://www.utexas.edu/its/news/features/022004/smfbirthday.html.

21. Ralph Blumenthal, "College Libraries Set Books Aside in a Digital Age," *New York Times*, May 14, 2005, http://www.nytimes.com/2005/05/14/education/14library.html. See also Kris Axtman, "Academic Libraries Empty Stacks for Online Centers," *Christian Science Monitor*, Aug. 23, 2005, http://www.csmonitor.com/2005/0823/p01s05-legn.html. Ironically, the ubiquity of laptops has meant that computer labs are currently being reconfigured as lounges at many universities!

22. Cora Bullock, "Eliot Has Left the Building!," *Alcalde* (Sept.–Oct. 2005), 68.

23. University of Texas Libraries, ALCTS CMDS Chief Collection Development Officers of Large Research Libraries, ALA Midwinter, January 2006, http://www.lita.org/ala/mgrps/divs/alcts/mgrps/cmds/grps/chi/06rpts/06_UTexas.doc.

RICHARD
CLEARY
AND
LAWRENCE
SPECK
} # Campus Architecture

Identity Crises

By 1945, the University of Texas had transformed its campus from a hodgepodge of mismatched buildings to a coherent ensemble of distinguished structures and gracious open spaces projecting confidence and ambition. This effort was led over a span of thirty-five years by inspired University administrators, including President H. Y. Benedict (1927–1937) and longtime chairman of the Faculty Building Advisory Committee William J. Battle (1922–1948), and three distinguished consulting architects: Cass Gilbert (1910–1922), Herbert M. Greene (1922–1930), and Paul Philippe Cret (1930–1945).[1] Among their most notable achievements are Gilbert's University Library and Education Building (known today as Battle Hall and Sutton Hall); Greene's Garrison Hall, Littlefield Dormitory, and Gregory Gymnasium; and Cret's Home Economics Building (known today as Mary E. Gearing Hall), Main Building and Tower, and Texas Memorial Museum. Although most of these buildings employed classical forms inspired by Spanish Renaissance and Spanish colonial architecture (notable exceptions are the Romanesque Gregory Gymnasium and the more austere classicism of the Texas Memorial Museum), they display considerable variety in detail and masterful accommodation of the campus's irregular terrain. Together, they provided the University a strong

---

Richard Cleary is professor and Page Southerland Page Fellow in Architecture in the School of Architecture at the University. He holds a PhD from Columbia University and specializes in the history of architecture and building technology. His published writings cover a broad range of architectural subjects. Lawrence Speck is the W. L. Moody, Jr., Centennial Professor in the School of Architecture and a member of the University's Academy of Distinguished Teachers. He served as the school's dean from 1992 to 2001. He has designed a number of important structures in Austin, including the Austin-Bergstrom International Airport terminal building and the Austin Convention Center. The present essay is drawn from material developed for the authors' The University of Texas at Austin: The Campus Guide *(2011), and serves as a continuation of Professor Speck's essay "Campus Architecture: The Heroic Decades," which is in the first volume of* The Texas Book.

image and, with the master development plan Cret completed in 1933, a model for future expansion. That model, however, was predicated on the continuity of familiar patterns of growth and enduring building types, but neither would remain constant in the second half of the twentieth century.

Veterans returning from World War II swelled UT's enrollment to 17,260 in 1946, nearly 7,000 more than before the war. This was the first of successively larger waves of men and women that over the next forty years would increase the student body to more than 50,000. The growth of the student population coincided with an equally dramatic expansion of the University's research mission, and both required larger and more technologically complex buildings than those erected before the war. A further challenge was the emergence of new architectural ideologies calling for the invention of forms exuding the spirit of modernity rather than allusions to the past. These demands reopened questions of architectural expression and institutional identity that Cret's visionary plan seemingly had settled before the war.

CRET'S SHADOW AND
THE MODERNIST CHALLENGE,
1945–1960

The postwar increase in enrollment was not unexpected. In 1944, President Homer Rainey approved revisions to the master development plan that supervising architect Robert Leon White had prepared with input from the ailing Cret, who would die the following year. Its most striking feature was the development of the East Mall as the new area for campus growth. As Cret had long anticipated, venerable B. Hall, the first men's dormitory, was to be demolished so that the University could establish an axis from the Main Building toward Waller Creek. To the east of Speedway, the mall was to have been lined with symmetrically placed buildings for the College of Engineering and terminated by a large auditorium shortly before the creek. The plan also called for a new building for the law school at the southeast corner of the Forty Acres; a group of buildings enclosing a courtyard at the southwest corner, where the Harry Ransom Center stands today; dormitories north of 26th Street (since renamed Dean Keeton Street); and a large building for the College of Engineering, facing the Power Plant across 24th Street. Although few

of the proposed buildings were realized as the plan indicated, it served as a reference for the next decade and, thus, maintained Cret's vision for the campus.

In 1948, the board of regents awarded the position of consulting architect to Dallas architect Mark Lemmon. A native Texan, Lemmon had studied geology at UT and received his bachelor's degree in 1912, a year after the completion of Battle Hall. He then attended the Massachusetts Institute of Technology (MIT), where he earned a professional degree in architecture. After employment with the prominent firm Warren and Wetmore in New York City and military service in World War I, Lemmon returned to Texas and began to practice in Dallas. He prospered, building one of the city's leading firms, with a wide range of clients, including large institutions such as Southern Methodist University and the Dallas Independent School District. During his eight years as UT's consulting architect, Lemmon had responsibility for fourteen buildings on the Austin campus, two buildings for the Southwestern Medical Center in Dallas, which became part of the UT System in 1949, and unrealized projects for the Medical Branch in Galveston.

Rooted in historicism, Lemmon sought to maintain a consistent character for the Austin campus, one faithful to the architectural vocabulary Gilbert, Greene, and Cret had devised. This was his approach at the Southern Methodist University campus, where Georgian Revival buildings set the dominant tone, and it met with the approval of the UT regents as well. However, the programmatic requirements, labor costs, and construction practices of building in the early 1950s were not those of the 1930s, and Lemmon's buildings are a pale reflection of the work of Gilbert, Greene, and Cret. The classical details of Blanton Dormitory (1954), for example, are sketchlike compared to those of Carothers Dormitory (1935), designed by Cret, on the other side of the courtyard, and the building's large size, necessitated by its population of twice as many residents as older dormitories, breaks with the scale of its neighbors.

Had Lemmon designed his buildings for the campus a decade earlier, he might have received unfavorable notice on stylistic details, but his conservative strategy would have been unexceptionable. By 1949, however, modernists critical of traditional forms in American architecture were becoming increasingly vocal, and when Lemmon's plans for the first of his projects on campus became public, architecture

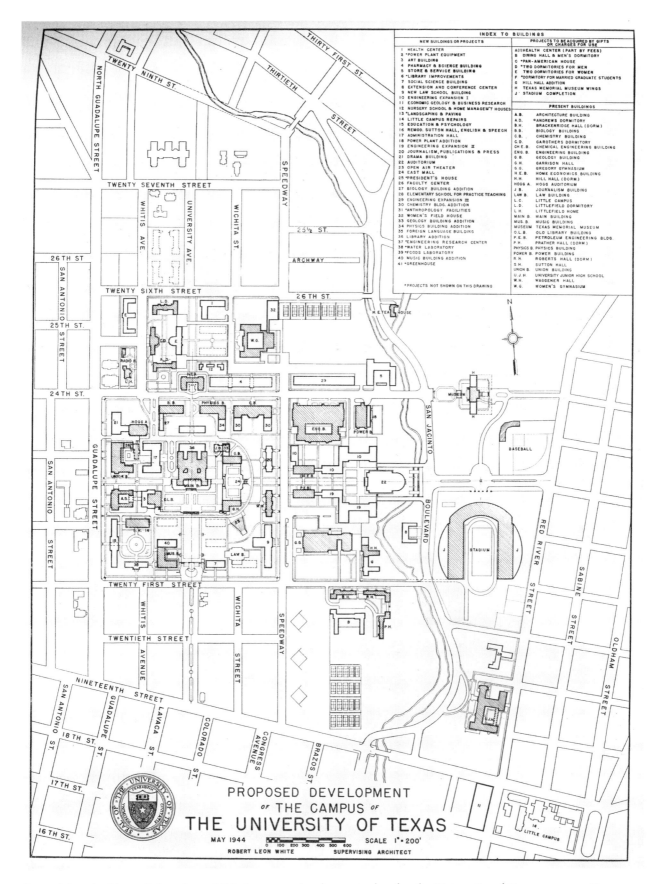

Supervising Architect Robert Leon White's master development plan for the University of Texas campus, May 1944. *Courtesy of the Alexander Architectural Archive, University of Texas Libraries, University of Texas at Austin. (University of Texas Buildings Collection)*

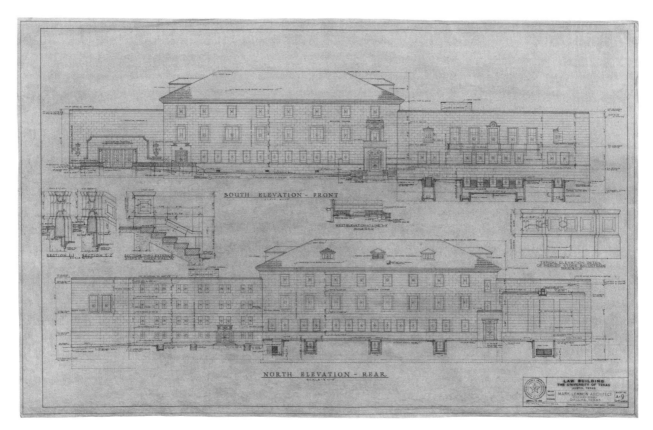

Mark Lemmon's elevation drawings for the Law Building, later named Townes Hall, 1951. *Courtesy of the Alexander Architectural Archive, University of Texas Libraries, University of Texas at Austin. (University of Texas Buildings Collection, Law Building sh. #A9)*

students fueled a protest that spread off campus and into the pages of the *Dallas Morning News.* "If the university is to fulfill its role in developing the cultural background of the coming generation," they wrote in a letter to the Faculty Building Advisory Committee released to the newspaper, "its entire attitude should be creative, not imitative."[2] They pointed to other universities that were "beginning to build in a free, rational and contemporary feeling," producing works then under construction such as the Harvard Graduate Center by Walter Gropius and the Architects Collaborative and Baker House by Alvar Aalto at MIT.

The student voices must have reflected growing opinion within the architectural establishment in Texas, because Lemmon's biographers Richard Brettell and William Winters describe him as profoundly shaken by the controversy, and while it did not lead to an immediate change in his position for the buildings at UT, his firm soon began to embrace

a restrained modernism in its work for the Dallas Independent School District. Citing buildings such as Casa View Elementary School in Dallas (1951), Brettell and Winters characterize Lemmon's modernist style as favoring large expanses of brick broken by horizontal groupings of windows surrounded by prominent bands of trim.

The exterior of Lemmon's most imposing UT commission, Townes Hall (1952), built for the law school on an open site on a hill above the east bank of Waller Creek, may reflect an unresolved struggle to find a middle ground between historicism and modernism. While its classical details would satisfy a checklist of features found on older campus buildings, they float as isolated objects on smooth expanses of limestone massed in good modernist fashion according to the building's internal organization. More successful is Lemmon's final building on campus, Kinsolving Dormitory (1958), which adopts the modernist vocabulary his firm devised for its schools in Dallas. This image suited University officials, who strongly promoted the dormitory as the latest word in student housing, replete with such modern amenities as air-conditioning, elevators, and hooded hair dryers on every floor.

Lemmon, like Cret, preferred an evolutionary approach to modernism, but architectural taste for institutional buildings in the 1950s increasingly favored more radical breaks with the past. The appearance of functionality, the absence of traditional ornament, and the prominent display of materials associated with modernity, such as brick, glass, and aluminum (all prominent in Kinsolving Dormitory), were hallmarks of the new order. Lemmon and others who had established their reputations as historicist architects struggled to master the new conventions, and architects educated in the 1930s and later often took the lead in innovation.

Among the younger generation was Louis C. Page,

Jr., who earned his bachelor's degree in architecture at UT in 1929 and a master's degree at MIT, where Louis F. Southerland, who had transferred from UT, was completing his undergraduate degree. Page and Southerland returned to Texas and formed a partnership that added Page's younger brother, George Matthew Page, following his graduation from UT in 1939. Page Southerland Page grew into a large practice in the postwar years, with many institutional and governmental clients, and when Mark Lemmon's contract ended in 1956, the regents hired the firm as consulting architect.

Page Southerland Page designed two buildings at the end of the 1950s that furthered the introduction of modernist design on campus. The W. R. Woolrich Laboratories building (originally known as the Engineering Laboratories Building) of 1958 is a straightforward expression of its construction—reinforced-concrete frame and brick infill—with no ornament

Kinsolving Dormitory. *From the Prints and Photographs Collection—UT—Dormitories—Kinsolving, Dolph Briscoe Center for American History, University of Texas at Austin. (DI 06859)*

Business Administration and Economics Building, viewed from the Tower, July 1967. To the right is Pearce Hall, the former home of the UT School of Law. Today, the Graduate School of Business Building stands where Pearce Hall stood. *Detail from photo of Jester Center construction site, UT News and Information Services Records—Jester Center, Dolph Briscoe Center for American History, University of Texas at Austin. (DI 06880)*

other than the patterns of the colored tiles facing the walls of the entrances.

The McCombs School of Business building (originally the Business Administration and Economics Building) was the first modernist building on the Forty Acres. Upon its completion, in 1962, it was the largest classroom building on campus and second in height only to the Main Building. It was composed of three distinct volumes provoked by separate programmatic needs: a five-story classroom building organized around an open courtyard; a compact office building for faculty and staff; and, linking them, a circulation hub containing the first escalators to appear in any building on campus.

Even though the building's plan, flat roofs, forthright expression of its structure, and crisp detail appeared refreshingly modern at the time, the design of the complex contains many gestures that tie it back to previous campus buildings as well. Its dominant material is a slightly toned-down version of the brick used in Waggener Hall and Gregory Gymnasium. Its first-floor base employs the familiar Cordova Cream limestone and Texas Pink granite, laid in horizontal bands similar to those along the base of Waggener.

The classroom portion has deep overhangs with coffered soffits, and the top floor was treated as a sort of belvedere with dark red clay-tile screens (removed in 2008) in the spirit of the Moorish quality Cret gave to several of his buildings. Recalling the polychrome terra-cotta work on many of the older buildings on campus, fifty ceramic reliefs with abstract designs created by Paul Peter Hatgil, a member of the Art Department faculty, serve as ornaments on the top of the façades of the office portion. Unlike Lemmon, whose Blanton Dormitory and Geography Building (formerly the Journalism Building, 1952) might be described as "Cret-lite," Page Southerland Page reworked the ingredients of the older buildings on campus in fresh terms.

Page Southerland Page served as consulting architect for only two years, although the firm retained close ties with the University and received additional commissions for individual buildings. At issue was the regents' reassessment of the role of the consulting architect, given the increasingly complex needs of the University of Texas System in addition to those of the Austin campus. No longer comfortable with making a long-term commitment to a single figure or firm, the regents sought to maintain flexibility by awarding more limited contracts. Jessen, Jessen, Milhouse and Greeven served as consulting architect from 1958 to 1962, followed by Brooks, Barr, Graeber and White from 1962 to 1966. The regents abolished the position of consulting architect in 1967 and instead relied on the administrative staff to coordinate the nomination of architects for building projects on a case-by-case basis.

By using many different architects, the University created plum jobs that politicians could, at times, auction off to the highest bidder. It is not unusual to hear stories from prominent Texas architects of the era who remember being visited by a bagman who offered the chance at commissions on the UT campus in exchange for campaign contributions. Shortened tenures, piecemeal commissions, and the politicization of the architect-selection process diluted the leadership role of architects in campus design and planning. From the late 1960s to 1994, when the regents commissioned Cesar Pelli to prepare a master development plan, the story of architecture and planning on the campus revolves more around administrators than architects.

THE HARRY RANSOM AND FRANK ERWIN YEARS, 1960–1975

Two giant figures in the University's history occupied center stage in the 1960s and 1970s: Harry Huntt Ransom, in his capacities as president and chancellor, and the regent Frank C. Erwin, Jr. Today, Ransom is best known for the extraordinary humanities research center that bears his name and stands as testimony to his commitment to fulfill the state constitution's mandate for a university of the first class. Ransom joined UT in 1935 as an instructor of English and rose through the ranks as a professor and, subsequently, as an administrator. He became dean of the College of Arts and Sciences in 1954 and provost in 1957. After naming him president in 1960, the regents made him chancellor of the University of Texas System a year later, a position he held for a decade. Highly respected by his faculty colleagues, Ransom also was effective in his dealings with regents and state legislators.

The building honoring Frank Erwin, the Frank C. Erwin, Jr. Special Events Center (1977), is no less fit-

ting a monument to its namesake than the Harry Ransom Center is to its. Large, confrontational, and resolutely populist, its attributes recall the man whose reputation continues to elicit strong reactions, pro and con, thirty years after his death, in 1980. Appointed to the board of regents in 1963 by his close friend Governor John Connolly, Erwin served on the board until 1975, holding the powerful position of chairman from 1966 to 1971. Erwin reportedly asserted that the greatness of a university rested on buildings, athletics, and funding, and he certainly saw to it that all three flourished on his watch. He engineered the University's most expensive building campaign up to that time and initiated an expansion of athletic facilities that has continued into the twenty-first century. His friendship with President Lyndon Johnson facilitated the University's access to sources of funding in Washington and encouraged the president to locate his library in Austin.

Among the first challenges Ransom faced as president was the preparation of a ten-year master development plan for the board of regents. With enrollment forecasts projecting an additional ten thousand students over the course of the 1960s (the actual increase would be higher—approximately twelve thousand), and a national educational policy calling for an ambitious agenda to expand research, especially in the sciences and engineering, Ransom sought simultaneously to manage growth and foster academic excellence.

A critical question was where to locate the new facilities required to support instruction and research as well as to provide parking for the automobiles of students, faculty, and staff, which by midcentury were clogging the streets and taking over open ground on campus and in the surrounding neighborhoods. Ransom's administration gave serious consideration to moving the College of Engineering's upper-level instruction and research programs either to the Brackenridge Tract along Town Lake (now Lady Bird Lake) or to a 210-acre property (now the Pickle Research Campus) on the northern outskirts of the city, acquired from the federal government in 1949. Both sites had ample room for the large buildings needed to accommodate modern laboratories, and precedents among other major universities for such a move included the University of Michigan's relocation of its engineering programs to the new North Campus at the edge of Ann Arbor, which began in

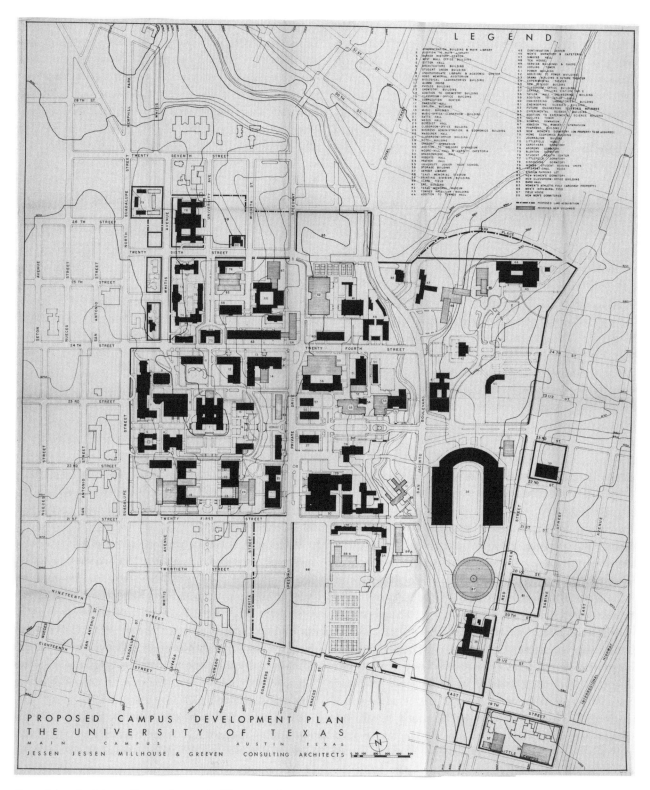

Consulting Architects Jessen, Jessen, Millhouse and Greeven's master development plan for the University of Texas campus, August 1962. *Courtesy of the Alexander Architectural Archive, University of Texas Libraries, University of Texas at Austin. (University of Texas Buildings Collection)*

1954. Despite the advantages offered by the outlying sites, Ransom resolved to keep all academic programs on the main campus, a momentous decision for future development.

The ten-year plan also set the objective that instructional facilities be situated no more than a walk of ten minutes (the interval between classes) from the Main Building. Future construction was to be directed to open areas within that radius. The demand for classrooms, laboratories, and offices was such that many of the new structures would require larger footprints and significantly greater heights than the older buildings on campus, thereby disrupting the carefully considered proportional relationships among the buildings and open spaces foreseen by Cret's master development plan.

A thorn in the scheme was the presence of the football stadium on a prime site near the edge of the boundary set by the "ten-minute rule." University officials triggered controversy in 1965 when they considered demolishing it and building a new stadium off campus, where there would be more room for parking and expansion. Heated opposition from students and alumni convinced the regents to abandon the proposal, and the stadium, ever increasing in size, remains a formidable presence as both a campus icon and an obstacle.

Ransom's decision to keep the College of Engineering on campus raised the question of where its new buildings would be located. The 1944 master plan of President Rainey's administration had proposed lining the East Mall with buildings for engineering, but while the long, thin structures indicated in the plan might have been adequate for classrooms, they were not large enough to contain modern laboratories and workshops. The women's sports fields to the north of 24th Street across from Taylor Hall (demolished in 2010), the College of Engineering's main building, however, offered ample room for such facilities, and a first step in occupying this area had been taken in 1958 with the construction of the W. R. Woolrich Laboratories on the north side of the street. It was followed in 1962 by the Engineering-Science Building, designed by Jessen, Jessen, Millhouse, Greeven & Crume with associate architects Phelps & Dewees & Simmons, which established the edge of the loose quadrangle of engineering and science buildings that, within a decade, extended to 26th Street (now named Dean Keeton Street). The main unit is

Architects' rendering of the Engineering-Science Building, ca. 1962. *From the UT News and Information Services Records—Engineering-Science Building, Dolph Briscoe Center for American History, University of Texas at Austin. (DI 06877)*

The Engineering-Science Building's pool, designed to shield scientific apparatus from solar radiation. *From the Prints and Photographs Collection—UT—Buildings— Engineering-Science, Dolph Briscoe Center for American History, University of Texas at Austin. (DI 06865)*

a blocky, brick-clad structure. Its small windows are operable, but unlike the earlier engineering and science buildings on campus, this is a building fully dependent on fluorescent lighting and mechanical climate control. Natural light and ventilation, now amenities rather than necessities, were made available only in the offices, classrooms, and small laboratories along the building's perimeter. Large laboratories and support areas requiring artificial climate control are located in the core.

The Engineering-Science Building was built at a time when progressive-minded architects and clients celebrated scientific and technological research with monumental architecture, such as Louis Kahn's Richards Medical Research Building (1957–1965) on the campus of the University of Pennsylvania, or the General Motors Technical Center (1946–1955) in Warren, Michigan, designed by Eero Saarinen. The architects of the Engineering-Science Building used its pair of particle accelerators—glamorous instruments in the atomic age of the early 1960s—as the key for aesthetic expression in the treatment of the low wing and slender tower that housed them, just north of the main unit. They transformed a pragmatic requirement—a water-filled pool to shield the apparatus below from solar radiation—into an element as delightful as the more traditional fountains Paul Cret had envisioned elsewhere on campus. Unfortunately, this architectural gesture proved more permanent than the research apparatus, and the forlorn state of the pool and the still-elegant canopy alongside it today reflects the difficulty of adapting the structure to new uses. Subsequent science and engineering buildings, such as Ernest Cockrell Jr. Hall (1971), lack the aesthetic ambition of the Engineering-Science Building, but offer greater flexibility in the arrangement of laboratory spaces. Indeed, Engineering-Science is marked for demolition to make way for a building better suited for twenty-first-century research and instruction.

Ransom and Erwin had neither the time nor the passion that William J. Battle could devote to the details of architecture earlier in the century, and the quality of the more than two dozen buildings realized on the campus during their administration is mixed. The two buildings most closely associated with Ransom's interests, the Peter T. Flawn Academic Center (originally named the Academic Center and Undergraduate Library when it was completed, in 1963) and the Harry Ransom Center (originally named the Humanities Research Center when it was completed, in 1972), illustrate the point.

Believing that great libraries are at the heart of first-class universities, Ransom vigorously promoted improved access to library materials for undergradu-

Architects' final rendering of the Academic Center and Undergraduate Library, as approved by the UT board of regents. Battle Hall is seen in the foreground. (Note that the two ornamental figures between the fenestrations were not included in the final construction of the building.) *From the Prints and Photographs Collection—UT Buildings—Peter T. Flawn Academic Center, Dolph Briscoe Center for American History, University of Texas at Austin. (DI 07327)*

ates and the expansion of UT's research collections for advanced study. He intended the Academic Center and Undergraduate Library to be a place where undergraduates would freely encounter the world of ideas embodied by books available in open stacks (an innovative concept at the time), art exhibitions, and readily accessible special collections.[3] Comfortable seating with areas set aside for conversation, including a rooftop terrace, contrasted with the study-hall atmosphere of the University's older libraries. Consulting architects Jessen, Jessen, Millhouse and Greeven, in collaboration with the versatile Dallas architect George L. Dahl, whose work at UT had begun in the 1920s as a partner of Herbert M. Greene and continued as associate architect with Paul Cret, rose to the occasion in their design for this innovative building. Ransom expressed his pleasure in a letter to Stark Young, a UT benefactor:

The architects have now finished their final perspective of the new building. I think that you will like the judicious combination of renaissance—with a small letter—and modern design. The Regents accepted the plan of the building with some argument;

a great compliment to their confidence in its function. They professed to believe that this is the most important building erected on the central University campus![4]

The glassy openness of the ground floor, which has contributed so significantly both to the interactive life of the building and its engagement with the West Mall and the Texas Union Courtyard, could have been managed only in a modern building, and the building's flexible, multipurpose character, which has enabled it to change responsively with the times, could not have occurred in a more traditionally planned structure. But the Flawn Center's cladding of Cordova Cream and Cordova Shell limestone locate the building firmly on the UT campus. Its tripartite composition—a base of glass and black granite, a plainer midsection with solar screens of cast stone, and an ornate cap—ties it to most of its predecessors of the prior fifty years. Its recessed top floor still carried a vague remembrance of the Spanish belvedere that inspired the crowns of Mary E. Gearing Hall, the Texas Union, and Goldsmith Hall until an unfortunate renovation in 2010. The rich blue mosaic tiles that lined those recesses recalled the colorful terra-cotta used in most of the buildings by Cass Gilbert and Herbert M. Greene. The broad coffered roof soffits repeat a motif characteristic of many of the earlier structures on the Forty Acres.

The Harry Ransom Center also has panels of Cordova Shell limestone and a tripartite composition of base, mid-section, and cap, but it took a leap of imagination to see it as an integral part of the campus until 2003, when Lake|Flato cut into its fortresslike walls and allowed passersby to realize that the treasures of what Ransom envisioned as "the national library of Texas" are to be enjoyed by the public as well as by scholars. The heavy, opaque character of the original building, designed by Max Brooks with Jessen, Jessen, Millhouse, Greeven and Crume, cannot be justified fully by the need to protect the vast collection of mostly paper artifacts from damaging ultraviolet light. Instead, this character reflects a shift in architectural taste that occurred in the course of the nine years separating it from the Flawn Academic Center. In contrast to the transparency and polished architectural finishes of the Flawn Center, the Ransom Center is an essay on the compositional themes of what architectural theorists of the late 1960s termed the

Harry Ransom's Humanities Research Center, 1978. *From the Prints and Photographs Collection—UT—Libraries—Humanities Research Center, Dolph Briscoe Center for American History, University of Texas at Austin. (DI 06856)*

New Brutalism. Loosely inspired by the late works of the Swiss architect Le Corbusier, which dramatically employed exposed concrete (the French term for raw concrete is *béton brut*) and devices such as slab-shaped sunscreens (*brises soleils*), a lugubrious treatment of this style became popular on North American university campuses just as the "dawning of the Age of Aquarius" was demanding that people "let the sunshine in." Another example of Brutalism on campus is the School of Nursing Building (1971), designed by Simpson and Lackey.

Big statements coupled with expediency marked Frank Erwin's attitude towards architecture. Both are embodied by the massive Beauford H. Jester Center, which opened in 1969. A persistent campus legend claims its architects specialized in prisons; however, this is not the case. The firms responsible for its design—the consulting architects Brooks, Barr, Graeber and White and the associate architects Jessen, Jessen, Millhouse, Greeven and Crume with John Linn Scott—are the authors of numerous buildings on the UT campus. Nevertheless, the expanses of blank wall and tiers of small windows surrounded by heavy limestone frames do suggest a facility that incarcerates its residents.

Such an intention was far from the minds of those

Architect's early conception of the Beauford H. Jester Center. *From the UT News and Information Services Records—Jester Center, Dolph Briscoe Center for American History, University of Texas at Austin. (DI 07017)*

who conceived the building. On the contrary, it was a bold experiment intended to foster a sense of community among freshmen and sophomores. Inspired by the house model of student dormitories, the Jester Center combined residential and academic facilities that, in the initial plans, even included faculty apartments. But unlike the typical college house with, say, two hundred residents, it was built on an unprecedented scale, housing approximately three thousand students. At the time of completion, it was the largest college dormitory in North America.

The planning of Jester Center coincided with nationwide interest in the use of high-rise buildings on college campuses to meet the demands of rapidly growing enrollments. These structures often were designed as freestanding towers in parklike settings, such as Harvard's Peabody Terrace (Sert, Jackson & Gourley, 1962–1964) and the Southwest Quadrangle at the University of Massachusetts (Hugh Stubbins & Associates, ca. 1966). Jester's proximity to the smaller-scale men's dormitories of the Cret era (Brackenridge, Roberts, and Prather Hall Dormitories) led its architects to follow a different strategy. They placed the two towers of ten and fourteen stories amid courtyards at the center of the block-sized site and lined the perimeter with three- and five-story buildings of brick with Cordova Shell limestone trim and red tile roofs, responding to the scale

and character-defining materials of the older dormitories. The low buildings contain classrooms, study areas, and offices for faculty and student services and open to an interior "main street" with shops, a movie theater–lecture hall, and access to the dining halls and the dormitory towers. Budgetary concerns that reduced the proposed amenities and raised the height of the towers in order to increase revenue diluted, but did not completely efface, the ideals to which the building aspired.

Frank Erwin proudly presided over the dedication of Jester Center in September 1969. A month later, he was center stage in a quite different gathering related to a new campus building: the "Battle of Waller Creek." The conflict erupted over the University's plans to remove trees along a portion of the creek in order to allow the relocation of San Jacinto Street as part of the expansion of Texas Memorial Stadium, which included the construction of L. Theo Bellmont Hall within the structure of the west side of the expanded stadium. When word spread that the removal was imminent, students surrounded the site and occupied the trees in defiance of orders to disperse. Erwin went to the scene and personally directed the police to intervene. "Arrest all the people you have to," he has been quoted as saying. "Once these trees are down, there won't be anything to protest." Twenty-seven students were arrested, and the trees were destroyed, but other students hauled branches up the hill and piled them in front of the entrance to the Main Building to prove him wrong.[5]

In the early 1970s, Erwin again raised the ire of students and faculty who criticized the enclosure of the southern and western edges of the Forty Acres with walls and planters, reducing the points of entry to the campus from the commercial district and disrupting the historic Peripatos, a tree-lined walk that had served as a campus boundary since it was laid out in 1891. Erwin maintained that the barrier was necessary to minimize damage to the landscape by uncontrolled foot traffic, but opponents saw the walls as an effort to control access to the campus. They argued that Erwin was using architecture as an instrument with which to inhibit dissent, linking this action with the contemporary redesign of the West Mall, which replaced a favorite rally point facing the Texas Union with a wide, circular fountain whose outer edge prevents sitting in this high-traffic pedestrian area.

Three Austin-based firms commanded the majority of the architectural work on campus during the Ransom and Erwin years: Page Southerland Page; Jessen, Jessen, Millhouse and Greeven; and Brooks, Barr, Graeber and White. Founded in the 1930s, all had flourished with institutional and corporate commissions in the decades following World War II. Most of the principals had earned their architecture degrees at UT. For those who went on to graduate study—notably Louis Page, Bubi Jessen, and Max Brooks—MIT was the favored institution (Louis Southerland received his bachelor's degree from MIT), where they received more thorough exposure to modernist architecture than they had encountered in Austin. By the 1960s, their firms had become adept in handling the prevailing idioms of modern design, but despite their expertise and familiar presence on campus, none of them received the commission for the University's most high-profile project of the 1960s, the Lyndon Baines Johnson Library and Museum and the adjacent Sid Richardson Hall. Instead, the Johnsons selected Gordon Bunshaft, a brilliant architect who was a partner in the New York office of Skidmore, Owings & Merrill. Among his prominent works is the Beinecke Rare Books and Manuscript Library at Yale University, which Mrs. Johnson admired. Brooks, Barr, Graeber and White, which at the time held the position of consulting architect at UT, was named associate architect. This appointment may have been smoothed by Max Brooks and Bunshaft having been classmates at MIT.

Like Cret's Texas Memorial Museum, the LBJ Library and Museum, dedicated in 1971, has a dual identity. It is both part of the fabric of the campus and a public monument to something larger than the University. Just as the Texas Memorial Museum honors the "heroic period of early Texas history," the LBJ complex celebrates the life and administration of the thirty-sixth president of the United States and attracts visitors who may not have any particular connection to UT. In both instances, the architects designed structures that powerfully convey their memorial purpose. The LBJ Library and Museum's solid, unornamented, and unpunctuated east and west walls, 200 feet long and sixty-five feet high, are faced in travertine and have the scale of a monument from an ancient civilization. The tenth-floor mass that spans the ninety feet between them and cantilevers an additional sixteen feet on either side

Lyndon Baines Johnson Library and Museum (*left*) and Sid Richardson Hall (*right*). *From the Prints and Photographs Collection—LBJ Library & Museum, Dolph Briscoe Center for American History, University of Texas at Austin. (DI 07010)*

establishes an elemental clarity for the building that is simple and timeless. In addition, the gentle curve of the flanking walls, the pin connections and glass slots that form the junction between the top floor and the walls, and the metal caps that indicate the girders have been post-tensioned all help elucidate the structural role of each of the building's components in a manner that is uncompromisingly modern. The gently curving walls are expressed as well in the Great Hall at the north end of the building, where the spatial volume and grand staircase focus attention on a five-story glass wall through which the display of 4,200 flag-red buckram manuscript boxes honor the historical record documenting Johnson's successes and failures.

The LBJ Library and Museum building is the focal point of a nineteen-acre ensemble: paved terraces, a rolling landscape of manicured lawns and stands of live oaks, and the 935-foot-long Sid Richardson Hall, which demarks the eastern edge. Although the architectural language is uncompromisingly modernist, the overall effect of the complex recalls an ancient Greek temple precinct, with Sid Richardson Hall acting as an enclosing portico that sets off and gives scale to the freestanding shrine of the presiding deity, reinterpreted here as the LBJ Library and Museum building. Just as the Parthenon on the Acropolis stood apart from the dense texture of ancient Athens, the LBJ complex presents a sense of building and landscape very different from the urban character of the campus at the heart of the Forty Acres. Each is masterfully composed and effective. The identity of the area between them, however, is less well defined.

At midcentury, a decade before planning began for the LBJ Library and Museum, the only University structures of note east of Waller Creek were Memorial Stadium, Clark Field (the baseball stadium, which was located approximately on the site now occupied by the College of Fine Arts Performing Arts Center), and Texas Memorial Museum. San Jacinto Boulevard wound its way along the stream, which still retained a country feel with stands of native trees. Beyond the stadium (approximately on the alignment of Robert Dedman Drive), the original Red River Street traced the crest of a low ridge and defined the western edge of a residential neighborhood platted on a grid of streets. Slightly to the south of the stadium stood University Junior High School (now the School of Social Work Building), and at the intersection of Red River and 19th Street (now named Martin Luther King Jr. Boulevard) was the historic Little Campus, built in the mid-nineteenth century as the state school for the blind and used by the University for a variety of purposes after World War I. Two blocks to the east of Red River was East Avenue, a north-south thoroughfare that became the right-of-way for I-35 in the 1950s.

The scattered University buildings and the low density of the neighboring private properties made the area east of Waller Creek a prime target for future expansion. The relocation in 1952 of such an important component of the University as the law school to a site east of the Texas Memorial Museum—one offering convenient automobile access to old Red River Street and, it was thought, wishfully, ample room for parking—was a decisive step. Simkins Hall (now known as Creekside Residence Hall) was built nearby in 1955 as the first unit of a never fully realized dormitory group intended for law students. Eight years later, the Art Building and Museum was completed at the intersection of San Jacinto Boulevard and the East Mall, setting the stage for the fine arts complex a decade later. The present University Police Building, built in 1960 at East Campus Drive and Manor Road (this is now the intersection of Robert Dedman

Drive and Clyde Littlefield Drive) as the Printing Division Building, was a demonstration of the ten-year plan's objective of relocating new service buildings outside the ten-minute-walk zone. This development was piecemeal, and the prevailing attitude for physical planning was to treat the area as a suburb, occupied by isolated buildings indifferently surrounded by lawns or parking.

The LBJ complex increased the importance of the campus's eastern edge. Shortly after its plans for the acquisition of land became public in 1965, the University and the City of Austin announced their partnership in a vast urban redevelopment project known as University East, which proposed extending UT's land holdings on both sides of I-35 and deep into the mostly residential neighborhoods of East Austin. Using federal funds and the power of eminent domain, the city was to acquire the land and transfer it to the University. The planners responsible for this scheme may have seen it as different only in scale from previous expansions that had enlarged the campus from the original Forty Acres. In those efforts, appeals to the inevitability of progress and the allure of buyout money had overcome reluctant property owners and justified the demolition of noteworthy buildings, but by the late 1960s, progress did not have same meaning or unquestioned authority that it had had even a decade earlier.

A racially segregated city at midcentury, Austin separated its black and white areas on either side of East Avenue, the alignment upon which I-35 was built. Many residents of the University East development area, predominantly African American, viewed the University's extension across that line as an institutional invasion of their neighborhood. They particularly took exception to the terms of redevelopment that required the wholesale declaration of the area as blighted. This assessment required the demolition of all properties in order to provide a clean slate for new development. Among the casualties in this politically charged process was the six-year-old Oaks Apartments by the noted architect and UT faculty member Roland G. Roessner—one of the few buildings in Austin to have received a national design award from the American Institute of Architects. Coincident with the tensions of desegregation at the University and elsewhere in the city, the development scheme also raised suspicions that it was an effort to push blacks away from the campus. Vocal opposition convinced the University to scale back its plans and concentrate its projects, which eventually included Disch-Falk Field (1975) and a group of service buildings, in the blocks closest to I-35. The University's presence in East Austin, however, remained a source of controversy for decades because of distrust regarding its intentions and the community's reservations about living adjacent to a miscellany of service buildings displaced to the edge of campus by the ten-minute rule.

A second urban renewal venture, initiated in 1967, encountered less resistance. Known as the Brackenridge Redevelopment Tract because of its proximity to Brackenridge Hospital on Red River Street, the site extended from San Jacinto Boulevard to I-35 and from 15th Street to Martin Luther King Jr. Boulevard (formerly 19th Street), including the Little Campus. As part of redevelopment of the site, a residential neighborhood was demolished and replaced with a park along Waller Creek, creating a new alignment of Red River Street that allowed for the expansion of the hospital and the construction of the Frank C. Erwin, Jr. Special Events Center (completed 1977). The Collections Deposit Library (1966), the School of Nursing Building (1971), and the Penick-Allison Tennis Center (1984) also were built on the tract. The historic Little Campus (now the Heman Sweatt Campus) was to have become a parking lot for the Erwin Center, but vigorous opposition by preservationists, prominent alumni, and a determined graduate student, Susan Barry, managed to save two buildings, the Arno Nowotny Building (1859) and John W. Hargis Hall (1888–1900).

DENOUEMENT, 1975–1990

Harry Ransom resigned as chancellor in 1971, and Frank Erwin stepped down from the board of regents in 1975, but buildings in which they had a hand remained in the pipeline. Acquisition of a tract of land south of 21st Street became the site of the Perry-Castañeda Library (completed 1977), which replaced the Main Building and Tower as the facility housing the central library. Whereas the older library had emphasized the storage of books in vertical stacks filling the Tower, the PCL emphasized the more contemporary practice of creating large horizontal spaces that facilitated the movement of readers, staff, and books

from section to section. From its opening, users consulting the building's posted floor plans have made a connection between the shape of its footprint and that of the state of Texas. While one might imagine Frank Erwin appreciating the image, the architects (Bartlett Cocke & Associates, Inc. and Phelps & Simmons & Associates) and library administrators who acted as clients for the PCL credited the singular shape to a functional response and an effort to reduce the apparent mass of the huge building.

One of the most impressive aspects of the PCL design is its climate responsiveness—a design priority that came in response to the energy crisis of the early 1970s. Though there is a fairly large amount of glass in the building, very little direct heat gain is received from the sun. Deep vertical fins block the low east and west sun from entering the building, while horizontal sunshades on the south face protect it from midday sun during the hotter portions of the year.

The tract containing the PCL also accommodated a new building for the College of Education. The George I. Sánchez Building, designed by Wilson, Morris, Crain and Anderson and completed in 1975, houses the formerly disparate units of the College of Education under one roof. Longer than a football field, this five-level structure was planned to accommodate 4,000 students with a flexible space wherein the only fixed elements were stairwells, elevators, escalators, and restrooms. Movable partitions, many of which were floor-to-ceiling clear glass with sliding doors, originally defined programmatic areas in the spirit of the open-classroom movement current in public schools at the time. Departments and levels were color-coded in a rainbow of hues, and brightly colored chairs contrasted sharply with white tables and desks and dark grey carpet. The building's brick exterior, however, reveals little of the vitality within.

The largest building project of the 1970s was the fine arts complex, which included a library, classrooms, faculty offices, and performance facilities for music and theater. Approved by the board of regents in 1972, the work took nearly a decade to realize. It completed the consolidation of the departments of the College of Fine Arts, which had been scattered across the campus, in a compact grouping extending from the F. Loren Winship Drama Building at the intersection of the East Mall and San Jacinto Boulevard to the Performing Arts Center.

George I. Sánchez Building. *From the Prints and Photographs Collection—UT—Buildings—Education, Dolph Briscoe Center for American History, University of Texas at Austin. (DI 06891)*

The University awarded the commissions for campus buildings in the 1970s to a larger group of firms than had been the case previously. Some of the firms were not new to UT. Bartlett Cocke, for instance, who designed Perry-Castañeda Library, had been associate architect for the Winship Drama Building (1960) during Jessen, Jessen, Millhouse and Greeven's tenure as consulting architect. Cocke, who received his architectural education at UT (1922) and MIT (1924), based his practice in San Antonio in 1931 and was an established figure in Texas architecture.

Among the newcomers was the Dallas firm Fisher and Spillman, founded by J. Herschel Fisher and Pat Y. Spillman in 1962. Fisher, a 1936 graduate of UT's architecture program, followed the well-beaten path to MIT for graduate study before going into practice in Dallas after World War II. Spillman was among the first generation of architects educated after the war. After completing his undergraduate studies at Texas A&M University in 1949, he went to Harvard University for graduate study in architecture and then to Yale University to study city planning. He worked for the prominent Chicago modernist Harry Weese before returning to Texas.

The firm received its first UT commission, the Thompson Conference Center, in 1968 and within a few years became a dominant presence, with a string of major commissions, including the fine arts complex, the Lee and Joe Jamail Texas Swimming Center, and the Recreational Sports Center. Like Bartlett Cocke's Perry-Castañeda Library, their buildings are imposing structures characterized by monumental, geometric forms clad in broad masonry surfaces (brick rather than the library's Indiana limestone) with deeply set fenestration. The work does not make overt reference to earlier buildings on the campus, but the blocky massing has antecedents (on a smaller scale) in Page Southerland Page's Art Building (1961) and even Paul Cret's Texas Memorial Museum (1936).

The building boom Frank Erwin put into motion helped the campus keep pace with the student population, which rose to forty thousand during his terms as regent, but the period of growth was not over—another ten thousand students would be wearing burnt orange by the end of the 1980s, adding stress to campus buildings and infrastructure. Seeking new sites for expansion, the University attempted to purchase sixteen blocks in the East Austin neighborhood south of Manor Road known as Blackland in 1982 and threatened reluctant property owners with eminent domain proceedings. As in the late 1960s, the residents, some of whom had been displaced by the University's first expansion in the area, protested, and a bitter dispute raged for six years until President William Cunningham and the neighborhood association forged an agreement that reduced the planned acquisitions by half. The site has been used for a child development center, the headquarters of the University Interscholastic League, and the Red and Charline McCombs Field for softball.

In the more central areas of the campus, several large new buildings were built in the 1980s, including the University Teaching Center, adjacent to the PCL, and the Chemical and Petroleum Engineering Building at the northern edge of the engineering group, but the decade is best characterized as a time of renovations to the buildings of the pre–World War II era. The renovation and addition to Goldsmith Hall, home of the School of Architecture, by Thomas, Booziotis and Associates is noteworthy for the sensitive handling of new construction alongside original fabric. At the end of the decade, a distinguished member of the architecture faculty, Charles Moore, reintroduced architectural whimsy, last seen in the buildings of Greene and Cret, in the extension to the Etter-Harbin Alumni Center, which he designed with faculty colleague Richard Dodge.

CONTROVERSIAL MISSTEPS AND THE PELLI PLAN, 1990–2000

Two projects initiated in 1990 highlighted the weaknesses in the University's approach to campus planning, which focused on functional allocations of space without due consideration for the relationship of each part to the whole and to the articulation of features that would contribute to a sense of campus identity. In late August of that year, University officials announced that the east wing of the historic Anna Hiss Gymnasium (Greene, LaRoche and Dahl, 1931) would be demolished to make way for a new molecular biology building. The architectural historian Blake Alexander of the School of Architecture decried the action in the *Daily Texan*: "We are now getting to the point that we're encroaching upon and

actually destroying the strongest element that holds the campus together—the original 1933 plan by Paul Cret. . . . There is no long-range plan, and without one, the campus will continue to deteriorate."[6] The issue for Alexander went beyond the loss of a historic building and took in the more grievous problem of planning without understanding how buildings and the spaces between them function as ensembles. No small part of the beauty of Anna Hiss Gymnasium was its location with respect to the series of terraces Cret had laid out from the Littlefield group of dormitories to Speedway, but over the years, they had been whittled away with the addition of new buildings, such as Burdine Hall (1970). The destruction of the Anna Hiss swimming pool removed another piece from the mosaic.[7]

At the same time, students were preparing a referendum to support the creation of a new student services building. After it passed in early 1991, the University selected a site north of Dean Keeton Street that was severely compromised by an adjacent decrepit apartment building and by difficult, even dangerous, pedestrian accessibility. When students saw the resulting "rat maze" design for the building, they initiated a referendum in late 1993 to withdraw their support. In response, newly installed president Robert Berdahl pledged to launch a campus plan that would examine the University's land and building needs in the hopes of preventing such problems in the future.

By the time a request for qualifications had been distributed to dozens of the top architectural and planning firms in early 1994, the ambitions of the new campus master plan had grown well beyond the scope of functionalist land-planning exercises such as that prepared for the ten-year plan of 1960. Quantitative assessments of space needs were now to be considered with respect to a primary qualitative goal of promoting "interaction and community" and identifying and defining "a system of lively, interactive public spaces for the campus which can provide an environment for community exchange."[8] President Berdahl regarded the physical design of the campus as a powerful vehicle for making the University a more humane, cohesive, and stimulating community and stood firmly behind the project.

After an extensive and unusually public selection process, the University selected Cesar Pelli and Associates of New Haven, Connecticut, as the primary master-plan consultant. Pelli was one of the most respected architects in the United States at the time, and the firm had recently completed an impressive master-planning effort for Rice University. In addition, Fred Clarke, a principal with the firm (later renamed Pelli Clarke Pelli Architects) and an alumnus of the UT School of Architecture, was highly invested in the project. After a fifty-year hiatus, the University of Texas had returned to its model from the early part of the twentieth century wherein it embraced comprehensive planning and sought out top talent to lead the effort.

Over a period of fourteen months, the Pelli team met regularly with a nineteen-member Master Planning Committee appointed by President Berdahl and chaired by physics professor Austin Gleeson. Aware of the poor communication that had engendered suspicion and controversy in the previous decades, the planners devised a participatory process. They held "town hall" meetings on campus and with neighborhood groups from the communities adjacent to the University; consulted city and state transportation agencies as well as advocacy groups for enhanced bikeways and light rail; and discussed various planning options with local and state historical commissions and other special-interest groups.

The completed plan made seven recommendations that reframed the direction of building on the campus and made a considerable contribution to creating the "sense of community" its framers had envisioned:[9]

1. *Reinforce the pedestrian character of the core campus.*

    By reducing daily automobile traffic and parking on the Forty Acres and beyond, a safer and more animated pedestrian environment would ensue. Speedway and several interior parking lots would be closed, and displaced parking would be located in new parking garages at the edges of the campus. Pedestrian-friendly paving, landscaping, lighting, furniture, and vending carts would animate the new car-free environments.

2. *Adopt design guidelines that respect the architectural heritage of the University and create a more cohesive character for the campus.*

    "It is intended," the document declared, "that the unique University of Texas fabric be the point of departure and aesthetic reference for future designers." The critical and, as it would later turn out, contro-

versial phrase in the statement was "point of departure." President Berdahl viewed it as a guideline, noting in his introduction, "We don't want to slavishly imitate all of the buildings on the Forty Acres, but we also don't want things that are different colors and textures."

3. *Establish a community of open spaces.*

    Prominent new linear open spaces with periodic nodes of activity were proposed along the pedestrian-friendly corridors of Speedway, University Avenue (between 21st Street and Martin Luther King Jr. Boulevard), a new North Mall, and an extended and improved East Mall. These, along with more intimate courtyards and plazas located at other points on campus, would create a fabric of diverse, lively places for both formal and informal campus activities.

4. *Increase student housing on campus.*

    President Berdahl considered this the most "critical aspect" of promoting interaction and community, namely, to have a higher percentage of students, especially freshmen, on campus more hours of the day and night. Large new communities of housing were proposed along Waller Creek near the men's dorms from the Cret Plan (Brackenridge, Roberts, and Prather) and on Whitis Avenue near the women's dorms from the Cret Plan (Littlefield, Carothers, and Andrews).

5. *Produce expanded unions and recreational activity centers.*

    Because of the growth of the campus to the east, Cret's Texas Union building on Guadalupe Street was distant from the focus of many students' daily lives. Three new centers of campus life were planned for the area near Waller Creek, more geographically central to the expanded campus.

6. *Increase the density of the core campus through the use of infill sites.*

    A number of locations for sizeable new academic facilities were identified near the center of the campus in an effort to keep the campus compact and walking distances between class changes to ten minutes, a principle retained from the 1960 master development plan. Building on these infill sites was also seen as a mechanism for reinforcing pedestrian activity and completing and improving adjacent open spaces.

7. *Strengthen identity and ease of way finding.*

    The plan proposed a range of new gateways that would announce entry to the campus and give a more gracious presence to the University in the city.

Among the most prominent of these were an enhanced approach to Littlefield Fountain along University Avenue (which had long been dominated by a weedy and desolate median where motorcycles parked) and a more dignified presence of the University facing the Capitol at the corner of Martin Luther King Jr. Boulevard and North Congress Avenue (which had long been flanked by open parking lots).

The campus community, the University administration, and the regents warmly embraced the Pelli Plan. Even before its formal adoption, it began to influence positively current projects like the Connally Center for Justice (1997) and the renovation of Gregory Gymnasium (1996). Over the next fifteen years, substantial advances were made on all seven of the plan's recommendations, and an era of phenomenal growth and physical transformation of the campus, rivaling the building campaigns of the 1930s and the post–World War II decades, would be conducted, for the most part, orderly and coherently.

Speedway was closed to all but emergency vehicular traffic in 1999, and much of the parking in the central campus was gradually relocated to four new parking garages at the periphery, as outlined in the Pelli Plan. Pedestrians began to reclaim the central campus in a way that had not been possible since before World War II. Festive new occasions like Gone to Texas, Forty Acres Fest, and a greatly enhanced spring graduation ceremony took full advantage of the transformation. Informal demonstrations, festivals, parties, and performances, especially in the plaza in front of Gregory Gym, were unimpeded by vehicular traffic.

The Pelli Plan did not solve all campus architectural or planning issues, however, nor did it prevent further controversy. By the late 1990s, there was a growing sense among campus leaders that the design guidelines in the Pelli Plan had been interpreted too literally and that the "slavish" imitation of earlier buildings that President Berdahl had sought to avoid had actually become a constricting factor, preventing the campus from enjoying architecturally distinguished buildings. This concern erupted into controversy in 1999 during the design of the Blanton Museum of Art when members of the board of regents balked at preliminary plans proposed by the Swiss architects Jacques Herzog and Pierre de Meuron, who took a free approach to the guidelines. The initial disagreement turned ugly, and the architects

resigned the commission despite efforts by President Larry Faulkner to mediate a resolution. Widespread coverage of the incident in the press did not portray the University in a flattering light, and the architects' winning of the prestigious Pritzker Prize (the equivalent of the Nobel Prize for architecture) in 2001 as well as the raves that surrounded the completion of their "Bird's Nest" stadium for the Beijing Olympics in 2008 underscored the sense that a great opportunity had been lost. The fiasco placed a heavy burden on the firm chosen to replace Herzog and de Meuron. Kallman McKinnell & Wood produced a building that reverted to a more literal approach to the guidelines in a way that neither offends nor excites, but that otherwise has provided an effective home for the museum's collections.

Though there seems to be no great sentiment on campus that might advocate building alien objects having more to do with their "starchitect's" career than with the University of Texas, there is also a desire to position the institution in a progressive leadership position. Prospective students who visit the campus probably do not get to see the state of the art labs where cutting-edge science is being done. But they do get a sense, from the buildings they experience, whether there is a spirit of exploration present on the campus—or not.

The controversy over the design of the Blanton Museum notwithstanding, the stage was set for addressing a dilemma that had plagued campus development since midcentury. For the first time in four decades, the University had adopted in the Pelli Plan a comprehensive plan for the entire campus, one that sought to achieve goals of cohesiveness and a strong sense of community while still accommodating the needs of contemporary building types, footprints, and technologies. The whole of the campus was clearly envisioned as being far more than the sum of its parts, and a strategy was in place to allow individual buildings some freedom of function and expression while still fulfilling their obligation to create coherent outdoor spaces and a connective campus fabric.

THE CAMPUS AS A HISTORICAL DOCUMENT

Just as the buildings of the heroic decades of UT campus development, 1910–1942, stand as a remarkable record of the ambitions and vision of political and educational leaders of that era, so the buildings of the latter half of the twentieth century provide an equally telling record of the political and educational intrigues of that conflicted period. Aspirations for advancement, innovation, and liberation from the tight strictures of the past are palpable in projects like the McCombs School of Business building and the Flawn Academic Center. They match UT's increasing struggle for a place on the progressive national and international educational stage in the 1960s. Yet the comfort of tradition and nostalgia crops up in other contemporary buildings virtually alongside them, such as the West Mall Building or Calhoun Hall, just as the conservatism of Texas as a state sometimes checked the ambitions of University leadership.

The power, dominance, and even bombast of colorful and influential figures of the era find physical expression in iconic structures like the LBJ Library, the Frank Erwin Center, and the Harry Ransom Center. They eschew dialogue and participation with other campus buildings in favor of a stand-alone monumentality, just as larger-than-life leaders of the time took the reins of the University forcefully and without compromise. They occupy outlying sites on the edges of the campus like big dogs guarding their own identifiable turf.

The fact that in the heroic decades H. Y. Benedict was president for ten years, William J. Battle was the longtime chairman of the Faculty Building Committee, and Paul Cret was the campus architect for twelve years—and that the three of them had great esteem for one another's perspectives and roles—is clearly evident in the long-term planning and coherent assembly of buildings they constructed. Likewise, the battles among regents, chancellors, presidents, athletic directors, and faculty leaders—as well as the revolving door of architects scrambling for political favor—during the years of identity crises is evident in the absence of comprehensive master planning, the fitfulness of architectural language, and the piecemeal division of the campus into various turfs. Too often their buildings were loud but not eloquent, and the denouement that followed was neither climactic nor satisfying.

By the mid-1990s, when President Robert Berdahl commissioned the Pelli master plan, there was fresh resolve to return to an era of strategic planning and design. There was a desire to tell a new story of the University of Texas in the twenty-first century, one that would be as compelling as the story of aspiration told by the best buildings on the old Forty Acres. The mood of campus leaders was hopeful and optimistic. Architecture had been identified as a tool to move the University forward and to project a standard of excellence and progress that would be inspiring and palpable to students, faculty, and visitors alike for decades to come.

NOTES ON SOURCES

Alongside the authors' *The University of Texas at Austin: The Campus Guide* (New York: Princeton Architectural Press, 2011), concise accounts of individual buildings may be found in Margaret C. Berry's *Brick by Golden Brick: A History of Campus Buildings at the University of Texas at Austin, 1883–1993* (Austin: LBCo., 1993).

The principal repository for material pertaining to UT's history is the Dolph Briscoe Center for American History. Archivists there have compiled readily accessible vertical files of press clippings and news releases for many campus buildings and campus plans, such as the urban renewal projects of the 1960s in East Austin. They also have prepared finding aids to guide researchers through the labyrinthine records of UT administration.

Some drawings and other architectural records from the mid-twentieth century have been deposited in the Alexander Architectural Archives, but many remain part of the working collections of campus agencies such as the Department of Project Management and Construction Services and the Division of Housing and Food Service. The lack of publications on the architectural and planning history of the UT campus since World War II is an obstacle that hinders the judgment of the campus community as it weighs decisions regarding the preservation, modification, and demolition of its mid- and late-twentieth-century buildings and landscapes.

NOTES

The authors thank Emily Freeman for her outstanding contributions as research assistant.

1. Editor's note: For a discussion of these three architects and their contributions to the campus architecture of the Uni-

versity of Texas, see "Campus Architecture: The Heroic Decades" by Lawrence Speck in the first *Texas Book*.

2. Lynn Landrum, "Thinking Out Loud," *Dallas Morning News*, 26 Nov., 1949; quoted in Richard R. Brettell and Willis Cecil Winters, *Crafting Traditions: The Architecture of Mark Lemmon* (Dallas: Meadows Museum and SMU Press, 2005), 74–75.

3. Editor's note: For more information about this building, see Richard W. Oram, "'Harry's Place': A Brief History of the Academic Center and Undergraduate Library/Peter T. Flawn Academic Center," in this volume.

4. H. H. Ransom to Stark Young, Mar. 15, 1960, Harry Huntt Ransom Papers, Box 3U356, Dolph Briscoe Center for American History, University of Texas at Austin. The authors thank graduate student Wei-Pei Cherng for bringing this letter to their attention.

5. For Erwin's remarks and a concise account of the incident, see Richard A. Holland, "Thirteen Ways of Looking at Chairman Frank," in the first *Texas Book*.

6. *Daily Texan*, Aug. 15, 1990.

7. Editor's note: For more information about Anna Hiss Gymnasium, see Brad Buchholz, "A Feminist, before Her Time: The Journey of Anna Hiss," in this volume.

8. Cesar Pelli & Associates, Balmori Associates, Inc., *University of Texas at Austin Campus Master Plan* (Austin: Univ. of Texas at Austin, 1999).

9. Ibid.

Gregory Gymnasium, ca. 1930s. *From the Prints and Photographs Collection—UT—Buildings—Gregory Gymnasium, Dolph Briscoe Center for American History, University of Texas at Austin. (DI 06866)*

RICHARD A.
HOLLAND

The Most Important
Building on Campus

These days the busiest place on the Texas campus must surely be the
Gregory Gym Annex. From 6:00 a.m. to midnight the building is full of
students, staff, faculty, and other Austinites lifting weights, walking on
treadmills, riding stationary bicycles and cross-trainers, playing the enclosed court games of handball, racquetball, and squash, and climbing
the artificial rock wall. A renovated indoor swimming pool is a popular
spot for early-morning lap swimmers, and in 2005, two new outdoor pools
opened—a "leisure pool" located northeast of the gym complex, and an
extravagantly handsome lap pool landscaped with date palms, just behind the gym. On the top floor of the annex are four full-length basketball courts, which can be used for volleyball, and above that is a walking
track whose east end looks down on the luxurious lap pool. It is hard to
image a better-designed or more heavily used university sports complex.

As one walks up the stairs from the entrance to the fourth floor, there
is a tangible memory of the old building. In the remodeling of the annex,
the original south exterior wall of the old gym was integrated into the
new building—the beautiful old brick is marked with stunning geometric concrete touches. The original gym is now the home of the nationally ranked Texas women's volleyball team. These exciting contests are
played on the same gym floor where the University's basketball games
once were. Before the fall of 1977, when varsity basketball moved to the
new Frank C. Erwin, Jr. Special Events Center, men's and women's hoops
were played on the same tightly confined court in Gregory. Just like then,

Editor of The Texas Book, *published in 2006, Richard A. Holland received
an MA in history from the University in 1967, and an MLS in library and information science in 1970. He was a bibliographer in the University's general
libraries for sixteen years before decamping to Southwest Texas State University (now Texas State University–San Marcos), where he was special collections librarian and the founding curator of the Southwestern Writers Collection. Today he is a senior lecturer in the University's Liberal Arts Honors
Program, where he teaches courses on Texas culture, American music, and
the decade of the 1960s.*

now there are solid balconies on three sides and, below them, bleachers that pull out to the edges of the floor. The front of the space features a raised stage with a curtain. For decades it was an extremely loud and intimidating place for Texas's archenemies, such as Texas A&M, to visit, and for several generations of University students, it was literally the place where everything happened.

Back in 1930, when Gregory Gym first opened, it was something of an outpost, located on Speedway just east of the original Forty Acres.[1] It and three other notable campus athletic facilities marked an expansion of the University's original master plan: the old

Atrium of the Gregory Gymnasium Annex, which connects to the original south exterior wall of Gregory Gymnasium, 2009. *Photo by Bob Childress; courtesy of the Division of Recreational Sports, University of Texas at Austin.*

baseball park Clark Field and Memorial Stadium were placed on the far eastern edge of the campus, and Anna Hiss Gym was built to the north. All four athletic facilities stretched the original Forty Acres, and all four bore the strong design ideas of Dallas architect Herbert M. Greene, who also designed two important women's dormitories, Scottish Rite and Littlefield, as well as the handsome home of the history department, Garrison Hall, placed on the east side of the main plaza.

For most of the University's history, Speedway was an operating Austin city street (as were San Jacinto and Red River), and this fact alone made the old campus feel approachable to the rest of the city and a part of Austin's everyday life in a way that is now hard to imagine. Long before the Business Administration and Economics Building, Jester Dormitory, and the Perry-Castañeda Library flanked the other corners of Speedway and 21st, Gregory Gym dominated the busy intersection.

There was no doubt that this southeastern corner of the campus was athletic in intent. Just across 21st Street from Gregory (where Jester Dorm is now) there were two full-length grass football fields with wooden goalposts. Just behind them were the men's tennis courts, set aside for physical education classes and for students who filled the courts, especially on Saturdays and Sundays. The tennis area corresponds to what is now the Blanton Museum and the parking garage behind it.

On the other side of Speedway was a mixed neighborhood of small businesses, boardinghouses for students, and a few somewhat rundown houses and duplexes. On the corner where the Perry-Castañeda Library opened in 1977, there was a friendly beer joint called Tony's Bar—the friendliness extended to its reputation for not checking student IDs too closely. Farther down the block was a small Holiday House, part of a local chain of quality hamburger restaurants famous for their chili burgers and apricot fried pies.

Going north on Congress Avenue toward the campus from the Capitol, a driver or pedestrian would cross 19th Street (now Martin Luther King Jr. Boulevard), where the street name changed to Speedway. It was not clear where the campus began until one saw Gregory Gym standing tall. Drivers or pedestrians traveling north on Speedway beyond 19th Street would encounter three stop signs on campus, at 21st, 24th, and 26th Streets; at the last of these (now Dean

Registration lines on the floor of Gregory Gymnasium, 1969. *Courtesy of the Division of Recreational Sports, University of Texas at Austin.*

Keeton Street) was a small group of women's tennis courts, called that because of their proximity to the women's dormitories on that end of the campus and to Anna Hiss Gym. There were no University Police buildings guarding access to the University and checking parking permits and, as a matter of fact, no parking permits. There was an attractive balance of buildings and green space that now is pretty much gone.

REGISTRATION

For generations of University students, Gregory Gym meant one thing: registration. Especially in the fall, when the weather was likely hot, waiting in line down the outside steps and then spending an hour or more inside the un-air-conditioned gym was something of an ordeal. Registration itself was literally a

maze of tables placed on the gym floor and arranged by department. Students would wait in line to get a card for the section of the class they needed.

If the class was full or otherwise not available, the student would be sent to a midlevel official called a "sectionizer," who would advise the student as how best to fix his or her schedule. If there were several sections of a lower-division class, this usually meant being assigned to a section that met on Tuesday, Thursday, and Saturday, often as early as 8:00 a.m. The sectionizers were usually graduate students who worked for fifty dollars a week and were thought to be notably unsympathetic to the desires or needs of hapless freshmen or sophomores.

After running the gauntlet on the gym floor, the registrant ascended to the stage in front, where the cashiers were enclosed in metal cages. In the early sixties, the cost for a full load of fifteen hours was usually about fifty dollars. The last step was to go

~Third Annual Intramural~
~Fite · Nite~
~1933~

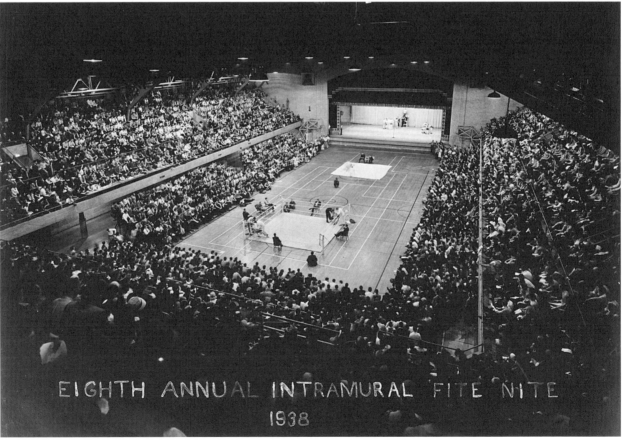

EIGHTH ANNUAL INTRAMURAL FITE NITE
1938

Fight Night, aka Fite Nite, in Gregory Gymnasium: 1933 (*top*) and 1938. *Both photos courtesy of the Division of Recreational Sports, University of Texas at Austin.*

up to the balcony in back to have a picture taken for the student ID, which indicated whether the student had bought a "blanket tax." The blanket tax was the biggest bargain at the University. Using it meant free admittance into all varsity sports events, including football, plus free admission into most campus lectures and concerts.

RECREATIONAL SPORTS

Activities in the gym and its annex have always been associated with intramural sports and what has been known since 1972 as Recreational Sports, the non-varsity branch of UT athletics. A good capsule history of these activities can be found on the bottom floor of the annex. Lining the halls in a serpentine fashion are framed photographs of intramural champions from the 1920s to the present. The inventor of the intramural programs at Texas was the legendary Berry Whitaker, who served in World War I, coached the varsity football team, and then began intramural sports in 1919. Whitaker's idea was to have the intramural finals happen early in the spring semester for boxing and wrestling, and later for volleyball and basketball. Other competitive activities included flag football and softball, but also fencing, badminton, table tennis, and, in the really early days, old-fashioned activities such as horseshoes. But for twenty-one years (1930–1951), the biggest event by far was Fight Night (aka "Fite Nite"), an evening of boxing matches held on the floor of Gregory Gym.

The boxing ring was set flat on the floor, not raised, in the middle of the gym. There were divisions by weight—lightweight, middleweight, heavyweight, etc.—and Fight Night was a must-see University event. The crowd was not just from the University—prominent Austinites flocked to Fight Night, including the most prominent of all, the governor. There was fencing on the stage during the fights, and some years there was a second ring on the floor, set aside for wrestling matches, also organized by weight. Other than Longhorn football and, in some seasons, varsity basketball, Fight Night was the biggest athletic event on campus. It must be remembered, however, that boxing, along with baseball and horse racing, was the most popular American sport during the thirties and forties.

Recreational Sports has always operated out of

Gregory Gym, but many of the competitions are held outdoors. For eighty years, the most intense and competitive sports have been football and basketball—just think of all the excellent high school basketball players and footballers who have attended the University and, for whatever reason, not played scholarship sports in college, but loved the competition to be found in intramurals.

Now as many as five hundred teams participate in the major team sports. Over the years, the competition has evolved from four divisions—Fraternity, Club, Housing, and Independent—to new divisions that include Open, Orange (A&B), White (A&B), Greek, and specialized leagues for basketball, such as the 6 Foot and Under (A&B). In addition there are women's leagues, a Law and Graduate School League, and, since 1974, three coed divisions. Some of the legendary fraternity teams have been the Fijis and the Kappa Sigs (thought by some to pledge new members based on their athletic prowess), and a housing winner year after year was the Oak Grove Men's Co-op. During a tour of the bottom floor "wall of fame," Bob Childress, the assistant director of Rec Sports, points out some of the notables who have participated over the years. Included are the legendary Dallas Cowboys

One of the photos included in the "Wall of Fame" on the lower level of Gregory Gymnasium, 1946. *Courtesy of the Division of Recreational Sports, University of Texas at Austin.*

coach Tom Landry, the Houston heart surgeon Denton Cooley, the philanthropist and UT donor Jack Blanton, and the actor Matthew McConaughey.

Teams name themselves, and during the sixties and seventies, some pretty frisky names appeared, including coed football teams named "The Cunning Linguists," and the "Holes and Poles." In the 1980s, an excellent football team made up of members of the Vietnamese Student Association called themselves the "Napalms." Bob Childress said that some names had been not approved because they were just too raunchy or politically incorrect. The subtlety of some names is evidenced by a law school football team that called itself the "Nads." It was their cheering fans ("Go Nads!") who completed the joke.

CHARLES ALAN WRIGHT
AND THE LEGAL EAGLES

At the end of each season, playoffs set up the league champions to compete against one another. By far the winningest intramural football team has been the Legal Eagles, a formidable law school aggregation coached by Professor Charles Alan Wright from 1955 to 2000, the year of his death. Professor Wright, who described himself as a "Philadelphia lawyer," had played football at Wesleyan University before attending Yale Law School. He joined the Texas law faculty at the age of twenty-seven, and when he learned that a group of law students was forming a football team, he volunteered his services as player and coach.

Wright was considered by many to be the most distinguished faculty member at UT, a campus well known for being home to prominent mathematicians, biologists, classicists, and historians. He was the leading expert in federal courts and procedure, coediting the fifty-four-volume *Federal Practice and Procedure*.[2] He was known to be a popular though somewhat eccentric professor who taught constitutional law and a famous class on federal courts and procedure. Wright lectured without notes, and students thought he had a photographic memory because of his habit of citing cases by page number and paragraph from memory alone. Late in his career, Supreme Court Justice Ruth Bader Ginsburg said in a tribute: "Like a Colossus, Charles Alan Wright stands at the summit of our profession."[3] But there is no doubt that Wright's greatest nonlegal passion was

UT professor of Law Charles Alan Wright and members of the Legal Eagles intramural football team, 1983. *Courtesy of the Division of Recreational Sports, University of Texas at Austin.*

his student flag-football team. He conducted practices wearing his customary three-piece suit, pacing on the sideline, smoking.

Recreational Sports has a glass exhibit case that summarizes Wright's forty-five-year career as an intramural coach. With the Legal Eagles record of 330 wins, 44 losses, and 5 ties under Wright, he is referred to as the "most successful football coach in Texas history." His practices were rigorous, and his teams quickly learned his three fundamental rules: the team is not a debating society, so do not argue with the referees; there should be no unnecessary penalties; no one on the team stops until the whistle blows.

The story goes that whenever Wright was visiting for a semester or a year at Harvard or Yale or Cambridge, he kept in touch with his wife, Custis, during Legal Eagles games, pacing and chain-smoking just as he did when he was on the field. In 2001, Recreational Sports established the Charles Alan Wright Trophy to be presented to the All-University Champion intramural flag football team. The trophy and other Legal Eagle memorabilia are on display in the back of the entry floor of the Gregory Gym Annex.

GYM PERFORMANCES: TOSCANINI, T. S. ELIOT, AND LOUIS ARMSTRONG

By the 1950s and 1960s, the University had something of a space problem when it came to hosting popular performers on campus. This was due to an exploding enrollment and a growing sophistication on the part of those responsible for booking literary and music attractions. There were four primary campus venues: the Texas Union main ballroom, Hogg Auditorium, Batts Hall auditorium, and, by far the largest, Gregory Gym. The popular spring Shakespeare productions directed by B. Iden Payne filled up Hogg, popular speakers including the political pundit William F. Buckley, Jr., and *Li'l Abner* cartoonist Al Capp spoke in the Texas Union, and Aldous Huxley, author of *Brave New World*, spoke to a standing-room-only crowd in Batts auditorium. But the big attractions were booked in the old gymnasium.

ARTURO TOSCANINI AND THE NBC SYMPHONY

In the spring of 1950, the NBC Symphony Orchestra, conducted by Arturo Toscanini, undertook a national tour that included three cities in Texas. After a concert in Houston, the symphony arrived in Austin by train. Some of the musicians thought the capital city had something of an Old West atmosphere, with a couple of seedy barrooms located not far from the train station. The Austin concert was to take place in Gregory Gym.[4] It was late April, and the weather was muggy when the orchestra rehearsed in the un-air-conditioned gym. It was the first time that orchestra members had seen the maestro remove his heavy alpaca jacket and conduct in his shirtsleeves—they stood and applauded. On the same day as the rehearsal there was a swim meet, and apparently the eighty-three-year-old conductor especially liked seeing the coeds walking around in the back of the gym wearing their swimsuits.

There were two local concerns about the concert: one was whether the gym would be filled to capacity (about 6,500 seats), and the other was about the program, which some members of the music faculty thought was a bit "dumbed down" (it included numbers like the *William Tell* overture). There should have been a third concern: the weather. The muggy weather broke on the day of the concert with one of Austin's trademark thunderstorms, which flooded many creeks and streets. The result, however, was a nice cooling down, so the gym was quite comfortable when the concert began. A special train from San Antonio brought hundreds of classical music fans, and there were fewer than two hundred empty seats. None of those in the audience had ever heard anything in their hometowns like the magnificent symphony conducted by the great Toscanini. Most of the reviews pointed out that the music sounded so fresh that it must have sounded just the way the composers had intended it to. Maestro Toscanini had such a fine time that he visited with fans until 1:30 in the morning before the orchestra left for Dallas.

T. S. ELIOT

By 1958, Harry Ransom's dream of a great literary center was becoming a reality; what would later come to be known as the Humanities Research Center (now the Harry Ransom Center) was acquiring some of its most important literary archives.[5] And during the spring semester of 1958, the three most prominent English poets of the day each made an appearance on the Texas campus: first W. H. Auden, then Robert Graves, both in February, and finally, in late April, T. S. Eliot himself. Of these three eminences, Auden, an Englishman, lived in New York City; Graves, an Englishman, lived on the island of Mallorca, off the coast of Spain; and T. S. Eliot, born in St. Louis, lived in London, where he was an editor at Faber and Faber. He was also considered the greatest living English language poet (he had won the Nobel Prize in Literature in 1948). In their appearances on campus, both Auden and Graves appeared in Batts Hall auditorium, a site for many important campus events. But with T. S. Eliot, only Gregory Gymnasium would do.[6]

The sixty-nine-year-old poet landed in Austin accompanied by his thirty-one-year-old wife, Valerie,

T. S. Eliot (*left*), with his American publisher Robert Giroux, in the Wrenn Library on the fourth floor of the Main Building, April 22, 1958. *From the Harry Ransom Papers, Dolph Briscoe Center for American History, University of Texas at Austin. (DI 07013)*

who had been Eliot's secretary at Faber and Faber. With them was the New York book publisher Robert Giroux. Eliot was given a very warm reception that included one of Provost Ransom's first literary exhibits, on Eliot and modernism, up in the Wrenn Library on the fourth floor of the Main Building, where now the presidential suite is located. During Robert Graves's visit to Austin, he had gone out of his way to criticize Eliot and his work, commenting that several of his recent poems he found to be "sordid."

At a small luncheon with students and faculty, hosted by Ransom on the terrace outside the rare-books rooms, Eliot shrugged off Graves's remarks. Shirley Bird Perry, who built a distinguished career at the University of Texas at Austin and the University of Texas System, serving as senior vice president of UT-Austin at the time of her death, in 2011, was one of the lucky students who sat with Eliot that day:

I was one of the students at Mr. Eliot's table and was, of course, thrilled. One bit of the conversation I remember was his response when a fellow student asked for his reaction to interpretations and to the assignment of deep meaning, etc. to segments of his work by critics, faculty members, et. al. He indicated that he was often amused and puzzled by some of the conjectures, noting that some were very far fetched and were not what he had in mind at all! I found that enormously interesting and refreshing![7]

More than six thousand were in the audience in Gregory Gym, some having driven from as far away as Louisiana. They heard the great man forcefully read his most notable poems, including parts of *The Waste Land* and "The Love Song of J. Alfred Prufrock." Before Eliot left the campus, he passed on to Ransom a manuscript copy of *The Waste Land* that contained an extra line. I have not been able to confirm the story about Eliot being presented with a Stetson cowboy hat.

LOUIS ARMSTRONG, THE DAVE BRUBECK QUARTET, THE COUNT BASIE ORCHESTRA, AND THE MODERN JAZZ QUARTET

Before the Beatles appeared on *The Ed Sullivan Show* and Bob Dylan went electric, some of us liked jazz more than anything else. By the early sixties, the campus Cultural Entertainment Committee regularly scheduled top jazz acts for Gregory Gym. Louis Armstrong had appeared in Austin a number of times in the past, but 1964 was the year that his hit "Hello Dolly" knocked the Beatles out of first place at the top of the music charts. For a young jazz snob, "Hello Dolly" was not the reason to see the show—it was his soulful playing and singing of "When It's Sleepy Time Down South," "Muskrat Ramble," "Struttin' With Some Barbeque," and a number that Pops introduced as one of the "good old good ones" he was playing for an old friend in the audience: "The Bucket's Got a Hole in It." Although somewhat past his prime, Louis could still hit the high notes on his trumpet, and he and the All-Stars were in fine form.

Both the Dave Brubeck Quartet and the Count Basie Orchestra played on the Gregory Gym stage. Brubeck had the most popular record in jazz history—*Time Out*—which played with difficult time signatures (⁵⁄₄, ⁷⁄₄, etc.) and featured jazz tunes that were played on the radio, such as "Take Five." The two great musicians in the quartet were Paul Desmond, with his lyrical tone and witty improvisation, and the precise yet swinging drummer Joe Morello, who could make the audience tap their feet to ⁵⁄₄ time.

The Count Basie group was a fully stocked big band: four trumpets, four trombones, five saxophones, and a rhythm section that featured Count Basie on piano and Freddie Green on guitar. This was the early-1960s ensemble that almost blew Frank Sinatra off the stage on the recording *Sinatra Live at the Sands*. Basie always opened his show with an old trick: a very soft piano solo by Basie accompanied by Freddy Green playing quiet rhythm guitar and then, about two minutes into the piece: pow! The whole

Louis Armstrong, with drummer Barrett Deems in the background, performing in Gregory Gymnasium, spring 1964. *From the UT Texas Student Publications, Inc. Photographs Collection—unprocessed negatives, 1963–1964, Dolph Briscoe Center for American History, University of Texas at Austin. (DI 07020)*

band came in playing fortissimo. There was nervous laughter from the audience because anyone who had never heard an honest-to-God big band could not believe how loud it was. Bands like Basie's and Duke Ellington's cut their teeth playing dances, and it did seem a little odd to just sit and watch, but no musicians were better at what they did than Basie and the members of his band.

For many jazz fans, the Modern Jazz Quartet was the pinnacle of "chamber jazz" in the early sixties, and it was hard to believe the group had been booked for old Gregory Gym. The quartet comprised the distinguished John Lewis on piano, Milt Jackson on vibraphone, the great Percy Heath on bass, and Connie Kay on drums. Lewis composed dignified songs that had contrapuntal elements, like "Django." Milt Jackson, a be-bop hero, composed and played soulful tunes like "Bag's Groove" (for the bags under his eyes) and "Bluesology." Connie Kay had the most elaborate jazz drum kit there was, ranging from huge Arabian-looking cymbals to tiny cymbals that had a

Dave Brubeck, right, being interviewed backstage in Gregory Gymnasium, February 20, 1964. *From the UT Texas Student Publications, Inc. Photographs Collection—unprocessed negatives, 1963–1964, Dolph Briscoe Center for American History, University of Texas at Austin. (DI 07022)*

very high pitch. The Modern Jazz Quartet largely ignored the audience and wore their customary tuxedos. In some ways, it was a minimalist Basie band—starting quietly and then, after five minutes or so, swinging like crazy. It was only years later that I learned that their spot in the middle of Gregory Gym was exactly where the boxing happened during Fight Night. The Modern Jazz Quartet drew just as big a crowd.

CODA

A return to the scene of the crime in old Gregory is possible when you buy a reasonably priced ticket to see one of the University's elite sports teams in action. Stepping into the gymnasium for a women's volleyball game is more than an exercise in nostalgia—it is a vital part of UT athletics as it currently

exists. In 2009, the Texas team reached the NCAA finals against perennial champion Penn State and lost in five sets. The player of the year in intercollegiate volleyball that year was junior Destinee Hooker, who left to play in the professional league.

Buying a ticket is easy, and the gym is packed—many other Texas athletes attend the game, and the spirit is high. In a recent match (fall 2010), a sold-out crowd saw the talented Horns beat nationally ranked Iowa State. It was good to see the old place packed and loud, watching an athletic event it was built to present.

NOTES

1. The gym was named after Thomas Watt Gregory, a Progressive Era attorney and politician who was part of Colonel Edward House's political coalition that worked closely with

The UT Tower, lit with a "1" after the Longhorns' victory over the University of Southern California in the Rose Bowl earned the team the 2005 national championship, as seen in the early-morning light from the new recreational pool behind Gregory Gymnasium, January 2006. *Photo by Bob Childress; courtesy of the Division of Recreational Sports, University of Texas at Austin.*

Woodrow Wilson. Before joining President Wilson's administration as U.S. attorney general, Gregory was a UT regent, from 1899 to 1907. He returned to Texas from Washington in 1918, and in the late 1920s, he headed the Ex-Students' Association. In that role, he helped raise and organize funds to build several important campus structures, including the gym later named after him.

2. An excellent summary of Charles Alan Wright's career at the UT School of Law is the UT Faculty Council memorial written by Professors Douglas Laycock, Roy Mersky, and Scott Powe: http://www.utexas.edu/faculty/council/2000-2001/memorials/Wright/wright.html.

3. Ruth Bader Ginsburg, "Statement Presenting the 1989 Fellows Research Award of the American Bar Foundation," Feb. 4, 1989.

4. The source for all information on Toscanini in Austin is Dorman Winfrey's charming book *Arturo Toscanini in Texas: The 1950 NBC Symphony Orchestra Tour* (Austin: Encino, 1967).

5. See Richard Oram, "'Going Towards a Great Library at Texas': Harry Ransom's Acquisition of the T. E. Hanley Collection" in the first *Texas Book*.

6. See Robert Robertson, "Critical Mass: T. S. Eliot and Other Giants of Literary Criticism Roamed the Forty Acres in the 1950s," *Alcalde*, January–February 2008, 36–38.

7. Shirley Bird Perry, e-mail to the author, September 23, 2009.

Aerial view of the McDonald Observatory in the Davis Mountains of West Texas. The two large domes in the foreground are the Struve Telescope (*left*) and the Smith Telescope atop Mount Locke; in the distance is the Hobby-Eberly Telescope, atop Mount Fowlkes. *Photo by Damond Benningfield; courtesy of the McDonald Observatory, University of Texas at Austin.*

FRANK N.
BASH

McDonald Observatory

Bigger and Brighter

The stars at night are big and bright,
Deep in the heart of Texas.
The prairie sky is wide and high,
Deep in the heart of Texas.

JUNE HERSHEY

The University of Texas at Austin is home to one of the world's leading centers for astronomical research: the McDonald Observatory. By any objective measure, the McDonald Observatory is not only first class, but world class. Its telescopic equipment, its team of researchers, and its contributions to science and the public good all rank among the world's best.

If one were to consider only the story of how McDonald began, this world-class status would seem quite remarkable. When a large—and completely unanticipated—private donation to fund the building of an observatory at the University of Texas was revealed at the reading of a bank president's will in 1926 in Paris, Texas, UT did not have a department of astronomy or any professors on its faculty whose primary work was focused on teaching or research in astronomy. In the eighty-five years since the reading of that will, the McDonald Observatory has flourished, through a fortunate combination of strategic collaboration, ongoing state support, generous private philanthropy, and the skill and dedication of generations of talented astronomers, telescope designers, technicians, and administrators. Though the observatory's founding may have begun with a stroke of luck, its continuing success has been the result of the vision and hard work of those generations of dedicated professionals. How-

Frank Bash is the Frank N. Edmonds, Jr. Regents Professor Emeritus in Astronomy at the University. From 1989 to 2003, he served as director of the University's McDonald Observatory. His work as an astronomer has focused on an interest in large-scale star-formation processes in spiral galaxies. An award-winning classroom teacher, he earned his PhD in astronomy from the University of Virginia, his MA in astronomy from Harvard University, and his bachelor's degree from Willamette University in his native Oregon.

ever, considering the enormous cost of astronomical research and the competition from outstanding observatories around the world, the future of that success can never be taken for granted.

The McDonald Observatory is a research unit of the University that provides research facilities for the University's Department of Astronomy and its own staff, and collaborates with leading observatories around the globe. The observatory's facilities are located atop Mount Locke and Mount Fowlkes under the clear skies over the Davis Mountains in West Texas, a 440-mile drive straight west from the University's main campus, in Austin. Texas is, of course, a big state. One must continue driving nearly another 200 miles from the McDonald Observatory, leaving the Central Time Zone and entering the Mountain Time Zone, to reach El Paso, Texas's westernmost city. The nearest town to the McDonald Observatory is Fort Davis, population 1,050, the unincorporated seat of Jeff Davis County.

The McDonald Observatory serves the global community of professional astronomers primarily by providing time on its telescopes, which are equipped with specialized devices to analyze the light that the telescopes have collected. In addition, the McDonald staff builds and installs special devices on its telescopes that are designed to solve certain important astronomical problems. For example, the Hobby-Eberly Telescope is being modified to collect data designed to solve the problem of "dark energy." Likewise, the observatory serves the community of amateur astronomers as well as the general public by operating a major visitors center and a large set of associated programs for visitors, by producing the *Star-Date* radio program in both English and Spanish, and by publishing *StarDate* magazine. I was the director of the McDonald Observatory from 1989 to 2003, during which time a lot happened—including an attempt to redefine the role of a major research institute in the society that supports it. Much of what I have to say in the following pages focuses on this more recent history of the observatory and the importance of its reconsideration of the role of public involvement in its mission.[1]

During my stays at the observatory, I like to spend time in the wonderful new visitors center—which, I am proud to say, bears my name. During such moments, I often reflect on the extensive public outreach and education programs that McDonald sup-ports and observe the many families with young children—families that have gone far off the beaten path of the interstate highway to get there. I see the aspirations that the parents have for their children and the eagerness and excitement in the children's faces (and those of the parents too). This trip is their adventure to the frontiers. The McDonald Observatory is in a remote, mountainous location, but to its visitors, it is a portal to limitless space—especially that part of space well beyond any regions that astronauts will ever conceivably be able to explore. Visitors' exploration includes the past and the future—their exploration through time as well as space. As I watch and listen, I see the role that astronomy plays in our society and I see how essential those outreach and education programs are.

When the idea of a major observatory in Texas was first conceived—by an East Texas lawyer and banker named William Johnson McDonald—the fledgling University did not have an astronomy department. William J. McDonald—a native of the Republic of Texas, Civil War veteran, and graduate of McKenzie College, a Methodist school near Clarksville, Texas, that went bankrupt a year after he graduated, in 1867—prospered first as an attorney, then as the owner of banks in Clarksville, Cooper, and Paris, Texas. He died in 1926, leaving an estate of more than one million dollars. Everyone was shocked when the executor of his estate, the cashier of his Paris bank, Eugene W. Bowers, read the will, revealing that McDonald had left virtually all of his estate to the University of Texas to build an observatory. When he first heard the news, the dean of UT's College of Arts and Sciences (and, later, University president), H. Y. Benedict, described the bequest as coming "like lightning out of a clear sky."

McDonald had no known connection to the University of Texas during his life other than paying his grandnephew's expenses at the UT Law School, but his library, part of which is now at the observatory, reveals that McDonald was a very widely read man. He owned a small telescope and observed the heavens with his landlord. He told his barber that astronomy was the coming science, the great wonder of the world, though neglected in the universities. All it needed was a bit of money. "If we had a big enough telescope, we could see into the gates of Heaven and see who was there," McDonald is reported to have said. Presumably, McDonald decided

William Johnson McDonald of Paris, Texas. *Courtesy of the McDonald Observatory, University of Texas at Austin.*

to give his money to the University of Texas because of UT's dominant position among Texas universities. Fortunately, Dean Benedict, a professor of mathematics, had a doctorate in astronomy from Harvard. The bequest was slightly more than $1.26 million, but it was contested by McDonald's relatives (in five consecutive court actions), and the University eventually settled for about $840,000.

After a complicated search for suitable sites for the observatory, University officials chose a location in the Davis Mountains in West Texas. This choice was very fortunate because, to this day, McDonald enjoys very dark skies. The University sought advice from a number of astronomical observatories, the Yerkes Observatory at the University of Chicago being especially influential. Yerkes was looking for a new, darker location and wanted a larger telescope than its forty-inch-diameter refractor. From this need, a fruitful partnership emerged.

Chicago had a collection of extremely distinguished astronomers, but its telescopes were located at Williams Bay, Wisconsin, near the shore of Lake Michigan, where the weather was often cloudy. Its largest telescope was the last representative of the old-fashioned kind of optical telescope, the refractor. Refractors, like most small amateur telescopes today, have lenses in the front, but as the telescope and the lens get larger, it becomes increasingly difficult to support the front lens to the required accuracy. The main Yerkes telescope has a front lens with a diameter of forty inches—the largest refractor ever built. By the time of the McDonald bequest, it had become clear to the Chicago astronomers that they needed a larger telescope located in the clear, dry southwestern United States. Even before any discussions with UT had begun, the Chicago astronomers had identified the area around Amarillo in the Texas Panhandle as an ideal site for a new telescope. UT's need for astronomers to operate and use the new McDonald telescope, and Chicago's need to have a large new telescope in a clear area, drove the two universities together. It was agreed that the University of Chicago would operate the McDonald Observatory for thirty years in a collaborative agreement with the University of Texas. In return, Chicago would get a portion of the time on the McDonald telescopes.

The funds were sufficient to build an eighty-two-inch-diameter reflecting telescope, its dome, and a set of houses and service buildings. There was no electrical power on the mountaintop, so an electrical generator had to be included. Construction was begun in November 1933, but construction of the telescope itself was delayed by problems in figuring the mirror. The mirror did not arrive until February 1939, and the telescope was not accepted until March of that year. At the time, the eighty-two-inch telescope was the second largest in the world. The largest was the one-hundred-inch Hooker Telescope on Mount Wilson, above Pasadena, California. The McDonald Observatory was dedicated in a scientific symposium and ceremony on May 5, 1939. The symposium was attended by most of the world's leading astronomers, and there are "home movies" of the event and the arrivals and departures surrounding it.

Astronomical telescopes are measured by the diameter of the lens or mirror. These days, professional astronomical telescopes all use mirrors rather than lenses. The light-gathering power of a telescope is related to the area of its mirror (specifically, it is proportional to the square of the diameter). Since astronomers seek ever-more-distant objects, which are very faint, bigger and bigger telescopes are being built. The largest are about four hundred inches in diameter. In addition, astronomers wish to reduce the amount of the Earth's atmosphere they have to look through, so modern observatories are being built on higher and higher mountains. The elevation of McDonald is about seven thousand feet (which is the highest point on Texas highways). The observatory on Mauna Kea, Hawaii, is at fourteen thousand feet, and sites are being looked at in the Andes of northern Chile at eighteen thousand feet. What still makes McDonald competitive is the dark sky in this thinly settled part of West Texas.

From 1932 until the early 1950s, the McDonald Observatory was completely, in essence, a Chicago show. The extremely distinguished Chicago astronomer Otto Struve was the director of the McDonald Observatory from 1932 to 1947. The eighty-two-inch telescope was responsible for a number of first-rate discoveries, including the discovery of "forbidden" spectral lines in the atmospheres of red giant stars; an early indication of the presence of "dark matter," implied by the motion of pairs of galaxies orbiting each other; and observations of the atmospheres of planets in our solar system, including the use of chemistry to understand the composition of those atmospheres. During the 1950s, it became obvious that Chicago's interest in McDonald was decreasing, as was its financial support of the observatory itself, apparently in anticipation of the possibility that the two institutions would not renew their cooperative agreement and the concern that Chicago might not be able to recover funds invested in McDonald. But the decision not to renew the agreement was mutual, since UT had begun to feel that Chicago was not "pulling its weight." Before I came to the University, I had heard complaints from Chicago astronomers that they were very unhappy when UT astronomers took over what those Chicago astronomers felt to be their observatory and UT began deciding who got time on the telescopes. Although the University had an astronomer on its mathematics faculty, E. J. Prouse, it didn't hire an astronomer who was expected to do astronomy until it hired Frank Edmonds, in 1952. In 1957, Chicago's director of McDonald, Gerard Kuiper, proposed a joint UT-Chicago Department of Astronomy, and the University divided its joint Department of Mathematics and Astronomy into two separate de-

Harlan J. Smith, director of the McDonald Observatory from 1963 to 1989. *Courtesy of the McDonald Observatory, University of Texas at Austin.*

partments so that could happen. Edmonds became the first faculty member of the new Department of Astronomy, in 1958.

The original UT-Chicago agreement was set to expire in 1962. In March 1962, the University reached a new agreement with Chicago. It included provisions that allowed UT the right to name the McDonald director, that called for the director to report only to the president of the University, and that required UT to take over full responsibility for funding the observatory. In 1963, UT appointed Harlan J. Smith as its first director of McDonald and named him chairman of the University's Department of Astronomy.

Upon arriving from Yale, Harlan Smith demanded that the University expand its efforts in astronomy, including increasing the size of the faculty. He also promoted the construction of a substantially larger and more modern telescope for McDonald. And he wanted to begin a UT program in radio astronomy, which would allow radio waves from celestial objects to be studied. The famous "quasars" were discovered by radio astronomers because, although they are quite faint and unremarkable on photographs, they are prodigious emitters of radio waves. I arrived in Austin in 1967 as a postdoctoral fellow to participate in the UT radio astronomy program and helped build a major radio-telescope facility south of the highway between Marfa and Alpine, Texas, about sixty miles southeast of McDonald.

In 1964, NASA signed a contract with the University of Texas to build an "80-inch class" telescope at the McDonald Observatory whose purpose was to add ground-based help to NASA's efforts to explore our solar system. It turned out that a larger mirror made of fused silica could be obtained from Corning Glass Works and that it would cool very quickly after being made, compared to other glasses. Characteristic of Harlan Smith's propensity always to push limits, the telescope mirror's diameter was increased to 107 inches. When dedicated on November 26, 1968, that telescope was third largest in the world. (The largest telescope in the world at that time was the famous 200-inch Palomar Telescope, and the second largest was the 120-inch telescope at the Lick Observatory, south of San Francisco.) The 107-inch telescope, especially with its magnificent coudé spectrograph, caused UT astronomy to remain very competitive and to attract first-rate young faculty members for a number of years. The UT program in radio astronomy also expanded, and its astronomers took over a program in very-high-frequency radio astronomy originally begun by UT's Department of Electrical Engineering. The Astronomy Department also added theorists, who use computers rather than telescopes.

In 1978, Harlan Smith relinquished the chairmanship of the department, and members of the faculty began to serve four-year terms as chairman. Each chairman is elected by the faculty and approved by the dean of the College of Natural Sciences; most of the senior faculty members have served a term. By the mid-1980s, it was becoming clear that UT needed to plan for a new telescope. After all, we seemed to build a new one every thirty years, so we would need to dedicate one in 1998. Harlan became intrigued by the notion of building a 300-inch telescope whose de-

tailed design and cost were not known—but it was certain to be expensive.

Harlan had also added a major program for visitors to the observatory. The W. L. Moody Visitor Center was built in 1980 and situated in the state highway right-of-way, forcing the highway to be moved over to accommodate it. He was an astronomical evangelist who warmly welcomed visitors to the observatory rather than locking them out. (Locking visitors out was the current fashion at the time at other observatories.) As a result, the observatory attracted thousands of tourists every year and began to appear on lists of favorite destinations for travelers. Under Harlan's directorship, McDonald began to produce the radio program *StarDate* and a magazine with the same name. These efforts were not warmly welcomed by some of the faculty, who felt that funds that should have been spent on research were being diverted to these frivolous efforts. But Harlan's efforts in public outreach are now regarded as perhaps his finest legacy, and he set an example now followed by essentially all other observatories.

Harlan Smith retired as director in 1989 and I succeeded him. Because of the high cost of a 300-inch telescope—coupled with the Texas oil bust, which had a severely deleterious effect on attempts to raise money—the observatory quietly abandoned that project. Although NASA was a major contributor to the 107-inch-telescope project, it had become clear that the federal government would not be participating in the Texas 300-inch-telescope project. To prevent federal agencies from having to deal with myriad requests for telescope money, national observatories had been established, funded entirely by the federal government through its National Science Foundation. Those observatories are located near Tucson, Arizona, and La Serena, Chile. As a result, UT would have to depend almost entirely on philanthropy by wealthy Texans, supplemented by operating funds from the University budget.

At about this time, the design of large telescopes was undergoing a major change. Computers were being used to design them so that the movement of a telescope's structure could be predicted as the telescope was turned to follow the star or galaxy being studied. As a telescope follows a star, its structure bends under the influence of gravity. The bending is slight, but the tolerances required for precisely holding the mirror's shape are very tight. Older telescopes were massively designed to resist this bending, but as they got bigger and bigger, the weight of all the steel caused the bending nonetheless. With the computer-design tools, very large telescopes could be designed with the absolute minimum of steel and the bending accurately predicted and held to a tolerably small amount. In addition, computers were being used to actively control the bending. That is, computers installed in a telescope could measure the changing bending as the telescope moved, and these computers were attached to devices that adjusted the telescope to compensate for the bending.

In 1989, I happened to run into an old friend and colleague, Dan Weedman, who had been on the UT astronomy faculty but who was then at Penn State. Dan and his Penn State colleague Larry Ramsey had designed a very large, very novel, and apparently very cheap telescope, and they were looking for a place to locate it. The telescope was called the Spectroscopic Survey Telescope. It would have a mirror composed of many smaller mirrors, all acting in concert to produce, effectively, one of the world's largest telescopes. The initial plan had the telescope housed in a grain silo, its mirrors, made of a cheap kind of glass, constructed by graduate students at Penn State. It was supposed to cost six million dollars. I brought this idea back to Harlan Smith just before he retired. Harlan agreed that this was a wonderful idea, that McDonald Observatory would be a perfect site for it, and that we should be a fifty-fifty partner with Penn State. He persuaded Bill Cunningham, who was then the president of UT-Austin, to put up $1.5 million of University money as a match for an equal amount to be raised privately. That arrangement would produce UT's half of the total cost. So when I took over, the project was underway—or at least it was started.

I was very concerned by the cost estimate and believed that the Penn State ultracheap plan was a recipe for disaster. I asked a group of McDonald Observatory engineers to look at the cost estimate, and they said that the telescope, properly done, would cost at least ten million dollars. That conclusion caused me to have to make a very difficult telephone call to President Cunningham and a mandatory trip, with him, to see Lieutenant Governor Bill Hobby. Hobby had had a distinguished tenure as lieutenant governor, but had announced his intention to retire from that job. The Texas legislature wished to honor him for his service, probably thinking of a statue or a similar honor. Hobby heard of the telescope project

and asked for the telescope to be the honor. That decision was probably the single-most important one in making the telescope a reality. The University was extremely suspicious of cost estimates from astronomers and knew the project would be very risky, but it was stuck once Hobby asked for the honor. So I had to tell Bill Hobby face-to-face of the revised, higher cost estimate. (I have defended astronomers' cost estimates by arguing that we build one-of-a-kind structures. In contrast, a building should be easy to estimate, since there is so much experience in building buildings. Of course, this comparison is little comfort to a university president whose rear end is hanging out to the tune of millions of dollars.)

To his credit, Hobby exploded only mildly when I told him of the higher cost. He also went with me to meetings with potential donors and helped "sell" the telescope. As we began the project jointly with Penn State, we hired a brilliant project manager, Tom Sebring. Tom improved the design and made a plan to have the telescope built by professional companies. Penn State found a donor, Robert Eberly, so in the spirit of the joint project, the telescope was renamed the Hobby-Eberly Telescope (HET). As Tom Sebring firmed up the cost estimate, the telescope's cost continued to rise, and Penn State was unable to fully fund its half of the higher cost. With the help of the

The Hobby-Eberly Telescope. *Photo by Martin Harris; courtesy of the McDonald Observatory, University of Texas at Austin.*

McDonald Observatory director Frank Bash (*left*) and Texas lieutenant governor Bill Hobby. *Courtesy of the McDonald Observatory, University of Texas at Austin.*

gave the University lawyers some nice trips to Germany. The final telescope cost was nearly twenty million dollars, but as I have said repeatedly to University presidents, such a cost is still a bargain, given that other telescopes whose mirrors are of a similar size cost in the neighborhood of one hundred million.

The Hobby-Eberly Telescope was dedicated on October 8, 1997. It took several years after that to get it running properly. It is extremely large, complicated, and delicate. Enormous credit goes to the McDonald Observatory engineers who finally got it running; they spent many long days and nights working on it. Time will tell, but it seems to have been a very good, though challenging, investment.

The design of the Hobby-Eberly Telescope seemed to be of interest to astronomers in the Southern Hemisphere. I was interested in potential deals in which we would contribute the telescope's plans and give advice and help in return for time on the southern brother of the HET. That way, the HET partnership would have access to the whole sky on an HET-like telescope at no financial cost. Sales trips were made to Chile, Australia, and finally South Africa, where the seed sprouted. That telescope is called the Southern African Large Telescope (SALT). The telescope is located at the South African Astronomical Observatory site near Sutherland. (Sutherland is a "twin town" with Fort Davis, Texas.) The country around Sutherland is remarkably similar to the country around Fort Davis. The design of the HET had to take into account the latitude of McDonald Observatory. Sutherland is at nearly the same latitude as McDonald, but south rather than north, so no design changes were needed for the SALT. The South African government, through its National Research Foundation, is half owner, approximately, of SALT. The other half is owned by a very diverse set of partners, including Rutgers University, the University of Wisconsin–Madison, the government of Poland, Canterbury University in New Zealand, the University of North Carolina at Chapel Hill, Dartmouth College, and others. The HET is a partner by virtue of its contribution of the telescope plans and its contribution of engineering help. SALT was dedicated on November 11, 2005. Getting the telescope running properly has proved to be a challenge, but it will be successful. The experience of dealing with our South African colleagues and the South Afri-

Texas legislature and very generous donors, we were able to find our half of the higher cost, but we had to find the piece that Penn State couldn't afford. At this stage, we went out to find new partners who could pick up the missing piece. Thus began an exercise that was like trying to find your future wife at a barn dance. Potential partners came and went as their potential donors went broke or lost interest, or as their administrations gave in to fear of the considerable risk involved. We ended up with three new partners: two in Germany—Ludwig-Maximilians Universität in Munich, and Georg-August-Universität in Göttingen—and Stanford University. Negotiating the legal agreements among the partners, especially the two German partners, proved to be a challenge, but

can government has had some ups and downs, but mainly has been wonderful. That country was just emerging from apartheid when we visited the first time. The government decided that it could not fund cutting-edge efforts in all sciences, but it could do so in astronomy, a discipline in which the country has a long history of excellent research. In South Africa, the telescope is not a university project, but a national project, and this state-of-the-art machine has generated national pride.

The other notable McDonald Observatory effort has been in public outreach and education. Tier 1 research universities in the United States are not well understood by the public, which supports them through their taxes. Tier 1 universities like the University of Texas at Austin award PhD degrees in many fields and have very active research programs. To do this, they require their faculty members to be experts in their fields rather than experts at teaching. (This is in contrast to, say, public schools, whose teachers are well trained in the process of education.) For example, the history faculty at a Tier 1 school is made up of historians, each having been required to write a book on some aspect of history; the better the university, the tougher the requirements. In the best universities, each faculty member is required to be an international leader in his or her subject. To achieve this standard, those universities must have facilities that allow the faculty to reach the goal of being in the front rank. So in history and other liberal arts, the library must provide the sort of scholarly materials that will allow faculty members to write their books. In the sciences, the university must have laboratories and other facilities that will attract and sustain the best intellectual talent in each science that the university wishes to teach. The theory is that university students are best taught by people who are international leaders in the subjects they teach. So the McDonald Observatory exists to attract the very best intellectual talent to the University of Texas at Austin so that they can do their scholarly work and teach the students at the University.

In addition, in the United States, the research that benefits society is done largely in universities. Medical research is done mainly in medical schools connected to universities. This model of university-based research is not universal. In Germany, much of the taxpayer-supported research is done in institutes, called Max Planck Institutes, which are stand-alone

and are separate from universities. But in the United States, the research that keeps faculties in the international front ranks of their disciplines and leads to discoveries that benefit society comes mostly from universities.

Selling the practical benefit of astronomical research is not easy. I have heard my colleagues make tortured arguments for the practical benefits of astronomical research, but these ring hollow. To my mind, the social benefit of astronomical research is in nurturing the human need to explore. We astronomers are society's explorers as we look into the distance and the past and as we try to understand where the universe came from and is going. Therefore, we have an obligation to tell the people who support us what we find.

In Texas, the operating funds for the McDonald Observatory come from the legislature through special line items. These items appear at the end of the budget for the University. The state legislature cannot veto or change items inside the University budget; however, it can and does adjust the funding for the whole budget. Likewise, it can change or eliminate special line items individually. These items are designed to fund research units, such as the McDonald Observatory, that don't grant academic degrees directly. (In astronomy, the Department of Astronomy grants academic degrees.) Every two years, when the legislature meets and when the state budget gets tight, the special line items are vulnerable. So the McDonald Observatory is much more exposed politically than, say, the Department of Astronomy. Part of our answer, as Harlan Smith knew, is to invite the public in, to welcome them and tell them what we have found.

It seemed to me that we needed a second answer, since we were asking the legislature for additional funds for operating the Hobby-Eberly Telescope. During my time in Texas, the state has gone from an oil-rich economy to one based on high tech. A growing fraction of our population is native Spanish-speaking. So, to support the new economy, we need to graduate more and better-trained engineers and scientists, and we need to include native Spanish speakers in this effort. Thus, the McDonald Observatory began a program in education in addition to our program in public outreach. The education program produces materials, lesson plans, and supporting help, such as summer workshops to help teachers

The Frank N. Bash Visitors Center at the McDonald Observatory. *Photo by Martin Harris; courtesy of the McDonald Observatory, University of Texas at Austin.*

use children's fascination with astronomy to interest them in studying science and math. This effort is not designed to produce future astronomers, but future engineers, doctors, and technicians. The materials are bilingual so that native Spanish speakers can participate more fully. I believe that future support for major U.S. universities—including the University of Texas at Austin—will depend on our willingness to identify and address major social problems and tackle them directly. So I hope that the McDonald Observatory has taken a leadership role in redefining the responsibility of a major research institute to the public that supports it.

The key to the success of these programs at McDonald is Sandra Preston, who is able to manage a set of very diverse people in a way that keeps them happy and productive. The programs fund themselves through, for example, admission charges to the visitors center.

While the Hobby-Eberly Telescope was under construction, it became apparent that the tiny W. L. Moody Visitors Center at McDonald was not adequate. As our public outreach programs grew, we needed to find money to support them. The sale of merchandise in our gift shop became a major source of revenue. But the visitors center had become almost all gift shop, and it had no space for our education program. Expansion of the visitors center required that we buy more land. The first step was to raise funds to buy three hundred acres from the Eppenauer Ranch. The new land allowed us to plan for a much larger visitors center with a large gift shop, but also with an interactive science museum, a large auditorium, and classroom space for our education efforts. We also included a café, since McDonald is far from any restaurant. The notion of the McDonald Observatory director running a café always worried me, but the staff has pulled it off. Many wonderful donors contributed to the construction of the new visitors center, but Bill and Bettye Nowlin were the principal ones. They came through even after I told them that we had a donor and didn't need their help. That donor later decided not to fund us. The Nowlins expressed concern that the original plans had been left too "bare bones" in an effort to save money, so they briefly conferred privately and asked to increase

Retired McDonald Observatory director Frank Bash shares his knowledge of astronomy with young Austin Dwain Sneed of Midland, Texas, during Austin's visit to the McDonald Observatory, September 2009. *Photos by Marc Wetzel; courtesy of the McDonald Observatory, University of Texas at Austin.*

their gift to allow better materials to be used in the construction. The new visitors center opened in February 2002. At the Nowlins' request, it was named the Frank N. Bash Visitor Center on July 22, 2006. I was and am extremely pleased and honored.

The University of Texas took an unexpected gift, which it saw as an opportunity, and by a clever collaboration, an investment in an Astronomy Department, and a continuing investment in operating costs and new equipment—often very expensive equipment—built a world-class research facility in astronomy. UT used funds earned by the University's endowment to support McDonald, as it did in a number of other areas, such as the Harry Ransom Center. Through the use of these funds, the University of Texas was able to distinguish itself in ways in which an ordinary state university could not. However, the legislature has in recent years chosen to reduce its support of the operating costs of the University, so UT has been forced to spend endowment earnings on basic educational resources, such as the University of Texas Libraries, which funds from the legislature used to cover. If Texas wishes to have a truly world-class university, then private philanthropy—like the extraordinary gift from a turn-of-the-century banker named William J. McDonald from Paris, Texas—will be instrumental in that goal.

NOTE

1. The history of the McDonald Observatory from its beginnings up to 1986 is covered beautifully in David Evans and J. Derral Mulholland, *Big and Bright: A History of the McDonald Observatory* (Austin: Univ. of Texas Press, 1986).

The inspiration for the name of the show. *Courtesy of* Austin City Limits.

MICHAEL
TOLAND
}
# *Austin City Limits* and the University of Texas

Enjoyed weekly by millions of viewers, *Austin City Limits* is the longest-running music performance show on television. That the program has had such a long life is in itself a tribute to both the distinctive presentation of its subject and its affiliation with public broadcasting.

What the majority of *Austin City Limits'* millions of viewers may not know is that for the first three-plus decades of its existence, this staple of the Public Broadcasting Service (PBS), produced by Austin public television station KLRU-TV, was filmed on the campus of the University of Texas at Austin. From the taping of its pilot in 1974 until the fall of 2010, the year the show's producers moved it to its new home in a theater in the new Block 21 development in downtown Austin, *Austin City Limits* was produced in Building B of the Jesse H. Jones Communication Center, the home of the University's College of Communication and its Department of Radio-Television-Film.

Housed in Building B, Austin's public broadcasting station, originally identified by the call letters KLRN, was founded in 1962 by the then director of Radio-Television-Film, Professor Robert Schenkkan. It was able to take advantage of the University's location and patronage in developing *Austin City Limits*. Bill Arhos was program director at KLRN at the time (the station would later be identified by the call letters KLRU) and one of the original minds behind the development of *Austin City Limits*; he taught courses in television production at the University also. The station was quick to call on students as interns and technical operators. In addition to the advantages it afforded KLRN (and, later, KLRU) in general, the campus location provided easy access to a ready audience for the performances on *Austin City Limits*. Indeed, the University acted as an incubator for the show: as a liberal-arts-oriented campus in the center of a

Michael Toland, who received his BA in English from the University in 1998, splits his time working for Austin public television station KLRU and writing music criticism for various outlets. He grew up watching Austin City Limits *with his father in the 1970s, attended his first taping (a performance by Dr. John) in 1991, and became the* ACL *archivist in 2004.*

medium-sized, music-intensive town, it provided the perfect atmosphere for the creation and development of the unique program that *Austin City Limits* has continued to be.

AN UNCOMMON APPROACH
TO TELEVISING MUSIC

Austin City Limits (sometimes known simply as *ACL*) presents an hour of popular music performance recorded onstage in front of a live audience. It is a simple concept, but one that was still fairly uncommon on television in the early 1970s. Jazz performances had appeared sporadically on television in the 1960s, but were often interrupted by the show's host. ABC's *Don Kirshner's Rock Concert* and NBC's *The Midnight Special* were already late night–early morning staples, but the former presented performances of only two or three songs by each act, while both heavily relied on rock radio staples of the day, with the occasional soul-R&B act mixed in. The most common productions for popular music on television were one-song segments on variety shows, which were usually lip-synched, or on talk shows, where they often suffered from poor sound mixes. More often than not, the artist found him- or herself ensconced in a colorful set that may or may not have been appropriate to the song's subject or the artist's image—precursors to the music videos of the 1980s.

The format for *Austin City Limits* was different. In an hour-long show, the artist was given either a half-hour slot (with another musician getting the second half) or the full hour. The performance was presented uninterrupted by commercials or a host, capturing the feel of the actual live concert from which the footage was taken. The band played to the crowd in front of it, rather than to the cameras floating around it. The show's producers also eschewed most of the camera tricks in vogue for music performance in the '70s—no soft lenses, extravagant fade-ins and fade-outs, or split-screen techniques found their way into the final edit. The result may have been considered raw or crude by some professional standards of the day, but it lowered the barrier between performer and audience more explicitly than any other broadcast. It is a format and standard that continues today, when most music television still presents acts either one song at a time or in a lip-synched video.

Furthermore, the show revolved not around the album rock and Top 40 pop music of the day, but around less slick, more traditional forms of American music. Originally created to showcase the folk and country-oriented talent found in its Texas base, *Austin City Limits* became, at least until the advent of networks like CMT and The Nashville Network, the television home for country music and other forms of what would come to be called Americana. While country and western had been presented to mainstream American audiences before on variety shows hosted by Johnny Cash, Glen Campbell, and Porter Wagoner, it hadn't been seen with the same concert feel as it was on *Austin City Limits*.

Finally, the show's presence on public television was significant. Since PBS did not have commercial considerations in mind when it broadcast and distributed programs, producers didn't face the same upward climb as they did with one of the major networks. If the subject of a program was not the kind that would capture millions of TV-watching eyeballs, and deliver those eyeballs to major commercial advertisers, NBC, CBS, and ABC would likely pass on its production. If the subject was deemed to have some kind of educational or artistic value, PBS was more likely to give it the green light. While there was argument among some of the decision makers about whether country and roots music followed the educational-artistic guidelines of public television, PBS was a logical home for a defiantly anticommercial music television show like *Austin City Limits*. The producers could take more chances with booking and production values than they would have ever been allowed at a major network in that era.

Austin City Limits' subsequent popularity brought new faces to PBS. Television consumers who may have found PBS's educational-artistic veneer off-putting, or even pretentious, discovered that there was programming for them as well, and found that PBS could be just as entertaining as—and possibly more enlightening than—the fare on the major networks. Other producers also took notice; while the old model of music television continues to dominate, shows like *Sessions at West 54th*, *Live From the Artist's Den*, and others have taken cues from *ACL*'s stripped-down presentation of music performance and emulated its successful formula. For the first decade or so of *ACL*'s existence, it was also generally believed (though no hard data have been forthcoming) that an artist's appear-

The Jesse H. Jones Communications Center, University of Texas at Austin, including (*left*) Building B (aka "Old Rusty"). *From the Prints and Photographs Collection—UT—Buildings—Jesse H. Jones Communications Center, Dolph Briscoe Center for American History, University of Texas at Austin. (DI 06855)*

ance on the show had a direct positive effect on that artist's record sales.

PUBLIC BROADCASTING ON THE FORTY ACRES

Just as a public television station was the most logical home for a boundary-stretching music show like *Austin City Limits*, so was the University the right place for a PBS station. There are reasons why universities are so often the hosts for public broadcasting organizations. The culture on a college campus encourages not only the pursuit of education, but also the dissemination of it beyond the campus borders—a mission shared by public broadcasting. The particularly liberal atmosphere of the University of Texas was a key factor in giving birth to KLRU, letting it become the kind of creative haven needed for the mavericks that created *Austin City Limits* to thrive.

In 1965, the University established the School of Communication, comprising the School of Journal-

ism, the Department of Speech, and the newly created Department of Radio-Television-Film. Construction on Buildings A, B, and C, which housed the school and surrounded a sun-baked central plaza, began in 1965, and the three departments took up residence in 1974. The School of Communication became the College of Communication in 1979, and the complex was officially the Jesse H. Jones Communication Center in 1982. Building A was devoted to radio-television-film classrooms and offices, while Building C, recently renamed the William Randolph Hearst Building, became the new home of the offices of the *Daily Texan* student newspaper and, later, Texas Student Television, the campus's in-house channel. Eventually known as "Old Rusty" because of the heavily oxidized coating of Cor-Ten that once covered its façade, Building B became the home of public radio station KUT-FM, the Longhorn Radio Network, and KLRN-TV, the Austin–San Antonio public television station. (Today's viewers recognize the call letters of Austin's PBS affiliate as "KLRU." KLRN split in two in 1979 because of the poor quality of signal from the single transmitter serving both communities. Outfitted with its own transmitter, the Austin station became KLRU, and the San Antonio station retained the original call letters, KLRN.)

Like many public television stations, KLRN enjoyed a unique relationship with its university host. Technically owned and operated by a community-based nonprofit corporation called the Southwest Texas Public Broadcasting Council (the University was prohibited by state law from owning a television broadcast license), the station contracted with UT for management services and provided practical training for radio-television-film students. Many of the station's workers were actually employed by the University—several even taught courses in TV production. Edwin R. Sharpe, then the UT vice president for ad-

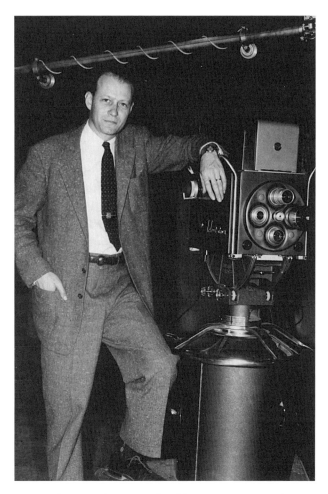

UT professor Robert F. Schenkkan, 1956. *From the UT Office of Public Affairs Records, Dolph Briscoe Center for American History, University of Texas at Austin. (DI 03249)*

ministration, oversaw the University's relationship with the station. In exchange, the University provided space, studios, equipment, and funding for the station until 1979, when UT severed its direct connection to KLRN because of a controversy over fund-raising practices and programming content.

The PBS affiliate was founded and managed by Professor Robert F. Schenkkan, sometimes called the father of educational television at the University for his hand in establishing KLRN and KUT. Thanks to Schenkkan's "vision and political savvy," as Clifford Endres notes in his book *Austin City Limits* (1987), KLRN staff had a major part in designing Old Rusty, in particular the sixth floor's two large studios. Designated Studios A and B, the rooms were unusually large for public broadcasting and contained brand-new equipment perfectly suitable for producing original programming.

In 1974, PBS began the Station Program Cooperative, an initiative that encouraged local affiliates to produce programs to air alongside the network's national shows, and KLRN wanted to participate. Both Schenkkan and program director Bill Arhos felt strongly that KLRN could produce significant national programming with a direct Austin connection. The first show the station produced was *Carrascolendas*, an award-winning bilingual children's program that ran for eight seasons. As that series found success with children and teachers, Arhos began looking for ideas for another show.

HOME WITH THE ARMADILLO

Bill Arhos, a Texas native who holds a bachelor's degree in science from Rice University and a master's degree in educational administration from Texas A&M, moved to Austin in 1961 and began working at KLRN in 1962 as an assistant instructional coordinator, teaching part-time at UT as well. He worked his way through nearly every position at the station—producer, director, camera operator, production manager—before settling into the unenviable position of trying to develop new programming. For ideas, he turned to producer Paul Bosner and director Bruce Scafe.

Scafe held degrees in both music and radio-television-film, often working as a professional jazz trumpeter as well. He came to KLRN by way of Dallas's ABC affiliate, but before that he had made his name directing *The Session*, a live-music program produced by public TV station WSIU-TV in Carbondale, Illinois. Bosner came to Texas after nearly two decades at the CBS studios in New York City, where he and his camera crew had won an Emmy for their work on the drama series *Studio One*. He lived in Dallas, but commuted to Austin to produce *Carrascolendas*. Described by Arhos as "pretty esoteric," Bosner liked to see movies at Austin's arthouse theater at the Dobie Mall on the edge of the UT-Austin campus, and he also began attending shows at the Armadillo World Headquarters, a music hall that had opened in 1970 in a converted National Guard armory located near Barton Springs Road and South 1st Street, just across the river from downtown. The Armadillo was home not only to touring acts that didn't fit the musical mainstream in the early 1970s, but also to a group of musicians building a local scene unlike any other in the country.

The story of Austin music in the '70s is one that has been told repeatedly by journalists, musicologists, and longtime Austin residents, but it is worth repeating because of its influence on the original direction of *Austin City Limits*. Austin's cultural melting pot, like that of many American cities in the early 1970s, was evolving, because of the mixing of the so-called straight culture and the counterculture. As the state capital, Austin had a large contingent of political and social conservatives and government officials, but the presence of a major university and low rental rates led to an influx of "hippies, radicals, artists and free spirits," as described by Thomas Fawcett in Endres's book *Austin City Limits*. The writer and historian Craig Hillis claims it was the influence of "cold beer, good dope and cheap rent" that led to Austin becoming home to Texas's countercultural representatives. The blending of these two cultures occurred at clubs like the Armadillo, where long-haired hippies and straight-laced cowboys could stand side by side, enjoying the same cold beer and country music.

That music reflected its audience. Performers and songwriters like Bobby Bridger, Rusty Wier, Steven Fromholz, B. W. Stevenson, Jerry Jeff Walker, and Michael Murphey (later Michael Martin Murphey) mixed country and folk with the trappings of rock and roll and hippie idealism. The Austin music veteran Doug Sahm found his blend of psyche-

delia and southwestern roots music fashionable and influential. Most importantly, longtime country-and-western fixture Willie Nelson moved to Austin and took up residence in the Armadillo, growing his beard, becoming more open about his marijuana use, and welcoming music fans of every stripe and creed to his shows. Although not yet a cultural force, Nelson was still a big enough star in the firmament of country music that his presence in Austin and acceptance of the countercultural lifestyle lent the scene enough weight to be called a movement.

The sounds bursting from Austin clubs were called progressive country or redneck rock. The latter phrase was borrowed from the title of local journalist Jan Reid's scene-intensive book *The Improbable Rise of Redneck Rock*, and its practitioners were often referred to as cosmic cowboys, after a Michael Murphey song title. The sound connected country to rock audiences, eventually infiltrating Nashville's country music establishment as the outlaw country movement. (Nelson and his friend and fellow Texan Waylon Jennings became the movement's most prominent figures.) Besides Reid, local journalists Joe Gracey and Townsend Miller tirelessly promoted the artists in their newspaper columns. Indeed, when Gracey heard that Dallas's PBS affiliate was planning a broadcast featuring a handful of what he called the "hippie-country bands," he used his column to issue a challenge to KLRN (as quoted in Endres's *Austin City Limits*): "Why didn't Austin's own public station do it first? The local media should be the first, not the last, to hear the news."

A fan of this music, Bosner was a regular at the Armadillo and had already read *The Improbable Rise of Redneck Rock*. Scafe wanted to direct a music program, no matter what type of music it featured. Arhos, stung by Gracey's criticism, pushed the two for ideas. A musical program featuring Austin's burgeoning progressive country scene seemed to be a clear choice, especially after Bosner gave Arhos Reid's book.

Arhos loved the book and shared Bosner and Scafe's enthusiasm. "You get an idea how far behind the scene I was when you realize that it existed long enough for a book to be written and published about it," Arhos remarked in Endres's *Austin City Limits*. "It was obvious. What was the most visible cultural product of Austin? It'd be like ignoring a rhinoceros in your bathtub." Arhos gave Bosner and Scafe the

The Austin music scene that helped inspire the creation of *Austin City Limits* was nurtured in venues such as the Armadillo World Headquarters, at 525 Barton Springs Road; the Soap Creek Saloon, at 707 E. Bee Caves Road; the One Knite Dive & Tavern, at 801 Red River Street; the Broken Spoke, at 3201 South Lamar Boulevard; the Texas Opry House, at 200 Academy Drive; and the Split Rail Inn, at 217 South Lamar Boulevard. *Photos of the Armadillo, One Knite, Broken Spoke, and Texas Opry House courtesy of Austin City Limits. Photo of the Soap Creek Saloon © 1979 Ken Hoge, www.kenhoge.com. Photo of the Split Rail Inn © 1977 Ken Hoge, www.kenhoge.com.*

green light, and the trio began to put together a television show.

AUSTIN CITY LIMITS IS BORN

KLRN's upper management, however, did not necessarily agree with the trio's enthusiasm for this new program, feeling that a show presenting "outsider" country music did not fit the mission of an educational station whose call letters were an abbreviation of "K-LEARN." Comments ranged from "It's too provincial to sell" to "Nobody likes that shit." Regardless, Arhos raised thirteen thousand dollars in pilot money (though he lost six thousand of it because of a poorly written proposal), and the project moved forward.

While Arhos worked on selling the show to his superiors, Bosner and Scafe confronted the technical challenges of bringing the same energy and magic of a live concert performance to a television screen. For Bosner, that meant capturing on videotape the unique relationship between the performers and the audience members, an elusive quality. Fortunately, Studio 6A—large enough to hold both a band and a substantial crowd, but small enough to be intimate—was almost perfectly suited for what Bosner had in mind. He, Scafe, and designer Augie Kymmel took materials liberated from KLRN's basement to build a set in 6A that would be an intimate space for both crowd and artist, with audience members sitting around and sometimes even on the stage. Perfectly happy to use UT students for crews and technicians, Bosner banned production techniques such as split-screen, freeze frames, and tricky zooms, stressing a basic, uncomplicated look over flashy technique. Bosner distributed a memo to the crew to emphasize what he wanted. "There will be no need to establish a visual point of view (reference) as to where the camera is," he wrote, as quoted in Endres's *Austin City Limits*. "It will be everywhere seeking out relationships, audience to musicians, musicians to each other, musicians to audience. . . . It is in this manner that we intend to capture the meaning, pleasure, the identification of the audience to this music."

Once the stage was set, the next task was to acquire artists. Bosner engaged Armadillo co-owner Mike Tolleson, who booked B. W. Stevenson and Willie Nelson in 6A on back-to-back nights in October

1974. Though Stevenson was the bigger star at the time, his performance drew poorly. KLRN wasn't yet proficient at spreading the news about tapings, and Stevenson's fan base was slow in responding. Though meant to be packed, 6A instead looked half empty on camera. Despite a strong performance by Stevenson, the recording was shelved.

The next night, October 14, was different. The budget was officially approved that day, raising the producers' spirits, and Nelson's fans packed 6A. Standing before a crowd similar to one they might face at the Armadillo—long-haired UT students and longtime country music fans—Nelson and his band essayed old hits and new songs that would become staples of his repertoire with exactly the kind of energy for which Bosner, Scafe, and Arhos were hoping. Normally leery of TV's slick production values, which did little for musicians like him, Nelson was quite happy with the way the show turned out. "We were all pretty pleased with ourselves and the results," wrote Arhos. Robert Schenkkan, the member of KLRN's management team most supportive of the new venture, sent a memo that simply stated, "Absolutely sensational job!" (Both quotations are found in Endres's *Austin City Limits*.)

The final piece of the creative puzzle was to find a title for the show, one that could best capture this unique Austin creation. Inspired by a marquee for the film *Macon County Line*, Arhos suggested a title with the same three-word ring to it. "Hill Country Rain," "River City Country" and "Austin Space" were all suggested, but not considered to be quite right. Finally, Bosner was inspired by his weekly commute from Dallas and the "Austin City Limit" sign he passed every trip. "The image gradually merged in his mind with the music he heard during his nights in the clubs," Endres notes. After enthusiastic approval from Arhos, the show's title became *Austin City Limits*.

Arhos took the pilot to the second-annual PBS Station Independence Project meeting, where it was acquired as a fund-raising special. During the spring 1975 fund drive, the pilot hit the top ten in dollars-per-minute and size of average pledge, giving Arhos the ammunition he needed in the fight to get *Austin City Limits* picked up as a series. He gained approval through PBS's Station Program Cooperative, and the dream of a nationally broadcast television series featuring Austin music and culture became a reality.

Willie Nelson performing during the taping of the pilot for *Austin City Limits*, October 14, 1974. *Courtesy of* Austin City Limits.

THE FUTURE OF *ACL*

Attending an *Austin City Limits* taping in Studio 6A, Building B, was a unique experience. The steps required to be a member of the studio audience were similar to those for any other concert event, with some subtle differences. Tickets are free; originally given away at KLRU a couple of days before a show, they are now reserved through an online drawing. The excitement felt by recipients built in intensity even more than for a show at a regular concert hall. The intimacy of the room was not only the hallmark of the show's feel, but also the reason why so few tickets were available—the University fire marshal limited the number of bodies that could be in there at one time. Waiting in line for the doors to open could feel like being part of an exclusive club, or being one of the luckiest people alive. It wasn't unusual for attendees to burst into huge smiles once they crossed KLRU's threshold. The good humor only increased once the fans arrived on the sixth floor, to be greeted by not only volunteers handing out programs for the night's performance, but also kegs of free beer, one of

the advantages to having a beer company as a sponsor. Inside the studio, beer cup in hand, the attendee noticed something else: no matter where one sat, it was a good seat—from any point in the studio, a fan could see the details of the artist's face. The rapport between audience and performer became a close one almost immediately, leading to shows that could rise to new heights and a fan experience as rapturous as could be imagined. It has been that way since the first show.

Austin City Limits has evolved since its first full season in 1976. Although production was nearly cancelled in season five and has suffered various funding crises over the years, it has never halted. The show's development has responded to periods of enormous growth in popularity, especially in the 1980s, when country music made inroads with mainstream music listeners. The 6A stage hosted landmark performances from American musical pioneers like Ray Charles, B. B. King, and Merle Haggard, unique singer-songwriters like Tom Waits, Van Morrison, and Leonard Cohen, and alternative rockers like My Morning Jacket, Wilco, and Coldplay.

After coming on board as assistant producer in season three, Terry Lickona became producer in season four, adding the current stage that same year and the famous Austin skyline backdrop in season seven; he became executive producer in season thirty-five. Leasing the show's title, Capital Sports and Entertainment (now C3) created an Austin-based music festival around it in 2002. The long lines of *ACL* fans that coiled around the Communication Center's plaza before tapings testify to the program's continuing upswing in popularity.

Longer lines, however, also meant greater demand for tickets. The resulting crowds of fans, funders, and friends of the artists grew larger than the studio could hold—by the mid-2000s, *Austin City Limits* had simply outgrown Building B of the Jesse H. Jones Communication Center on the UT campus. As a result, in 2006, KLRU made the difficult decision to seek new accommodations for the show. As part of a new development in downtown Austin called Block 21, a 2,500-seat theater, dubbed ACL Live at the Moody Theater, was built with the specific intent of housing production of *Austin City Limits*. The bigger capacity made it easier to meet ticket demands and increase attendance.

Yet, even though *Austin City Limits* was leaving the UT campus, the producers wanted to take to the new theater the original studio's distinctive feel, which had developed on the Forty Acres. This presented the challenge of, as Lickona stated for the *Austin City Limits* Oral History Project, "figuring out how to take the atmosphere of this room [6A], the vibe, the history, and transplant it to a new facility in a new building that we've made from scratch." In the end, the producers of the show have re-created and updated the famous backdrop of the Austin skyline at the Moody Theater, and used familiar lighting and sound production to capture the feel of the original location on the UT campus.

The relationship between UT and *Austin City Limits*, however, has not been severed by the relocation. From *ACL*'s beginning, the University's support has been an important factor in the program's success. It was UT's provision of then state-of-the-art facilities in 1973 that allowed KLRN to move confidently into national production. "Would there have been an *ACL* without that kind of space and equip-

ment?" mused Arhos in a recent e-mail to me. "Probably not. It certainly made it a lot easier to originate and produce."

Just as significantly, student interns at UT have worked on the program since the first season and will continue to do so now that the production has moved off campus. As the media tide shifts constantly, it will be up to the next generation of producers and directors to navigate the often-treacherous waters. The future expression of *ACL* will rest on future media platforms driven by that generation. The next producers of *Austin City Limits* might very well be sitting in classrooms in the Jesse H. Jones Communication Center right now.

NOTE ON SOURCES

For the basic narrative of the show's origins, I am heavily indebted to the first two chapters of Clifford Endres, *Austin City Limits* (Austin: Univ. of Texas Press, 1987); all of the story's principals agree with this account. Many additional details were filled in by Bill Arhos's unpublished essay "Austin City Limits: A Retrospective" (1985), as well as by invaluable e-mail exchanges with Arhos himself throughout 2009 and 2010. Documents at the Dolph Briscoe Center for American History clarified points about Arhos, KLRN, KLRU, and the College of Communication. Also helpful was the Austin City Limits Oral History project, researched by Maggie Rivas-Rodriguez's 2007 class Journalism as Oral History and published on its website: http://journalism.utexas.edu/coursework/acl. Finally, e-mail correspondence with the playwright and screenwriter Robert Schenkkan, Jr., in April 2010 was crucial in gathering details about his father.

Other works about *Austin City Limits* include *Austin City Limits: Twenty-Five Years of American Music* by John T. Davis (New York: Billboard Books, 2000), and *Austin City Limits: Thirty-Five Years in Photographs* by Scott Newton and Terry Lickona (Austin: Univ. of Texas Press, 2010). For more background on the Austin music scene of the early 1970s, Jan Reid, *The Improbable Rise of Redneck Rock* (Austin: Heidelberg, 1974) is essential.

Reminiscences

Barbara Smith Conrad in performance: (*clockwise from top left*) *Aida* (1976; DI 07142), *Porgy and Bess* (1985; DI 07143), *Rigoletto* (1982; DI 07144), and *Yerma* (1966; DI 07145). *All images from the Barbara Smith Conrad Photograph Collection, Dolph Briscoe Center for American History, University of Texas at Austin.*

BARBARA
SMITH
CONRAD

} # I Had No Reason to Believe Otherwise

My college education began at Prairie View A&M College of Texas. It was exciting to be away from home and pursuing something you thought you were going to do. I was going to be a math major. I was serious about that because my father was so good at it—but the music always won out.

Music had been a dream, a passing fancy sort of thing, as I learned about other African Americans who had excelled in this field—Marian Anderson being my absolutely ultimate heroine. This dream was greatly nurtured when I came to the University of Texas. I had the love, the passion. I had been exposed to quite a lot of music, but I didn't have the history of it. I didn't have the links to music's European roots, which I got at UT—talking to people who spoke those languages, so that the music of Fauré, Debussy, Mozart, Puccini, Verdi—all those—became something different as the language began to emerge.

Everybody in my family, practically, had gone to Prairie View. My father had two brothers—Uncle Curtis and Uncle Duree—who had gone there. They each became superintendents of schools in Texas—one in Gilmer and the other in Pittsburg. Duree Smith was a beloved uncle. He thought it would be a good idea for me to go to Prairie View, and that was all I needed to know. My brother Dinard went to Prairie View, as well.

Dinard was our family's child prodigy. He was playing Mozart sona-

---

Barbara Conrad is a world-renowned mezzo-soprano who performed with the Metropolitan Opera for eight years, from 1982 to 1989, and has performed leading operatic roles in Europe and the Americas with the world's foremost conductors and orchestras. She lives in New York City, where she is codirector and cofounder of the Wagner Theater Program and complements her performing activities with artist residencies, master classes, and her private vocal studio. David Dettmer drew this reminiscence from interviews Ms. Conrad recorded with Erin Purdy for the University's Oral History Project on May 10 and 11, 2006, at the Ebenezer Baptist Church on East 10th Street in Austin. These interviews, which were used extensively to produce the documentary film When I Rise *(Alpheus Media, 2010), are available for study at UT's Dolph Briscoe Center for American History.*

tas at age six, Mama said. I don't remember that, but I just always knew if Dinard walked into a room, the first thing he looked for was a piano. Dinard really had the greatest influence on my early musical development. He spoon-fed me.

He was in the male chorus at Prairie View, and once he went up to Dallas for a concert. The performance was Beethoven's *Christ on the Mount of Olives*, which is an oratorio piece. There's a great soprano solo in there; he just remembered it, and he came home that night at one o'clock in the morning and he taught it to me. He didn't remember all the German words, because we spoke no German, but got the melody right and all the rest of it. He was that kind of person. Any kind of music you wanted to know about, any song, you'd say, "I want something, an old Irish ditty," and he would just start playing it. It didn't matter. That was his talent.

Growing up, music was everywhere. I discovered that I had a talent for it and people to support me. My teacher in Queen City, Mrs. Hatten, quickly discovered my singing voice. She was a big, big supporter of the music itself. I had my first public appearance, on radio, in Texarkana, thanks to Mrs. Hatten. Technique for vocal, as I understand it now, wasn't part of my early education. Just imitation. My sister Connie was a beautiful singer, so I could imitate her. I used to try to imitate anyone who had what I now would call the lyric art of singing—that way in which the breath spins out its songs—and a lot of people had that. My grandmother—my Big Mama—had that. She could sing anything.

Several years ago, Ross Perot invited Dinard and me to a ceremony in Dallas. It was a big tom-tom, attended by several people we knew. (So many of the people who grew up in small Texas towns of my youth—Pittsburg, Atlanta, and Queen City—live in the Dallas–Fort Worth area now.) They adored Dinard, and I was their little hometown celebrity. Fannie Mae, an old classmate who used to listen to me practice at lunchtime with Mrs. Hatten, was talking with me about my singing and my career. She said, "Barbara, I knew you could get up and do this. You know, I would have been out there screaming and hollering just like you did when we were kids. Girl, you were screaming and hollering—we didn't know what to make of that sound!"

Whenever anyone in the little communities of my youth had a gift—being the best cotton chopper, whatever—it was lauded and applauded and appreciated. It didn't matter what it was. Likewise, when I first became established in my professional career, my aunt Maggie—who is my mother's favorite aunt, my great-aunt—used to call me "Miss Fine," "Big Shot," and "Miss International Fine." That was the community. There was so much of that love and respect. We grew up feeling pretty secure about ourselves.

My hometown is the tiny East Texas community of Center Point. Growing up there was magical. The land that we lived on—the community—was founded by freedmen. One of them was my great-grandfather, so it's precious to us. It's in the beautiful part of the state—piney woods, piney wood country, red dirt. Yummy clay dirt; we loved to smell it as children. Farming land. Lots of manmade lakes, and lots and lots and lots of little farms. Soft, rolling hills. Beautiful. A beautiful, beautiful part of the country. I can smell the pine trees now. The honeysuckle is outrageous. Fresh air. Freedom. Freedom in a way that only the soul knows—and my feet! I immediately pull off my shoes; I'm barefoot from the moment I get there.

I was born in Atlanta, Texas, because my parents' work took them there when school was in session. My parents named me Barbara Louise Smith. My father, Conrad Alphonso Smith (my professional name honors him), was the principal of the schools in the Honey Grove and Shady Grove communities, northwest of Atlanta, in rural Cass County, at that time. My mother, Jerrie Lee Cash, was the teacher and drove the bus as well, I'm told.

Back in Camp County, the home seat was Pittsburg. Center Point, a rural community a few miles east of Pittsburg, is where my mother was born and where my father came to school. Center Point had the first black accredited school in the state. It was a boarding school, so that was pretty exciting—an accredited boarding school. My parents' work took the family to live in Cass County during the week; we went back home to Center Point on the weekends and during summers and holidays. Being the youngest, I spent most of my time in school at Queen City, two miles north of Atlanta. The tiny rural schools I attended during my grade-school years consolidated when I was in eighth grade, and so I graduated from high school in Queen City.

The boarding school in Center Point had a farm attached to it. My father and his brothers, as I un-

The Smith family of Center Point, Texas: (*in front, left to right*) Dinard, Barbara, Peter; (*behind, left to right*) Big Mama, Connie, Mrs. Goodman, Johnnie, Mama. *From the Barbara Smith Conrad Photograph Collection, Dolph Briscoe Center for American History, University of Texas at Austin. (DI 07146)*

derstand it, had no shoes and no clothes practically when they came to that school from Leesburg, ten miles west of Pittsburg, but they worked on the various things they could do around the school, around the farm. My mother was amazing in that she grew up in a fragmented family situation, raised by her mother and Big Mama's fourteen or fifteen siblings. (Big Mama had a third-grade education.) They all raised her up, as they used to say.

In our community, education was very important. Both my parents went to Bishop College, in Marshall. My mother was a marvelous teacher, determined, caring, nurturing—very much the English schoolmarm. She was tough, but you were prepared! (We used to call her "the Sergeant" behind her back.) You had to be very careful with your language around her. Everybody talked about her insistence that you be able to speak well, read well, reason well, and that you treat people well. That was important. It was a community.

Not long after I was born, my father went into the military service—in part, I think, because my par-

ents had lost their first child, my sister Margaret Lewis, to adolescent diabetes when she was twelve. Her death changed our lives. My father felt so hampered. He said, "Lou, I felt like I failed my child. I couldn't provide what she needed." (In Center Point, I'm known as Lou.) There was just no money. But going away to the military meant that the farm and all the kids were left in the hands of Mama and that extended family—both relatives and nonrelatives.

My father had quite a distinguished military career, graduating number two or three in Commander General Staff School and achieving the rank of major. (Ross Perot once told me that that was like being a colonel today.) He was a veteran of World War II and the Korean War, terribly injured in both by mortar shock. My father was revered because he was a leader. He was a true, wonderful leader: compassionate, brilliant, tough. A father you could admire. And I forced him to hug me. It got easier. ("Hey Lou, where's my hug?")

My father came out of the military service for a couple years when I was eleven or twelve to try to be home with the family, but he found that that situation wasn't adequate for us and returned to the military. So we were teachers, farmers, military—all of that together. Mama was a huge part of that community, as was my father. My father was a hero. Mama was the glue.

I was the youngest of the four surviving children, and there was a time, when I was three, that Mama simply couldn't feed and take care of all of us. So some of the time Connie and I stayed with Aunt Maggie and her husband, whom I called "Pappy," in Quanah, out in West Texas. There I was a little princess. Aunt Maggie and Pappy had no children, and they adopted me and spoiled me rotten—I was royal and spoiled! That poor man, Pappy! One time I wanted cowgirl boots. He traveled eighty miles. Do you know how far that was in those days to get me some cowgirl boots? My sister and I stayed in Quanah

Little Barbara Smith with her uncle and aunt, Arthur and Maggie Goodman, in Quanah, Texas, 1942. *From the Barbara Smith Conrad Photograph Collection, Dolph Briscoe Center for American History, University of Texas at Austin. (DI 07147)*

some, but I came back and joined the family when I was five. I was gone so much that my older brother, Howard, whom we called Pete, didn't know who I was. He asked my younger brother, Dinard, "Who is she? Who is that girl with all that long hair?" "That's your sister, idiot!" He used to love to tell that story.

It was in Quanah that I first came to understand that I had musical abilities. Aunt Maggie would get me all dressed up in my pinafores, and Pappy liked to show me off. I remember first singing in the front yard on a Saturday evening, holding my dresses like so in front of my uncle. "Yes, Jesus Loves Me" was the song, and I sang every little song I knew because he wanted me to, dressed up in my beautiful little pinafores made by my Aunt Maggie from this beautiful fabric from flour sacks. I still have one of those dresses.

I was born during the Depression, but I never felt like a Depression child. It wasn't possible. There was too much to be thankful for, first of all. I mean, we didn't have the things you could buy in the store, but you had fish, you had eggs. I remember the worst time was when we had to sell everything we raised to survive. We ate a lot of potatoes that summer. For a while, I did not want potatoes and eggs. But the way it hurt was when I saw my mother so worried—when I saw her pain, when she couldn't afford to buy a new pair of shoes. That hurt. That bothered me.

In the same way, I guess segregation bothered me—through my mother more than directly myself—having to watch her in Queen City, where we stayed during the week. For example, there was a lady, some yards away, who was white, who was an excellent dressmaker, and my mother employed her to make some clothes for her from time to time. But to collect them, she had to go to the back door. Those were the things that used to absolutely take me from rage to sadness, or sadness to rage. The embarrassment, the indignity for my mother, who was smarter than most people I knew. And my mother, oh. For that—to this day, I go: "*Um . . .*"

But we had these balances in our lives. Some of my father's best friends that came and hung out with him, and went fishing together, hunting together, were white. But there were times where it was hard to watch that. I personally feel it some days even more, certain moments that come up. ("What do you mean I can't afford to pay $500 for a pair of shoes? Of course I can. But am I going to? No.") Stupid stuff, but it's there. Going to a department store in Texarkana and not being able to try on a hat because your hair was "greasy." ("Don't get oil on my hats." "Well then, put something under it so people can try them on.") We didn't have anything. Books were hard to get.

Here's a story about a lesson learned: When I was a child, we could not afford band suits. We were, obviously, attending segregated schools. So another school finally gave us their castoffs—which might not have been so bad had they been in good condition and didn't stink to high heavens. I just remember going, "You've got to be kidding! We can't—" I was thirteen at the time. I was so livid. We went back home to Center Point that Friday evening, as we did every Friday, and I went directly to my Big Mama's house. She had this rocking chair, which seemed huge to me as a child; I guess it was normal-sized, with a stool next to it. Every time we had a problem, she'd make you sit on that stool and she'd read from the Bible. "Come. Let us reason together." A thirteen-year-old child is not interested. I just wanted to rant and rave, and she let me do a little bit of that. Then she said, "Lou, you don't know it yet, child, but you have a built-in motivation for living and you just don't realize it yet." And, of course, with me you always had to break things down. She said, "Well now, you know, what can we do with this?" Big Mama remembered that we had just learned in home economics class how to make piecrusts. She said, "Make something. Sell something. Make your own suits." And that's what I did. I went back to Queen City, spoke to my teacher, Miss Hilmon (who is still alive and wonderful), and we made gazillions of potato pies, and little individual pies, and sold them everywhere. And we made our own suits. They weren't suits; they were skirts and blouses, and whatever. But they looked good on us. They were ours.

The balance was the joy in our lives. There was so much of it. Maybe we had to love each other a little bit more. Maybe we had to care about each other a little bit more. Maybe we had to try harder to understand our circumstances. Maybe we had to work harder as students to survive and to excel. Through these experiences, though, you learn to persevere, and be creative, and live within yourself. You understand that if you want something to happen, it starts with, as the Germans say, *selbst*—it starts with self. It develops a certain character. I appreciate that. It served me well in my career.

I grew up surrounded by music—voices, voices, voices, and pianists—Dinard being the most outstanding. Center Point Baptist Church had a fine music program because Dinard's piano teacher was also a teacher in that school. Center Point was a community of music-makers, and the church was our platform. We had anthems and all of that wonderful music as well as gospel and hymns and revivals. And so that developed everything that we had to offer—I and all of my siblings. We sang all the time at prayer meetings and revival meetings. And then we had the Interscholastic League competitions, which were a great opportunity. You had to prepare to compete—first at the preliminaries, and then at the state meet. I did that, and won a few times. But it made you get up and sing—or play or debate or spell or whatever you did. The UIL was a good program—it still is.[1]

Barbara Smith and Big Mama. *From the Barbara Smith Conrad Photograph Collection, Dolph Briscoe Center for American History, University of Texas at Austin. (DI 07150)*

We had wonderful opportunities to perform in so many venues. Most important, though, was to perform as a soloist. It's the best platform possible. There is no more difficult an audience than a church full of black people who all know how to sing better than you do! You've got to come up with something. That was Dinard's great gift. He knew how to program. He knew what song to sing, when, and where. He could also sing. He didn't like to, particularly, but once in a while he'd do it. When he'd do it, he'd whisper to me, saying, "All right. They want me to sing. I'm going to make all those old ladies faint," and he'd rear back with his gorgeous profile and start singing and playing, and that's about what they did. They didn't faint, but they swooned a lot!

There was music everywhere in our family. Connie was our Leontyne Price, the soprano. She had a great voice. My mother had an uncle—Uncle Ruff Floyd, who later became a cobbler—who was sold for a thousand dollars as a slave because he could play the fiddle. I was enchanted by him. I think I was seven or eight when I met him—the one and only time I saw him. I can't think of one cousin that my mother had, or her brother, who didn't have a beautiful singing voice. Just a community of music makers—Center Point, that is.

I also can't remember a music I don't enjoy singing. But, obviously, I grew up with certain kinds of music. I slipped off and went to a few clubs that I wasn't supposed to go to. I heard some real good—what is it called?—gutbucket blues. I heard all of that music in little shacks somewhere in the woods. But the obvious music was the spirituals, which I just love. The hymns—which were like prayers in celebration. And, of course, gospel music was . . . Dinard, once again, was the champion. Good Lord, could he play.

And then, of course, because of him and my sister, particularly, I grew up learning the most complicated music—Bach, Mozart, Stravinsky—though not realizing it. I learned hard music. I didn't know it was hard; I just went with my ear. But then, luckily, it got developed as I went along to school, particularly at the University of Texas.

I had some good teachers at Prairie View—in music, specifically—very good teachers. But the scout came and visited us, and wanted to know my interest in coming to the University of Texas. I don't remember the man's name or where exactly he came from; I assume it was UT, or that he was connected

Barbara Smith in Center Point, Texas. *From the Barbara Smith Conrad Photograph Collection, Dolph Briscoe Center for American History, University of Texas at Austin. (DI 07149)*

to those concerned with bringing undergraduates to UT. There were several of us interviewed, and those of us who were chosen to come. I talked it over with my folks and decided: why not? It was a great opportunity to advance in something that I was clearly enamored with, which was singing.

I came to Austin in 1956, the fall semester, among the first group of black undergraduates to be admitted to the University of Texas. The famous *Brown v. Board of Education* case had been decided a couple years earlier.[2] Gosh—even now my heart beats just a little bit faster thinking about it. It was exciting. It was terrifying. We were like a little . . . well, we surrounded each other, those girls and boys who came. I don't remember how many came or how many stayed. I know that a certain number came. There were not many—and quite a few left before the semester was over.

The first day on campus started off as a very beautiful day. We were an attractive group of young people because we thought we were so smart and so bright and so wonderful. Everybody made us feel that way. We were supported by our housemother, Almetris Duren, to actually come to the campus.

Residents of the Almetris Co-op, 1958. Almetris Duren is seated in the middle of the second row. Barbara Smith is standing directly behind Ms. Duren. *From the Barbara Smith Conrad Photograph Collection, Dolph Briscoe Center for American History, University of Texas at Austin. (DI 04391)*

As we were walking toward the Main Building, toward the Tower, there was some jeering. Very little, but there is one sentence that I wish I could erase from my memory. Some boy screamed out, "Oh, look at them. Our pappies probably messed around with all of their grand-mammies," or their mammies, or something like that. My heart stopped, and the fury I felt—I have a classmate who said, "You turned purple." We had been drilled to stay silent, to stay dignified, and ignore anything like that. That was the only incident; aside from that, we felt the same excitement and anxiety and all the things that any youngster feels.

The University segregated the housing, with the

African American boys staying in the old ROTC barracks. We girls lived in a dormitory that UT had leased from Huston-Tillotson College in East Austin, across the highway. It was wonderful—big, spacious rooms. You didn't have to share with anyone if you didn't want to. But we were a great family. We quickly bonded.

Mama Duren was our housemother.[3] She was mama—protective. She could be stern when she needed to be. She just protected us all in every way she knew possible, from nutrition to your class work to your health; every aspect of your life was her concern. She could make you laugh. She had these dimples, which I loved. I'd take my finger and move it just so. "What are you doing—burrowing a hole in my face?" I was a very serious girl—she'd make me laugh.

My classmates were mostly wonderful. Among my teachers, John Silber—who later became the dean of the College of Arts and Sciences—was a huge, huge supporter. Most of my music faculty, and Dr. William Doty, dean of the College of Fine Arts, tried to be. Outside there, though, it was another world. There was some roughing up with me walking to East Austin. Just scary—scare tactics. But, boy, I must have some Irish in me. (I do, in fact.) Don't make me mad. Not good. Ask my nieces and nephews!

At UT, I found a community that was magical in parts and difficult in others. I found the heartbreak of not being well prepared. I faced things. Kids knew things that I had never heard about in music. I had to learn a lot, real fast.

In the School of Music, I studied under Edra Gustafson. She was a very fine teacher. Very fine teacher. Swedish. Lutheran. I went to her church a lot. She was a good disciplinarian, in the best sense. I really started to learn what it was to develop ways to make my voice operate better, to help it. I learned technique—vocal technique—and she introduced me to some incredibly beautiful music.

It was Miss Gus, we called her, who first introduced me to the French song repertoire, particularly "L'invitation au voyage," which is a beautiful French art song. It was that whole world where you could just disappear into another culture. It was wonderful and beautiful, and struck my artist's soul somewhere. I learned a lot from Miss Gus. I learned how to appreciate my gifts. I never thought of this as a gift particularly. Miss Gus used to say, "Every time you stand up to sing, Barbara, you must thank God first." And to this day, I do that. She fed me a lot—I was about *that* big. She made great Swedish meatballs. Miss Gus enriched my life. She fostered me until long after I left UT.

Dean Doty was my counterpoint teacher. As an instructor, he was the best—clear, no nonsense—but he knew how far he could push you. He knew that you knew things that you didn't know. He would do little exercises that clearly would suggest whether the student understood or didn't understand counterpoint, and I just did it. He would give little exercises, and before you knew it, you could trust your own ear.

Dr. E. William Doty, dean of the College of Fine Arts, entering the Music Building (today named Homer Rainey Hall) on the South Mall, ca. 1953. *From the UT Texas Student Publications, Inc. Photographs Collection—E. William Doty (dean, College of Fine Arts), Dolph Briscoe Center for American History, University of Texas at Austin. (DI 06867)*

For me, my time at UT was always a little bit of a schism. (I use the word a lot, but it's true.) When I would go to the music school, I felt very much at home and accepted. That's because, number one, most musicians had evolved a certain way. Many had gone on to other parts of the world; and there were lots of Europeans in the UT music department. But then I'd go outside that little cocoon, and it was not easy. I couldn't go to any restaurants on campus.

Here's a "wow" story. I had an assignment for drama class that involved going to see the film *The Bad Seed*. The Paramount Theater downtown was segregated, so we had to get permission for me to go. I got there, and the girl in the ticket booth freaked. She exclaimed, "You can't. You can't, you can't." Then she screamed, "You can't!" I realize now that she was probably afraid she was going to lose her job. Whatever. A young man witnessed this and introduced me to whoever was in charge of makeup and costumes at the drama school. He said, "Here's an idea." I had long, long hair, which was straightened. They parted it down the center, and put a dot on my forehead, and put some gauze around me, and I went back to that theater and saw that movie. Now did I remember much of it? No. It was a kind of adventure, but then I got there and sort of—well, it was scary—because I realized—you know—I had seen the results of lynchings, and I thought, "Oh, God, what am I doing? I'm putting my family at risk." I saw the movie, though. Same person. So those were some weird times. Weird, weird.

You had to do what you had to do. For example, if you wanted a chili cheeseburger, then you sent the one or two who could pass as white, and they would go get the chili cheeseburgers. We would do anything—we would cross all lines—to get a chili cheeseburger. But the incident at the Paramount was my breakthrough performance!

My life, as I had grown up with it, was pretty wonderful. It was not an unhappy life. It was a wonderful life, and I didn't see any reason why that shouldn't continue when I was at the University. It was just going to get richer, I thought, because, God, I read all the time about all these marvelous things that could happen when races come together. So I was dreaming the same dream everyone else was dreaming in that period: we really will overcome; we really will be brothers and sisters. I thought that was a great ambition, a great cause. Part of that is what I felt, and part of that is what my community felt. The combination was pretty powerful. That's the core: you knew what you were fighting for.

You knew you were fighting, in some small way, for the right to be. The right to higher education. The right for equal education. The right to be heard. The right to be productive. Imagine that—I can make a difference. To anyone. I learned that from my parents. So with all of its drawbacks, I learned exactly what I needed to learn—and it could have been far worse. I might not have survived. Those were violent times we were going into.

The man I had my crush on when I was ten died a violent death. His body was dragged out of a lake in Louisiana. There were people who said he had made a pass at some white lady. I don't know if that accusation was true or false, but I know he was killed. I didn't want to live in a world like that. It was too painful. I wept for him for years because he was a very kind man. I said I had a crush. My father wasn't there, so he was almost a daddy to me—certainly old enough to be. I wanted a world different from that. I had wanted to have a big family. I was the one who was going to have a bunch of kids. I didn't want them to grow up like this. I did not want to see them watch their mothers go up to somebody's back door one more time.

{ }

It was less than two months into my first semester at UT, in October 1956, that the audition for the opera occurred.

The College of Fine Arts was auditioning for its student production of the opera *Dido and Aeneas*, by the English composer Henry Purcell, which was to be presented to the public at the end of the spring semester. I had never heard of it until that moment. Josephine Antoine had heard about me and seen me—I'm not quite sure where. One day I was practicing in the Music Building, which today is named Homer Rainey Hall there on the South Mall, and she barged in. She said, "My dear, you would be a wonderful Dido." I hadn't a clue. ("Who is this wild woman, coming in here?") Clearly, she was someone who was a theater person. Anyway, she asked me to come and audition. I did.

Ms. Antoine was on the voice faculty at UT when I joined. It turns out that she was also a very good friend of a woman who became an absolutely wonderful supporter and protectress of mine, Dr. Inez Jeffrey, in whose house in West Austin, on 19th Street, I spent many, many hours.[4] Ms. Antoine thought I had real promise. She had sung at the Metropolitan Opera, and I later learned she had told Inez that she thought—how did she put it?—that "the girl has that *iks* factor"—that thing that says, you know, that you've got it. It's a very European expression—it's just German for *X*. But I just thought this was the greatest word anybody ever used to describe me—the *iks* factor—and it was very encouraging to me. She told Inez she thought I would have a career. She told me that many years later.

I was in a big general-music class that first semester. The day after the audition, I arrived to class, making it just in time (often we walked all the way from East Austin), and the class started to applaud. I was ready to do battle, of course—or I was confused, let's put it that way. I wasn't quite that reactive. The professor at the time completely got it that I was about to go into protective mode, and said, "Barbara, you need to go and look at the bulletin board." "Okay." Having forgotten that the roles were supposed to be posted the next day, I went to look at the bulletin board. There it was. I had been chosen. That's the way it began.

It was a school production. In fact, I had gone to Dean Doty to ask for special permission to take it, because they had to give me credit, since I was allowed to perform. It was very, very . . . I mean, can you imagine doing your first opera? I was absolutely convinced I was going to win the Academy Award for this. I don't know what I was thinking! I just knew it was an exciting time. I had read enough to understand how opera worked, up to a point. But to be cast in one was really quite something. We started rehearsing, and did so throughout the year.

You had to fit rehearsals in with the rest of your class work. But oh, was it exciting. I can't really tell you why I was that excited, as I had at this point never seen an opera. I just knew that opera was my world. A cousin of mine in Houston got me a ticket to go see *Elektra*, of all things—a Strauss opera—in Houston, and then I was bedazzled.

The storyline of *Dido and Aeneas* was significant. My role was Dido, the queen of Carthage. Carthage was, of course, a city on the northern coast of Africa in the days when Troy fell to the Greeks, and in the opera, the Trojan hero Aeneas has escaped the burning city and sailed to the African coast. It's a love story between Dido and Aeneas. We thought that was perfect timing—capturing the usual Sturm und Drang between races and the overcoming of those insurmountable things between cultures. Dido was the queen and had reigned, but she had to die, of course. Somebody has to die in opera, and she had to die.

One of the famous arias from this opera is "When I Am Laid in Earth," and that is the aria that really captured me. As it turns out, it is one of the great pieces ever written just as a pure vocal piece and pa-

thos. The melody will make you cry; you don't have to know anything about it. Dido's handmaiden is there onstage with her, and Dido says, "Remember me, but ah! forget my fate." She commits suicide. I trained to do it very well, I thought. I remember one of my teachers saying, "Barbara, your arms are so long! You can't leave them up there forever." It was a great time. It was a process that opened up, little by little, and I'm glad for it, because it got me acquainted with what that felt like, to develop a character with singing. It was a very exciting time.

My relationship with my fellow cast mates developed very nicely—or so I thought, anyway. I was treated well. We were just students learning music together and learning how to perform it. We were learning about staging and about developing characters together. Occasionally I would get a little feeling of "Why is she here?" from the others, but I get that still—and it has nothing to do with race! I got my first taste of "I am the prima donna here." "No, I'm the prima donna."

We were going to do an opera with an orchestra. Oh, my goodness. That was just heaven for me—for all of us, I'm sure. Then I started getting phone calls.

The calls happened once in a while late in the first semester, but nothing that really made me that nervous. We would occasionally just get crank calls—the usual ugliness that comes spewing from people. We mostly would pass it off as another sad soul. But then it became a little bit more ominous because the callers would talk about places I had sung. I remember having sung for Miss Gus's church, the Lutheran church on 19th Street. The callers said that it was not permissible to have a "Nigra girl" sing at this church and I needed to go home—that I needed to go back and be with my own. I heard ugly names. Hard to say them, even today. Not necessary.

But here's a wonderful thing that happened. The students' support of me was so heartwarming. I did not expect to have that kind of support. I didn't know that others were observing what was going on in that way. They felt something about it, and students—in the department, especially—started to reach out.

That's when I met Carolyn Graves, my sweetheart for life. I had asked for someone to help me—a tutor in subjects that I just couldn't catch up with—and she had been chosen. She and her parents were huge supporters. Her father offered to let me stay in their home when all these things happened. Along

Barbara Smith and Carolyn Graves. *Courtesy of Carolyn Graves Good.*

the way, there were so many people in the department—faculty members—who were just unbelievably supportive.

I was very frustrated during this time, sometimes, because we were all together in the Music Building, and then we went our separate ways and we no longer had that unity. I missed that, because the people I saw the most were the people I went to class with every day. Outside of class, we couldn't "hang out" together. You felt—and we were advised—that it would not be prudent or safe to try to mix too much. "Let it come gradually," they said. Youngsters don't do things gradually. We were kids, teenagers. You like somebody and you respond. Luckily, there were enough people who weren't afraid.

I remember Carolyn and the man who was courting her—her future husband, Earl Good—invited me to their church. And little by little, we would do little things. God bless Dr. Blake Smith and Frances Carr. Dr. Smith was the minister of University Baptist Church, and probably more than anyone in my life—certainly in that period—he recognized how important it was for me to "Make your heart happier," as he used to say.[5] In his mind, Christ was the way to go. He didn't preach to me a lot of theology or any of that stuff—he simply did everything by example. He stood up for me; he insisted that I sing there.

He was sort of my guru for a while. I trusted him, and I could talk to him about anything. And he gave me good advice—solid, sane advice. He knew I was not the person to just throw out a lot of goodness—I was not that. It wouldn't work. ("Love thy neighbor as thyself." "Well, maybe.")

Frances Carr was the music director at University Baptist, and she invited me to come and sing with the University Baptist choir. That opened a lot of hearts and doors and possibilities. I never knew that people got paid for singing in church choirs! I got paid to sing for the first time. Frances was a staunch supporter, and we did a lot of good work.

But there were those who were just "agin" it, and I would get those inevitable ugly calls. We all got some of that. A couple times, when I was walking to the dormitory across the highway after rehearsal, there were three or four big burly guys waiting along my path—they were there, I guess, for the purpose of frightening me. They did that very well. UT did not have the mighty sports complex it has now on the eastern edge of campus; the area around Texas Memorial Stadium was hills and lots of rocks. So I just dropped my books, picked up a couple rocks, and waited. What was I going to do? It's amazing, though; the human spirit is really quite something. It never occurred to me that I was not big enough to do anything; I was strong enough, maybe. Those burly guys didn't do any real damage that time, but they scared me. There was a man who had a little store at the top of that hill, where we bought sodas and stuff. He saw the end of it and helped me get home. Things got more ominous as time went on.

It was my very own state representative from northeast Texas, Joe Chapman, who informed everybody that this just can't happen, this "Nigra girl." (I tell you—of all the derogatory names, that one is my least favorite. It's a good thing my father didn't know who that was. If he had, I probably wouldn't have had my father any longer.) But mostly I had great support from students and a lot of the faculty. That was a good thing. Just the life outside the campus, or outside the classroom, wasn't so great. But life went along. Classes went along. You did the best you could. I guess if I have one huge resentment—other than the obvious one, which is the racism of the period—it is that I spent so much time trying to survive here that I sometimes couldn't be the student that I wanted to be.

We were often very frightened because we were always being threatened about being raped and all kinds of ugly, ugly, horrible things. (Was somebody going to storm in that dormitory and do something?) And then it would disappear. But you banded together. There was the Austin black community. Boy, did they come to our aid. They clothed us and fed us and tried to make us feel that we had a place here somehow. That's how I became an AKA, Alpha Kappa Alpha. But they were looking after us. Our housemothers and several of the community ladies made themselves available to take us around and to feed us. (Aren't college kids always hungry? I seemed to be one of them.) They made sure we were decently attired and that we trusted in God. I remember one lady saying, "Even if you don't believe in God, try it out for a little while. It might help." That was a very good thing to say to me, because I was always questioning that. We were told: "These are your circumstances. If you should lose your temper, try your best; don't go to the violent part of it, because then it's hard to protect you. You have every right to speak your truth and be proud. Ignore anything that has no relevance to you."

Without that community, we had no place to go. The average student can't afford much anyway, as you know. So what did you do—stay in your dorm or hang around what later became Almetris House? Not a lot of activity in that. So it became the black people of Austin and a few white ones who really helped to nurture that part of our lives: a little bit of social life, a little bit of spiritual life. Some of that was really important.

I didn't get hurt too much more after that. Just once. It was one of those incidents that just makes you stop and think, "What makes a person do that?" I was coming from the Littlefield House, there at 23rd and Whitis, walking toward 19th Street, and saw a man coming toward me on the sidewalk. (The Littlefield House is my favorite building on the UT campus. It was the Music Annex when I was a student, and I took piano lessons there. It was a safe haven, and it was so simple, full of music and all sorts of lovely things.) This man just walked up and he said, "Oh, you're one of those. You're Barbara Smith." I'm sure he recognized me because I had been in the newspaper, because I had sung in the church—probably Miss Gus's church, I don't remember. And he just spat in my face.

At first I was stunned. I didn't know what had hit me. I started to wipe off my face, and my first reaction was to take this spittle off my face and aim it towards him. Of course, there wasn't enough left to do any damage. I have never known such rage. I blurted, "Why are you doing this? If I had done something to you personally . . . why are you doing this?" By the time I recovered from that little outburst, he was long gone. I just remember he had red hair. I don't remember much else. He certainly had to be pretty tall, because I had to look up to see his face. I don't know anything about it. Nothing. I don't think he was a student. Students would or would not speak with us—but I don't remember a student doing anything horrible like that.

Two weeks before the May 10 opening performance of *Dido and Aeneas,* I was removed from the cast.

Dean Doty called me in for a meeting. It was his least proud moment, I'm sure. Well, he said so. He called me in and said that the UT Board of Regents, the UT president, my housemothers, and a few interested citizens had met, and they were concerned about my well-being. They knew of some of the incidents I had faced and that I had been pretty badly damaged on my left ribs once in a tussle. And so they were afraid that it would just break into something uncontrollable.

I remember saying, "Dean Doty, not that many people are going to come to this opera." That was my take on it. But the part that was not pleasant, and still to this day is not pleasant to remember, is that he had been persuaded to convince me that I was getting some kind of academic credit for this course and my removal was for my own good. None of that was true. Then he told me that I was not allowed to tell anyone except my parents. I thought, "You take away something that is that meaningful for a young person, and then you stuff their mouths with cement." I was beyond heartbroken. I lived in a place of heartbreak and rage—rage at a system that could let that happen with a man I absolutely adored. I loved Dean Doty—I really did. I had to listen to him tell me those things, which we both knew were not true.

President Logan Wilson had already made the decision, but I was not informed of it until April 24. We had been rehearsing since October. All of those organizations across the country that were concerned with integration had their eyes on places like the University of Texas, so no one at UT wanted any big tom-tom going on the subject. So waiting until nearly the end was, in the minds of the administrators, a simpler way to do it, I guess. I can only guess. The thing I resented most is that they made all those decisions and never told me. I never once met President Wilson. I don't even want to call him president—he doesn't deserve it, in my opinion. It's not that I dislike him. I don't respect him.

I left Dean Doty's office that day, and I was different. I was changed, because if Dean Doty could do that to me, then whom could I trust? Several people in the black community, a couple of my classmates or housemates—and Mama Duren, of course. That's about it. It took me many years to understand the position Dean Doty was in. In later years, he came to New York several times to visit me; he came to the church where I sang a solo, and to concerts I did early in my career. Nonetheless, those were my feelings at the time.

I wrote to my parents a long, long, long letter trying to figure out what I was going to do and what I should do before I called them, because I didn't want them to hear me so upset. All my mother needed at that point was for me to say, "I'm not happy here," and she would have been so glad, because, I later learned, she was terrified the whole time I was here. When I finally did call, I spoke to Mama first, because she was the one who always answered the phone. Her first reaction was "Are they protecting you sufficiently?" and her second was "Do you want to come home?" I really didn't have the answer for either one, because I wasn't sure what to do. Running away was not something that was built in my nature, so I was determined to stay here and do whatever. My father, on the other hand, said, "Lou, all you have to do is remember your name. That means you're proud of yourself: who you are and where you come from. You don't have to be afraid of any of this." "Okay, Daddy." He talked further, but those are the words that will ring in my ears forever. That's where I got my little backbone. I stood up and said, "I'm going to do what I have to do to survive all of this."

No one, of course, figured that this story would break.

I don't know exactly how, but word of the decision got to a reporter named Mathis at the *Houston Post*.[6] All of a sudden, a day or so later, I couldn't go anyplace without meeting reporters. I look outside my window, there's someone outside my classroom; I would be stopped along the road; I walked in my dorm, and there was one in my closet. We had a big laugh about that. One girl said, "He wasn't even cute." Girls were very into cute men at that point.

My tongue was not my friend. "How did you get the role?" a reporter would ask. I would answer, "Because, obviously, I was the best one they could find," or something like that. "Because I deserved it," I would say. Bob Jacobson, whom I had met the night of *The Bad Seed* and who was a pre-law student at the time, suggested that I ought to talk to someone and tell my story. He suggested I tell it to Nancy Mc-Means, who was the editor of the *Daily Texan* at that time. The decision was to squirrel me away and write my story as I understood it.[7] It was empowering to write my own response, but I felt so trapped. I wanted to say everything that came into my mind, but I was also trying to be that person who is a healer. That was part of my upbringing. You try to make peace and not war. But writing the response helped. It certainly got people off my back. It's also how Harry Belafonte, the internationally famous calypso singer and ardent social activist, read about me.

Every door you went by—white, black, or otherwise—had a poster of Belafonte on it because he was so gorgeous! He had read the article about my situation that had appeared in the *New York Times*, and he called. Everybody in the dorm got to enjoy that call a lot more than I did! He mentioned himself and Sidney Poitier and Mahalia Jackson and Sammy Davis, Jr. He had discussed me with them. They were all pulling for me. He wanted to know if I wanted to get out of the land of white people (I will not use that word that he used). He said, "I would be willing to help you go to the school of your choice if you want to leave."

Leaving UT was not an option for me. You see, this is my home. I'm a Texan. This is supposed to be a state university to all people. Now that is something I learned all my life and believed in—or tried to. I had to believe it, that we could overcome this.

Staying at UT was not the easiest decision, since most of my childhood I had wanted to go to Fisk University, in Nashville, which was *the* school for music folks—for black kids. A very good school. But I couldn't have lived with that decision. Aside from which, I had fallen in love with some of my teachers at UT, and I had made friends with some of the students. I was very much in the middle of The Cause, in my own way. My way was to stay and fight—fight in the way that I knew how, which is to try to do something to excel.[8]

I received a lot of support. One of the people who stands out is Fania Kruger. (I just recently learned she is the aunt of Bernard Rapoport; I read it in his book, and I thought, "You've got to be kidding!") She read about my situation and invited me to her home. She served me high tea, my first. A Russian Jewess, she understood suffering and became a beacon of a kind that I'd never known—a poetess, a writer, a European with whom I had real, close contact. Someone who really understood my soul—probably better than I did, in a way. She was an amazing, courageous woman. You didn't dare question that I could come to her house anytime she chose to have me there. It wasn't that many times, but they were unforgettable. She was a music lover and caring of human beings.

I also received a letter from eight members of the Texas legislature. The line that everyone remembers, and that was reported in the newspaper, is "You are to be highly commended on keeping your head when others about you are losing theirs."[9] In the same spirit, some student groups at UT adopted a resolution directed at the administration and regents, reaffirming their belief in equal opportunity for students to participate in the life of the University.[10]

I was very touched by the responses of many of the students—including those you wouldn't expect. You don't expect some jockey boy to come up and say, "You . . . you are . . . you're a member of this community," or something like that. I don't remember his exact words—he couldn't get them out right. He was sort of stuttering, but making his point very clear: "We're behind you." I got that. Not right away, but soon after. It just started to pour in. There were lots of offers for movie deals, offers for my life story. But I wasn't interested. I didn't want to be a token for anybody. Music was the center of my universe. My life story? What could you possibly learn? You could sensationalize it and make, maybe, a little money off of it, I guess. But it wasn't sensational to me. I was this kid from northeast Texas getting a chance to do her thing. So.

After all of the commotion, the opera was performed that weekend, with a reduced number of performances. There was great interest around campus and in the press whether I would attend. I did not.

During the course of all these events, there was a moment when I happened to be talking with my housemother and some of the girls in the dorm, and one girl said, "You know, Barbara, you have at this moment a tremendous amount of power." And I said, "I guess I do. And how am I going to use it?" With me, it always came down to, number one, your personal sense of self—your pride, in other words, and the fact that I wanted to make this mean something. Don't forget, I came from a community that struggled so hard to get anywhere, to excel in any way. So here was my opportunity. I couldn't run from it—I just couldn't. I'm glad I didn't.

I graduated from the University of Texas midterm, in January 1959. The time between the *Dido and Aeneas* episode and my graduation was frustrating, chaotic, wonderful. I was not a student anymore—I was a person. I was supposed to show everybody how wonderful I was, and that takes away a little bit of the joy of the exploration. I became the person everybody wanted to show off. In spite of that, there was the marriage between relationships you develop and the music you're trying to create—learning to create. My

Barbara Smith at the organ, September 1959. *From the Barbara Smith Conrad Photograph Collection, Dolph Briscoe Center for American History, University of Texas at Austin. (DI 07148)*

vocal development came along nicely, though I just didn't enjoy it as much as I had before. There were too many distractions. You need to be quiet to develop as an artist. There was a point where they thought I should go to another teacher, which made me very unhappy. I eventually went back to Miss Gus.

My junior recital had by far the greatest sense of "Victoria! I did it!" By the time I got to my senior recital, the balance had changed somewhat. There was a lot of pressure, but I loved the music I was doing. My senior recital was fraught with a lot more drama because of all that had happened before. There were all these people who were in that audience who were pursuing me still to do a film or whatever. The houses were packed those nights. Nevertheless, my recitals represented a certain kind of achievement— singing in foreign languages, for example, something I had known nothing about before. You work at something, and you hold it, and you hold it, and suddenly it's really a thing of beauty for you, or for somebody at least. It's a great sense of accomplishment. It was flying into zones I had never explored.

I didn't feel anything when I graduated. It's a terrible thing to say, isn't it? The diploma per se didn't mean anything to me. But the friends I had made, the things I had learned through my teachers and colleagues at the school, were deeply meaningful. My diploma arrived, all nicely framed, and I put it away. My heart froze a little bit—to protect myself. Once I was finished, the question became "What was it all about?" "Why did I live through all of that?" "I could have done this—or I could have done that." The inevitable anger, betrayal. I felt betrayed. I think Dr. Doty understood that, which is why he would come fairly often in those early years after I left to try to heal this anger, because it was all connected with the people. Trust was a huge issue for me; I think it is for most people, but it certainly was for me. Now I'm very proud of my diploma. Did I get it? Yes. And I'm very protective. I'm a very loud Texas Ex now. It took awhile.

Right as my final semester was ending, Harry Belafonte called again and asked if I wanted to come to New York to meet him. I asked Miss Gus what I could send him to say thank you, because by this time I had received a couple of scholarships at UT from him. I said, "What do you send Harry Belafonte? He has everything." She said, "Why don't you send a tape of your junior recital"—and that's what I did. His present wife is a cousin of Barry Morell,

who was a very fine tenor at the Met for a long, long time (I eventually would sing with him). He listened to the tape and passed it on to Morell. He listened to it and thought I should be heard by some of the masters. So there was Giuseppe Danise, the great baritone in Italy, and Bidu Sayão, the incredible soprano, and Fausto Cleva, who was a conductor of great import. I had won a talent competition and got to go to St. Louis to participate with a lot of other kids from other parts of the country, and from there I went on to New York. I met Mr. Belafonte for the first time. Oh, my God, what a day that was!

I was so nervous—I don't think I've been more nervous about anything. Everybody had given me something to wear: from my mother, her watch and her best coat (which was not nearly warm enough) for the winter; a little perfume from my Aunt Maggie; and so forth. I forgot it all except for the dress and the coat! I arrived in New York, and Belafonte had put me in the Waldorf-Astoria, but I wanted to be with a friend I had just made in St. Louis, so I stayed at the International House instead. Belafonte couldn't get over that! I went down the next day to meet him. Gloria Cantor, his secretary, said, "Ah, you finally made it. I'll call Harry and tell him you're here." He came in. He looked at me and said, "Kind of skinny." And he said, "How's our Texas nightingale?" and gave me a hug. And then he pulled back, he sniffed, and said, "Gloria, she used Ivory Soap this morning."

Talk about a magical day! Oh, my God. I met Sidney Poitier that day. I met Sammy Davis, Jr., that day and he gave me a Swiss watch—that was a long story, but it was a lovely little Swiss watch. They took me to the theater and great restaurants. What a time. We sang for this bevy of people at the Ansonia Hotel, which is a very famous hotel; people like Caruso stayed there. After it was over, Giuseppe Danise said, "Yes, she has talent. She has wonderful talent. She has no balcony, but she has talent"—which means it was a little flat on top. He prescribed 75 percent hard work, and the rest would be talent and luck.

We went downstairs, and Harry took off one of his famous caps that he always wears. He put it on my head and he said, "Hot dang, Barbara, we made it." That was the beginning of New York and that whole journey.

Dreams come true. It's as Maestro Danise said when I auditioned for him at the Ansonia all those years ago: "Seventy-five percent hard work, and the rest is talent and opportunity." I don't know that I agree with those percentages. It doesn't matter. Hard work is a big part of it. And not giving up.

In 1985, during my time with the Metropolitan Opera in New York, I made a life-changing decision. I had just been offered a four-year contract at the Hamburg Opera in Germany when I received a call from Roy Vaughan of the Texas Exes about being named a Distinguished Alumnus of the University of Texas. My manager at the time, Thea Dispeker, still doesn't believe it, but had I accepted that contract, I would not have been able to accept the Distinguished Alumnus Award because the conflict was huge—and Germany is not just across the bridge.

Peter Flawn, who was president of UT at the time, had reached out to me the year before. My manager, Bess Pruitt, had called me and said, "You've been invited by the president." All of a sudden I had this invitation to come to UT. Priscilla and Peter Flawn had arranged this very lovely luncheon at the Littlefield House, which was just so perfect for me because that's my sweetest memory on campus, that place. The Flawns set the stage so wonderfully—it was so well done that I hardly noticed I was being wooed. I just knew it felt good to be here and appreciated. And Bess, in the meantime, had been in touch with Earl Stewart, a musician, composer, and lecturer at UT, about the possibility of this piece that he was writing, *Al-Inkishafi*. How those things tied together, I really don't know—but they are somehow connected. Being invited back to UT—something just ripples right through my solar plexus every time that moment comes up for me.

My first response was, "Why would I want to go back?" And truth was, I probably always did. I think you always—if you're honest, at least if I'm honest with myself—feel like a part of your family has rejected you, and you in turn rejected them somehow and just closed the door until something happened. Hearts opened. Minds opened. Things changed. And most of the time over all those years before that, I didn't think about the University of Texas. But boy, when I decided I would do it, there was a floodgate of emotions, from absolute delight that this was a possibility to heal some of these wounds, to knowing that I was coming back as a successful artist. That felt good, and it felt daunting, because I also didn't know if I was going to be able to deal with anything that looked like rejection to me. I was allergic to it. But it was a very exciting time.

I performed in the première of *Al-Inkishafi* at the Performing Arts Center, which had opened on the UT campus across the street from Texas Memorial Stadium just a couple years earlier. It was a grand moment—a hard moment. I'll never forget it as long as I live. You walk out onstage; you feel thousands of arms around you. I was not alone.

Then the next year, I returned to Austin to be named a Distinguished Alumnus of the University. In terms of dollars and cents, it made no sense compared to the contract I had turned down. Hamburg was one of *the* premier places to jump off from. But being named a Distinguished Alumnus had a historic significance—it was something I couldn't ignore. Not only to be the first African American to receive that award, but also to be a fine arts major receiving the award, no less, is what it meant. You can't have grown up through those years and not understood the significance of that moment. That was a tough one. It was my toughest career moment. You have to consider who you are and what your life's journey has been. Then it's not so complicated. I can't really, honestly say I've ever regretted the decision. It was just too clear.

I have my angels who visit me and tell me what to do. These angels are my ancestors. They follow me always. That's not a fantasy; that's where I am. Things do change, so I don't feel I carry the responsibility of them so much as I carry a banner in honor of them. And this is my chance to carry that banner.

Many people have no idea what it is like to dream of having an education. It's huge. No opera contract would ever compare. In my career, I meet very distinguished people, but I usually spend only a second with them—usually in the line, shaking hands. When I came back to the University to be named a Distinguished Alumnus, all of a sudden at the ceremony I'm meeting people like Bob and Nancy Inman, Dr. Ruth Hartgraves, Bob and Angelina Dorsey, Roy Vaughan, and so many other wonderful and interesting and accomplished people. My family was there, too. I think the thing I enjoyed most about that time was their faces—the pride in my mother's face. My father was deceased already—but to receive that honor was a glorious, glorious moment. I realize that this is what my diploma means to me now.

Patricia Sage, my dear friend and sister who happens to be a great musician and singer, has said for a number of years, "You have not sung your best song yet." And I think she's right—in fact, I know she is. I have a passion for learning as I do, for keeping my own development going. I never thought that I would be this strong at this point in my life. Much of this strength comes from my teaching, and my work helping to preserve our nation's rich musical heritage. The University has been a wonderful resource—providing me with additional opportunities to teach and to promote the study of American spirituals. Yes, I talked with all of my angels, with all of my ancestors, before I made that decision to return to UT.

Texas taught me a lot. Growing up here taught me a lot. The University of Texas taught me far more than I ever realized. My appreciation for human beings who stand up for something that is right is deep and growing all the time. I guess that's what's on my mind right now. I know it is.

Trust. What is trust? It's like knowing that you have looked into a person's soul. The eyes are the soul as far as I'm concerned. With trust, you know that somewhere you have a mutual truth, a mutual caring. And through that, whatever you have to do next will happen as a result of it. It's powerful. I feel very powerful right now. It's sweet.

{ }

On the morning of February 5, 2009, during the regular session of the Eighty-First Texas Legislature, Representative Bryan Hughes, District 5 (which includes Pittsburg and Center Point, Texas), brought to the floor House Concurrent Resolution 31, honoring Barbara Smith Conrad on her career as a world-renowned opera singer. Joining Representative Hughes in authoring HCR 31 were Representatives Dawnna Dukes, District 46; Elliot Naishtat, District 49; Senfronia Thompson, District 141; and Susan King, District 71. Senator Kirk Watson sponsored the resolution in the Senate.[11]

Chair (Representative Thompson): The Chair recognizes Mr. Hughes for a motion.
Representative Hughes: Thank you, Madam Speaker. Members, I move to suspend all necessary rules to take up and consider at this time House Concurrent Resolution 31, honoring Barbara Smith Conrad.

Chair: Members, you heard the motion. Is there an objection? The Chair hears none. *[gavel]* The Chair lays out HCR 31, to be read in full.
Reading Clerk: HCR 31, by Hughes:

WHEREAS, A gifted opera singer, Barbara Smith Conrad, has been delighting audiences for the past four decades, achieving worldwide acclaim and recognition; and

WHEREAS, Raised in the East Texas community of Center Point, Barbara Smith began exploring music as a child; she and her siblings practiced playing a variety of genres on their family's piano, from sonatas by Mozart to the gospel hymns they heard at their local Baptist church; she went on to attend The University of Texas at Austin, and as a sophomore, she won the lead role in the campus production of *Dido and Aeneas*; however, in an incident that drew national attention, Ms. Smith was advised by school administrators that she could not perform in the opera; despite an offer from actor Harry Belafonte to underwrite her studies at the institution of her choice, she chose to remain at the university and earned her bachelor's degree in music from UT in 1959; and

WHEREAS, Pursuing a career as a vocalist in the years that followed, she took her father's first name, Conrad, and toured with various opera groups; in 1977, she was cast as Marian Anderson in the ABC television movie, *Eleanor and Franklin: The White House Years*; she also garnered praise for her work in the Houston Grand Opera production of *Carmen*, and she became a performer with the prestigious Metropolitan Opera from 1982 to 1989; this exceptional mezzo-soprano continued to play leading roles with the Vienna State Opera, New York City Opera, Teatro Nacional de Venezuela, Pittsburgh Opera, and others throughout the United States, Canada, Europe, and South America; moreover, she has been accompanied by such celebrated orchestras as the New York Philharmonic and the symphonies of London, Boston, Cleveland, and Detroit; and

WHEREAS, In 1984, Ms. Conrad returned to her alma mater to lend her voice for the premiere of *Al-Inkishafi*, and the following year, she was named a Distinguished Alumnus by the Ex-Students' Association of The University of Texas; she has also been honored with invitations to sing at the White House for Lady Bird Johnson's 75th birthday and to perform for Pope John Paul II during his visit to New York City in 1995; and

WHEREAS, Today, among her other pursuits, Ms. Conrad spends time at her vocal studio in Manhattan and works closely with the Manhattan School of Music as the cofounder and codirector of its Wagner Theater Program; she also regularly participates in the Distinguished Alumnus Awards at UT, where she often sings "The Eyes of Texas"; fittingly, the university has created an endowed presidential scholarship in fine arts in Ms. Conrad's name, and in 2005, the Dolph Briscoe Center for American History at UT announced the Endowment for the Study of the American Spiritual, for which Ms. Conrad serves as the national ambassador; she released a recording of spirituals in 1995 with the choir of the Convent Avenue Baptist Church and remains dedicated to preserving this art form; and

WHEREAS, With talent and perseverance, Barbara Smith Conrad has become a world-renowned mezzosoprano, and in realizing her dreams, she is an inspiration to countless individuals; now, therefore be it

RESOLVED, That the 81st Legislature of the State of Texas hereby commend Barbara Smith Conrad on her accomplished musical career and her role in the movement toward civil rights in the United States of America, and extend to her sincere best wishes for continued success and happiness; and be it further

RESOLVED, That an official copy of this resolution be prepared for Ms. Conrad as an expression of high regard by the Texas House of Representatives and Senate. *[standing ovation]*

Chair: The Chair recognizes Mr. Hughes.

Representative Hughes: Thank you, Madam Speaker. Members, I don't have to tell you folks that the things we do here are important and it's always a big deal, but today is a really big day—it's a really big day.

Let me introduce some of the people that are on the dais: of course, our honoree, Ms. Barbara Smith Conrad; we're so delighted to have her. Bill Powers, president of the university, would have been here, but he's testifying in front of Senate Finance; and he has put this together, he sends his regards—he'll be with us later. We have Dr. Don Carleton, executive director of the Dolph Briscoe Center for American History. We also have Dr. Robert DeSimone, director of the Sarah and Ernest Butler Opera Center in the College of Fine Arts at UT. We have Dr. Gregory J. Vincent, Vice President for Diversity and Community Engagement at The University of Texas at Austin, and Dr. Glenn Chandler, director of the Butler School of Music at UT. Also joining us in the chamber today on the dais are Chief Justice Wallace Jefferson, Justice Dale Wainwright, and Railroad Commission chair Michael Williams.

And I've got to introduce some special guests that are in the gallery today—some of Ms. Conrad's friends and family and supporters who are with us. Would you please rise in the gallery so that we can recognize you and welcome you to *your* Texas House. *[applause]*

Chair: The Chair recognizes Representative Dukes.

Representative Dukes: Thank you, Madam Speaker. It is a great day for us to have Ms. Conrad here in the Texas House.

Fifty-two years have passed, and it was in this body that much of the discussion was to prevent her from her opportunity—as a human being who had the skills and the capability to take the lead—from being in such a position. It is amazing that in this period of time she is able to come back to the Texas House of Representatives, where she is recognized for her talent, her skills, and her strength.

In that year that she had to endure, it was not an easy choice, I'm sure, for Ms. Conrad to choose to remain at The University of Texas. My grandfather's first cousin was Heman Sweatt, and he was one who was part of *Sweatt v. Painter*. I recall Heman telling us how difficult it was for him with the threats and the abuse that he had to take, and discrimination. It caused him to have ulcers, and it changed the course of his life immensely. But Ms. Conrad was a *strong woman*, and she maintained throughout all of it. We welcome you back to the Texas House of Representatives with open arms.

And I would be remiss if I did not add that one of the reasons I believe she is probably also a strong woman is because she is a sorority sister of Representative Thompson and myself—an Alpha Kappa Alpha woman. *[applause]*

Chair: The Chair recognizes Mr. Hughes.

Representative Hughes: Thank you, Madam Speaker. I want to make sure everyone is aware that at noon today, in the Rotunda, Ms. Conrad will be singing for us. There's also going to be a reception for her from 12:30 to 1:30 in the Legislative Conference Center.

She experienced things that most of us can't really imagine. But rather than making her bitter or gnarled or angry, you can just look at her countenance and see how she trusts God, how she works hard, how she uses her gifts. We're so honored to have her here.

Members, as we welcome home this great Texan

Barbara Smith Conrad singing "Amazing Grace" in the Texas House of Representatives, February 5, 2009. On the dais with her are (*left to right*) Rep. Senfronia Thompson; Robert DeSimone, director of the Sarah and Ernest Butler Opera Center at the University of Texas at Austin; Gregory J. Vincent, vice president for diversity and community engagement at UT-Austin; B. Glenn Chandler, director of the Butler School of Music at UT-Austin; Texas Railroad Commission chair Michael Williams; Texas Supreme Court chief justice Wallace Jefferson; and Texas Supreme Court associate justice Dale Wainwright. Standing below either end of the dais are Rep. Bryan Hughes (*left*) and Rep. Dawnna Dukes. *Photo by Rick Patrick, rickpatrickphotography.com.*

I want to read you a quote of hers I found in doing some research about her. She lives in New York, and she was asked, "What's it like to come back to East Texas?" She's from Camp County, Center Point, House District 5. "What's it like? Is it a shock to the system to come back to East Texas?" She said, "Oh, no. I'd live there in a snap if I could." And here's what she said: "I love it—I love home. I love Texas."

Madam Speaker, I move adoption of House Concurrent Resolution 31.
Chair: Members, you heard the motion. Is there objection? The Chair hears none. [*gavel*] All names will be added by Representatives Dukes and McClendon. Is there objection? The Chair hears none. [*gavel*] The Chair one more time recognizes Mr. Hughes.
Representative Hughes: Thank you, Madam Speaker. Now at this point I'm going to put Ms. Conrad on

the spot. Again, she's going to sing for us in the Rotunda, but Representative Dukes suggested that she might also sing for us here. Ms. Conrad, can you offer something for us here from the floor? Would you sing for us? [*encouragement and applause from the floor*]

Barbara Conrad: Thank you very much. [*pause to collect her emotions*] Give me a moment. [*pause*] I am proud to be a Texan. I always was, which is why they couldn't take it away from me in the first place. It was always my home, it was always my state, it was always my community, you are all of my people. [*looking up to the gallery*] Carol, are you here? Carolyn, girl. Yes. [*waves*] Earl? [*returning to her address to the members of the House*] My folks have always dwelled here.

Some of the people at the time didn't know I was basically harmless. [*laughter*] Basically. My mother said I was her angel with a forkèd tail. There's a reason.

[*turning to the state dignitaries and university officials accompanying her on the dais*] I am proud to share this moment with my distinguished "escorts"—I just love it!

[*turning back to the members of the House floor and the visitors in the gallery*] What I'm most proud of is that those of you who fought the fight continue to do so for *all* human rights—for *all* human rights.

You know, for me it was monumental because I was young, I was dreaming, I was hoping to have this illustrious career. Well, that came later, actually. I didn't know that much. But I knew that this was my course. And I was blessed with people who referred to me as "Miss Fine," "Big Shot," all of those wonderful things. And I had no reason to believe otherwise.

[*sings, soulfully:*]

Amazing grace! how sweet the sound,
That saved a wretch like me!
I once was lost, but now am found,
Was blind, but now I see.

Through many dangers, toils, and snares,
I have already come;
'Tis grace that brought me safe thus far,
And grace will lead me home.

[*great applause*]

HCR 31 was read and adopted by the Texas Senate on February 10, 2009, and signed by Governor Rick Perry on February 20, 2009.

NOTES

1. Editor's note: See Bobby Hawthorne, "The UIL and the Integration of Texas High School Athletics," in the first *Texas Book* for a discussion of the University Interscholastic League, which was created by the University of Texas in 1913 and today operates under the auspices of UT-Austin's Division of Diversity and Community Engagement.

2. Editor's note: The University of Texas Board of Regents planned for official integration of undergraduate students at UT beginning in the fall semester of 1956, but John Hargis (and two others, who soon withdrew) blazed the trail for African American undergraduates by enrolling in June 1955. See Richard B. McCaslin, "Steadfast in His Intent: John W. Hargis and the Integration of the University of Texas at Austin," in this volume for an account of the larger story of the arrival of the first African American undergraduates at the University of Texas.

African American students were first allowed to enroll at UT in 1950—but only in certain graduate and professional programs—following the decision in *Sweatt v. Painter*, a landmark case involving the University of Texas Law School that the U.S. Supreme Court had decided earlier that year. For an account of the arrival of the first African American students at UT, see Michael Gillette, "Blacks Challenge the White University" in the first *Texas Book*.

The *Sweatt* case stemmed from a lawsuit filed in 1946 against the University of Texas by Heman Marion Sweatt after he had applied for and been denied admission to the UT School of Law. (The named respondent was the president of the University of Texas, Theophilus Shickel Painter.) The U.S. Supreme Court's decision in favor of Sweatt did not overturn the "separate but equal" interpretation that it had given the due process clause of the Fourteenth Amendment in *Plessy v. Ferguson* in 1896. However, the 1950 decision did give African Americans the opportunity to be admitted to UT, but only in graduate and professional programs not offered at Texas State University for Negroes in Houston (renamed Texas Southern University in 1951) or Prairie View A&M College in Prairie View. (There were African Americans enrolled in undergraduate classes at UT before 1955. African Americans admitted to UT after *Sweatt* were allowed to enroll in undergraduate courses if the courses were necessary for the student's completion of his or her graduate or professional degree.) The U.S. Supreme Court's decision for the petitioner in *Brown v. Board of Education of Topeka* (1954) overturned the principle of separate but equal, and the subsequent *Brown II* ruling in 1955 required the Texas legislature and UT regents to "proceed with all deliberate speed" in allowing African American applicants to be admitted to UT as undergraduates on the basis of academic qualifications, regardless of race.

3. Editor's note: Almetris Marsh Duren (1910–2000) was a towering and beloved figure in the lives of students at the University of Texas, most notably in the lives of African American students during the period of racial integration on campus. A 1950 graduate of Tillotson College in Austin, she became housemother at Huston-Tillotson's Eliza Dee Dorm, located at 12th Street and East Avenue, in 1956. When Eliza Dee Dorm was demolished in 1958 for construction of the Interregional Highway (I-35), "Mama" Duren and her African American students were relocated to an existing house on Whitis Avenue, which became known as Almetris Co-op. When that structure was demolished in the late 1960s to make way for the Jesse H. Jones Communications Center, one of the houses in the University's new Women's Co-op—a block north on Whitis Avenue, between 26th and 27th Streets—was named Almetris Co-op.

Duren served in UT's Office of the Dean of Students as a counselor and adviser to students and student groups from 1968 until her retirement in 1981. She founded the University's first minority recruitment program as well as the Innervisions of Blackness Choir, and in 1979 was a recipient of the inaugural Presidential Citation, which recognizes persons whose contributions have brought great distinction to the University and who exemplify the values of the institution. UT's Almetris Duren Hall, the massive 588-bed coed residence hall at the corner of 27th Street and Whitis Avenue, which opened in 2007, is named in her honor.

4. Editor's note: 19th Street was renamed Martin Luther King Jr. Boulevard by the City of Austin in 1975.

5. Editor's note: University Baptist Church, under the leadership of Dr. Blake Smith, was an early leader in integration and racial reconciliation in Austin. Joseph Martin Dawson reports: "In 1945, after there had been an exchange of worship with a Negro congregation, University Baptist voted to 'abandon separated seating forever'" ("I Belong to a Southern Baptist Integrated Church," *Christian Century* 57, no. 46 [November 12, 1958]). In 1950, University Baptist formally integrated when a Sergeant Wilson of Kelly Field in San Antonio joined the congregation. According to Dawson, "Dr. Smith had been authorized by the church to baptize any convert on his frequent missions to military bases in the United States and Europe. The Negro flier asked Smith to baptize him, and when no Baptist church in San Antonio would consent to the use of its baptistry for the purpose, the soul-winner baptized him at midnight in the swimming pool of the Y.M.C.A. Upon returning to Austin the pastor related the incident to his church amid cheers, and the sergeant was welcomed into membership." University Baptist Church was ostracized by some Baptist organizations during this period because of its decision to end racial segregation in the church.

6. Editor's note: Jim Mathis broke the story in his article "Negro Girl Out of UT Opera Cast," which appeared on the front page of the *Houston Post*, on Tuesday, May 7, 1957, three days before the opening performance of *Dido and Aeneas*. According to Mathis's article:

Rep Joe Chapman of Sulphur Springs precipitated the removal [of Barbara Smith from the cast] when he called Dr Logan Wilson, University president, after a denunciatory and threatening speech by Rep Jerry Sadler of Percilla before a 40-member East Texas legislative delegation. The decision to withdraw the Negro girl before the public performance came from the top administrative echelon. At the same time, all faculty members, Miss Smith, and a student director of the opera were directed or advised not to talk about the incident. All comment on the removal was to come from the president's office. . . .

Sadler told The Post Monday that he was called about the inclusion of a Negro girl in the cast by a woman university employee. He would not name his informant. Sadler, a former Texas railroad commissioner, said he checked the report, then made his speech at the weekly East Texas delegation breakfast. A fiery speaker, Sadler spoke for 10 minutes on his theme. "I mentioned appropriations, and as a matter of fact, voted against those for the university because they have Negro undergraduates," Sadler said. (The appropriations bill passed the House and the Senate. It is now in a conference committee. Both chambers must vote again on the bill, however.) "Two hours after I spoke, Chapman came to tell me that Wilson said the Negro girl would not be in the cast," Sadler added.

Both Sadler and Chapman have been in the forefront of the prosegregationist ranks in the House, but frequently differ in methods. Chapman told The Post that he had called Dr Wilson and discussed casting of the Negro girl for a public performance. Chapman said he thought it "probably wouldn't be good public relations to have a Negro star with a white person."

"I talked to Dr Wilson myself casually, and I understood the policy was that there would be no personal contact," Chapman explained by telephone from Sulphur Springs. "All I wanted to do was to keep them out of controversy. I'm a Texas ex myself. He assured me that had always been the policy, and that they would not do anything to start a controversy," Chapman added. Chapman said he had made no mention of the university appropriations, and denied that the segregation bloc in the House had threatened to cut funds to the college of fine arts. "I think he (Dr Wilson) is handling a delicate situation in an excellent way. They've got a bunch of left-wingers in the university but they are doing a pretty good job of holding them down," he ended. Chapman blamed the NAACP and "a whole bunch of rabble rousers" for seeking publicity on the removal and in doing so to "put Dr Wilson on the spot."

On Wednesday, May 8, 1957, the *Daily Texan* reported in a front-page article, "Negro Girl Withdrawn from UT Opera Cast," that state representative Jerry Sadler had been "approached by a Texan reporter and commented only: 'I've got nothing to say to your paper—I think you got a scandal sheet run by a bunch of left-wing liberals!'" Mark Smith, the paper's news editor, then noted: "Representative Chapman stated his opinions of the issue, when asked, 'Do you sincerely believe that the state of Texas has the right to dictate policies of the University?' He answered, 'There's no question about it—we (the legislature) control the University through appropriations. And if given bad publicity in the Texan—well, we wouldn't stand for that.'"

President Wilson vigorously denied in public—most notably in prepared, carefully argued remarks to the faculty at its May 14 meeting—that there had been any pressure from the legislature or individual legislators forcing his decision, or that he had first spoken with Joe Chapman about the matter on the day after he had made the decision to remove Barbara Smith from the cast.

7. Editor's note: Barbara Smith's carefully considered, conciliatory response appeared on the front page of the *Daily Texan*, on May 9, 1957, the day before the opening performance of the opera, under the headline "Barbara Smith Came to UT for Education," with the byline of and a brief introduction by Nancy McMeans.

8. Editor's note: In his article "I Belong to a Southern Baptist Integrated Church," Joseph Martin Dawson shares a telling anecdote related to Barbara Smith's removal from the cast of *Dido and Aeneas*: "By a singular coincidence, on the Sunday Miss Smith's problem came into public notice, the church calendar which had gone to press the preceding Friday announced that she would sing, 'Let Us Worship Together on Our Knees.' She sang the solo in her usual modest manner, and after the service an elderly lady of the Old South said tearfully, 'When I heard Barbara, my prejudices fell off like an outworn garment.'"

9. Editor's note: On Friday, May 10, 1957, the *Daily Texan* reported the full text of the letter in a front-page article, "8 Legislators Express Regret to Miss Smith," by staff writer Don Knoles:

> We deeply regret the incidents of recent date which have resulted in your not being able to play one of the leads in a Student Opera at The University of Texas.
>
> We particularly regret any part of it which may have been caused by actions on the part of any member of the Texas Legislature.
>
> It is most unfortunate that some people have lost their sense of values, are more interested in personal advancement and the applause of the folks back home, than they are in Christian principles of right and wrong.
>
> You are to be highly commended on "keeping your head" when others about you are losing theirs, and on accepting the decision of the University at such a high personal sacrifice to yourself.
>
> It is most unfortunate that this incident has arisen, but we hope we can all arise from the ashes of these broken hopes and dreams stronger than ever in our determination "to live and let live" and to follow the God given principles of right and wrong, rather than the whims of selfish groups and individuals.

On Friday, May 10, 1957, Jim Mathis reported in the *Houston Post*:

> Rep Maurice S. Pipkin of Brownsville wrote the letter after plans to protest the ouster on the House floor were abandoned. "We want her to know that the person who caused her difficulty did not think for the entire Legislature—that he represented only his own peculiar thinking," Pipkin said.
>
> . . . Pipkin did not begin circulating the letter until the House adjourned at 4:15 PM. The House had restlessly awaited a planned series of personal privilege speeches to protest the ouster. Rep Eli[g]io ["Kika"] De La Garza of Mission was to lead off the outburst. Rep [Jerry] Sadler said he and [Rep Joe] Chapman were prepared to answer in kind any floor challenges. Sadler said Chapman would open and he would close the segregationist speeches. But the day waned and the objectors, fearful that their speeches would only fan the flame of student discontent and national interest, never did kick off their verbal barrage. . . .
>
> Besides Pipkin the seven other signers were Reps De La Garza, Menton Murray of Harlingen, Malcolm McGregor of El Paso, W. N. Woolsey of Corpus Christi, Bob Wheeler of Tilden, Bob Mullen of Alice and Oscar M. Laurel of Laredo. ("8 Solons Apologize to UT Negro Singer")

Mathis also reported that "Chapman and Sadler both were singled out for student disdain in the form of effigies. Crudely made effigies were hung both in the capitol rotunda and the university's Littlefield Fountain early Thursday. Both effigies bore Chapman and Sadler's names. The one found on the campus labeled the two 'demagogue.'"

10. Editor's note: On Thursday, May 9, 1957, Jim Mathis reported in the *Houston Post*:

> A resolution demanding a Student Assembly investigation of the ouster of Barbara Smith from her role in a University of Texas undergraduate opera was approved here Wednesday night by the school's Young Democrats and Young Republicans. The resolution by the two groups also called for an inquiry into "all other incidents in the recent past of action by the administration to remove duly qualified and selected students from campus activities."
>
> The action, taken by about 100 students meeting at the University YMCA, was taken despite efforts to prevent it made by Student Assembly officers, who said they approved of the administration's action in ousting the Negro student from the cast. . . .
>
> Student Body President Harley Clark and Bobby Jacobs, chairman of the university's Human Relations Commission, came under fire at the Wednesday night meeting when they appeared to defend the administration's actions. Clark told the group that [UT president Logan] Wilson's action in ousting Miss Smith might appear as a sacrifice of principles but that under the circumstances it was all he could do. Clark said the university officials had tried to meet each particular problem of integration as it came up rather than lay down a specific policy. Clark termed Miss Smith "a pretty great person for going through things as she is."
>
> A moderate resolution was hammered out at the meeting. There were demands from extremists that the opera performances be boycotted and the opera be performed off campus. These motions were beaten down. . . .
>
> The Daily Texan, university student newspaper, ran the story of Miss Smith's removal Wednesday, a day after it had been revealed in The Houston Post. In a long editorial, the Texan said the faculty committee which named the Negro co-ed to sing the role displayed "striking naivete" in not recognizing the "temper of the times." ("Student Groups Urge Probe of Co-ed Ouster")

11. This transcript of the proceedings in the House chamber was transcribed by David Dettmer from the online recordings of House hearings and debates posted on the website of the Legislative Reference Library of Texas: http://www.house.state.tx.us/video-audio/chamber/#81 (see recording for February 5, 2009, 10:00 a.m.–11:00 a.m.). The text of HCR 31 included here is posted by the Legislative Reference Library of Texas at http://www.legis.state.tx.us/tlodocs/81R/billtext/pdf/HC00031F.pdf#navpanes=0.590

VANCE
MUSE
The Arcadia That Was Austin

I remember the fall of 1971 as being particularly crisp and colorful, the sharp air and crystalline skies adding extra spark to the new school year. The semester had hardly begun when I found my go-to spot on campus, an ideal afternoon recharge zone: the dappled South Mall, where I could chill out (or cram for exams) beneath that extravagant canopy of live oaks. Propped up against a tree or lying on the grass, I might wrestle through a bit of Marshall McLuhan for Joseph Kruppa's controversial English class (its very name shook all of my assumptions about curriculum— Twentieth-Century Literature and Electronic Media), dive into Lefebvre's history of the French Revolution for my Western Civ course (taught by the other amazing Dr. Kruppa, Patricia), or simply gaze up at the clouds, feeling fortunate to be where I was. And so that semester went, one remarkable day, and discovery, after another.

Not all those discoveries were academic in nature. One afternoon I realized that I had begun making a slight detour in my regular route. Heading back to class, I found that I was now walking all the way down the Mall and circling Littlefield Fountain for the sole purpose of stealing glances at the muscular bronze equestrians emerging from the spray. This, it seemed, would also be a year of self-discovery.

At twilight, friends and I would gather at Les Amis—our own Les Deux Magots, or so we fancied. Crowded together at jolly tables under the café's

Vance Muse attended the University from 1970 to 1973. In New York, he worked as a copywriter at Simon & Schuster and an associate editor at Rebus, Inc., and was a staff writer for Life *magazine. He is the author of* Old New Orleans *(1988), two volumes of the* Smithsonian Guide to Historic America *(Northern New England, revised edition, 1998; Deep South, revised edition, 1998), and* We Bombed in Burbank: A Joyride to Prime Time *(1994), as well as coauthor, with Raymond W. Daum, of* Walking with Garbo: Conversations and Recollections *(1991). He has contributed articles to the* New York Times, Texas Monthly, Preservation, *and other magazines. He is at work on a new book,* We Were Here, *about an early twentieth-century gay summer colony in New England.*

Details of the male figures within sculptor Pompeo Coppini's Littlefield Fountain Memorial on the South Mall of the UT-Austin campus. *All photos courtesy of Marsha Miller.*

Les Amis, 1971. *From the Restaurants, Lunchrooms, Etc. file, Austin History Center, Austin Public Library. (PICA 08569)*

bright red awning, we compared notes on professors and reading lists, politics and film, usually agreeing but sometimes arguing into the night—the conversations could go on for hours, covering all things curricular and extracurricular. This was everything I wanted my college experience to be—bookish and bohemian, stimulating and somehow sensual. I had found my groove on the enormous, ever-expanding University of Texas campus, and wished that I could stay in school forever. I felt embraced—by the camaraderie of like-minded people and also by the natural and man-made beauty of the place, from the great gnarly trees and gorgeous sunsets to the warm, harmonic architecture of the original forty acres. The only thing missing, I dimly and only occasionally thought at the time, was a romantic relationship of any kind, though I didn't dwell on the lack. In that department, like Garbo, I just wanted to be alone. Or so I thought.

The fraternity-house scene, I had learned, wasn't for me, but neither was dormitory living. And so,

starting junior year, I set out to find a room of my own. Bicycling one morning past a small compound of green-shingled, well-kept houses two blocks west of campus, I spotted the hand-painted sign: "Efficiency Apartment, $77/month." I couldn't brake and get off my bike fast enough.

I can still smell the flat's paste-wax-scented air, see the amber light slanting through wooden blinds, and feel the warmth of the little fireplace on a chilly day. But its most alluring feature by far was the Murphy bed, stashed upright behind double closet doors. "Very *La Bohème*!" exclaimed my friend Robin when she appeared one day bearing a housewarming gift (a hideous, smiling, crescent-moon candle I thought was beautiful). The sound track of our lives, however, was no opera but *Getz/Gilberto*, Joni Mitchell's every LP, and Laura Nyro's dark and mysterious *New York Tendaberry*. (These and a few other essential album covers I displayed on the fireplace mantel, perfect twelve-inch-square works of art.)

I was twenty. And gay, though I hadn't come to

terms with that fact or expressed my true orientation and desires—not to Robin, to my family, or to myself. But the University atmosphere was making the prospect of doing so easier to contemplate, even inevitable. Two summers before, the Stonewall riots in Greenwich Village had given birth to an empowering gay consciousness that was beginning to filter down to our part of the country. At Columbia, Berkeley, the University of Michigan, and other schools, gay student organizations and national groups such as the Gay Liberation Front were making noise and demands ("Proud to be a Gay American" and "Out is IN" proclaimed two of the battle cries). Even in Austin anyone could see, like Dorothy in *The Wizard of Oz*, that we weren't in Kansas anymore; one afternoon, browsing the University Co-op newsstand, I was astonished by the headline blazoned across the cover of the latest issue of the *Washington Monthly*: "Gay Is Good for Us All." The bold words—orange-pink on a dark green background—were shocking in their matter-of-factness.

Over coffee at Les Amis one evening, Robin—who turned out to know me better than I knew myself—mentioned a friend who was visiting from San Francisco. Without telling me exactly what was on her mind, she set us up on a date. On the appointed evening, a green-and-white Volkswagen bus—peace symbol gleaming in place of the round VW ornament—pulled up to my apartment house. Out stepped Craig, a handsome emissary from Haight-Asbury, sporting beads, sandals, a tie-dyed shirt, and hair down to his shoulders. We went off to Bag End (the name came, of course, from *The Hobbit*), a classic college-town vegetarian restaurant of the era, occupying a grand Victorian heap whose wainscoted rooms dripped with macramé. After much, um, revealing conversation (over plates of tofu and brown rice and chipped cups of chamomile tea), Craig and I ended the evening back at my place, where I pulled down the Murphy bed with new purpose. The gesture—and the mechanism of that novel piece of furniture—added some dramatic flair, and literal meaning, to my coming out of the closet.

That indelible night was also a sleepless one for me. At some point I slipped out of bed, careful not to awaken Craig, pulled on a pair of jeans, and made my way over to campus for a barefoot stroll in the moonlight. How different the world seemed: I now saw that I was living in a romantic Mediterranean village, fragrant with cedar and filled with terra-cotta archways, wisteria-covered pergolas, chiming bell towers, red-tile rooftops. Not to mention baroque fountains brimming with male nudes.

What might have been fearsome—expressing "the love that dare not speak its name"—turned out to be not so scary after all. I felt at ease with, even emboldened by, my newly realized minority status. Boy, did I; as a witty commentator put it at the time, in one of the many national news stories about the burgeoning gay-rights movement, homosexuality was fast becoming the love that wouldn't shut up. I felt compelled to share my self-revelation with the world, coming out to anyone who would listen—family, friends, classmates, and some of my professors. To a person, they all pretty much shrugged in response. It was a charmed, intoxicating time, when proclaiming one's identity, including sexual orientation, was a requirement of the new world order, post–Age of Aquarius. Gay liberation, to the most inclusive and progressive ways of thinking, was brother and sister to feminism and a child of the civil rights movement.

Positive reinforcement was not hard to find at UT for anyone who knew where to look. I was fortunate to have teachers who encouraged the study of topics ranging from the complicated domestic relationships of the Bloomsbury group to nascent gay politics. In Kursten Dodge's English literature class, our analysis of the novels of D. H. Lawrence included a riveting discussion of Ken Russell's flamboyant film version of *Women in Love*, with its famous wrestling match (or was it a love scene?) between a naked Alan Bates and Oliver Reed. My government professor, Robert Hardgrave, turned me loose on a single-topic tutorial, resulting in a long paper in which I (no doubt laboriously) drew comparisons between different minority-group struggles to achieve equal opportunity and legal protection in matters of housing, employment, and public accommodation. For a marketing-class project, my friend Joanne and I came up with a public-service advertising campaign designed to combat negative gay stereotypes in the media. One of the posters we plastered around the journalism building featured curly-haired characters who looked a lot like the two of us, down to her granny glasses, my moustache, and our ridiculously short cutoff jeans (I shudder to think what we all wore to class in those days). "Two-four-six-eight," went our unoriginal slogan, "Gay is OK—just like Straight."

In the Arcadia that was Austin, Craig and I would

sneak off after my classes to watch the sunset from a secret spot we called "The Ledge," an idyllic rocky perch somewhere high above and west of Barton Springs (that would one day vanish into a real estate development). Though he hailed from a small West Texas town and spoke in a soft country-boy accent, Craig to me was most cosmopolitan and worldly, my guide to the pleasures of the counterculture as well as the flesh. We spent languid afternoons at my flat, pondering Castaneda and gazing at Cadmus's once-censored illustrations of Cavafy poems. Wearing down its grooves in the background was Craig's favorite album, *Tumbleweed Connection* (I didn't believe it when he told me that the new artist, with the interesting name of Elton John, was gay). This was my dizzying first crush; when it came time for Craig to head back to San Francisco, I ached.

Single again, I made a point of getting out—dropping in on the nightly salon at Les Amis; crashing fraternity-house parties with Robin on my arm (I had to admit, those Delts knew how to blow off steam); making something not very tasty from the one cookbook I owned, Adele Davis's *Let's Eat Right to Keep Fit*, for Sunday potluck suppers. Some nights I hunkered down with homework in a turquoise-vinyl window booth at Nighthawk (where you could picture yourself as one of the all-night-diner figures in Edward Hopper's classic painting of almost the same name, *Nighthawks*). Afterward, I might venture over to Pearl Street Warehouse, a friendly gay club a few blocks south of campus, where I watched, enthralled, as lanky Texas boys joyously executed the fast-and-fancy footwork of the "Love Train" line dance and the two-step.

And I couldn't get enough of Cinema Texas and Varsity Theater offerings. One night I walked over to catch *Sunday Bloody Sunday*. It's a daring film, in which Glenda Jackson and Peter Finch are in love with the same young man, played by Murray Head. In an early scene Finch and Head embrace, then kiss—on the mouth. Many in the audience groaned or gasped. I gasped, too, but in wonder: here was homosexuality honestly presented on the big screen, without apologies or stereotypes. Exhilarating and affirming as that moment in cinema history was, those groans also made me slink down into my seat. To be sure, I was aware that to most people, even those who dwelled in zip code 78712, gay was not good. But UT seemed to be—to me—a safe haven from homophobia (a word not yet in currency); I had

begun to see the walled campus and its immediate environs as Austin's gay neighborhood, an answer to New York's Greenwich Village, the French Quarter in New Orleans, and Houston's Montrose.

In the spring, I made a new friend, a young woman deeply involved in the antiwar protests that were still rocking college campuses across the country and that at UT would culminate in the 20,000-strong moratorium march. Coming from a proper San Antonio family and an East Coast school, she was a glamorous radical; beautiful, fiery, and eloquent, she galvanized crowds. "I love the antiwar movement," she proclaimed through a bullhorn at campus rallies. "But I'd rather not have to do this job!" Given her militancy and her devotion to myriad social causes, it seemed only natural that we discuss my very personal interest in gay activism. One night, at a small gathering in her candlelit, incense-filled garage apartment, I announced my homosexuality to all present—a bit too bluntly, apparently. Our host—that rock of radicalism—blinked and made it clear that I should leave—and never call again. That such a revolutionary, someone seemingly so caring and daring, could be shocked by the confession—and not sense the kindred political issues at hand—might have made me wonder whether I ought to rein in my confrontational ways. It didn't, and I didn't, more than getting by with more than a little help from my friends.

Had I needed a formal support group back then, I would have been out of luck. Today, tellingly, anyone looking into the history of the gay experience at UT is directed to the Student Counseling archives, where evidence shows that not all students had such an easy time of it. Many struggled with their sexuality, to the point of needing crisis intervention. This, after all, was during an era when homosexual acts between consenting adults were criminalized. And the American Psychiatric Association still classified homosexuality as a mental disorder (along with illnesses such as schizophrenia and anorexia nervosa). It wasn't until 1973 that UT's first gay student organization was founded. That same year's *Cactus* reflects the effort at inclusion in its introduction to the section on student life: "Whether a University lifestyle included health foods, homosexuality, hard drugs, hard liquor, Hippie Hollow, or the Broken Spoke, an individual in most cases could find other people with similar interests. Although these lifestyles may not be condoned by everyone, the individual could usu-

Vance Muse (*left*) and Bob Speer, 1972. *Courtesy of Vance Muse.*

Vance Muse and Sherri Grasmuck, in West Campus near 21st and Rio Grande, 1972. *Courtesy of Vance Muse.*

ally act without much opposition and perhaps with some acceptance." The well-meaning words are both unintentionally hurtful and hilarious. I wince at seeing homosexuals (and boot-scooters and eaters of whole grains, for that matter) lassoed in along with druggies and drunks, but such words and sentiments are simply, painfully enough, accurate reflections of their time.

At the start of senior year, I met Bob, a graduate student who worked half days at Garner & Smith Bookstore, a cluttered, bibliophile's Eden located across from the newly built Humanities Research Center (the hulking, fortresslike structure, according to all the talk, was designed to withstand the force of student riots). The owners—courtly gentlemen of a certain age and longtime companions—filled the shop with well-read clerks who unfailingly knew, and kept in stock, all the books you were looking for (and many others you didn't realize you wanted or needed). A sandy-haired jock standing six feet two, Bob struck up a conversation with me one day about

Maurice, E. M. Forster's posthumously published gay novel, which was making much literary news. I bought the book on the spot and was soon sharing a rambling Arts and Crafts bungalow with Bob and two good friends, also UT students and newly hitched, Sherri and Michael. We called it a commune, and our theme song was "Our House" (along with the requisite two cats in the yard, as the song goes, we also had a very fine rescue puppy, Blanche). Bob and I were as out as a couple could be on campus, marching with friends behind Gay Pride banners and taking it upon ourselves to "liberate" events like the Fall Mall Ball, where we danced together (not always fearlessly, but never inciting incident). Mostly, though, he and I just lived our lives as an openly gay couple, on and off campus. I suppose that was a pretty bold thing to do at the time, but it never seemed that way to us.

I eventually followed Bob to New York City, where we both worked in book publishing—he at Viking Press, I at Simon & Schuster. Though we had landed smack in the middle of the nation's gay mecca just as openly homosexual candidates were beginning to run for municipal office and Bette Midler was moving her "Divine Miss M" act from the Continental Baths to the Palace Theatre on Broadway, I felt no more at home in madly progressive Manhattan than I had in my other, gentler Oz.

Visiting Austin now, years after Les Amis and so many other haunts and hangouts are gone, that is still the case. As I stroll the South Mall, thinking back on those dreamy days, another sweet lyric from Crosby, Stills, Nash and Young plays in my head: "All my changes were there."

Alice Gordon as Queen Gertrude in a scene from *Hamlet*, with Jerald Head (*left*) as Polonius and the late Blake Steinberg as King Claudius, 1975. *Courtesy of Alice Gordon.*

ALICE
GORDON

Barn Dance

The Early Years of
Shakespeare at Winedale

ROMEO: I dream'd a dream to-night.
MERCUTIO: And so did I.
ROMEO: Well, what was yours?
MERCUTIO: That dreamers often lie.
ROMEO: In bed asleep, while they do dream things true.
MERCUTIO: O, then, I see Queen Mab hath been with you.
        She is the fairies' midwife, and she comes
        In shape no bigger than an agate-stone
        On the fore-finger of an alderman,
        Drawn with a team of little atomies
        Athwart men's noses as they lie asleep.
                        ROMEO AND JULIET, ACT I, SCENE 4

In the fall of 1972, when I first took the English course that would come
to be called Shakespeare at Winedale, it was barely two years old and already had an air of myth. During our first few classes, Dr. James B. Ayres
talked about the highlights of the previous two summer-class stints at
the Winedale Inn Museum, halfway between Austin and Houston—philanthropist Ima Hogg's gift to UT of about ninety acres of gently undulat-
ing farmland scattered with oak and pecan trees and historic vernacular
buildings. As we would discover soon enough, "museum" would figure
little in our experience of Winedale. Dr. Ayres told us a string of anecdotes
about class performances in the property's old cedar barn. One in particular still fills me with longing to have been there: at dusk, for the Queen
Mab scene in *Romeo and Juliet*, English major Carl Smith made an en-

---

*Alice Gordon (BA, English, 1974) was in the UT English Department's
Shakespeare at Winedale classes of fall 1972 and summers 1973, 1974, and
1975, and years later—knocked out by the summer-class performances in
1990—returned to Winedale as program director Jim Ayres's summer assistant in 1991 and 1992. She also participated in the reunion classes and performances of 1990, 2000, 2005, and 2010. She has had a long career as a writer,
editor, literary programmer, performer, and artist-colony administrator.*

trance from the roof, opening and climbing through the slatted-wood shutters of the hayloft window and, against a backdrop of sky, released a full glass jar of fireflies into the darkened barn. How could someone come up with *that* while studying Shakespeare? I wondered. Thirty-seven years later, I have been in that barn, as performer and audience member, countless times, and wonder still comes upon me every time I pass through the rough wooden doorway.

Coincidence of chance and an impulse for self-improvement had landed me in Dr. Ayres's Shakespeare class. I was fresh off a twelve-month break from college, back in Austin for my senior year. All my friends had graduated. An English major, I walked into the department office in Parlin Hall to look at the upper-class courses pinned to the bulletin board. My eye landed on English 379M: The Play: Reading, Criticism, and Performance. The class description mentioned two weekends of "workshop performance" at Winedale. To my surprise, I thought: This will help me to be less shy.

Dr. Ayres was thirty-nine that fall—twenty years younger than I am at this writing. Now he is nearing eighty, and Shakespeare at Winedale is a familiar program throughout the University and beyond as a stop on Central Texas's summer theater circuit. When he retired from teaching the class in 2000, handing it over to his former student James Loehlin, he was well known and possessed multiple awards. Typical of him, though, he didn't *really* retire. He took up teaching at Texas A&M for a bit, and returns to UT to teach Shakespeare when the need arises. He lives not far from Winedale, where his brainchild (or perhaps brain-grandchild) Camp Shakespeare, founded in 2001, meets for a couple of two-week sessions every summer. The ten- to sixteen-year-old campers usually include children of his former Shakespeare at Winedale students.

But to see Dr. Ayres today is still to reconnect with that formative character I first encountered in a classroom of Parlin Hall. He came across as not so professorial a professor: tall and commanding and serious, but prone to unexpected jokes; possibly diffident; a bit of a mumbler. His athleticism struck me as unusual for a faculty member. Years later in the *Austin Chronicle*, his student Lana Lesley called him "a scholar wrapped in a jock suit." He had played minor league baseball until an injury sidelined him, and was a friend of UT's most famous football coach, Darrell Royal. Those two facts seemed to explain as

Dr. James B. Ayres and Terry Galloway at the picnic tables near Lauderdale House, 1975. *Courtesy of Alice Gordon.*

much about his teaching methods as did his advanced degree and his unwavering passion for Shakespeare.

At Winedale that fall and the following summer, my first as a student in the six-week class in the countryside, he transformed. He was like Scarlett O'Hara reunited with Tara—Winedale was in his blood. Now (and forever after) he was "Doc," for that is what the repeat students and everyone in the Winedale area called him. Studying with him there suddenly seemed more like spending an action-packed camp term with a cool counselor. This was the early 1970s, which is to say, still the '60s, and he was too young to be on the other side of the generation gap; so although he wasn't particularly political, as far as I could tell, and didn't smoke dope or listen to Led Zeppelin, he was just as excited by the era's crazy-creative freedom as the students who claimed it by virtue of being alive on a big university campus in

America at that time. He seemed to want both to be in charge and to be one of us, lecturing us one minute, walking like a duck the next, staring intently at the floor, then breaking out into a completely physical, contagious cackle. In hindsight decades later, he would say he *was* one of us then—Shakespeare was teaching all of us about ourselves in those early years, when not even he knew how to harness the impossible energy, inventiveness, and insight recompounding the very air at Winedale.

In 1972, there was nothing in my young experience to compare to either Doc or Shakespeare at Winedale except, perhaps, a church retreat nine years earlier, when an equally compelling young canon took the teenage congregation to the country and, after a little religious talk, really put the spirit in us with an unforgettable game of Capture the Flag in a huge field under another dark Texas sky.

For spiritual sustenance, Winedale was about to lead me to a far deeper well.

I knew that first October weekend we traveled to Winedale, after we had taken our suitcases up to the new dormitories added onto the historic Lauderdale House, that I was in for a challenge I might not be able to meet. We had been studying *Henry V,* and our afternoon assignment was to prepare group presentations of the choruses—soliloquies of action using words to paint scenery, muster armies, move time, and people the world of the play in the audience's imagination before the characters themselves enter. The students would perform for one another after dinner. We followed Doc to the barn.

Some have called it a sacred space, and if "sacred" can describe the explosion as well as the hush of life, I agree. In its early days as a theater, the barn was an empty space to lure even the great, "holy, rough theater" proponent Peter Brook himself; the British director's seminal book *The Empty Space* was among our most important texts beyond the plays. My 1973 classmate Robert Jackson (also in the classes of 1971 and 1972) describes the barn as a jungle gym and remembers it as being "like a character or a presence." (Shakespeare at Winedale was a collaborative experience, and I couldn't write about it without offering other early students' memories as well.) "The barn led you to try things," Robert says, "like some older kid daring you to drink longer in the night, whispering, 'Risk?'" A big wooden square with a clay floor,

it centered on four foot-thick posts and crossbeams that were barely higher than our heads, bolted to the posts to support the soaring rafters (and seduce us to sit on them and swing our legs or scrabble along them like spiders above the audience's heads). From the exterior, it looks like a wooden tent, and inside it feels like one, too: in fair weather, four wide wooden flaps, two on each side, were propped open on hinged posts to let the sun and stars and air in and to allow sneakier entrances for student performers than the three aisles dividing rows of several hundred folding wooden chairs set in a curve to demarcate the thrust clay stage for the public performances.

That small clay playing area, I believe, grounded us—as if the nothing between us and the earth itself drew us closer to the words. I can still taste the poignancy of Jan Notzon playing the deposed King Richard II, rooted in place, bringing to bear all his young knowledge of grief and shame as he invited his

A peek backstage from inside the Theater Barn at Winedale, 1975. *Courtesy of Laura Smith.*

The original clay-floor performance space in the Theater Barn, 1975. *Courtesy of Laura Smith.*

few remaining loyal followers: "For God's sake, let us sit upon the ground / And tell sad stories of the deaths of kings." The upper stage, what remains of the foreshortened hayloft, seemed to draw us there for scenes in which characters plotted or escaped or looked back in misery on a life before banishment. I remember Nick Andrews as Macbeth and Dali Villarreal as Lady Macbeth mesmerizing as they conspired to murder, teetering at the edge, both dressed in black, their faces eerie in the light of the candles they had carried up the stairs hidden behind the curtain; I think again of Carl Smith releasing those fireflies; and I can still see many another landing from the roof through the big wooden shutters—entrances by fairies, thieves, lovers, and madmen. Alas for the players of at least the last two decades, climbing on the roof and through the windows (and on the beams) has been prohibited—a freedom that waned as institutional concerns over safety, liability, and historic preservation grew and rules kicked in to address them. How lucky we were to have a barn with no rules.

The direction I take in this seminar-workshop proceeds from the rather obvious but too often overlooked assumptions about the relationship between life and dramatic art. . . .

I hesitate to explain what happens at Winedale, for it is, in a very real sense, unexplainable. We have space, quiet, clean air, and a rare opportunity to know the value of play. Winedale itself is a theater, if the world is.

DOC

Three or four groups of five or six students took our stations around the barn to tackle the *Henry V* choruses. We gathered outside the rear entrance and dressing rooms where, in summer sessions to come, I would stand with others and hold hands to make a ritual circle before performances, wearing the costumes we had made, filled with excitement and dread, tossing out lines from the plays, wishing each other well, waiting for an affectionate joke and good word from Doc or our fellows to break the tension, to propel us, prepared, into the barn. Where, after the play had begun, we would wait for our entrances, whisper our lines, smoke cigarettes, play on a tractor by the barn, check details of costumes or makeup—hiding this one's bra strap or safety pins, regluing that one's peeling beard. (There were plenty of these to keep an eye on, since Doc introduced every new batch of female students to cross-dressing, equitably parceling out roles in plays with far more male than female characters and, of course, turning the Elizabethan convention of an all-male troupe on its head.)

Someone suggested we recite our chorus together, a first step to get our mouths around the words—*O for a Muse of fire that would ascend / The brightest heaven of invention, / A kingdom for a stage, princes to act, / And monarchs to behold the swelling scene!* Reciting the words became chanting them, then chewing them, and by the time we had reached the end, our loose formation had closed into a huddle, and our voices were louder, and our own words bubbled up: "Okay, you take this line"—*Then should the warlike Harry, like himself, / Assume the port of Mars*—"I'll take this one"—*and at his heels / Leash'd in like hounds, should famine, sword, and fire / Crouch for employment*—"Why don't we say this one together"—*Or may we cram / Within this wooden O the very casques / That did affright the air at Agincourt?* We started moving our bodies, trying to embody the verse, and, breathless, at a certain point I was looking over my shoulder and hearing my voice chime in among the others and watching myself move with them into this or that crouch or leap or march or proud stance. The sensation wasn't bad or frightening; it was just odd and exhilarating to see both what seemed to be me and not-me as assertive and opinionated as everyone else trying to work this performance out in half an hour. One part of me saying the words that came next, the other part listening to them so intently. We had so many ideas. *I* had so many ideas!

It took some time, years perhaps, for me to realize what was going on in that out-of-body experience: the twenty-two-year-old me, cavorting behind that barn, had reencountered after a very long separation the eight-year-old me who, in a yard, a meadow, the middle of the street, like the young imaginers we all once were, knew instinctively, unconsciously, unfetteredly, how to *play*. Now, I was playing with Shakespeare and his imaginary castles, kings, and horses! This stranger who was me, I began to realize on that crisp fall day, was the person I wanted to live with for the rest of my life.

Turning left from FM 1457 onto the last mile of road to Winedale still makes my stomach flip with anticipation. In those early years, one entered through the second gate to get to Lauderdale House. From the small porch between the restored Greek Revival farmhouse and the new dorm and classroom wing, we could watch the comings and goings of fellow students—laden with notebooks, props, costumes—across the mown quarter mile of grass between house and theater barn, see them disappear into the passageway through the former slaves' quarters or head between that building and Hazel's Cottage—which had a congenial porch for practicing a scene. Soon enough we learned not to say "rehearsing" because, to Doc, it spoke of "acting" rather than "play" or "discovery." For the same reason, we didn't put on a show, but "gave a performance." It wasn't hard to toe that line. We had no theater training. We were English, science, German, math majors. But Doc had spent a summer as a dramaturge at the Shakespeare Festival at Stratford, Connecticut, and had found the experience dispiriting. The performers and directors sometimes seemed more concerned with applied and gimmicky staging than with trusting that a world would grow organically when a group of open minds committed itself to tending the many clues planted in the rich dramatic soil of every Shakespeare text.

Two lusciously spreading pecan trees stood—still stand—just outside the barn, and the broad shade below their meeting canopies invited scene practice and afternoon exercise on two once-brick-red canvas tarps faded to soft orange by the Central Texas sun. This was also the spot where audiences for Saturday and Sunday matinees escaped the heat and relished the free keg beer and lemonade at intermission and after the performance. The kegs were tapped and shared by a contingent of local German Americans whose ancestors had settled this area of Central Texas. Doc had befriended the majority of the community. They belonged to families that had been there since statehood, and they had names including Rollie, Rosalie, Verlie, Delphin. Some of them were the same age as we were, although their early and continuing labors made them seem older.

They would occasionally wander into the barn to watch us work, and sometimes snicker at lines we

Farm-to-Market Road 2714—the road to Winedale. *Courtesy of Laura Smith.*

Lauderdale House, where students lived in the early years of Shakespeare at Winedale, 1975. *Courtesy of Laura Smith.*

Rollie and Marilyn Wagner's store, across the road from Winedale, 1975. *Courtesy of Laura Smith.*

Daily exercise beneath the pecan trees outside the Theater Barn, 1975. *Courtesy of Laura Smith.*

knew were supposed to be funny but not why, leaving it to Doc to explain, after our neighbors had left, that such plays as *The Winter's Tale* and *As You Like It* had ancient pastoral references that even modern rural residents needed no Shakespeare professor to translate. Rollie, who, with his wife, Marilyn, lived above their store and café across the road from Lauderdale House, was only one of the community members we recruited to take part in the plays; rolypoly, tall, carrot topped, and with a slapstick gene, he was as game and crazy as any other member of Dogberry's watch in the 1975 class's *Much Ado About Nothing*. Terry Galloway, who played Dogberry, and her hapless officers inserted a long, appropriately nutty chase scene. To music from John Addison's score for the film *Tom Jones*, they whooshed by in a canvas boat, pursuing the troublemaker Don John and his weasely cohort, chased and chasers sprinting up and down stairs and in and out of every barn door and window, in the process whipping up colliding breezes to cool the audience, who probably didn't notice, being doubled over with the resonant silliness of it all.

How, Camillo,
May this, almost a miracle, be done?
THE WINTER'S TALE, ACT 4, SCENE 4

Terry Galloway, sending me recollections of her years at Winedale, concluded with, "Oh, Al, we have been part of an on-going miracle, haven't we?" Yes. Yes we have. But not the kind of miracle that just happens. At Winedale, miracles come down to hard, messy, intellectual, physical, and emotional work. Everything we needed to know for playing a scene was in the text, Doc told us. To bring the words to life, we had few props but a pair of handmade stools, one of them a tree stump. Our attention was our only tool. As often as he guided our way, Doc left us alone—in the barn, under the trees, in a field, on a porch—to confront ourselves in the mirrors of one another's reactions or lack of them as we grappled with using our voices and bodies to tease out the meaning, the dictates, the implications of the words and the simultaneously archetypal and intricate stories they tell.

I know I wasn't the only one who cursorily had studied a few plays by Shakespeare before this class and still thought them ancient and exotic creatures whose language was not so much an exalted version of our own as a puzzle next to impossible for any but

seasoned scholars to solve. By this time (1972), Zeffirelli's *Romeo and Juliet* had opened up a few cracks of perception, as did the earlier films Doc treated us to with screenings in the barn (popcorn included), such as Olivier's *Hamlet* and *Henry V*, and a pirate video of the New York Shakespeare Festival's triumphant *Much Ado About Nothing* with Sam Waterston. I remember marveling at Akira Kurosawa's *Throne of Blood*, inspired by Macbeth. Shakespeare inspired even the Japanese!

But, in short, we had to experience the play ourselves for a chance to really get it. Later that fall of 1972, Doc cast my Hungarian scene partner and me as Lysander and Demetrius in what should have been one of the most hilarious scenes in *A Midsummer Night's Dream*. Our hearts sank in mortification as we watched another group of students so easily find the comedy in the play. We had played it as if we had been transplanted to *King Lear*. My friend Mary Collins was yanked from a cluelessness not quite as dire when our late classmate Donald Britton (1971–1975) told her to fling herself on the floor of the barn and scoop up and passionately kiss the pieces of paper she had just thrown down as Julia in *Two Gentlemen of Verona* (act 1, scene 2). "I was aghast," Mary writes in an e-mail:

> WHAT? I'd . . . I'd get dirty, and I'd have to forsake my careful, tony sound and even more careful way of moving like a lady. "Too bad," said Donald. "Get dirty, get hysterical, go back and forth—love him, hate him." Laura Smith and I were pretending to play croquet, and Donald could see that I had nearly no idea of what the scene was really about—Julia's passionate feelings! The cues for what he was demanding of me were in the text, but to me, they were invisible.

Every such recalled experience of a former student is dear to me because almost everyone felt that helplessness. The few students with prior theater experience were the exception, but they had to rethink their approach at Winedale. As far as Doc was concerned, drama training got in the way of a direct connection with the words. The highest form of dramatic *literature* was the point. Winedale was about a group of sixteen students learning to see the world through the kaleidoscopic filter of Shakespeare, learning to engage life. Learning how to live in community, learning where our limits were, and how to leap over them. Or how to accept our limits and—as we now know our very brains physiologically do—bypass them to prospect for some other part of ourselves that could take the leap.

And it was supposed to be fun!

The students who repeated the course from one summer to the next helped initiate the new ones by their example. Everything started in the classroom. All our fat Penguin, Pelican, or Riverside editions of the complete works of Shakespeare added close to 125 pounds to the weight of the long wooden table at which we sat. During my first summer, awe unto alarm at the confidence of such repeat students as Donald Britton, Dali Villarreal, Robert Jackson, Liz Atkinson, and Terry Galloway made me a spectator at these daily sessions. Their knowledge of the plays, not to mention Doc's, was thorough—no remedial Shakespeare here. Their hunger for them was insatiable. The conversations that framed the reading aloud of scenes now make me think of a kite contest—quick, bright, colorful opinions rising and circling, jockeying and sometimes colliding with one another. This freewheeling study began with the very first class. Doc remembers:

> I've lovingly thought of the eleven kids in summer '71 as motley (I had to recruit them from just about everywhere to get started) but they developed a wonderful ensemble spirit through their struggle with the scenes and with one another. For some ten days (and late nights), they argued, challenged, demanded, searching for the "something" in the something in the scene. There were tears and yelling. But there was always respect, hugs, back-rubbing, and relaxation exercises on the wet clay barn floor, and wonderful improvisations at night. Reprieve. The next day they entered the arena again with the same fighting spirit. It is no wonder to me that several students have described the experience as "heroic."

With the same bravado they showed in the classroom, the seasoned students lit up the barn. Once, in 1973, we got on our feet with the scene in *The Taming of the Shrew* (act 4, scene 1) that has Petruchio's servants scramble to prepare for their master's return home with his new bride, Kate. Nick Andrews morphed into Curtis as an overeager minion who scurried around on tiptoe, running on- and offstage with this or that housekeeping prop, and one time swerving back into the scene with a full bucket of water perched on his shoulder. He's going to spill it and ruin the floor! I thought, Boy, is HE ever going to get into trouble. Well, by "accidentally" dumping the bucket all over Kate the shrew, Nick instantly raised the stakes of play. Every other servant—now real players in the scene—climbed over one another to new heights of frenzied ineptitude.

Let go, let 'er rip, the answer's not in holding back. That lesson had to be learned over and over again at Winedale.

One summer day a torrential downpour threatened to flood the barn and ruin the floor's smooth evenness. Doc recruited Michael Barker and a few others to dig a trench around the building to divert the rising river of rainwater. Michael dubbed the project the Wiffy Canal—who knows why now, but who cares? The jokes flew and flew. For six weeks, favorite lines from the plays conveniently and obsessively popped up in our conversations. *Midsummer*'s "You bead, you acorn!" was perfect for mock outrage. *The Tempest*'s "The best news is . . ." for any positive report. Work and play had the same purpose, power, pleasure.

For some of us, though, the humor in the Winedale enterprise could be elusive. The expectation of constant improvisation threatened to wash away all our defenses, leaving puddles of exposed vulnerability behind. Every night until the week before the

(*Left to right*) Terry Galloway, Rob Lallier, Judy Knowles, and Jerald Head (as Falstaff). *Courtesy of Laura Smith.*

public performances began, Doc would assign different pairs of students to devise class improvisations for after dinner, using *Improvisation for the Theater* by Viola Spolin or taking off from that classic text to make up their own, often more audacious games. Many a night was marked by brilliant ephemeral performances you wish you could see again and again. At other time, improvs "could go spectacularly wrong," as Gail Palermo told me in an e-mail. "I remember Robert Jackson and I invented a game but were silent about the rules (we were under the spell of Grotowski or Artaud) and people got really angry and there were tears and so forth. Here was a case where we tried out theory only to find that reality yielded unwelcome results." But most improvisations had rewards as well as pitfalls. I wrote my first poem (later published!) during an improvisational circle in a meadow for which everyone was given thirty seconds to do so using a word drawn from a hat. Terry Galloway drew "mellifluous," and having no idea what it meant, left the runway with it: "Mellifluous here and there, Mellifluous everywhere."

When improvisations weren't on the schedule, the barn offered some unscheduled challenges. Once Carl Smith proposed we all meet and "do mime" in the barn after dinner. He was sprite-like, with twinkling eyes and an elfish grin, a musician who played and performed as though life depended on it. Only the dim punched-tin houselights that had been made by Rollie's father, Papa Wagner, lit the barn. When I arrived, people were already silently moving every which way, everywhere in the barn. Someone whispered to me, "We're being animals." Good God! I thought and then, for lack of any other idea, became a deer. It is obvious to me now that I was just embodying my fear by choosing a naturally nervous, cautious creature ready to sprint away from the slightest threat. Which came in handy when other "animals" crept too close. Sexual tension crackled through the humid air. Now and then, distracted enough by moving around, my body would remember that a deer was graceful as well as skittish, curious as well as jumpy. Still, I kept being caught in the metaphorical headlights. I thought the entire barn would turn into an orgy. Of course, it didn't. Of course, it could have! At least an orgy of two: at Winedale in those days, furtive pairs of amorous students were known to return to the barn late at night to find privacy in a corner of the hayloft.

Lauderdale House, 1973. *Courtesy of Alice Gordon.*

Downtime was more abundant then than it has been since the classes began putting together three entire plays in nine weeks, compared to the original two-weekend programs of linked scenes. Or did our hard work just meld with downtime? "We played constantly," writes Terry Galloway. "All the world our stage. And Doc let us. He let us go. We'd get up on the roof of the barn and slide down it during rainstorms. We danced around in our tights as the lightning was striking trees just over the rise and probably killing cattle." ("There was always at least one or two cows that got killed," confirms Carl Smith.) After one such storm, Carl remembers running out into a field with the fairy contingent of *A Midsummer Night's Dream* (he was Oberon) to experiment with Puck (Terry) and Titania (Sally Charlton). They slapped mud and leaves all over their clothes, Carl writes, then "spent a good while frolicking as some kind of insect/fairy combination until Dr. Ayres came out with a can of Raid and pretended to spray us. We writhed appropriately and that was the end of that 'rehearsal.'"

In the late afternoon or at night after work in the barn, we would often cross the road to Rollie and Marilyn's perfect little country store to drink beer and play pool and feed quarters into the jukebox. A few locals always sat at several tables and chairs in the bare-bones wooden building with its dim, naked lightbulbs and the cheery glow of neon beer signs. Gail Palermo picked up how to dance the Cotton-Eyed Joe there, she says, and remembers, "When every other place was blisteringly hot, the store was cool. I can smell the wooden floorboards now." I will wager she can still feel the rough shingles of the barn roof on a clear night, too, when the last stop before bed was stargazing from Winedale's highest perch.

Every day we cleaned the barn and swept the floor, from doors to doors, windows to windows, then dampened the clay with a light spray from a hose, just enough to keep the dust down but not make it sticky or impressionable. And if you tried to cut corners on the mundane tasks, Doc would call you on it. Moment by moment, he stressed, fed our larger purpose. (I think the intentional, meditative quality of sweeping that Doc urged us to find led to one of the more wonderful moments in 1974's *A Midsummer Night's Dream*: When the Rude Mechanicals met for the first time, Peter Quince entered with a broom, sweeping. The others followed one by one, sounding the tools of their trades in a soft cacophony, then gradually hammering tin, sweeping broom, and stropping blade found the same rhythm and climaxed in a percussive little hymn to manual labor.)

We all learned how to sew at least a straight seam, some of us even to put in sleeves, and the classroom filled with people using or waiting to use the sewing machine. During costume-making week in 1975, it was a particular hot spot. Buddy Steele had brought along a record by the Carolina-born, Austin-based Uncle Walt's Band. We fell in love, boom, only to have Buddy tell us that Uncle Walt's, like the Beatles after they had completely captured our hearts, had just broken up. We played that record over and over and over, and sang along to every song, and stitched and stitched. Michael Barker dubbed us the Sewing Fools.

KING LEAR: Dost thou call me fool, boy?
FOOL: All thy other titles thou has given away, that thou wast born with.

KING LEAR, ACT I, SCENE 4

How does one capture the excitement of the nuts and bolts that go into doing the world's best plays justice when in the performance of one's heart's desire the nuts and bolts don't show? That is where Doc was a natural genius, believing in no less than the expenditure of all our energy every time—not just before the public—we did a scene. I think he expanded his own ideas of what was possible because he had told us *we* could, and had seen us do it. While we hunted for the inner blueprint of a play, he surveyed new territories of study in our quest and presented them back to us, mapped with all his scholarship, his own playfulness, and his facilitator's remove.

While many early students worked on the twentieth-anniversary reunion performance of *The Comedy of Errors*, all Doc had to do to jolt life into a helplessly lifeless crowd (some "comedy"!) was spend three goofy seconds walking among us, gesturing broadly and gossiping in gibberish. We got it! He was the one who created the atmosphere for an evening improvisation meant to conjure the *Tempest* shipwreck, hunting down a piece of sheet metal for two students to rattle thunderously, and rigging the exercise tarp with rope slung over the rafters so we could make the canvas billow in the imagined high winds—all hands on special effects! We opened the play in performance that way.

The parade as prologue to *Much Ado* was his idea. He recruited the high school marching band the Polka Dots from the nearby town of Burton, borrowed one of Winedale manager Gloria Jaster's horses and a harness to carry a Texas flag, and found a wagon and driver to bring the play's soldiers home from the war to Messina-at-Winedale. Our characters invited the whole audience to leave their seats and step outdoors for the occasion, and we all lined the road and drive from the gate to the barn. "This is how I understand a necessary theater," writes Peter Brook in *The Empty Space*, "one in which there is only a practical difference between actor and audience, not a fundamental one." With our *Much Ado*, an imaginary celebration merged with a real one, and as Doc later said, the whole play "exploded with just everything imaginable, or unimaginable. You had to be there."

Of course, we learned, it is one thing to understand the words, whether in our heads or hearts, and another to touch an audience with that understanding. We were our own most critical, most loyal, most feeling audience. The moment of watching fellow students get it was as thrilling as getting it ourselves. In 1973, with five weeks of Shakespeare under our belts and one week left to work, we committed to Shakespeare at Winedale's first performance of a whole play: *The Tempest*. After a lengthy discussion of its themes, especially magic versus nature, we concluded that Ariel, "the airy spirit," and Caliban, "the monster," would be the only characters played by the same two students for the duration. The rest of us would switch roles from act to act, playing both speaking parts and "strange Shapes" who spent our offstage time circling the barn, emitting caws and shrieks and growls to create an "isle . . . full of noises." Donald Britton as Ariel and Liz Atkinson as Caliban took hyperspeed journeys into character. As ensemble witnesses, we all felt the failure when Donald quickly discovered that running around the barn like a pixie couldn't capture Ariel's supernatural dissolves. The next day, we all were awed by the brilliance of his alternative: to quietly, peripherally—almost unnoticed—materialize, by a post, in a window, at Prospero's elbow. The profound calm of it seemed to overtake Donald, from the expression on his face to the confidence and focus he drew from the language. It lent both an otherworldly and almost threatening quality to Ariel: this is a character who innately has more power than his master, who needs a spell to control him. Donald taught me that with his performance. The best Ariels I have seen in performance since have known it too.

Meanwhile, Liz underwent a more difficult transformation: from a tall, lovely woman to the "deformed slave" of Shakespeare's dramatis personae. Caliban is an enraged, self-hating character, and Liz's trouble with finding it gave her a little of that malady herself. But at Winedale, she must have felt safe to be so stricken; one night it led her to the inspired idea to costume her character by rolling around in the dirt. The next night, she turned the dirt into mud and rolled around in that. Every night as we approached our first performance, she would make the mud muddier and roll around in it longer. She emerged bent over with enough physical and psychic weight to roar into being as Caliban.

Doc wrote to me: "The thing that made the '73

summer was not the final performance of *The Tempest*. It was what everyone had undergone in getting to the end."

To most of us, Doc's approval was as important as three square meals. He was a goofball. But he could just as easily become the coach and dress us down like so many losers in the locker room. Each summer there was at least one major crisis of complacency at about the midway-to-first-performance point, when the balance between deepening new friendships and finding our way to ensemble tipped too much toward the former. Apparently only Doc noticed the slip. He pointed his finger and named names. Usually, the majority of students hurried to carry the guilt of his disappointment and swiftly acted to expiate our sins with a renewed burst of energy and focus. Any stragglers got swept up in the majority's interest. Almost twenty years later, as Doc's summer assistant, I saw that although he may have come honestly by his frustrations with a class veering off course, he had learned to use a sign of complacency as his cue to manipulate us back in shape. "Creating a disturbance," he called it. It is a risky way to restore a group's wholeness. Inevitably, there were those who found it unfair. But they, too, ultimately were pulled along into renewed focus. During that stressful time, most difficult personalities winningly found their places. There was no better place to go than deeper into the plays. When we surrendered, when we gave ourselves wholly to the words—perhaps understanding for the first time in our lives what giving ourselves wholly meant—"imaginary forces at work" (*Henry V*) filled the barn to the rafters.

I remember once running towards the mats under the old pecan trees that make a canopy outside the barn and being so suddenly happy . . . that I just spontaneously did three hand flips—one, two, three! . . . [Winedale] was a place where I felt understood, as if some desire in my heart that I didn't even know was there had not just been awakened but answered at the same time. Joy. Complete Joy."

TERRY GALLOWAY

In 1975, I had the fearsome honor of being chosen to play Beatrice in *Much Ado About Nothing*—Winedale's third full-play presentation—and underwent an enormous struggle with finding the lightheart-

Summer class of Shakespeare at Winedale, 1975. Dr. Ayres is leaning on the roof of the vehicle, fourth from the right. *Courtesy of Laura Smith.*

edness that shielded her passion. One day, eight of us cast as the four dancing couples in the play tackled the logistics of the masque scene, our goal being to figure out how to continually dance while highlighting one couple after the next as they made sly repartee. We met after lunch one day on the grass behind Lauderdale House. Our classmate accompanist was one Christine, a flutist (or was she a guitarist?) who had studied the scene and composed for it a sweet, simple, rhythmic tune. (To this day I can la-la-la it in its entirety.) For just a couple of hours on the grass, we devised steps and twirls and bows as we spoke the words and listened to the music of those four brief exchanges merge with the music Christine played, and the dance took on a life of its own. Every day until performance we practiced and practiced, and each couple arrived at center stage when it was their turn to speak their lines, still dancing, of course, as if our characters had been dancing this dance since they were children training in the social graces. In the end, the words and music seemed to

have choreographed us, not we them. We had earned our citizenship in the world of the play.

Our audiences could feel it. We loved them for that, and they loved us back. One of them patted Terry's backside when she went down an aisle as Puck in *Midsummer*. Another begged to know from Carl Smith at a reception following a performance of *The Merchant of Venice* who had "done" this Shylock's gorgeous curly hair. When Mary Collins first performed Dromio of Ephesus in *The Comedy of Errors* for the public, a clown it took every fiber of her being to engage, she says, "I did my little trick with a bag and a ball and the audience *laughed*, loudly! I felt adorable, acknowledged, exonerated!" And after *Much Ado About Nothing*, a man greeted me outside with, "You sent me to nirvana!" You and me both, sir. We all went together.

O joyful day!
I would not take a knighthood for my fortune.

SAM
HURT
with
additional
material by
PAUL
BEGALA

Hank the Hallucination's Campaign Trail Remembered

Confessions of a Traitorous, Politically Agnostic Opportunist

My first encounter with Hank was long before he had a name or a hard-earned place on the printed page, much less his shadow of a rumored echo somewhere in the musty Halls of History.

It took place in our living room when I was about six or seven. I was looking through our living-room window, watching a tree across the alley dance disjointedly in the wind. The individual parts swiveled back and forth with no apparent connection to the other parts or to the whole. I was watching this—spellbound, I guess you could say—when I noticed that the tree had frozen completely still and the living room—walls, window frame, furniture—everything in my peripheral vision—was now "dancing" (except it was too haphazard to be a true dance.) This was very interesting, and I continued transfixed for some time, holding perfectly still, as one would upon encountering an exotic wild creature. At some point, it crossed my mind that instead of worrying that I might scare it away, maybe I should be more concerned about seeing whether it would eventually leave. I got up and climbed the staircase nearby. The house around me had returned to stationary normalcy, but where did that chorus of voices come from? I didn't remember it starting, but the tiresomely repetitious phrase was annoying. When I reached the top of the stairs, it stopped abruptly, and in the same instant, I realized that I couldn't remember the words that still echoed in my ears. Three or four words, about six syllables. I can still almost bring it into focus, but not quite.

Sam Hurt earned his BA in the Plan II Honors program at the University in 1980 (with "Special" Honors) and a JD from the UT School of Law in 1983 (squeaked by). While a student at UT, he created the daily comic strip Eyebeam *(1980–1989) and later developed the strip* Queen of the Universe *(1990–1992). He currently produces* Eyebeam *weekly for the* Austin Chronicle, *and* Root Causes *quarterly for* Edible Austin *magazine. He enjoys (very much) his inactive status with the State Bar of Texas. His current focus is on painting, and his paintings, mugs, and note cards can be found at Avenue Gallery in South Austin and on the Web at samhurt.com. Archives of his work and current strips can be found at eyebeam.com.*

Upon hearing about all this, my mom concluded that I had been hypnotized by the movement of the tree, but I like to think that the Enigmatic Other, who serves as a muse for many artists in many mediums, had blessed me with a close encounter.

Years later, Hank appeared for the first time in lines I was making on paper. He still didn't have a name. He showed up in a Father's Day card I was drawing. He needed a face in order to be partially anthropomorphized while maintaining his Otherness. I liked him. He looked so happy, even though his physical presence was quite intimidating. This was probably around 1978, about the time I was first getting a few cartoons printed in the *Daily Texan*. I worked hard for the next few years to have my strips printed sporadically. I took any illustration job and played at political cartoons, anything to be in print. Over time, the strip gradually took shape and acquired the name *Eyebeam* and a small cast of characters. At long last, I got the chance to write and draw the strip daily. By this time, I was a law student.

It occurred to me that the weird creature—the Other from the Father's Day card—might be a fun foil for Eyebeam, in which case he would need a name. I thought of him as a "Startling Disturbance in What Was Previously Thought to Be Reality," but brevity being both a virtue and a necessity for a cartoonist, I eventually dubbed him "Hank the Hallucination." He was a lot of fun, taking up so much space in those little boxes Eyebeam inhabited. (He generally appeared only to Eyebeam himself, but this was not strictly enforced.) He seemed to go over well.

Soon afterward, when the first student-government election in some years was approaching, I was lounging outside the Tarlton Law Library with a handful of fellow law students. "I went out and voted against the Students' Association year after year, and we finally got rid of it, and now it's back," said someone. "Yeah. We should run a joke candidate." Some years before, a law student had put Amy the Wonderdog forth as a candidate, and the Arts and Sausages party had put on brilliant absurdist campaign theater. "Sam—you should run Eyebeam for president." This struck me as a terrible idea—my alter ego sticking his neck where I would never want my own to go—but something occurred to me. If we were going to run one of the characters, it would have to be Hank, no question.

A crazy cacophony of disorganized unity followed. Someone complained at an election-commission hearing that by appearing in the comic strip, Hank was campaigning before the designated

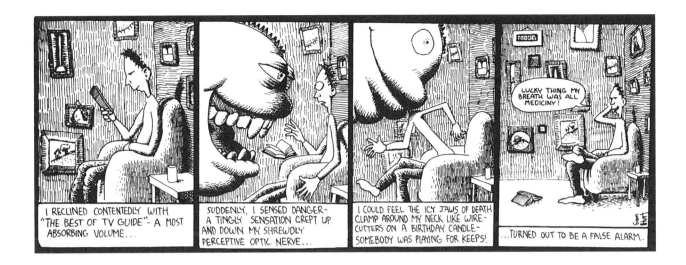

time. John Schwartz pointed out that a law passed during the Amy the Wonderdog aftermath, banning animals from running for office, arguably made Hank the only legal candidate in the field. Someone created an official student record for Hank so that he could be eligible for office. It was a school transcript, signed by actual teachers. (I was interested to find that, scholastically, Hank was doing far better than I was in the School of Law. Perhaps he had fewer distractions.) Steve Patterson, with a background in politics and a keen sense of Technicolor reality-bending media-circus management, served as Hank's campaign manager. The Society for Hallucination Integration of Texas was formed. A live music concert on the East Mall: Hankstock! It must have been a slow news month, because there was lots of press—not just on campus or locally, but even some national coverage.

For me, it was both a story line to drive the strip and the ultimate connection with the experiences of a captive student-body audience—even better than jokes about dorm food. For many, it was a vehement protest against allowing some of their classmates to run a varsity government organization. For others, it was just a really good excuse for a party.

In the back of my mind, I think I was a bit uneasy about my alliance with those who hoped Hank's candidacy would result in reabolishing the Students' Association. They may have been the largest group (hard to measure—the categories not being mutually exclusive), and I benefited from their efforts. But something about it always nagged at me, and after all this time, I can clearly see what it was: I don't really see the argument against a college having some sort of organized student-government activity for those

who want to explore their interest in that field or hone their skills there. After all, it seems like a good idea for other endeavors, like, oh, say . . . aspiring cartoonists. (I understand the frustration with what the politicos were actually up to. I think most people feel a similar frustration with the politicians in the "real world"; and our different ideological leanings determine which individual officeholders we disapprove of more. I agree with the old saw that democracy is the worst possible system, except for all the other choices.)

I was also a bit uncomfortable about how mad we were making some people. One of the guys running for office was especially vociferous in demeaning us in letters to the editor. And the editor herself, Lisa Beyer, who had been the first to give me my treasured daily slot back when she was assistant to the editor, and who had become a good friend, was strongly against the Hank campaign, and editorialized stern reproach (even though I don't recall ever discussing it with her in person, and if memory serves, we continued to party together quite jovially).

Another candidate seemed to take it more in stride. Paul Begala walked up to me at a UT Friar Society cocktail party and asked me how the heck does a guy run a campaign against a hallucination? It was a pretty good setup, and I riffed about how one would attack his vacuous positions on the issues, nonexistent platform, and illusory policies. Or something along those lines. A day or two later, a letter appeared in the *Daily Texan* and the *Austin American-Statesman* in which Mr. Begala, as an actual human candidate, begged to take his nebulous opponent to task. He followed with a series of one-liners that were very clever, so I took them for verbatim quotes from my own cocktail-party riff. Since then, I have learned what a funny guy Paul is, and it occurred to me that he probably polished and improved and built on my gags. In any case, he had gotten in on the joke by playfully taking on Hank instead of attacking his supporters, and he had made it funny. It shifted things around—gave him a place in the constellation of characters apart from the other human candidates. If it didn't determine the ultimate outcome, it at least presaged Paul Begala's prowess in political consultation and punditry. Meanwhile, I had become a double agent—or at least an unwitting strategist for Hank's nominal opponent.

Probably because it meant different things to different people, the campaign has become something that everyone seems to remember differently, and when it comes to the official outcome, and how Begala ended up in the office Hank had vied for, accounts differ drastically. Hank received more votes than any two human candidates (and unlike those of the other candidates, voters had to write his name in), but his total was just barely under 50 percent—a strong plurality. The officials that be declared a runoff between the top two land-mammal candidates.

As part of the many ways in which Hank's supporters had made him their own, someone had written an account of an assassination attempt. You know—just for fun. The idea of an assassination attempt being an aspect of politics I hadn't explored yet, I thought it would be fodder for a story line in the strip. A creepy would-be assassin appears as Hank and Eyebeam walk through campus and shoots his gun directly at Hank. The gunman says "Is he there? Did I get him?" and then Hank and Eyebeam continue their conversation. A good solid gag, a daily deadline fulfilled. The logical follow-up—a little girl points her finger at Hank, says "bang," and he collapses, shrivels, fades, and disappears—seemed like a good idea. Another good gag, another day's deadline. I didn't think of it as a permanent dispatching of Hank, but I guess I should have known it would be given significance. Headlines, mountains of flowers, a funeral procession by numerous Hank supporters. It sort of hurt my feelings to hear about the last of these after the fact, but I guess they saw my execution of Hank as a way of wresting control of him back into my own hands, and his funeral was their way of putting to rest the part of Hank that was theirs. Maybe I am reading too much into all that. Anyway, some see that juncture as an end to his campaign. Since the whole premise of his being was that he didn't exist in the first place, I was surprised to find that killing him off was such a big deal. But it was in some respects a hot potato that I didn't know what to do with, so maybe, unconsciously, some part of me was trying to find a way to put it to rest.

Anyway, somewhere in there was the runoff. I assume some voters wrote in Hank, but I don't remember anything about these being counted or reported, and Paul Begala won the runoff and became president of the reinstated UT Students' Association.

A number of interesting things happened in the wake of the election. The first paperback collection of

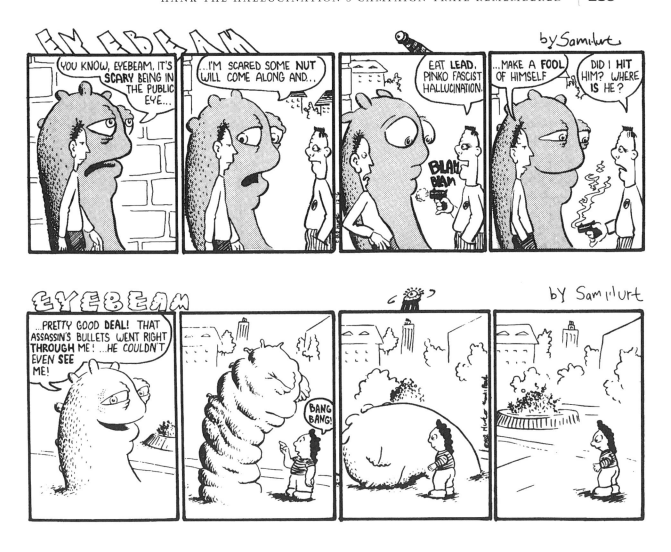

Eyebeam comic strips came out about then. (A coincidence—I had started working on it the previous summer while I was working at a law firm in Houston, before student government was even reinstated.) The campaign had generated extensive coverage in the press, which had to be good for book sales. I have always assumed that Hank's fifteen minutes prompted the *Austin American-Statesman* to invite *Eyebeam* onto its daily comics page shortly afterward.

From there, *Eyebeam* was slowly picked up by dozens of papers across the country, more paperback collections were published, and these made their way to hallowed repositories in lavatories around the world. I hope I led many profound excursions into the Unknown. At the very least, I had fun observing things we don't know but generally go around behaving (and especially talking) as if we did.

Through the years, various elements of *Eyebeam* have resonated with readers and bounced back to me. It is one of my greatest pleasures. Ratliff's turning up the volume during commercials; "Are you boring yet?"; Studmuffins; Wimpy Downstream Beer; Queen of the Universe (self-appointed). But of all of these, the Hank election bounces back in its own special way. Instead of hearing about adopted catchphrases or resonating scenarios, people tell me they *participated* in Hank's campaign—by voting, organizing, building a giant statue of Hank in the fountain, playing at Hankstock. He became a part of their lives to a degree when they worked *with* Hank outside the comic strip, in *their* world. Sort of.

In looking back on the Hank the Hallucination episode and researching it a bit for this piece, I have learned that Hank has worked his way into stories of subsequent elections and found his way into not only Paul Begala's but also Mark McKinnon's story of origin, leading to a pleasant discovery. I always thought that Hank's campaign was a minor footnote in history, and I am delighted to learn that it is actually a full-fledged *regular* footnote!

These days, *Eyebeam* is a weekly feature in the *Austin Chronicle*, my way of keeping my pinkie toe in the world of cartooning, in addition to a quarterly strip called *Root Causes* in *Edible Austin* magazine, and my participation in *Frank and Ernest*, mostly as colorist for the weekly Sunday strips. My main focus is painting; I'm still attempting to lead the viewer on a mysterious journey, unencumbered with the decisive clarity of a punch line, and trying to encour-

age more participation from that viewer in the destination of the open-ended narrative. The Enigmatic Other usually lurks somewhere just out of view. I like to think Hank would approve.

Everything I Needed to Know about Politics I Learned from Hank

PAUL BEGALA

In 1982, when students were debating whether to reconstitute student government at the University of Texas, a primary argument against student government was that it would "merely train a bunch of junior politicos."

Boy, were they right.

In the twenty-five years I have been in politics—from the Capitol in Austin to the White House, from Africa to Europe to Latin America to the Caribbean—the lessons I learned in campus politics have stood me in good stead.

Sitting at lunch with Palestinian leader Yasser Arafat, I recalled working to garner the votes of both the Jewish fraternities and the Palestinian students. In confronting Newt Gingrich and the nihilists who shut down the federal government, I thought of those at UT who bitterly opposed having any student government at all. And when I watched the meteoric rise of heretofore-unknown outsiders, from Ross Perot to Sarah Palin, I relied on the lessons I learned from Hank the Hallucination.

There are at least six lessons I learned from the Hank experience:

1. Government exists to make a difference in people's lives. This is the most important lesson of all. Convinced that student government had become nothing more than a debating society for résumé padders, UT students in 1978 abolished student government. But in its absence, millions of dollars in student fees were being allocated with scant input from students. It was a classic case of taxation without representation. The Hank movement embodied that frustration—to the extent a disembodied hallucination can embody anything. Hank's slogan, "Get Real," said it all. Students weren't cynical, but they were damned

skeptical that a bunch of campus politicos could make a difference in their lives.

Ever mindful that Hank had garnered twice as many votes as I did, I set about to ensure that student government make a real difference in the real lives of real people. We established a child care center for students who had young children, and that today is caring for its second generation of little Longhorns. (In fact, the student senator who created that child care center, Diane Friday, has been married to me for twenty years and is now raising our four children.) We created SURE—Students United for Rape Elimination, the campus walk program that continues to this day. We successfully lobbied the legislature to kill a tuition increase, keeping tuition at four dollars a semester hour. We helped stop legislation to raise the drinking age to twenty-one (pretty relevant when more than half of your constituents are eighteen to twenty years old).

Perhaps the reason I was so drawn to Bill Clinton, even when he was a little-known small-state governor, was his belief in this principle. He understood that when politicians become self-referential—when they act like politics is an insider's game, and not the only legitimate way to allocate public resources—folks feel alienated, and then angry.

2. People project their own needs onto their leaders. Like successful leaders from Ronald Reagan to Barack Obama, Hank was able to be all things to lots of people. Right-wing libertarians saw him as a rejection of governmental paternalism. Lefty dope smokers saw him as a joyful frolic, a vacation from reality. Alienated, acne-plagued underclassmen saw him as a way to stick it to the cool kids. Hank was all those things and more.

3. Take your work seriously, but not yourself. Nobody likes an arrogant politician. Corollary: everyone likes someone who thumbs her or his nose at the system. In the 2003 film *School of Rock*, Jack Black says the purpose of rock and roll is to "stick it to the man." That was Hank's purpose as well. I believe the reason I prevailed over my fellow human rivals was that I refused to join them in a pompous, prissy letter that decried the entire Hank movement. I celebrated Hank, loved the attitude that animated his candidacy (and as a cartoon, he was especially animated), and shared Hank's eye-rolling response to the standard political BS. I think I became student body pres-

ident because I was the only guy running who didn't have a corncob up his butt.

4. When a movement loses touch with its vision, it perishes. Something strange and awful happened to Hank. He lawyered up. It wasn't Hank's fault; he'd died tragically at the hands of a little girl's imaginary finger-gun. And it wasn't Sam Hurt's fault. From the first to the last, Sam maintained the perfect pitch, a blend of satire and silliness that helped Hank resonate with thousands of people. Nor was it Hank's campaign apparatus, such as it was. I recall Steve Patterson (who later went on to be a top executive in the NBA) keeping his sense of humor through the whole enterprise.

But still, they came. Law nerds and sticklers. Sure,

Paul Begala, Students' Association president, 1982–1983. *Courtesy of University Communications, University of Texas at Austin.*

you expected them from the anti-Hank forces. But somehow they infected the Hank movement. They wanted to litigate more than laugh, they searched for loopholes and codicils in the student election code with the very pomposity Hank delighted in puncturing.

I've never forgotten that. Indeed, when I work on a campaign, my Election Day ritual is to reread the candidate's announcement speech. If, on Election Day, it still serves as the basis for the victory (or concession) speech, I know the campaign stayed true to its original vision. If not, well, then perhaps we compromised too much, strayed too far, forgot what we were all about.

5. A movement beats a person every time. Thanks to the miracle of Google and *Wikipedia*, I am often introduced as "the man who lost a campaign to a cartoon character." I don't cringe; I love it. It's rare, but sometimes—as with Hank—a campaign becomes about more than a candidate. It becomes a movement. I saw that when I was campaigning with Bill Clinton in places like Vandalia, Illinois (population 7,000), and Parrott, Georgia (population 156). Clinton drew crowds that doubled or tripled the entire population of the town. People literally came from miles around. Saw the same thing with Barack Obama. They come not to see a man, but to be part of a movement. One of the enduring laws of politics I learned at UT is that people tend to support that which they help create. Students had ownership of Hank, and they made his candidacy a cause. Applying that lesson to student government, I made sure every committee had a majority of students who were not student senators. I figured the more student government was a movement and not a monument, the more effective we would be and the more support we would have.

6. Twenty-seven years later, it is still rocking on. I had breakfast with Pat Baker, my UT roommate, a few weeks ago at the Driskill Hotel. Pat was an engineering major, not a budding politico. But he threw himself into the fray and busted his butt for my campaign. Decades later, over eggs and chicken-fried steak, he shook his head in amazement and told me his daughter is now active in student government at UT.

As Eyebeam said, "It's not a small world. It's just folded over so many times."

Vote Amazes Ex–Student Body Leaders

MIKE COX

Austin American-Statesman, Friday, March 3, 1978

It can now be said that two rather remarkable governmental events occurred in Texas on March 2.

On March 2, 1836, of course, Texas declared its independence from Mexico.

And on March 2, 1978—at about 1 a.m.—the final vote count at the University of Texas showed that students favored doing away with their student government.

It was a stunning event on a campus used to stunning events, though student government won't really be abolished unless the Board of Regents agrees with the campus electorate.

The vote represents a departure from the days when student government at UT tracked—or almost tracked—prevailing national attitudes. In the years prior to the late 1960s, student government was conservative, even if sometimes it seemed a bit liberal-leaning to more conservative Texas politicians.

In 1970, UT got a radical student president, Jeff Jones. At least he was called a radical back then. Today he's quietly teaching English at Austin Community College.

In 1976, student government briefly played with absurdism, the so-called Arts and Sausages platform of student President Jay Adkins.

Last year, the government got more traditional, except for the rise of Amy the Wonderdog, a pet who netted more votes than some people in the student elections.

Now, well, former UT Student Body President and former City Council member Bob Binder could hardly believe it.

"I'm absolutely amazed," he said of the vote to abolish the student government. "I'm very disappointed to see that. It's the old story of cutting off your nose to spite your face."

He said he didn't think the notion had a

Jay Adkins (*with hat in left photo*) and Skip Slyfield (*scattering coins in both photos*) campaigned on the Arts and Sausages ticket for president and vice president of the UT Students' Association in the spring of 1976. One of their campaign promises was to change the inscription on the Main Building from "YE SHALL KNOW THE TRUTH AND THE TRUTH SHALL MAKE YOU FREE" to "MONEY TALKS." *Both photos from the UT Texas Student Publications, Inc. Photographs Collection— unprocessed negatives, Dolph Briscoe Center for American History, University of Texas at Austin. (Left: DI 06888; right: DI 06886)*

chance of passing, but added he hadn't thought the Arts and Sausages candidates had a shot, either.

"Student government provides a lot of services," he said. "It deals with health insurance, it allocates auditorium space for campus movies, it plays a role in keeping concession costs down at football games . . . it offers direct benefits."

The vote, he said, may reflect a general disenchantment with all types of government. "I guess the students don't want input," he said.

Binder was president of the student body in 1971–72. Clif Drummond, a former aide to U.S. Rep. Jake Pickle, was student body president in 1966–67, 30 years behind Pickle, who was student body president the year before John Connally.

Texas and national politics is virtually a Who's Who of former UT student presidents.

"The students have taken a very short-sighted action," Drummond said. "The student government has never run, nor should it run, the university. But students should have a say and offer some pretty important policy input."

If there was no student government, Drummond said, there would be "no recognized mechanism for more than 39,000 students to have their say."

He added, "I trust this is a transitory decision."

In the spring of 1976, UT Students' Association president-elect Jay Adkins (*in top hat*) and vice president-elect Skip Sly-field (*wearing scarf*) led a demonstration in front of the Main Building in which they offered SA senators-elect, bound in chains, for sale after the UT board of regents decided not to reinstate mandatory funding for student government. *Both photos from the UT Texas Student Publications, Inc. Photographs Collection—unprocessed negatives, Dolph Briscoe Center for American History, University of Texas at Austin. (Top: DI 06885; bottom: DI 06887)*

West Mall dialogue during the campaign for 1976 Students' Association elections. *From the UT Texas Student Publications, Inc. Photographs Collection—unprocessed negatives, Dolph Briscoe Center for American History, University of Texas at Austin, DI 06889.*

UT Reinstates Student Government

KEN FRITSCHEL

Daily Texan, Thursday, October 7, 1982

University student government was reinstated Wednesday after the student body approved amendments to the Students' Association constitution by a 1,707–1,178 count.

Student Government at the University was abolished in 1978.

UT Election Commission Co-Chairwoman Michelle Gradwohl said the commission has received no complaints about the results and, to her knowledge, no plans have been made for appeals. The Election Commission will meet Tuesday to set a date for student government candidate elections, she said.

Last spring the student body approved amendment proposals to the Students' Association constitution submitted by Group Effort. The student-approved amendments, plus several revisions proposed by UT President Peter Flawn, were presented to the UT System Board of Regents at its Aug. 12–13 meeting.

Flawn's revisions included toughening minimum GPA requirements for prospective student government candidates, increasing the required course load for each candidate and striking a clause that dictated the vice president of the Student Senate would serve as chairman of the Senior Cabinet.

A panel of five law professors was commissioned by the regents to determine if Flawn's changes warranted another vote. A unanimous yes vote necessitated Wednesday's election.

Hank Vote Forces Begala, Duval into Runoff Election

KEN FRITSCHEL

Daily Texan, Thursday, November 11, 1982

An unusually high voter turnout in Wednesday's student government elections that slowed vote tallying to a crawl has resulted in a runoff between presidential candidates Paul Begala and Pat Duval, though both were out-polled by write-in candidate Hank the Hallucination.

Duval, business senior, got 1,486 votes to 1,327 for Begala, a government senior, and second-year law student J. Wray Warren garnered 644 votes. Hank, a character in Sam Hurt's *Daily Texan* comic strip "Eyebeam," received 3,013 votes, election commissioners announced early Thursday.

Election commissioners said a runoff date has not been set, and that pending petition, Hank will not be included in the runoff.

In conclusion . . .

CAT
OSTERMAN } **A Perfect Game**

The eyes of Texas are upon you,
All the live long day.
The eyes of Texas are upon you,
You cannot get away.

In the fall of 2001, shortly after I arrived on campus to begin my freshman year at the University of Texas at Austin, the UT Women's Athletics Department held its annual student-athlete orientation in the Centennial Room on the ninth floor of Bellmont Hall. During one portion of the
orientation, we spent twenty minutes learning the words to our beloved
school song, "The Eyes of Texas." Little did I know, at that point, how
true the words to this tune are.

As a girl born and raised in the northwest suburbs of Houston, out near
Katy, Texas, I walked onto the UT campus expecting to be unknown. Having had success in softball as a pitcher for my travel team, the Katy Cruis-
ers, and our team at Cypress Springs High School, I was highly recruited
during my high school career, and I chose UT over virtually every school
in the country. My second choice was Stanford—but being born and raised
in Texas, I never really felt that I could be that far from home. But regard-

---

Catherine Leigh Osterman is one of the most decorated athletes in the his-
tory of collegiate athletics. During her four seasons (2002–2003, 2005–2006)
as a pitcher on the Longhorn softball team, she was named USA Softball
National Player of the Year three times, setting the NCAA career strikeout
record and breaking virtually every record at UT for pitchers. She was also
a three-time Big 12 Conference Female Athlete of the Year, the only athlete
from any men's or women's sport to earn Athlete of the Year honors more
than once. In her career at UT, she pitched seven perfect games and twenty
no-hitters. As a member of the U.S. Olympic team, she won a gold medal at
the 2004 Olympic Games in Athens and silver at the 2008 Olympics in Bei-
jing. A three-time member of the Big 12 Academic Team, she received her
BA in psychology from the University in 2007.

less of my success at the high-school level and the attention I had received from college coaches, I didn't expect the attention that a Parade All-American coming to play basketball for Jody Conradt and the storied UT women's basketball program would get. In my mind, I was just using softball to get an education—making McCombs Field my home under the direction of UT's softball coach, Connie Clark. Even though I had been named a high school all-American by the National Fastpitch Coaches Association, I thought, "Who at Texas really follows softball that closely to know who I am?" Over the course of my six years on the Forty Acres, however, I would learn the meaning of bleeding burnt orange, the definition of being a true Longhorn fan, and, most importantly, how amazing life can be as a UT athlete, even if you are not on the football team.

Fall of 2001 was the first time in my life I truly felt pressure. No one would know that I felt it—because I didn't want people thinking I couldn't handle it—but the pressure was definitely on. The summer before I donned burnt orange, the *Austin American-Statesman* had run an article in conjunction with the Texas high school all-star game, which was being held at McCombs Field. There were four of us from my incoming class of nine that were participating in this game. However, the article centered around one person: me.

To understand the pressure I felt, it is important to know that UT's softball program fielded its first team in 1997. The University had established the program with the goal of eventually becoming a national power, once the program had had time to grow and build up a winning tradition. However, it was vaulted almost immediately into the national spotlight when pitcher Christa Williams transferred from UCLA to UT and led the team to two amazing seasons—1998 and 1999—during her two years on the Forty Acres. In fact, in her first season at UT, the Longhorns advanced to the NCAA Women's College World Series, the youngest program ever to do so. After Christa forewent her senior year, Texas softball endured a trying year in 2001, suffering the program's first (and to date, only) losing record after some remarkable and unexpected success in those first four years of the program.

So here was an article proclaiming that I was going to bring this program back to national prominence. You may call it foreshadowing or just being

knowledgeable, but I thought this prediction was just outright crazy. Expectations were never something I wanted to know about. My father and I had expectations of our own, most centering on work ethic, competing hard, and having fun. Early on, we never expected that I would receive a scholarship; in fact, I vividly remember a discussion in my driveway about whether I would be good enough to walk on at Texas. We definitely never envisioned my career unfolding the way it did. But now, in my mind, I was being expected to do big things. To be honest, until the summer of my junior year of high school, I never comprehended my talent. I just worked hard, and played harder. I hated to lose, and I loved to win. Both of

Cat Osterman pitching in her final game for the Texas Longhorns, in the Women's College World Series in Oklahoma City against first-ranked UCLA, June 3, 2006. *From the Sports Photography Department, Intercollegiate Athletics for Men and Women, University of Texas at Austin.*

those qualities made me fit right in with Texas athletics.

That summer day in July 2001, many of the Longhorn faithful came out to get a glimpse of what was to come. They cheered for us by name and even expressed excitement about our return to Austin in a few months. The four of us in the class of 2001 played our friendly all-star game and left Austin with excitement of what we thought was to come. After all, who watches high school softball? Well, as we learned, Longhorn fans do.

Fast-forward to the scene from orientation. For two days, the Women's Athletics Department had us learning anything and everything we could about the school, Texas athletics, and one another. The support for female athletes was incredible. We had our own academic advisers, whom we didn't have to share with the men. We had our own athletics director, which was the case at only a few other universities around the country. More importantly, we were treated with the utmost respect, class, and dignity, and, basically, viewed as just important as any football, basketball, or baseball player on campus. If you know Texas—the state as well as the University—you know that football is religion. Quickly we all learned that in the Athletics Department, it didn't matter whether you were male or female or what your sport was—you were a UT athlete: a Longhorn for life.

My memory of my time on the Forty Acres is vivid. So much occurred on the field, in the classroom, socially, and on trips. I remember receiving our media guide as a freshman. Media guides are the bound booklets our Sports Information Department puts together to send out to media and opposing universities and to sell to fans. Inside are details of the University itself and the city of Austin, but also, and more importantly, the players' bios and the stats and records of the program. I am big on setting goals, or having something to aim for. I had grown accustomed to striking out batters in high school, so I quickly looked up the record for strikeouts in a single season and in a career. I can vividly remember calling my dad saying, "Six hundred thirty-four: that's the number of strikeouts you need to break the career record." My dad gave a short laugh—not a mocking laugh, but more of a "you shouldn't worry about that—just go out and pitch your best" kind of laugh. Again, little did I know how soon that record

would be broken, nor did I know the magnitude of the record I would leave behind.

I remember waking up at six a.m. to stroll across the street to the Moncrief-Neuhaus Athletic Center for weights and conditioning drills. I remember Wednesdays at four in the afternoon when we had to do our conditioning in the heat of the day on the track at the Mike A. Myers Track and Soccer Stadium. These are the times, unseen by the fans, during which we came together as a team, during which we developed our character, during which you become the athlete that fans expected you to be. Knowing we were all in this together made getting through workouts that seemed impossible possible. Struggling together, passing conditioning tests together—that's what made us the athletes we are.

Study hall was my least favorite part about being at UT, but I will admit it was the most essential. I never fail to mention that it was mandatory for us as freshmen, but for me it was highly recommended after that first year as well. I was not a bad student by any means—I graduated with a 3.05 and rarely was in danger of failing. I just have problems concentrating and multitasking; simply put, I get distracted too easily. Many times I sat in the academic offices doing my homework, or in the white-walled room of the Dana X. Bible Academic Center, reading my chapters for class. While I loathed these times during the day, I look back and realize that without them, I would probably have had a harder time academically. Conditioning drills and study hall are essential to being a successful collegiate athlete, though they are the part of winning softball games that the fans typically don't see.

UT fans are, in my opinion, by far the most loyal fans in the country. Of course, they enjoy success as much as we athletes do, but even in defeat, they are there supporting their athletes. There were numerous occasions throughout my career when I looked in the stands and was just amazed at the number, enthusiasm, and love of our fans.

In the spring of 2002, our team had kicked off the season, and surprisingly, our stadium was pretty full for a doubleheader against the Ladyjacks from Stephen F. Austin State University. Those in attendance had no idea what was in store, just as I had no idea what had occurred once the first game of the doubleheader was over. On this particular day in February, I toed the rubber with ear warmers on because it was actually cold enough for me to need them, even though we were in Austin. I don't remember much about the game, other than the ending. With the last out recorded, Coach Clark had us hold up by the entrance to the dugout before heading into the locker room for our typical in-between-games snacks and talk. Before fans could get out of their seats, our announcer came over the loudspeaker. As we are standing there, Lindsay Gardner, my teammate from travel ball and an instrumental part of my choosing to go to Texas, starts hugging me and getting excited. Finally, I hear it, barely, over the cheers, "Ladies and gentlemen, with the completion of game one, freshman Cat Osterman has just thrown the first perfect game in the history of the University of Texas softball program." Lindsay tried to push me out for a curtain call of sorts, and I probably flashed a quick smile and wave before I retreated to the locker room. I can't even recall whether my parents were in attendance that night, but I do remember the fans' roar of approval. I remember the standing ovation, and I remember the cheers as I came out from the dugout in my jacket to huddle up before the next game. I couldn't have been more than ten games, if that, into my Longhorn career, and the Longhorn faithful had already rallied around. I knew the next four years were going to be truly remarkable.

Over the course of my career, I started being the running joke of our team—not in a cruel way, but because my teammates constantly laughed or poked fun every time I was noticed, usually with me being completely oblivious of the fact that I was being noticed. I remember a team meal my freshman year at EZs, a casual restaurant on North Lamar that we frequented. A young boy, probably about ten years old, said "Dad, that's the softball team." The dad looked at his son and said, "Did you read their jacket or something?" At this point I tuned out, but later I was informed that the little boy said, "No dad, the tall girl is that new pitcher. I read about her." Of course my teammates often gave me their "Geez, we can't take you anywhere!" teasing, and my response every time was, "Yeah, right." This is just another demonstration of how loyal Longhorn fans are. Over the course of six years around Austin, I learned that Longhorn fans follow every sport with passion. They embrace their athletes with continual support, and if there were some that didn't follow softball, they quickly jumped on our bandwagon. It became a lit-

tle more "normal" to be recognized around town as time went on—a true testament to how dedicated Longhorn fans are.

The fact that we played many of our home games in front of sold-out crowds at McCombs Field is testament enough to how Longhorn fans love their programs! But two of my favorite Texas-fan moments were in other sports venues on campus. Our record in 2005 set us up nicely for a great postseason run. We were named the host of our regional, meaning that we got to enjoy the luxury of sleeping in our own beds, playing on our own turf, having our fans in their everyday seats, and also being able to partake in our normal lives in Austin. For most of us, we followed the men's baseball team as closely as we followed our own season. Our softball regionals ran at the same time when Texas baseball hosted a series with the Texas A&M Aggies. Friday night of the postseason tournament, I pitched a no-hitter, and Saturday morning I followed that up with a perfect game to advance us to the regional's championship game. As usual, I went to eat after the game, then my catcher, Megan Willis, and I decided to catch the baseball game with a few friends. It's not unusual for the Longhorn baseball team's fans to recognize us and share their congratulations, but this day was particularly different. Megan Willis and I arrived early with friends, sat with some of the baseball players' parents up higher in the bleachers than we normally sat so that we could chitchat, and after a few innings, decided to make our way down to some lower seats to watch the game. We had done this routine several times, but this time, as we walked down to lower seats, we noticed that fans were clapping, but nothing had happened in the game at that time. When we reached the lower level, I looked up to see all of the fans at Disch-Falk Field that day standing and clapping. The entire baseball stadium was giving us a standing ovation for our last two performances. Hearing the ovation, I believe Craig Way, the radio announcer, had seen me walking in the stadium and mentioned the results of our last two games, but I don't know many places where they would recognize their athletes informally that way. To this day, that is one of my favorite memories at Texas—minus the ribbing I got from the baseball guys after that.

My other favorite recognition from the University was during a football game. After winning my third USA Softball National Player of the Year award, I was

Cat Osterman (*center*) is congratulated by her Texas Longhorn teammates after pitching a perfect game against Mississippi State in the NCAA Regional Tournament in Austin, May 21, 2005. *From the Sports Photography Department, Intercollegiate Athletics for Men and Women, University of Texas at Austin.*

honored that next fall on the football field. It was always nice to be down on the field to see some of the game, but this time was particularly special. During one of the breaks in the action, the announcer informed the crowd that I was in the stadium, and then a short feature of my highlights played on the enormous video screen. The USA Softball representatives presented my trophy, but the response that followed wasn't just courtesy applause. The cheers and clapping and love I heard and felt that day put into perspective what my life at UT had become. Hearing the entire crowd at Darrell K Royal–Texas Memorial Stadium cheer for you is a pretty breathtaking moment.

Of course, there is also the academic piece of a student-athlete's life. I enrolled at UT wanting to do something different. I originally wanted to double-major in psychology and sports management, because sports psychology is my deep passion. But after mapping out the courses, I decided one major would

be enough, and added a business foundation minor. I encountered many professors who were more than willing to work around the classes I had to miss for games and travel, but none I remember more than Lynda Cleveland. Professor Cleveland, who taught management information systems for the business foundation minor, had a good number of athletes in her class, which she enjoyed. She never hid the fact she was an avid sports fan. I took her class in the fall of 2004 after returning from our Olympic run in Athens. I had not yet formally introduced myself, since I had missed the first few days of class because of being out of the country, but my first day back, she called my name and made me stand up in front of the class while she congratulated me.

Her class was not the easiest, but she reached out to us any time we needed help, and when the much-talked-about Business Career Fair arrived, she was always checking in to make sure we were on top of it. I had numerous conversations with Professor Cleveland throughout my semester in her class, and we exchanged e-mails throughout my academic career at Texas. When it came time to apply for graduate school, she even wrote a letter of recommendation for me. I always tried to "hide" in class, but the fact that she didn't let me just blend in made an impression, and I actually appreciated her support for us athletes.

Another of my most memorable experiences in the classroom was in my statistics class for psychology. This might just have been one of the hardest classes I took at UT. I had just returned from the 2004 Olympics, and I often slunk into my chair and tried to be unnoticed, which was relatively easy in the psychology classes. After class let out one day during the first week, a guy from my class caught up to me outside the building and started asking about Greece, the Olympics, etc. He was genuine in his inquiry, and after the first round of questions, I realized I could just be me with him. I quickly took comfort in knowing someone in class. I looked forward to the days I had class with Josh. We ended up doing our group project together with two other classmates, and I am proud to say Josh and I remained friends. After our statistics class, we started trying to plan what other psych classes we could take together that fit in both our schedules. The next two years, Josh and I took two or three more classes together, and on top of our classes, Josh exposed me to other extracurricular activities going on at Texas, such as the time I went to see Josh and his girlfriend perform in the Madrigal Dinner.

I met a good number of people in class with whom I stayed in contact for a little while. It was always nice to be accepted by my peers academically, because oftentimes student-athletes feel as if we are athletes only, and I have always wanted to be more than that. I was fortunate enough to be inducted into the Friar Society, a prestigious UT honor society, which is a comical story. I had no idea what the Friar Society was, and when I got an e-mail about being inducted, I blew it off, thinking it was something completely different. Soon Randa Ryan, our academic counselor, called me in and put me on the phone. I soon learned what it meant to be a Friar, and after induction, my eyes were wide open to the University of Texas as a whole. I am still friends with quite a few of my fellow inductees, most of whom were in student gov-

ernment. I was amazed to hear what they had accomplished, and felt as though my athletic achievements shouldn't have put me in their company. Either way, it was another experience at Texas that I wouldn't trade for the world.

When I finally graduated, I walked across the stage of Gregory Gym with my friend Montana in front of me. We met in one psych class and planned to take a couple others together as well. We found each other on graduation day and had a good time enjoying our last moments as UT students. While I am known for my on-field accolades, walking to get my diploma was one of the highlights of my career at Texas. UT athletics turned my world upside down, more than I could imagine, but UT academics gave me a chance to feel as though I accomplished something on my own, and allowed me to fit in with students on a different level.

As I reflect back on my time at UT, I realize how my success and the support I received were normal for the times. I know that this hasn't always been the case for female athletes, and all of us today who have benefitted from collegiate women's athletics owe a lot to the female athletes who preceded us and to the leaders who have worked to bring opportunities in women's collegiate athletics closer to being on par with those of the men. Female athletes of past generations didn't always have an opportunity to compete in their chosen sport, opportunities that my generation has always known to be there for us.

UT athletics gives all of us a chance to be seen on the national stage. Texas has the tradition of being great, and with that tradition come the perks of playing nationally televised games and drawing attention all across the country. During my time at the University, I was recognized more as "that pitcher from Texas" than anything else—and that is sometimes still true. I am not so sure had I gone somewhere else that my career would have been as widely viewed as it was because I was a Longhorn. Longhorn sports connect so many people across this country: some who have direct ties to the school, some who long to be in our shoes, and some who just decided one day that they were Longhorn fans.

When you become an athlete at the University of Texas, you become part of history. Wearing burnt orange is an honor, and being able to join athletes like Earl Campbell, Ricky Williams, Roger Clemens, Huston Street, Vince Young, and many others is almost unimaginable to me. After my career as a player at Texas was over, I was astonished by how many people spoke my name in the same breath as Earl, Huston, Vince, and many others. In 2008, I was on the "Bound for Beijing" pre-Olympic tour with the National Softball Team. We stopped in Midland, Texas, for an exhibition game, and here one of the most astonishing moments in my career happened. As we still do after every game, we had a forty-five-minute autograph session, and since we were in Texas,

I expected to see some UT hats, shirts, and memorabilia to sign. Halfway through our autograph session, a man handed me his hat and said, "Only Texas legends sign this thing." I looked down, and only two other signatures were on that hat: Earl Campbell and Huston Street. I went to school with Huston, and respect him a ton, but to be considered on the same level as Earl Campbell made me feel especially proud to be a Longhorn.

Aerial view, looking south, of Married Student Housing's Brackenridge Apartments, situated between Lions Municipal Golf Course and the Colorado River, near Red Bud Isle. *From the UT Office of Public Affairs Records, Dolph Briscoe Center for American History, University of Texas at Austin. (DI 07018)*

WAYNE
BUTLER

Before the Bulldozers

Life in Married Student Housing

You can all go to hell; I'm going to Texas.
DAVID CROCKETT

I arrived in Austin during the late afternoon of an insanely hot day in August 1985. I was one and a half years married; my wife, Sara, was four months pregnant; and we pulled up to a dilapidated duplex in a very shady neighborhood (and not in the leafy sense), a place we had rented sight unseen via telephone before the advent of the Internet, in a chugging U-Haul loaded with scraps of hand-me-down furniture from newly introduced Houston in-laws. We were coming off an expatriate experience as teachers at the American School in Mexico City, where we eloped four months after encountering one another at the kickoff faculty meeting. In the quest for higher education and our next adventure, Sara, a corporate gypsy child who had spent many of her formative years in Texas, suggested we move to Austin, which she sold to this Yankee as "the Boston of the South," to attend the University of Texas at Austin.

I had never been to Texas, but I knew something, or so I thought, about hot dusty high plains with somnolent banditos and heroic Marlboro men and tumbling tumbleweeds. Knew spacemen came from Texas to land on the moon. Knew something about a sniper and a Tower. Knew something about a cow with long horns, a Royal coach, a wishbone, and a back named Earl who could run around and over everyone. In New York, I was taught to remember the Alamo, but I couldn't remember why. Heard about a dope-smoking country singer named Willie. Knew something about the place names, having grown up in a Texan-developed subdivision in the

Wayne Butler received his MA (1987) and PhD in English curriculum and instruction (1992) from the University. He serves currently as an assistant director in UT's Continuing and Innovative Education. From 2002 to 2011, his office was in the University's Lake Austin Centre, just a short walk from Deep Eddy, Lions Municipal Golf Course, and the site of his former home on the Brackenridge Tract.

New York City suburbs where all the streets were named after Texas cities. I grew up in Alamo Court. My first girlfriend lived in Austin Circle. Drove from one to the other—my Chisholm Trail, so to speak—along Texas Avenue and Dallas Drive.

The day I arrived in Austin, with a few thousand dollars in savings, some ambition, a pregnant wife I barely knew, and an acceptance letter to the graduate program in UT's College of Education, I opened the back of the U-Haul, and the heat blinded me. I squinted at the furniture that wasn't mine from people I didn't know, saw the car on blocks in my duplex neighbor's half of the driveway, and grew concerned that I had made the mistake of my life.

In a few days, we would buy a slab of polyurethane foam at the original Academy on I-35 and East 41st Street for our bed; I learned I would be eligible for neither financial aid nor health insurance; and I took a job slicing bologna in the old HEB supermarket in Hancock Center on Red River Street, where they made me shave my cherished expatriate's beard in the name of hygiene. I suppose my New York accent gave me credibility as a deli man. I was now *convinced* that I made the mistake of my life.

But Sara, a full-moon siren and seeker of silver linings who sips from half-full glasses, started making some calls. She learned about what was then called Married Student Housing, a name for a category of University apartments (Brackenridge, Gateway, and Colorado) that changed to Family Housing and then to University Apartments in the ensuing years to reflect the fact that single parents were raising families there, too. That the apartments were in West Austin. That there was a free shuttle bus to campus.

Two weeks before classes were to begin, we made our way to the Division of Housing and Food Service and completed an application.

How big and how much, we asked.

Let's see, you're a pregnant couple, so you qualify for an unfurnished two-bedroom, one-bath apartment with kitchen and combined living-dining room. No openings now, but we'll put you on the waiting list.

How much, we asked.

While I vaguely remember the price coming in at about $300, it was substantially cheaper than comparable Austin rental property, especially for West Austin.

A few days before classes began, we got the phone call. There was an opening in the Brackenridge Apart-

ments, the newest of the three complexes. By the first day of school, we had settled into 3354-C Lake Austin Boulevard, a 600-square-foot, two-bedroom, one-bath apartment on the second floor in the 1980s version of the Brackenridge Apartments, bounded on the northeast by Lake Austin Boulevard, on the southwest by Town Lake (since renamed Lady Bird Lake in honor of the former first lady), on the northwest by Redbud Trail, on the southeast by the UT Biological Field Lab. From our living-room window, if you looked at just the right angle, you could see the fourteenth fairway of Lions Municipal Golf Course across Lake Austin Boulevard.

I didn't realize it at the time, but we were in a pretty nice part of town.

We stuffed our second-floor apartment with the hand-me-down 1960s furniture and the folk art and masks we had collected in Mexico. The beige, double-decker rectangular prefab-looking buildings were arranged in clusters of two five-unit buildings with a sidewalk running through each cluster to form a courtyard, each one strewn with faded kick balls, bicycles, tricycles, Big Wheels, baby strollers, laundry racks, and Little Smokey barbecue grills. To get to the second-floor apartments, one ascended a utilitarian steel staircase a few steps up to a landing, where staircases flared left and right to reach the upper floors. The apartments were heated and cooled

Wayne and Sara Butler's apartment, 3354-C Lake Austin Boulevard (*second floor, left*), in UT's Married Student Housing, ca. 1989. *Courtesy of Wayne and Sara Butler.*

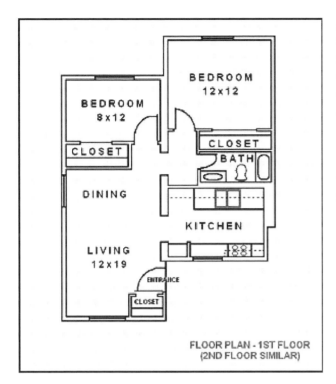

BEDROOM
12x12

BEDROOM
8x12

CLOSET

CLOSET

BATH

DINING

KITCHEN

LIVING
12x19

ENTRANCE

CLOSET

FLOOR PLAN - 1ST FLOOR
(2ND FLOOR SIMILAR)

Floor plan for the Married Student Housing's Brackenridge Apartments in the 1980s and 1990s.

200,000 miles out of a car. It was the car I drove to my high school prom in New York when it was the new family sedan, then from New York to Mexico City after my parents bequeathed it to us as a wedding present, then up to Austin after navigating the ancient Aztec and Spanish colonial roads of Mexico and the cacophonous labyrinth of its capital city.

It fit right in.

The lot was full of faded and dented '70s-era Detroit gas-guzzlers affordable for families who had more kids, brains, and ambition than money.

As sometimes happens in life, an innocent phone call led to a happenstance that led to, for this Yankee, the road less traveled by—and that has made all the difference. Although I didn't know it at the time, for the next seven years, this would be my Austin, my little piece of Texas. I would become a Longhorn, an Austinite, and a Texan without ever wearing boots or a ten-gallon hat. I would earn a master's degree and a PhD and achieve the highest level of education in my family. I would learn to be a husband. I would become a father two times. I would become a man.

A CHERISHED AND MEMORABLE PLACE

For nearly fifteen years, these memories went wherever the details of our mundane experiences go as they melt into the larger narratives of our lives. Upon earning my PhD, in 1992, I landed a teaching job at the University of Michigan, where we also lived in the university's family housing in a quest to extend the cost-effective quality of life we had experienced in graduate school at UT. Five years later, I returned to Austin to rejoin several graduate school colleagues and ride the dot-com wave during the early years of the Internet. When the wave crashed a few years later, I was back at UT and an office building on Lake Austin Boulevard, nearly adjacent to the Brackenridge Apartments. The basic infrastructure of the physical places that encased my memories—Lake Austin Boulevard, the Brackenridge Apartments, Lions Golf Course—remained intact.

But in 2006, the UT Board of Regents formed the Brackenridge Tract Task Force to see whether 305 acres between Town Lake, Enfield Road, and Deep Eddy might be transformed into the new Aus-

by heat-exchange pump units, the kind found in cheap motels. (A drive-by in 2010 revealed the apartments had been retrofitted with central AC units.) They were lit with long florescent ceiling lights encased in rectangular covers of opaque, textured plastic. The walls were white and textured, with acoustic popcorn on the ceilings. The kitchen cabinets were painted dark brown. The floors were covered with gray-and-brown-speckled vinyl tile. The bathroom fixtures were the same ones used in the Perry-Castañeda Library. No dishwashers. No washer-dryer hookups, but the complex did provide a community coin laundry.

The grounds were dotted with ancient live oaks and grass patches between worn footpaths. No landscaping, no flowers, no frills. The northwestern quadrant, on the southwestern side of Lake Austin Boulevard and south of Redbud Trail, was undeveloped—an open field with broadly crowned live oaks scattered about, parklike. The Brackenridge Apartments were utilitarian, functional, and institutional.

In the parking lot sat our 1975 Chevy Malibu, a road-weary rolling bucket of rust with 115,000 miles on the odometer, back before you could expect to get tin. That is, there was once again renewed interest in leveraging the prime lakefront real estate in order to fortify the University's coffers as a way to underwrite the University's mission in the face of the perfect fiscal storm of ever-increasing costs and reduced state funding for higher education. The board retained the New York City (I cringe at the irony) urban design firm Cooper, Robertson, and Partners to develop a conceptual plan to "create a model of land stewardship through the creation of a forward-thinking, environmentally sustainable, life-enriching, and financially successful new community [and] to realize the full potential of the property as a cherished and memorable place."[1]

The plan was ambitious, reached far into the future, and was not without its virtues, no matter what side of the passionate debate one was on. Among the details, which included dense urban planning, public green spaces, and a boardwalk along Lady Bird Lake, was the imminent destruction of the Brackenridge Apartments. The news unleashed memories of who I was before and while I lived there, the people I knew, and how the place served as not just a vessel of, but also a catalyst for, who I would become. As the nineteenth-century American poet Walt Whitman wrote in "There Was a Child Went Forth":

> There was a child went forth every day,
> And the first object he look'd upon, that object he
>   became,
> And that object became part of him for the day or a
>   certain part of the day,
> Or for many years or stretching cycles of years.

I am one of the tens of thousands of UT alums who, since World War II, have come to life, come of age, and gone forth on journeys both mundane and monumental from one of the versions of the low-cost, temporary apartments within the Brackenridge Tract as we passed through the University, through Austin, through Texas, and, in many cases, through the United States en route to our dreams and destinies. We became part of Brackenridge, and it part of us. And while the complex where I metamorphosed from a young adult to a grown man—a person shouldering responsibilities and obligations and promises and expectations—may be gone, Brackenridge became part of me for the cycle of years.

THE BRACKENRIDGE TRACT: ADVANCING AND PROMOTING UNIVERSITY EDUCATION

The Brackenridge Apartments sit on a piece of land known as the Brackenridge Tract, a property steeped in the themes and histories of Texas, Austin, and the University. The apartment complex and the tract were named after Colonel George Brackenridge, who served several terms as UT regent over twenty-six years, between 1886, during the University's infancy, until his death in 1920. Born in Indiana in 1832, Brackenridge moved to Texas in 1853 and started a trading business, which became the foundation of his fortune and power. While his brothers joined the Confederate Army during the Civil War, he was a Union sympathizer and war profiteer. By 1866, he was a prominent San Antonio banker, and when his bank invested in the cattle business, his fortunes and power grew. In 1886, the nascent University of Texas called upon him to serve as a regent.[2]

His business acumen helped improve the University when he found ways to leverage the vast West Texas landholdings that, up until Brackenridge's tenure, had been considered useless and were being vastly underutilized by the University. He became known as the University's patron saint, according to the legendary Texan Roy Bedichek, by investing his own wealth to underwrite buildings and programs on the UT campus. As the University's population grew, the campus's original Forty Acres became crowded, so Brackenridge unleashed a new vision for the University.

A sophisticated investor and speculator, Brackenridge had over several years acquired significant parcels of Austin real estate. He believed a particular parcel, about 500 acres straddling the Colorado River west of downtown Austin, in conjunction with the adjoining 500 acres of the Pease estate to the northeast, would make an ideal location for a new UT campus, one bordered on the west and south by the river and up to approximately what is today Windsor Road. In December 1909, Brackenridge wrote to UT president Sidney Mezes: "I tender to the University . . . land . . . amounting to somewhere in the neighborhood of (500) acres, provided it could be occupied for University purposes advantageously. . . . I am perfectly willing and ready to do this if it meets any of

The original, barracks-style housing units of Married Student Housing's Brackenridge Apartments. *From the Prints and Photographs Collection—UT—Housing, Dolph Briscoe Center for American History, University of Texas at Austin. (DI 06848)*

the wants of the University, but would be unwilling to give it to them to be sold or exchanged for other property."[3] On June 17, 1910, Brackenridge did in fact deed the land to the University "for the purpose of advancing and promoting University education." His vision was that one day the UT campus would cascade down from Tarrytown to the Colorado River.

One would think the University would have embraced such a generous offer of a bucolic piece of riverfront property with unencumbered boundaries in order to give the institution's physical plant room to grow along with its student population, but Brackenridge's vision would never be realized, thanks to political wrangling among University benefactors, UT leadership, and state legislators and governors. UT's other great late nineteenth- and early twentieth-century benefactor, George Littlefield, a son of the South, Confederate war hero, secessionist, and rival of Brackenridge, wanted to keep the University in

its original location and, perhaps more importantly, to trump Brackenridge's bid to become the "alpha" benefactor.

Over the years, and as a result of Brackenridge's deed clauses that forbid the University from selling the property if it is not to be used for education, parcels of the land were leased out while the University used sections for ancillary educational purposes. In 1924, the University leased a parcel to the Austin Lions Club to build a golf course. To meet the needs of married World War II veterans who were enrolling in college in record numbers, in 1947 the University received from the U.S. government wooden bachelor-officer quarters, which it converted into apartments. It erected some of them on a parcel of land northeast of Lake Austin Boulevard, northwest of Hearn Street, and southwest of 7th Street. These structures were known as the Deep Eddy complex. It erected the rest of them on the parcel of land between Lake Austin

The Colorado Apartments, located a short distance southeast of the Brackenridge Apartments on Lake Austin Boulevard. *From the Prints and Photographs Collection—UT—Housing, Dolph Briscoe Center for American History, University of Texas at Austin. (DI 06849)*

Boulevard and the Colorado River, northwest of Deep Eddy Pool and southeast of Red Bud Trail. These structures were the original versions of the Brackenridge Apartments and their neighbor to the southeast, the Colorado Apartments.

The World War II generation planted the seeds of the 1960s baby boom, and UT's original Forty Acres became increasingly overcrowded. The UT Board of Regents and administrators once again looked to the Brackenridge Tract for ways to expand the University. One parcel was considered for a presidential residence. Given the distance of the Brackenridge Tract from the main campus, campus planners quickly dismissed the notion of erecting academic buildings on Brackenridge, but some thought was given to making space near the original Forty Acres by moving the football and baseball stadiums to the Brackenridge Tract. In 1966, the Colorado Apartments, a low-slung, flat-roofed redbrick complex just northwest of Deep Eddy Pool, replaced the original wooden military structures that had stood there. In 1983, the new

Brackenridge Apartments were erected to replace the old barracks.

A CHILD IS BORN

The heat in Austin is like the cold in New York. It is the indoor time of the year, when people are seen only when they are shuffling or scurrying between climate-controlled environments. So during our first month or so in Brackenridge, we busied ourselves with our school and study schedules, only occasionally interacting with our new neighbors. Both my wife and I were mid-twentysomethings who had not been in a college classroom in several years. Our days and nights were filled with finding libraries, and books and articles in those libraries, and reading more for individual classes than we might have for a semester's worth of our undergraduate classes, and writing more in one semester than we had in our lives before that—all on legal pads and a portable Sears electric typewriter, since we had not yet been introduced to the nascent world of the personal computer and word processing. And struggling to pick up graduate school jargon, even though our professors' and classmates' words sounded like English and they all seemed to know what they were talking about. And trying to pay bills. And trying to find an OB/GYN we could afford.

When we had time to notice, we realized many of the women were pregnant. We would hear and see children running, riding, and screaming gleefully among the buildings in twilight in that short time when the evening air cools slightly before darkness falls. Since we were childless, we had not yet joined the young-parents-of-young-children set, but we were encouraged by what we saw and quickly realized this would be a good place to have children.

In late January 1986, our first child, Alexis, was born at Seton Hospital on 38th Street. When a child is born within a community of family and friends, the birth is cause for celebration. Cooing new grandmothers cradle the child while congratulating and offering advice to the new mother. Peacock-proud new grandfathers surround the new father, passing around a bottle of beer or whiskey or tequila and accepting cigars. Excitable new aunts surround the sibling who has passed into motherhood with giggles and promises of free babysitting. Friends surround the father with back slaps and the mother with advice about pediatricians. Childbirth is one of the great family and communal rituals of the human experience.

But we were alone. After assisting in my daughter's birth, taking the requisite pictures, and cuddling the new baby, I shivered with the chill of epiphany. I was overwhelmed when first looking into my baby's eyes and realized instinctively everything was different forever. I handed the swaddled bundle over to the pediatric nurse, cradled my wife's face in my hands, and whispered, "You did good, baby. Congratulations. I love you," and gave her a good-night kiss. I drove back to Brackenridge to an apartment that would be empty only a few days longer, called my parents and in-laws with the news, and sat alone in the wingback chair next to the window, staring out across Brackenridge's winter landscape of litter skimming across brown grass and dormant gray-green live oak leaves fluttering in a cold wind in the gray dusk.

I need to celebrate, to hand out cigars, to accept the accolades of new parenthood, I thought.

I jumped back in the Malibu and drove down Lake Austin Boulevard towards Miller Dam to a spot called the Lakeview Café, with its view of the dam and Lake Austin, which formed behind it. I ambled up to the bar, ordered a whiskey, and toasted myself. As I had learned in New York pubs, barkeeps learn to lend an ear to those drinking alone, so I shared with the man behind the bar my cause for celebration. "Congratulations," he said. After an hour or so, I returned to Brackenridge.

While writing this reminiscence in 2010, I would drive along Lake Austin Boulevard and through the Brackenridge complex to evoke the memories. One day in late February, a few weeks more than twenty-four years after I welcomed myself to parenthood, a demolition crew surrounded the building that housed the Lakeview Café. When the Lower Colorado River Authority built its new facilities on the shores of Lake Austin, the café lost its view, the clientele moved to newer bars, coffee shops, and restaurants built on what had been parkland on the lake, and the building was converted into an LCRA meeting hall. Over a few days, all that remained was a scar on the landscape, and within a few weeks thereafter, the sod had taken hold. To those driving by today, the place never existed.

On January 27, 1986, the Butler family drove from Seton to 3354-C Lake Austin Boulevard in the sunshine, and my daughter laid her head on her first pillow in her first home. So she went forth, and Brackenridge became part of her and she part of it.

I HEAR BRACKENRIDGE SINGING

Over the next several weeks, we learned to enjoy the warm Texas winter as we joined the throng of parents and their children who strolled among the buildings with baby carriages for the fresh air and sunshine and hoisted colicky babies on shoulders late at night in the hope they might fall asleep in time for you to finish that paper due in the morning. Day by day, we were greeted by more of our neighbors: "Ah, you had the baby. Congratulations. We saw you were pregnant. How beautiful! She looks like you. She looks like her father. Do you need a car seat? We don't need ours anymore. Do you have a high chair? I'm selling ours cheap. Have you found a pediatrician?"

We became part of the comings and goings, the ebb and flow, of the community that was Brackenridge. In "I Hear America Singing," Whitman celebrated the voices of his fellow Americans.

> I hear America singing, the varied carols I hear,
> Those of mechanics, each one singing his as it
>   should be blithe and strong,
> The carpenter singing his as he measures his plank
>   or beam,
> The mason singing his as he makes ready for work,
>   or leaves off work,
> The boatman singing what belongs to him in his
>   boat, the deckhand singing on the steamboat
>   deck,
> The shoemaker singing as he sits on his bench, the
>   hatter singing as he stands,
> The wood-cutter's song, the ploughboy's on his way
>   in the morning, or at noon intermission or at
>   sundown,
> The delicious singing of the mother, or of the young
>   wife at work, or of the girl sewing or washing,
> Each singing what belongs to him or her and to none
>   else,
> The day what belongs to the day—at night the party
>   of young fellows, robust, friendly,
> Singing with open mouths their strong melodious
>   songs.

Our neighbors were the academic rather than the working class, but much like Whitman's characters, many were newcomers to America. Their work was solitary and often done in silence, but when we all gathered outdoors or when windows were thrown open to catch a breeze, we heard the varied carols. Small groups of Asian men hustled silently to catch the first shuttle bus in the morning and returned on the last bus late at night. We would overhear Spanish phone conversations. We heard a couple arguing in Hebrew, the guttural sounds coming off more serious than the content probably was. We heard children scolded in Portuguese. We heard Asian tongues, but were too unsophisticated to distinguish Korean from Chinese, or from Japanese. We spoke with Indian and African neighbors in their British- or French-accented English. Brazilian music danced out of win-

dows. Of course, we heard English too. Americans were the majority, but having just come off an international experience, we were more tuned in to the international students. Children laughed and cried in their own universal language all parents understand, whatever their native tongues.

What was clear was that almost none of our neighbors were from these here parts, as they say around these here parts. We were all foreigners—regardless of whether we were Americans or internationals—gathered together there in West Austin, in Central Texas, in what amounted to a public housing complex, far away from who and what we knew and who and what we were or would become, pursuing a universal dream to improve ourselves and our lots in life through education. Despite our differences, we merged into a multicultural community bound together by shared values for education, by our relative poverty, and by the shared first steps away from the childless early-adulthood days into the serious business of starting families, raising kids, and building careers.

In a way, then, Brackenridge had much in common with the New York I came from. While I was raised a suburbanite, an hour up the Hudson River from New York City and just a few miles from the eighteenth-century farm where J. Hector St. John de Crèvecoeur penned *Letters from an American Farmer* and introduced the concept of the "melting pot," my mother infused us with tales of her parents, immigrants and first-generation Americans, who came to New York with little money or education. And many of my childhood friends, also first-generation suburbanites, heard the same stories, often from the widowed grandmother with a thick accent who lived in the finished basement. Those of immigrants who ended up wherever they could afford, chasing some rumor of work to be had, among the other Spanish-, German-, Polish-, Hebrew-, or Gaelic-speaking families who ended up in the same place. Those of immigrants with large families living in small five- or six-story walk-ups where the Irish family lived next to the Jewish family that lived above the Puerto Rican family that lived across the hall from the German family. I remember the tales of living in Manhattan tenements, of immigrants tightly packed together in small rooms with little privacy and few luxuries, like air-conditioning to fight the swelter of steamy

New York summers. They told the stories of running up and down the narrow side streets where people lived between the avenues and boulevards, playing tag, hide and seek, box ball, hopscotch, and ring-a-levio, riding shared bikes, playing stickball. Young couples with furtive glances, hidden hand holding, and perhaps a stolen kiss in the alley between buildings. The parents and adults sat on stoops or on folding chairs on sidewalks, drinking icy cheap beer and lemonade, the kind made with lemons and sugar, telling jokes and stories, sharing recipes and the secrets of happiness and love and pain and loss and life and death. Planning futures of better apartments in better parts of the city or perhaps a house in the suburbs, always tales of better lives someplace in America as an antidote to the poverty, persecution, or suffering from their homelands and the suffering of the present, which was at least better than their homelands. The 169th Street of my mother's Manhattan youth was a village where the eyes of all the parents watched out for all the children and for one another in times of illness or job loss, and on birthdays, bar mitzvahs, or *quinceañeras*.

Brackenridge had stoop culture in the time before the Internet and cell phones and one hundred–plus channels on cable TV. Cool and balmy evenings were spent sitting on the staircases leading to the upper apartments while the kids learned to crawl, walk, run, stumble, and ride bicycles, like lion cubs practicing to be adults someday. During these evenings, on the shuttle bus rides, in the shared laundry room, and the occasional al fresco potlucks in which neighbors contributed their ethnic specialties, I learned much about my neighbors and the lands and traditions that shaped them.

AN IVORY BRACELET

Our next-door neighbor, Lupenga Mphande, his wife Mary, several children, and his sister-in-law hailed from Malawi, a landlocked nation in southeast Africa. Lupenga lived in the northern district of Mzimba. He was at UT to pursue a PhD in foreign language education. Lupenga was a slight man who favored sleeveless white t-shirts, Bermuda shorts, and sandals while at home. He spoke British English flavored with the rhythms and tones of his native Af-

rican language, reminiscent of Nelson Mandela. He laughed heartily and grinned widely. On pleasant evenings after dinner, he would sit on his steps and I would sit on mine, facing each other across the landing perched above the courtyard, where we could keep an eye on the children and the neighbors working their way home from school. At times we spoke about nothing, but often we would engage in real conversations. Lupenga educated me about the Africans' view of apartheid and the sovereignty of African nations. When we discussed education, he told me he first went to a local school when he was big enough to touch his left ear with his right arm across the top of his head. When he exhausted the local educational options, he traveled elsewhere in his nation to attend a British school run by missionaries.

Over time, I noticed Lupenga wore a white, unclasped bracelet. One evening it came up in conversation as he explained that his father was a tribal elder, and hence he was descended from royalty in his land. Young men of his standing had the hand-carved ivory bracelets slid over their hands at puberty. As the hand grew, the bracelet would become too small to ever be removed. The bracelet was a status symbol, a marker of one's place in his native culture. Lupenga and I ended up in a class together, and he wrote about pumpkin myths, legends, and rituals, since the pumpkin was the subsistence crop of his homeland.

My daughter became playmates with his daughters. My wife and his wife helped with each other's children. When I turned thirty, my wife threw a surprise party in our apartment, and Lupenga and Mary attended. Burned in my memory is an image of Lupenga, a descendent of African royalty, singing "Happy Birthday to You," wearing a brightly colored conical birthday hat, eating sugary birthday cake, laughing heartily, and smiling broadly.

Despite our limited resources, we still had more than many, and most winter breaks we could make a road trip to visit relatives. Most of the international students could not afford such journeys. We would buy a Christmas tree before our holiday travels and enjoy it for the days we were still in Austin. Once, on departure day, I took the tree, fully lighted and decorated, across the landing to the Mphendes to share the joys of an American Christmas. They accepted joyfully, especially the children.

FROTH AND SWIRL

Ofer Shavitz was an Israeli of German descent. His Israeli wife Ilana traced her roots back to Arab peoples. Her use of halal meats spoke to her heritage. They met in the Israeli army, where she was a helicopter mechanic. At UT, Ofer was working on a master's degree in electrical engineering. They had two children, Inbar and Tal, and lived across the courtyard in a first-floor apartment. The Shavitzes were gregarious, garrulous, and generous. Ilana was a homemaker, and when windows opened, exotic aromas from her kitchen filled the courtyard, as did her high-pitched Hebrew admonishments of her children.

It was not unusual for the graduate student spouse in Brackenridge to pull typical student hours of late nights that ran over into the early mornings. During the hottest times of the year, the most tolerable time to be outdoors was after midnight. Those of us cramming for the next day's exam or typing up handwritten manuscripts to deliver them hot off the presses the next day would emerge from our apartments for breaks to stretch legs and necks, breathe fresh air, or simply look up at the stars. Many a night, Ofer and I would greet each other in the streetlight shadows of the courtyard, make small talk, and lament exhaustion levels resulting from packed schedules and crying kids.

One night, Ofer invited me to his silent apartment while his wife and children slept. "I have something for you to keep you awake," he said. We went to the kitchen. On his stove top was an *ibrik*—a Turkish coffee urn—a fluted metal pot with a narrow opening, a broad bottom, and a long handle. He filled the pot about two-thirds of the way with water, spooned in finely ground French roast, a couple of spoonfuls of sugar, and a couple of cracked cardamom pods. He brought the mixture to a boil, and just as the froth was about to overflow, he removed the pot from the stovetop and swirled. When the froth retreated, he returned the pot to the heat. He repeated the process twice more, and then filled two demitasse cups. It was sweet and bitter, aromatic and acidic, delicious and fortifying. After we finished the pot, I thanked him for his hospitality, walked out into the moonlight, and never slept a wink. Within days, I found myself at the second iteration of Whole Foods supermarket—the one on 12th and Lamar—buying an

ibrik, which I use to this day to make Turkish coffee just the way Ofer showed me.

BROTHERS AND SISTERS

Our first Brackenridge friends, Antonio and Helene Simoes—he Brazilian, she French—lived across the courtyard on the second floor. He was tall and strong-jawed with a Portuguese accent, and her eyes showed a hint of her Chinese ancestry. She laughed joyfully. He was pursuing a PhD in romance languages, and she was a Spanish lecturer. When we moved in, they had one son and Helene was pregnant with their second. My wife delivered Alexis and Helene delivered Bruno within two months of each other, and thus we had much in common. Helene and Sara bonded over motherhood and Helene's recipe for what we call flan, the rich custard we developed a taste for in Mexico, but which was probably closer to crème brûlée in its eggy creaminess. It was one of Helene's stock contributions to the potlucks. Our families bonded as we raised our children together. From time to time, we would care for each other's children if we needed a break for studying, shopping, or just enjoying a night out. Fabio, the eldest son, was a swimmer and a fan of American sports. He was a Chicago Cubs fan. A New York Mets fan and a ballplayer myself, I spent time with Fabio talking about the game. We had a friendly rivalry when the Mets won the World Series in 1986. The Simoeses and Butlers together hired Vivian, a young South American early-childhood educator married to another graduate student. On alternating weeks, Vivian (or BeBe, as the children called her) would sit the children in one or another of our apartments. On days when Vivian couldn't help out, one of us four parents would take the day off to sit the children, speaking and reading to them, feeding them, bathing them, and changing their diapers.

When the children were ready to move on to preschool, together they went to Lake Austin Montessori on Hearn Street, on a lot where today a McMansion stands. For the first three years of their lives, Bruno and our daughter were raised as brother and sister, taking baths together, sharing meals, seeing the world together for the first time, and communicating together with their first words, the patois of toddlers blending the English, Portuguese, French,

Bruno Simoes and Alexis Butler, ca. 1989. *Courtesy of Wayne and Sara Butler.*

and Spanish of their parents and caretakers. Upon completion of their degrees, the Simoes moved on to professorships at the University of Kansas. Watching the children say good-bye was poignant as they hugged and kissed without understanding that this was the last farewell, that they would not see one another tomorrow or perhaps forever. I gave Fabio one of my baseball history coffee-table books as a farewell present. Helene gave Sara the flan recipe, which is the hit of every potluck Sara brings it to. We inherited their daybed, which our children both used as their first beds and our houseguests slept on for another twenty years. Years later we learned Helene had been diagnosed with a cancer, to which she succumbed. Through the miracle of social networking, our daughter and Bruno reunited online, sharing childhood photos. When I got on Facebook, I reconnected with Antonio, Bruno, and Fabio, who upon friending me, asked whether I was still a Mets fan.

A BLUE CARPET

David was an English professor at a Japanese university married to a tall, thin Japanese woman whose name I could never pronounce and can't remember. We were casual acquaintances, and our only real interaction occurred as they were preparing to leave Brackenridge to return to Japan. They were selling a light blue carpet cut to fit a typical Brackenridge living room, and my wife wanted it so our daughter wouldn't have to crawl on the cold tile floor. We went to their apartment on moving day to inspect the carpet and possibly close the deal. The Japanese woman stood in the corner, forlorn. She shared with my wife, in broken English, that she was sorry to be leaving because she would be going back to the tiny apartments of her native land. Six hundred square feet was palatial to her. I was hesitant about the purchase, not because the carpet was unacceptable, but because of the anticipated hassle of rolling it up, lugging it down the sidewalk and up to the second story, moving the furniture, rolling it out in our apartment, and replacing the furniture again. I said we would think about it. The next day, after returning weary from a long day of library research, writing, and classes, I opened the apartment door to see the blue carpet laid out in front of me. David had rolled up the carpet in his apartment, lugged it down the sidewalk and up to the second floor, moved my furniture, rolled out the carpet, and replaced the furniture.

A BICYCLE

Below us lived an Indian family. The husband, who was slight, mustachioed, and bespectacled, was home infrequently, since he was an industrious engineering student. The wife was fulsome, and she wore traditional saris. They were quiet, pleasant acquaintances who didn't mingle much with the courtyard crowd, but were cordial and smiled eagerly the few times we chatted in passing. They had one daughter, a dark-haired preschooler with wet brown eyes and tiny gold-stud earrings. More socialized than her parents, she joined the other children in the courtyard while her mother concocted exotic curries in the kitchen, enticing the entire courtyard. For her birthday, her parents bought her a bicycle with training wheels. One evening as I was returning from school, the father in his traditional garb was working on the bicycle while his daughter implored him impatiently to fix it somehow so she could join the posse of courtyard bike riders. I offered a neighborly hand. The training wheels were out of line, the rear wheel out of balance, and the chain was tangled around the sprocket. The father was working on the bike while it lay on its side like a wounded animal. I went out to the Malibu and pulled out my hodgepodge tool kit. I flipped the bike wheels up on the handlebars and seat, loosened the training wheels and the rear axle, threaded the chain between the sprockets, and aligned and retightened everything. Gave the pedal a triumphant crank and watched the rear wheel spin true. I turned the bike back on its wheels, and rolled the bike to the girl. She smiled thank you. Her father gave me a giddy thank you and said gleefully, "You Americans are so resourceful!"

THE BRACK MARKET

Brackenridge had its own sort of economy. When people completed their stays, especially the international students returning to their home countries, they would often sell their used goods cheaply, furniture and sundries they had probably bought cheap on the Brackenridge black market. Our child's first car seat we found lying beside a Dumpster. Her first high chair we bought from a neighbor. As children grew out of clothing, families passed outfits along to other families with smaller, younger children.

Shortly after Alexis was born, we were invited to join the grassroots babysitting co-op. The system had been set up long before we arrived, and the founders did not even live in Brackenridge anymore. The system involved scrip. Upon enrollment, a new family received red, green, and blue slips of paper, a simple set of rules, contact information and child-care forms, and a table used to calculate how much scrip it would cost to babysit, or could be earned by babysitting, how many children for how long. Thus, when parents needed breaks to study, to work, to exercise, or just to get out of the house for a few hours for an evening without children, we did not have to pay for babysitting. The co-op brought its members closer as we met monthly in one another's apartments on a rotating basis to work on process improvements, to coffee-klatch, and to otherwise bond with those with whom we would be entrusting our greatest assets—our children. As communal caretakers of one another's children, we got to know the children very

well and could then serve as surrogates in the event a child fell from a bicycle, scraped a knee, and cried within earshot of your apartment. The "Brack" market, so to speak, kept costs down while keeping the quality of life higher than we could have otherwise afforded.

HIKE AND BIKE

Nostalgia deceives and distorts memory, and despite my reflections on a past that bordered on the idyllic, there were gray days and dark nights. Graduate school can be a grind, even in Brackenridge. In many ways, striving for an advanced degree is risky, for failure to cross the finish line triumphantly can result in unrecoverable debt, lost time you might have spent pursuing other more lucrative pursuits, and a battered ego. You are on unsteady ground, not always knowing exactly the secret language of your academic discipline while you walk in the shadows of classmates you envision as brilliant. In your dreams, you dread the day you are discovered as the academic fraud you surely are. At home, given your age and parenthood, you are a full-fledged adult. But by day, you are an apprentice, sometimes mentored and sometimes lorded over by the acclaimed professors you were trying to one day become. You did their research, wrote papers to their standards, or not, passed their tests, or not, learned their codes, or not, and sought their approval, or not. Unless you were funded by your country, your company, your family, ample savings you were lucky enough to scrape together in a previous life, or the wages of your fully employed spouse, you borrowed. You mortgaged your future with school loans and credit cards with the utter blind faith that when you earned the degree, the rewards would handle the debt. You scrimped where you could, and the children would not always sleep when you needed them to. Otherwise-loving spouses bickered. Stress surrounded your insecurities, real and imagined, like ether.

So we hiked and biked.

Brackenridge's community-building layout was not its only, or perhaps even its best, feature. As they say in real estate, it was about location, location, location. While the land tilts gently down to the stretch of the Colorado River then known as Town Lake, for the most part the land is flat. Thus, with infants in baby carriages, toddlers in jogging strollers, or youngsters on bicycles, parents alone or together could walk southeast along Lake Austin Boulevard a short distance to what was an Apple Tree supermarket, one with an atrium built around an old oak, at the intersection with Exposition Boulevard. Another half mile or so beyond that Apple Tree (a Randalls as of this writing) lay the 1960s-era Colorado Apartments. At the east end of those apartments was Deep Eddy Cabaret, a long-standing nightspot with arguably the best jukebox in town but no live music, sitting at the entrance to Eilers Park, the gateway to the ancient Deep Eddy Pool, where Sara's mother swam in the 1940s when she was earning her master's in English under Harry Ransom's tutelage. On the hottest days, the family could refresh itself in the cold spring waters in the shallow wading end. Both my children swam there. On one side of the pool was the original Austin Nature Center, with its small cages of indigenous small animals and tanks of fish, snakes, turtles, and frogs. On the other side lay the path leading to the hike-and-bike trail that loops around Town Lake, and if you had the energy and endurance, you could walk or ride your bike all the way to Pleasant Valley Road and back along the lake's banks, passing under bridges housing bats, along Auditorium Shores, and past the ever-changing Austin skyline, which in the 1980s was dominated by construction cranes.

In the seven years I lived in Brackenridge, I made that walk scores, perhaps hundreds, of times, engaging in internal dialogues about literary and rhetorical theory, about research designs and statistical problems, about my life and the life I was making with my wife and children. I am sure the passersby saw my furrowed brow and far-off gaze and questioned my sanity, assuming, of course they themselves were not looking within as they looked into the horizon. I would emerge from the trail a happier man, whether I had worked out the knots in my mind or not, because a good nature walk along water is always restorative.

ONLY AS GOOD AS WE WERE

So someday down the road, perhaps during my lifetime, the Brackenridge Apartments will be demolished and exist only in the minds of those who lived there and in their fading photos, in their happy and

sad tales, and in the words of this essay. If all goes as planned, the apartments will be gone, as will Lions Municipal Golf Course, and even the route of Lake Austin Boulevard, which replaced the dam road built in the 1890s during Austin's earliest attempt to tame the Colorado River, will be altered. As leases expire, the stores and shopping centers will be destroyed to make way for a planned community where manufactured green spaces will break up dense urban living built around exclusive condominiums and pedestrian-friendly retail experiences. The Lady Bird Lake Hike and Bike Trail might be extended from Deep Eddy all the way to Red Bud Isle. If all goes as planned, future UT student families will live in new apartments on the Gateway property, a terraced, landlocked complex whose sole entrance leads onto the three-lane, one-way westbound West 6th Street, where cars speed by on their way to the nearby MoPac Expressway entrance ramp. A complex segregated from the surrounding community by a tall barbed-wire-crowned cyclone fence. Kids don't ride their bicycles much there because of the hills, and you don't see parents with strollers off the grounds much, since there is no place to walk to or a pedestrian-friendly way to get there. The apartments will grow higher and denser, with less open space for children to roam. Its residents can't walk to the store or to the lake from there.

This is not to say, however, they paved paradise and put up a parking lot, for young student families from Texas, the other forty-nine states, and countries around the world will flock to Gateway for the safe and relatively low cost of living, and create their own communities, friends, and memories. The University will reap the profits, and the spirit, even if not the letter, of Colonel Brackenridge's deed will be complied with. Through some fancy legal work, the University will be able to say the proceeds from the Brackenridge Tract made the University a wealthier, and thus better, place.

When Ernest Hemingway reflected on the places where he wrote his best works, he noted that while some places were better than others, a place is only as good as you were when you were there. Agreed, but a place can also empower, inspire, and nurture us to be the best we can be. UT Married Student Housing, UT Family Housing, the Brackenridge, Deep Eddy, Colorado, and Gateway Apartments launched some of the University's, Texas's, the United States', and the world's best and brightest. Antonio Simoes became a tenured professor of romance languages at the University of Kansas. Lupenga Mphande became a renowned and respected poet and tenured professor of African American studies at Ohio State University. The Shavitzes settled in Austin, where Ofer entered the software business while Ilana had several more children. Their daughter, Inbar, like my daughter, Alexis, became a UT alum. I, the Yankee with immigrant and New York City roots, have made a career at UT, attending all UT football and basketball games and wearing burnt orange whenever the occasion calls for it. I say with pride, "I'm not from Texas, but I got here as quickly as I could." Sara built a career in the Austin Independent School District, making a difference in the lives of at-risk students. Those I knew personally were much like other family-housing alums who left UT to make a difference in various ways. Former federal judge Timothy Johnson, former Texas state senator Gonzalo Barrientos, Dr. Andre Avots-Avotins, the chairman of the board of Scott & White Hospital in Temple, and the Latino

studies pioneer and celebrated UT English and folklore professor Américo Paredes nurtured their families at Married Student Housing. I don't doubt those of less renown went forth to be, even if not leaders in their fields, productive citizens of Texas and the world. Perhaps not exactly what Colonel Brackenridge had in mind in 1909, but perhaps even more than he expected.

NOTES

1. "Conceptual Master Plan: The University of Texas System—Brackenridge Tract," http://www.utbracktract.com/?q=node/17.

2. Editor's note: For further discussion of George Washington Brackenridge and his contributions to the University of Texas, see Richard A. Holland, "George W. Brackenridge, George W. Littlefield, and the Shadow of the Past," in the first *Texas Book*.

3. Quoted in Frank C. Erwin, Jr., "U.T. Austin—Brackenridge Tract—Regent Erwin's Review of the History of the Tract," July 10, 1973 (UT System files); available at http://www.utsystem.edu/bor/files/bracktract/erwinhistory.pdf.

Acknowledgments

The creation of this second volume of *The Texas Book* would not have been possible without the generosity of the talented writers who contributed to it, primarily out of their own particular appreciation for the University and its programs. I am grateful for the time, the effort, and, most importantly, the creative energy that each of them lent to the project.

My first thanks go to my friend Richard A. Holland. In 2000, Kate Adams, who was the associate director at the Center for American History in those days, told me that a fellow was going to be in the center quite a bit while doing research for a book and that I was to give him some occasional assistance when he asked for it. (I had recently started working at the center, and Kate was my supervisor at the time.) It so happened that I had been learning a lot about UT history from Jim Nicar of the Texas Exes, who is today the Exes' director of campus relations and remains an indefatigable discoverer and disseminator of UT's history; on one occasion, Jim had ordered some reprints of photos of B. Hall, and as I helped him with his order, he showed me the prints and told me some of the lore associated with the old dorm. I mentioned to Dick how interesting the B. Hall story seemed to me (I had survived four years of living in all-male dorms at my alma mater, the University of Kansas), and Dick encouraged me to write a piece about B. Hall for the book.

I am sincerely grateful for Dick's trust in me to contribute to the first book and for allowing me to help him with it as extensively as I did, as well as his ongoing encouragement for my writing and editing projects. I am also grateful for the many meals I have shared with the assortment of folks who show up every year at the home of him and his wife, UT Law School clinical professor Cynthia Bryant, for Thanksgiving. In addition to the wonderful company, it is a special treat to spend an afternoon in a house—the "crumbling manse of Speedway Heights," just north of campus—made of Old Main bricks.

I am grateful to Dave Hamrick at the University of Texas Press for believing that a second volume of *The Texas Book* would be both something that people would like to read and an important addition to the preservation of the University's history. I appreciate recently retired UT Press director Joanna Hitchcock's support for the project as well.

My thanks go to my editor at UT Press, Allison Faust, whose good cheer, positive feedback, and patience with an editor who, midproject, became a father for the first time have helped make this finished product possible.

I am also grateful to Lynne Chapman, manuscript editor at UT Press, and Kaila Wyllys, production coordinator at UT Press, as well as copyeditor Kip Keller and my two excellent first readers for all that they have done to invest this book with quality and precision.

Special thanks go to Ralph Elder, my former colleague at the Center for American History. Ralph's knowledge of Texas history resources is surpassed only by his cheerfulness and generosity. And no one's blood runs a truer shade of burnt orange (or is it focal orange?) than Ralph's.

I would also like to make special mention of Marsha Miller's contributions to the book. Marsha is director of photography for University Communications at UT-Austin and, in my opinion, one of the most talented people on campus.

The procurement of the illustrations in this book in large part is the result of the hard work of Linda Peterson, the recently retired head of photographic archives at the Dolph Briscoe Center for American History, and Aryn Glazier, the center's photography services coordinator.

Further assistance at the center came from associate director Alison Beck, who was instrumental in helping me create the Barbara Conrad reminiscence that appears in this volume, as was Don Carleton, the center's director. One of the highlights of my time at the center was working directly with Ms. Conrad to organize a performance she gave in 2005 in the old board of regents meeting room in the Main Building for some of her friends in Austin.

Mark O'English, an archivist in Manuscripts, Archives, and Special Collections at the Terrell Library at Washington State University, and his staff went above and beyond to capture, from coaches' archived game film, still images of Duke Washington running through Longhorn defenders and scoring a touchdown in UT's Memorial Stadium.

Many other folks lent their assistance by helping me track down information or by putting me in touch with potential contributors to the book. Joel Barna and Marc Wetzel at the McDonald Observatory helped me procure photographs; Jennifer V. Ebbeler, an associate professor of classics at the University, helped me with my Latin; Texas A&M alumnus Paul Taylor tutored me on the history of University Baptist Church; Steve Darby, the head pro at Hancock Golf Course, and Tinsley Penick filled in details about the history of the Austin Country Club.

Others whose name deserves a mention are Tom Zigal, my former colleague in the Office of the President at UT-Austin; Tim Taliaferro, the editor-in-chief of the *Alcalde*, the official magazine of the Texas Exes; Beth Palazzolo in the Office of the Vice President for University Operations at UT-Austin; Nancy Sparrow in the Alexander Architectural Archive at UT-Austin; Martha King, director of Endowment Services and Compliance at UT-Austin; Patrice Fox at the Harry Ransom Center at UT-Austin; Cindy Slater, Associate Director for Library Services at the H. J. Lutcher Stark Center for Physical Culture and Sports at UT-Austin; Scott Sayers of Austin, Texas; Becky Johnson at the Texas Legislative Reference Library; Julie Moody, former reporter at KUT radio; Kent Calder, director of the Texas State Historical Association; and Gloria Jaster-Hickey, former manager of the Winedale Historical Complex, whom I have known for almost twenty-five years now.

The late Shirley Bird Perry, my former colleague who was a senior vice president at the University at the time of her death in 2011, was always a dependable and enthusiastic source of knowledge about UT's history. Likewise, Susan Clagett, associate vice president for University events, is always a graceful font of advice, support, and positive vibes—and, as Larry Faulkner explains in his foreword, was a central figure in the genesis of this book.

Although it is important to know that this book does not in any way speak for or represent the views of the Office of the President, I am grateful for the encouragement I received from president emeritus Larry Faulkner and current UT-Austin president Bill Powers, who is my boss at my day job at the University, regarding this project.

Finally, I'm grateful once again for the opportunity to work directly with the people who contributed to the contents of this book. Universities of the first class are an indispensable part of a free and healthy society, and working closely with these champions of the work produced here at the University of Texas at Austin has been an honor and a privilege.

Index